The Business Cycle

# The Business Cycle

## GROWTH AND CRISIS UNDER CAPITALISM

*Howard J. Sherman*

PRINCETON UNIVERSITY PRESS

PRINCETON, NEW JERSEY

Copyright © 1991 by Princeton University Press
Published by Princeton University Press, 41 William Street,
Princeton, New Jersey 08540
In the United Kingdom: Princeton University Press, Oxford

*Library of Congress Cataloging-in-Publication Data*

Sherman, Howard J.
The business cycle : growth and crisis under capitalism / Howard
J. Sherman.
p.   cm.
Includes bibliographical references and index.
1. Business cycles.   2. Capitalism.   I. Title.
HB3711.S4722   1991    338.5′42—dc20    90-43440

ISBN 0-691-04262-4

ISBN 0-691-02721-8 (pbk.)

This book has been composed in Linotron Caledonia

Princeton University Press books are printed on acid-free paper,
and meet the guidelines for permanence and durability of the
Committee on Production Guidelines for Book Longevity of the
Council on Library Resources

Printed in the United States of America

10   9   8   7   6   5   4   3   2

DEDICATED TO THE MEMORY OF
KARL MARX
WESLEY MITCHELL
JOHN M. KEYNES
MICHAL KALECKI

*Four giants of business cycle research.*

# Contents

## PART THREE: *More Realistic Approximations*

# List of Figures

# Preface

THIS BOOK was written out of a strong feeling of the need to understand why capitalism is so unstable and why so many millions of people are frequently and involuntarily unemployed. Most of the present literature on the business cycle is unsatisfying because it does not answer these questions. This book attempts to place the instability of the business cycle at the center of macroeconomic understanding, a position that is exactly contrary to the present dominant view in macroeconomics. Therefore, the reader should not be surprised to find that this book has a very different approach than that of most of the current literature and rather takes its inspiration from the great pioneers in this area of economics: Karl Marx, Wesley Mitchell, John M. Keynes, and Michal Kalecki.

Arthur MacEwan, John Miller, Barbara Sinclair, and Martin Wolfson gave me a great deal of encouragement at crucial times. Shirlee Pigeon and Sandy Schauer did a wonderful job of typing, as well as editing some of my mistakes. For constructive criticisms of the manuscript (or articles that led to it), I wish to thank Rhon Baiman, Samuel Bowles, William Darity, Jr., Jeanne Diaz, John Duffy, Gary Dymski, Howard Engelskirchen, Keith Griffin, Robin Hahnel, Lawrence Harris, Craig Justice, Azizur Khan, John E. King, Philip Klein, Arthur MacEwan, John Miller, Terry McKinley, Robert Pollin, Christine Rider, Sheldon Stein, Frank Thompson, Andrew Winnick, Martin Wolfson and Kenneth Woodward. I would like to thank Lyn Grossman for editing the manuscript.

I thank the publishers for permission to use some material from the following: Howard Sherman, "Theories of Economic Crisis: Demand-side, Supply-side, and Profit Squeeze," *Science and Society* (1989); Howard Sherman, "The Business Cycle of Capitalism," *International Review of Applied Economics* (1987); Howard Sherman, "Profit Squeeze in Marx, Keynes, Mitchell, and Kalecki," *Review of Radical Political Economics* (1989); Howard Sherman, "Cyclical Behavior of the Labor Share," *Review of Radical Political Economics* (1990); and Howard Sherman, "Real and Monetary Factors in the Business Cycle," *Review of Radical Political Economics* (1990). I am also grateful to Gary Evans for permission to use some material from Howard Sherman and Gary Evans, *Macroeconomics: Keynesian, Monetarist, and Marxist Views* (New York: Harper and Row, 1984).

I also thank the UCR Research Committee for their support.

# PART ONE

# Overview

# CHAPTER 1

# The Waste of the Business Cycle

IN THE GREAT DEPRESSION of the 1930s, millions of people were involuntarily unemployed. The unemployed did not have enough money to buy the food, clothing, and shelter that they so badly needed. To the degree that this human misery repeats itself—to a much lesser extent—in the contraction phase of every business cycle, there is a major social problem arising from a seemingly irrational economic situation.

All capitalist economies suffer from business cycles. A business cycle may be defined as an expansion in economic activity (measured by such indicators as output, employment, and profits) followed by a contraction in economic activity (including declining production, massive unemployment, and business losses and bankruptcies). It has no regular periodicity, but the same sequence of economic events does take place time after time. Each cycle is different, but there are many regularities or similar sequences found in every business cycle. Although alleged long-cycle and long-run trends are discussed in this book, the focus is on the short-run cyclical behavior of cycles ranging from two to ten years.

Since the business cycle includes a period of expansion, most economists of the neoclassical school emphasize the sunny side of the picture—that growth does occur through the business cycle. Neoclassical economists see recessions or depressions as merely a momentary, temporary problem. They view the contraction phase of the cycle as a necessary evil, which resolves some problems of the system, but opens the way to new and more vigorous growth. They contend that the present system is the only possible efficient system leading to growth, so cyclical downturns are a small price to pay. Moreover, neoclassical economists believe that people choose to be unemployed—that there is almost no involuntary unemployment.

Contrary to the neoclassical view, one hypothesis of this book is that the waste and misery of business contractions are not necessary in all efficient economic systems and could be totally eliminated in a more rational economic system. One problem of the business cycle is that it leaves workers, capitalists, and other citizens in a state of uncertainty much of the time. The problem of uncertainty is stressed as a business cycle problem throughout this book, but it must be emphasized that it is also a human problem. The other main problem is that cyclical contractions cause losses to society, business, and individual workers—especially involuntary unemployment. If the hypothesis of this book that capitalism is inherently unstable and generates cyclical unemployment is correct, then all of macroeconomics should be reconstructed around this focus. The dominant neoclassical view of equilibrium, clearing of all markets, and no involuntary unemployment should be replaced by a dynamic, historical, cycle-oriented view.

## LOSSES TO SOCIETY

Society suffers many types of losses from the contractions that occur during business cycles. Thousands of factories stand idle, and millions of workers are unemployed, so society loses an enormous amount of potential output for current consumption. Society also loses because very little new plant and equipment are produced, so there is very little, if any, growth of productive potential for future expansion. For that reason, every recession or depression lowers the long-run rate of growth. Although the overall, long-run U.S. trend has been one of economic growth, the rate of growth has been lowered by these losses, according to the findings of this book. Society loses the new inventions that are not discovered because there is less motivation and less money for research and development. Society loses because millions of people are unable to work and to create to the best of their potential. Society loses because millions of people are frustrated and unhappy and the social atmosphere is poisoned.

## LOSSES TO BUSINESS

In every contraction, many businesses cannot sell their goods at a profit. The number of bankruptcies skyrockets. The number of new businesses declines drastically. Millions of small businesses are forced out of business, and their owners are often left unemployed. Even a few large corporations go out of business, leaving all of their employees out of a job.

## LOSSES TO INDIVIDUAL WORKERS

The greatest scourge of the business cycle, however, is the involuntary unemployment of millions of workers. Every one of these individuals suffers the disruption of a useful life. Heads of families cannot feed their children. The unemployed feel useless; each believes that he or she is a personal failure. There is a calculable increase in mental and physical sickness among the unemployed and their families. Increased unemployment causes increases in alcoholism, divorce, child abuse, crime, and even suicide.

A study for the Joint Economic Committee has documented the grim facts. A sustained 1 percent increase in unemployment is associated with the following statistically significant percentage increases: suicide, 4.1 percent; state mental hospital admissions, 3.4 percent; state prison admissions, 4.0 percent; homicide, 5.7 percent; deaths from cirrhosis of the liver, 1.9 percent; deaths from cardiovascular diseases, 1.9 percent (Brenner 1976, v).

## THE CONTROVERSIES AND A FRAMEWORK FOR THEIR ANALYSIS

Chapter 2 presents a measuring system for the empirical description of the cycle, based on the approach of Wesley Mitchell. Chapter 3 argues the institutionalist position that the business cycle is uniquely caused by the institutions of capitalism. After contrasting capitalism with precapitalist institutions, the chapter demonstrates that the history of the cycle changes with the changing stages of capitalism.

No subject in economics is more controversial than unemployment. Chapter 4 explains the dominant view in U.S. economics: that involuntary unemployment does not exist, except for an irreducible frictional, or "natural," level. This view is based on the argument that the capitalist system automatically adjusts demand to supply so that there are only brief deviations from full employment equilibrium, due to factors that are external, or exogenous, to the system. This view is rejected in favor of a mainly endogenous approach.

Chapter 4 then considers briefly the main hypothesis of this book: that internal, or endogenous, factors are the main cause of the business cycle of capitalism. Some endogenous theories emphasize the lack of consumer demand; others emphasize the cost of supply, including high wages, interest rates, or raw material prices. Both demand-side and supply-side theories have made major contributions to understanding, but it is shown that each is inadequate by itself. A synthesis is proposed, based on the theories of Marx, Mitchell, Keynes, and Kalecki.

Part Two of the book discusses the more detailed controversies involving the behavior of each important variable and the theories associated with the different aspects of the cycle. Thus, Chapters 5 and 6 discuss consumption and investment behavior, and Chapter 7 explicates the multiplier-accelerator theory based on the behavior of these two variables. Chapter 8 discusses the behavior of income distribution between labor and capital over the cycle, and Chapter 9 contains an exposition of demand-side theories, such as underconsumption, that build on the behavior of income distribution, consumption, and investment.

Chapter 10 details cost behavior of raw materials, plant, and equipment. These data set the stage for Chapter 11, which presents supply-side theories based on the cost of capital (overinvestment) or the cost of labor (reserve army theory). Chapter 12 examines how profits and profit rates behave over the cycle, providing the foundation for a new type of profit squeeze (or nutcracker) theory in Chapter 13, which attempts a synthesis of the empirically supported elements of demand-side and supply-side theories.

Part Three of this book adds more complex reality to the theoretical framework. It does this by considering money and credit in Chapter 14, monopoly power in Chapter 15, international relationships in Chapter 16, and governmental behavior in Chapter 17. Some economists would argue for introducing each of these levels into the very first model of the economy, but that would mean an enormously complex model from the very start. If the model involved every important relationship from the start, it would be difficult, or impossible, to understand any of it. Using successive approximations starting from simple models and proceeding to more complex, realistic ones, makes the analysis both clearer and more rigorous.

Finally, Part Four considers what changes in institutions and in policies are needed in order to ameliorate or totally eliminate the waste of the business cycle.

# CHAPTER 2

# Measuring the Business Cycle

THE PIONEER in empirical description of the business cycle was Wesley Clair Mitchell. Indeed, he helped develop many of our present national income accounts. With the help of Arthur Burns (see Burns and Mitchell 1946), he created a method specifically for measuring the business cycle. The method was used in several cycle studies of the National Bureau of Economic Research (NBER), which he founded. Alas, the NBER no longer follows Mitchell's method, but it is still usually called the NBER method.

Mitchell's NBER method depicts the exact path of a single variable over the average business cycle. Mitchell's method, the details of which are presented in this chapter, is still the best method for getting a clear picture of the business cycle. The NBER method may reveal a simple visual relationship of variables, which is helpful in suggesting a hypothesis for testing, but it should be stressed that it does not provide a statistical test of relationships. After the NBER method shows the typical cyclical behavior of a variable, then the next stage of analysis is often the use of econometric regression and correlation analysis to test its relation to other variables.

## DEFINITION OF THE BUSINESS CYCLE

Before a phenomenon can be measured, it must be carefully defined. Wesley Mitchell presented the most useful definition of the business cycle; it is as follows:

> Business cycles are a type of fluctuation found in the aggregate economic activity of nations that organize their work mainly in business enterprises; a cycle consists of expansions occurring at about the same time in many economic activities, followed by similarly general recessions, contractions, and revivals which merge into the expansion phase of the next cycle; this sequence of changes is recurrent but not periodic; in duration business cycles vary from more than one year to ten or twelve years; they are not divisible into shorter cycles of similar character with amplitudes approximately their own.
>
> (Burns and Mitchell 1946, 3)

It is worth examining separately each of the points in Mitchell's definition. First, it is clear that the business cycle is a phenomenon found under capitalism, and not under other systems (as will be seen in the next chapter). Second, the business cycle is not limited to a single firm or industry, but is economywide, expected to show most clearly among aggregate indicators. It is widely diffused and is expected to show in most series. Third, one cycle follows after another; they are marked by regularities and similar sequences of events. Fourth, cycles differ, however, in many ways, including how long they are, so there is no regular periodicity.

Fifth, Mitchell mentioned time periods for a whole business cycle of anywhere from one to twelve years. Some authors have found shorter, mild three- or four-year cycles as well as longer, sharper ten-year cycles. Mitchell does not find that distinction in the evidence, nor does this author. Cycles vary in length from a year to ten years, each repeating roughly the same sequence of events, so that they are qualitatively similar in their pattern and relationships. There are, of course, some very mild cycles and some very severe cycles, but there is no evidence of two or three mild cycles within each severe, longer cycle. Mitchell proved in detail that cycles of shorter duration than those identified by the NBER would show no regular sequence of events, so their alleged patterns would be statistically insignificant.

On the other hand, some authors claim to have found long cycles of fifty to sixty years in length. The first person to argue this view was Kondratief, for whom they are named. Their most famous advocate was Schumpeter (1939). Little evidence was found for their existence, and discussion of them died away in the prosperous 1950s and 1960s. In the difficult times of the 1970s and 1980s, there has been a revival of interest in long cycles (see the sympathetic survey by Kotz [1987]).

Best known of the advocates of long waves in the present revival are Gordon, Weisskopf, and Bowles (1983), who argue: "The U.S. and world capitalist economies are currently in [the] midst of the third long swing crisis of the past century" (p. 152). How do they define long cycles? They admit that long cycles cannot be dated by total output or investment, but they claim long cycles can be dated by changes in the "social structure of accumulation." This concept is a multidimensional political-economic concept of great complexity, so their empirical estimates remain highly controversial.

Mitchell found no evidence of such long cycles, nor has this author in his own research. How could there be much scientific evidence of "long cycles" when even their advocates have discovered at most three of them? In the next chapter it will be shown that—rather than long waves—capitalism has passed through various stages and that the business cycle shows important differences in these stages.

We must distinguish between different types of movements over time. First, in the very long run, there is an evolution of economic systems from one mode of production to another, for example, from ancient Roman slavery to medieval feudalism in Europe. Second, each economic system evolves and goes through various stages, involving considerable changes, but still recognizably the same system. For example, the U.S. economic system was characterized by very small economic units at one time, but is now in a stage characterized by giant corporations with varying degrees of monopoly power. Third, we may identify many long-run trends, such as the increasing percentage of women in the labor force, generally under one stage of one system, but sometimes crossing over several stages. A long-term trend is almost always completely interrupted when there is an evolutionary or revolutionary change from one system to another. Fourth, there are the alleged long cycles. Fifth, there is the business cycle as defined by Mitchell. Sixth, many economic series have seasonal variations, such as higher growth of construction in warmer months. Seventh, there are also erratic movements of each economic variable, not directly connected to any of the above systematic movements. This book concentrates only on the business cycle, but does introduce long-run trends and stages of capitalism when necessary as a background.

### DATES OF THE CYCLE

Mitchell's method begins by establishing the trough and peak dates of each cycle, using all available evidence, with heaviest reliance on the main aggregate series. Mitchell's work on dating the cycle was taken over by the NBER and then by the U.S. Department of Commerce, which publishes the dates in the *Business Conditions Digest*. The quarterly dates since reconversion from World War II are given in Table 2.1.

Table 2.1 reveals that cycle troughs (the lowest point of each cycle) were reached in 1949, 1954, 1958, 1961, 1970, 1975, 1980, and 1982. The most serious of these were in 1975 and 1982. Notice that the quarter of the year in which the trough occurs varies widely, with no pattern.

These dates are used throughout this book as the best available dates of the business cycle. There are many things that could be criticized about these dates (see Sherman 1986). For example, they do not distinguish in any way between a major depression and a minor recession. They simply record each case where aggregate business activity has continuously declined or continuously risen for some lengthy period. The exact criteria used for dating the peaks and troughs are complex, including a number of indicators; the criteria are clearly explained by Burns and Mitchell (1946, ch. 4) and by Moore (1983, ch. 1). These dates are used both because no better series is available and because they are accepted and used by most scholars in the field. The NBER dates for troughs and peaks go all the way back into the nineteenth century; these

TABLE 2.1
Quarterly Cycle Dates

| Cycle | Initial Trough | Peak | Final Trough |
|-------|---------------|------|--------------|
| 1 | 1949.4 | 1953.3 | 1954.2 |
| 2 | 1954.2 | 1957.3 | 1958.2 |
| 3 | 1958.2 | 1960.2 | 1961.1 |
| 4 | 1961.1 | 1969.4 | 1970.4 |
| 5 | 1970.4 | 1973.4 | 1975.1 |
| 6 | 1975.1 | 1980.1 | 1980.3 |
| 7 | 1980.3 | 1981.3 | 1982.4 |

Source: U.S. Department of Commerce, Bureau of Economic Analysis, *Handbook of Cyclical Indicators, A Supplement to the Business Conditions Digest* (Washington, D.C.: U.S. Government Printing Office, 1984). The dates are derived from the table on page 178 of the source.
Note: 1949.4 means the fourth quarter of 1949.

earlier dates will be given in the next chapter, which deals with the history of the business cycle.

The quarterly dates are used throughout this book because this is probably the best time unit for cycle analysis. As Burns and Mitchell (1946) point out at great length, data given daily, weekly, or even monthly tend to have too much static; in a different metaphor, they lose the forest and show only the trees. On the other hand, annual data leave out many cyclical turning points and are not sufficiently detailed.

## REFERENCE CYCLES VERSUS SPECIFIC CYCLES

The dates given in Table 2.1 determine what the NBER calls a reference cycle. A reference cycle is the average business cycle for all sectors of the U.S. economy. Unless stated otherwise, all empirical analyses of cycles in this book refer to reference cycles.

Each specific economic series, however, has slightly different peaks and troughs from the average cycle. Sometimes it is necessary to look at performance of an economic variable over its own particular cycle dates; this is called a specific cycle. It is used rarely, usually for a variable that differs considerably and systematically from the reference cycle. For example, profit rates almost always *lead* the reference cycle, that is, they turn down before the peak. Some interest rates usually *lag* after the reference cycle, that is, they turn down after the peak.

Note that a cycle may be measured from trough to trough or from peak to peak. Because it is the more common procedure, all cycles in this book are measured from trough to trough.

## DIVISIONS OF THE CYCLE

Mitchell called the rising period of the business cycle, from the initial trough to the peak, the *expansion* period. The declining period of the business cycle, from the peak to the final trough, is called the *contraction* period.

In the business cycle, as defined by Mitchell, there are four phases: two in the expansion period and two in the contraction period. Starting from the low point, or initial trough, of the cycle, there is a rapid upturn, called a *recovery* (or revival). Next, there is a further expansion, called a *prosperity*. This is followed by a downturn, called the *crisis*. Finally, the crisis turns into a contraction, called a *depression*. Mild depressions are sometimes called recessions, but this book will use Mitchell's term of "depression" to describe the final phase of the cycle.

In a more detailed analysis, Mitchell then divides the cycle into nine stages. The number of stages is arbitrary, but has a logic to it. Stage 1 is the initial trough of the cycle, the low point from which it begins. One could measure peak to peak, but that is not as convenient for illustrating most theories of the business cycle, so this book uses trough-to-trough cycles exclusively. Stage 5 is the cycle peak, where most business activity reaches its highest point. Finally, stage 9 is the final trough, from which a new cycle begins. Stages 1, 5, and 9 are, by definition, just three months or one quarter long.

The expansion period lasts from stage 1 to stage 5. The whole expansion (excluding stages 1 and 5) is then divided up into three equal time periods. The three periods of equal length in expansion are called stages 2, 3, and 4. Thus, if the whole expansion is 15 quarters long (excluding stages 1 and 5), each of the three stages will be five quarters long.

Similarly, the contraction period lasts from stage 5 till stage 9. The whole contraction (excluding stages 5 and 9) is then divided up into three equal time periods. The three periods of equal length in contraction are called stages 6, 7, and 8. Thus, if the whole contraction is six quarters long (excluding stages 5 and 9), then each of the three stages will be two quarters long. Since expansions are normally longer than contractions, stages 2, 3, and 4 are normally longer than stages 6, 7, and 8.

The four phases may now be more precisely defined in terms of the nine stages. Thus, recovery is stages 1 to 3, prosperity is stages 3 to 5, crisis is stages 5 to 7, and depression is stages 7 to 9. The entire expansion period is stages 1 to 5, while the entire contraction period is stages 5 to 9. In other words, recovery is the first phase of expansion (stages 1–3),

TABLE 2.2
Pattern of Real Gross National Product (in billions of 1982 dollars)

| | | | | | Stage | | | | |
|---|---|---|---|---|---|---|---|---|---|
| | Trough | | | | Peak | | | | Trough |
| | 1 | 2 | 3 | 4 | 5 | 6 | 7 | 8 | 9 |
| | | E X P A N S I O N | | | | C O N T R A C T I O N | | | |
| PART A. | 1970–1975 Cycle Data | | | | | | | | |
| Original data | $2,414 | $2,485 | $2,588 | $2,721 | $2,762 | $2,747 | $2,737 | $2,695 | $2,643 |
| Cycle relatives | 91.8 | 94.5 | 98.4 | 103.5 | 105.1 | 104.5 | 104.1 | 102.5 | 100.5 |
| PART B. | Data for Average Cycle, 1949–1982, 7 Cycles | | | | | | | | |
| Original data | $1,987 | $2,071 | $2,200 | $2,301 | $2,336 | $2,323 | $2,297 | $2,289 | $2,280 |
| Cycle relatives | 89.6 | 93.9 | 100.1 | 104.7 | 106.4 | 105.8 | 104.7 | 104.3 | 104.0 |

Source: Same as Table 2.1. Gross National Product is Series #50 in the source.

while prosperity is the second phase of expansion (stages 3–5). Similarly, crisis is the first phase of contraction (stages 5–7), while depression is the last phase of contraction (stages 7–9). Mitchell considers that the task of business cycle theory is to explain how each phase leads to the next.

CYCLE RELATIVES

Table 2.2 shows the data for the real gross national product (GNP in real terms, that is, in constant dollars deflated for price inflation). Part A presents the figures for one cycle, namely the fourth quarter of 1970 through the first quarter of 1975. The first row, called "original data," simply indicates the dollar amounts averaged for each of the nine stages of that business cycle.

The second row of Table 2.2 shows the cycle relatives. The cycle relatives are the original data for a variable divided by the average of that variable for the whole cycle. The average for the whole cycle is called the *cycle base*. The average GNP in this cycle was $2,629 billion, so the original data for each stage were divided by that amount to get the nine cycle relatives (which are each multiplied by 100 to make them percentages). For example, GNP in stage 1 was $2,414 billion, which was divided by the cycle base of $2,629 billion (and multiplied by 100) to obtain the cycle relative of 91.8. Thus, a *cycle relative* is just the original data as a percentage of the cycle average (or base) at each stage. This procedure normalizes the data around an average of 100 for the whole cycle. Hence, we can compare the pattern of two entirely different series, such as GNP

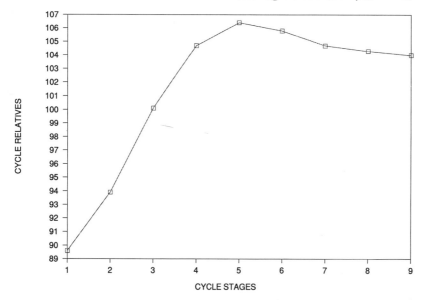

Fig. 2.1. Gross National Product: Amplitude by Stage Averaged across Seven Cycles, 1949–1982 (from series 50, Appendix C)

and interest rates, even though the original units are quite different. We can also compare or average several different cycles of the same variable, even though the cycle base is different in each cycle.

Part B of Table 2.2 and Figure 2.1 present the average GNP data and the average GNP cycle relatives for all seven cycles from 1949 through 1982. We see that GNP is lowest in stage 1, at the initial trough. GNP then rises to its peak at stage 5. GNP then falls to the final trough at stage 9. But since there is growth, the GNP is higher at the final trough of stage 9 than it was at the initial trough of stage 1. That will be true for all growing economic variables, but will not be true for those that are declining or those that are purely cyclical (such as the unemployment rate if it has no secular trend).

Whereas GNP peaks at the cycle peak (stage 5), not all series have individual peaks at the cycle peak. Some, such as profit rates, are leading indicators, which normally turn down *before* the cycle peak. Others, such as interest rates, are lagging indicators, which normally turn down *after* the cycle peak. The broader and more aggregate a variable is, the more likely it is to behave with regularity and in the same cyclical manner as the average of all business activity. GNP is the broadest aggregate variable, so it normally reflects the business cycle, moves smoothly upward in the expansion and smoothly downward in the contraction, and neither leads nor lags.

TABLE 2.3

Growth of Real Gross National Product

(average, 7 cycles, 1949–1982, as percentage of cycle base)

| | Segment | | | | | | | |
|---|---|---|---|---|---|---|---|---|
| | 1–2 | 2–3 | 3–4 | 4–5 | 5–6 | 6–7 | 7–8 | 8–9 |
| | EXPANSION | | | | CONTRACTION | | | |
| Total change | 4.3 | 6.2 | 4.6 | 1.7 | −0.6 | −1.1 | −0.3 | −0.3 |
| Number of quarters | 3 | 5 | 5 | 3 | 1 | 1 | 1 | 1 |
| Change per quarter | 1.4 | 1.2 | 0.9 | 0.6 | −0.6 | −1.1 | −0.3 | −0.3 |

Source: Same as Table 2.1.

Note: The average number of quarters is rounded to the nearest whole number.

RATES OF GROWTH

To study growth or decline, we must examine the change from one period to another. For this purpose, a *segment* is defined as the period from the middle of one stage to the middle of the next. While GNP rises in all segments of expansion and falls in all segments of contraction, it does so at different rates of growth or decline.

In Table 2.3 we measure the total change in the cycle relative from one stage to the next (that is, each segment). The first row of Table 2.3 depicts these amounts of total change in GNP in one segment. The second row shows the average number of quarters in each segment (rounded to be whole numbers). Note that in this period, from 1949 to 1982, the number of quarters in the average expansion varies from three to five quarters per segment, but in the average contraction, there is only around one quarter per segment. Thus, expansions are much longer than contractions in this particular period. This situation—greater length of expansions—does not hold in all periods. In ten of the last twenty-five business cycles, the contraction was longer than the expansion (for example, the latest contraction, 1981–1982, was longer than the preceding expansion).

Finally, we divide the total change in each segment by the number of quarters in that segment to find the rate of growth (or decline) per quarter. These rates of growth are presented in Table 2.3 and Figure 2.2. In the four segments of expansion in the average for all seven cycles, the GNP grew 1.4, 1.2, 0.9, and 0.6 per quarter (as a percentage of its average cycle base). This pattern is typical of most private economic activity in expansions under capitalism. In other words, economic growth is most rapid in the first segment of expansion, less rapid in the second segment,

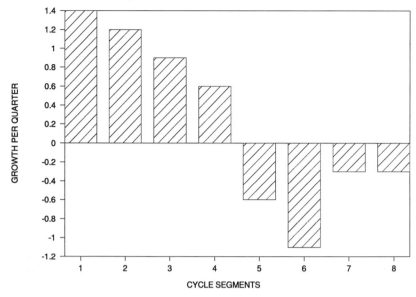

Fig. 2.2. Gross National Product: Growth by Segment Averaged across Seven Cycles, 1949–1982 (from series 50, Appendix F)

even slower in the third segment, and slowest in the final segment before the peak.

Wesley Mitchell noted that the economy always gets slower and slower until it reaches zero growth and then begins to decline. This pattern is not mathematically ordained unless God decreed sine curves. It could be different in every cycle and every variable. It could be imagined that growth is most rapid in the final segment—then there could be an external shock, followed by a sharp downturn. On the contrary, in our actual economy, in the early expansion, even major external shocks can be survived. Normally, it is only after the peak that an external shock will exacerbate the downturn. The pattern of growth is less well defined in contractions, simply because they are usually shorter. Usually, however, the first half of contraction witnesses more rapid decline than does the last half, as illustrated in Figure 2.2. Thus, in the average of all seven cycles, GNP fell at −0.9 per quarter in the first half of contraction, but at only −0.3 per quarter in the last half of contraction.

## CYCLICAL AMPLITUDE

How can we measure the amplitude (or amount of rise and fall) of a cycle so that we can compare different cycles? In most investigations, there is

TABLE 2.4
Cyclical Amplitude of Real Gross National Product

| | Expansion Amplitude (Peak – Initial Trough) | Contraction Amplitude (Final Trough – Peak) |
|---|---|---|
| 1949–1954 cycle | 25.7 | −2.8 |
| 1954–1958 cycle | 10.6 | −3.1 |
| 1958–1961 cycle | 9.4 | −0.3 |
| 1961–1970 cycle | 35.6 | −0.4 |
| 1970–1975 cycle | 13.3 | −4.6 |
| 1975–1980 cycle | 19.8 | −2.5 |
| 1980–1982 cycle | 3.3 | −3.3 |
| Average | 16.7 | −2.4 |

Source: Same as Table 2.1.

always the problem of comparison of percentages derived from different bases. Cycle relatives, however, always start from a base equal to 100, so it is easy to compare amplitudes. Table 2.4 shows cycle amplitudes.

An *expansion amplitude* equals the peak minus the initial trough of the cycle in terms of cycle relatives. The expansion amplitudes shown here—in the second column of Table 2.4—reflect (1) the rate of growth of GNP and (2) the very different lengths of expansions in different cycles. Thus, GNP grew most (35.6 percent) during the long, eight-year expansion of the 1960s, in which the stimulus of the Vietnam War played a major role. The next biggest rise in GNP was during the Korean War in the early 1950s. Notice that the rise from 1980 to 1981 was both brief and weak.

A *contraction amplitude* equals the final trough minus the peak in terms of cycle relatives. It is normally negative, indicating a decline from peak to final trough. The third column of Table 2.4 shows the contraction amplitudes of GNP for each cycle. The sharpest declines in real GNP were in the severe recessions of 1975 and 1982.

## LEADING, LAGGING, AND COINCIDENT INDICATORS

Wesley Mitchell began a research program focusing on those series that usually, on the average, lead the cycle (with peaks before the cycle peak and troughs before the cycle trough), those series that are roughly coincident with cycle peaks and troughs, and those series that usually, on the average, lag behind the cycle (with peaks after the cycle peak and troughs after the cycle trough). The U.S. Department of Commerce now compiles these indicators. Tables 2.5 and 2.6 and Figures 2.3, 2.4, and 2.5 picture the leading, lagging, or coincident behavior of these series.

Table 2.5 shows that the leading indicators peak in stage 4 (peaks are marked by a P), the coincident indicators peak in stage 5 at the cycle peak, and the lagging indicators do not peak until stage 7. Similarly, the leading indicators reach a trough in stage 8 (troughs are marked by a T), the coincident indicators reach a trough in stage 9 at the cycle trough, and the lagging indicators keep falling until stage 2 of the next cycle. In Table 2.6 and in Figures 2.3, 2.4, and 2.5, the rates of growth of each type of indicator are shown. Note that each has its lowest growth rate just before it peaks and begins to decline (this is similar to the behavior of GNP and most other economic variables). Tables 2.5 and 2.6 also show exactly which series are used by the Department of Commerce as leading, lagging, and coincident indicators.

Geoffrey Moore (1983) has done the most work on leading indicators to follow up on Mitchell's pioneering efforts. He says that leading indicators tend to measure anticipations or new commitments, while coincident indicators tend to be comprehensive indicators of economic performance. He explains some of the particular reasons why series normally turn at different times:

> More specifically, series that represent early stages of production and investment processes (new orders for durable goods, housing starts, or permits) lead series that represent late stages (finished output, investment expenditures). Under uncertainty, less binding decisions are taken first. For example, hours of work are lengthened (shortened) before the workforce is altered by new hirings (layoffs). (Moore, 1983, p. 27)

Some of the lagging indicators lag because they represent activities that are influenced by the cycle. Thus, interest rates usually lag behind the cyclical downturn because the downturn causes emergency credit needs, which are accommodated in part but are charged at higher interest rates. The long-term (more than fifteen weeks) unemployment rate lags at the downturn simply because it takes fifteen weeks to add to this group as far as the records are concerned. In the upturn, long-term unemployment lags because it is harder for the long-term unemployed (on the average) to find jobs.

Moore (1983) examined indicators in six foreign countries (Canada, United Kingdom, West Germany, France, Italy, and Japan), using U.S. turning points as benchmarks. He found that "the sequence of turns among the leading, coincident, and lagging groups in each country corresponds roughly to the sequence in the United States" (p. 77). The most extensive survey of indicators, by Klein and Moore (1985), looked at both

TABLE 2.5
Leading, Lagging, and Coincident Indicators: Cycle Relatives
(average of 7 cycles, 1949–1982)

| | | | | | Stage | | | | |
| --- | --- | --- | --- | --- | --- | --- | --- | --- | --- |
| | | | | | Peak | | | | |
| | 1 | 2 | 3 | 4 | 5 | 6 | 7 | 8 | 9 |
| Indicators | | EXPANSION | | | | CONTRACTION | | | |
| 12 Leading (910) | 87 | 95 | 102 | 106P | 104 | 103 | 100 | 99T | 100 |
| 4 Coincident (920) | 87 | 91 | 100 | 107 | 109P | 108 | 106 | 102 | 100T |
| 6 Lagging (930) | 93 | 90T | 96 | 106 | 111 | 112 | 113P | 111 | 109 |

Source: Same as Table 2.1.

Note: Series numbers: The number in parentheses after the name of the series is the number of the series in the source. Peaks and troughs: The peak of each series is indicated by the letter P. The trough of each series is indicated by the letter T. These are reference cycle dates given by the NBER and Department of Commerce. Components: According to the Department of Commerce, the twelve leading indicators (in an average index in series #910) are as follows: #1—Average weekly hours of production workers in manufacturing; #5—Average weekly initial claims for unemployment insurance; #8—Manufacturers' new orders for consumer goods and materials in constant dollars; #12—Index of net business formation; #19—Index of stock prices, 500 common stocks; #20—Contracts and orders for plant and equipment, in constant dollars; #29—Index of new private housing units authorized by local building permits; #32—Vendor performance, percentage of companies receiving slower deliveries; #36—Change in manufacturing and trade inventories, in constant dollars; #99—Change in sensitive materials prices; #106—Money supply (M2) in constant dollars; #111—Change in business and consumer credit outstanding. According to the Department of Commerce, the four coincident indicators (indexed in series #920) are as follows: #41—Employees on nonagriculture payrolls; #47—Index of industrial production; #51—Personal income less transfer payments, in constant dollars; #57—Manufacturing and trade sales, in constant dollars. According to the Department of Commerce, the six lagging indicators (indexed in series #930) are as follows: #62—Index of labor cost per unit of output, manufacturing; #77—Ratio, manufacturing and trade inventories to sales; #91—Average duration of unemployment in weeks; #95—Ratio, consumer installment credit outstanding to personal income; #101—Commercial and industrial loans outstanding, in constant dollars; #109—Average prime rate charged by banks.

TABLE 2.6
Leading, Lagging, and Coincident Indicators: Growth per Quarter
(average of 7 cycles, 1949–1982)

| | | | | | Segment | | | | |
| --- | --- | --- | --- | --- | --- | --- | --- | --- | --- |
| | 1–2 | 2–3 | 3–4 | 4–5 | Peak | 5–6 | 6–7 | 7–8 | 8–9 |
| Indicators | | EXPANSION | | | | CONTRACTION | | | |
| 12 Leading (910) | 2.6 | 1.5 | 0.7 | −0.4 | | −1.8 | −2.3 | −1.5 | 1.2 |
| 4 Coincident (920) | 1.6 | 1.8 | 1.3 | 0.8 | | −1.3 | −2.6 | −3.4 | −1.7 |
| 6 Lagging (930) | −1.1 | 1.3 | 1.8 | 1.9 | | 1.8 | 0.5 | −2.0 | −2.5 |

Source: Same as Table 2.1.
Notes: Same as Table 2.5.

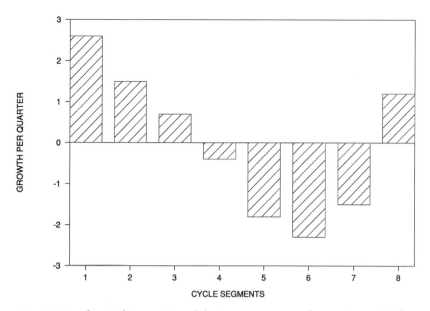

Fig. 2.3. Leading Indicators: Growth by Segment Averaged across Seven Cycles, 1949–1982 (from series 910, Appendix F)

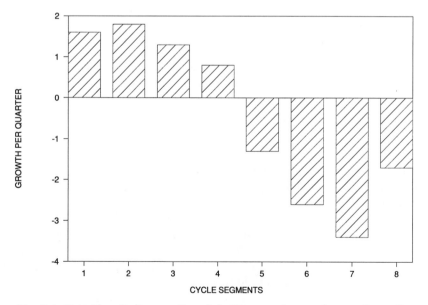

Fig. 2.4. Coincident Indicators: Growth by Segment Averaged across Seven Cycles, 1949–1982 (from series 920, Appendix F)

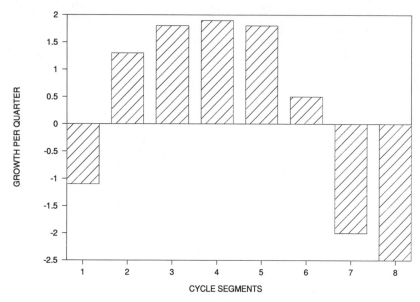

Fig. 2.5. Lagging Indicators: Growth by Segment Averaged across Seven Cycles, 1949–1982 (from series 930, Appendix F)

so-called classical cycles (actual upturns and downturns) and so-called growth cycles (upturns and downturns in growth rates). When the U.S. economy suffered classical downturns, Europeans and Japanese sometimes suffered only growth rate downturns. Klein and Moore found:

> So far we have seen that most of the leading and lagging indicators that display consistent behavior at classical turning points in the United States have a similar record of leading and lagging growth cycle turning points in at least nine additional countries. . . . The indicator systems we have developed suggest that the cyclical interrelations among economic processes are quite similar in each of them. (p. 109)

Thus, we find clear regularities in sequential processes over the cycle, not only in the United States, but in all of the leading capitalist countries. Moreover, they turn at roughly the same time in all of these countries, as we shall see in detail in the chapter on international processes.

The reader should be cautioned that, while the leading indicators always correctly predict a depression or a recovery, this can be known with certainty only by hindsight. In the first place, there is a time lag from the peak of the leading indicators to the cycle peak, but it is quite variable and unpredictable except as an average. Second, a dip in the leading indicators always forecasts a dip in aggregate activity, but the amount is quite variable, from a small decline in the growth rate to a major depression. Thus, the leading indicators are a useful tool for understanding the past, but a very doubtful tool for predicting the future.

## THE BUSINESS CYCLE AS A UNIT

Mitchell's method forces us to look at an entire business cycle, not just the expansion phase or the contraction phase separately. This means that it is not scientifically justifiable to examine a business cycle that is still in progress and not completed. As this book is being written, the present business cycle, which commenced in 1983, has not yet completed its expansion phase. Therefore, the author must resist the temptation for a full-scale examination of the present situation. As a result of the decision to examine each whole business cycle as one unit, *this book covers systematically only the time span ending in 1982*, with a few exceptions for long-run trends.

## APPENDIXES FOR REFERENCE TO DATA

Appendixes A through H refer to cycles in certain time periods bounded by the initial troughs and final troughs as determined by the NBER and the Department of Commerce; these cycles are called *reference cycles*, as opposed to specific cycles for each variable (which could differ from the reference cycles). The cycles in the Appendixes—and throughout the book—are always dated by quarter and always use quarterly statistics.

The original data are not presented because they are so easily available, but Appendix A does provide brief definitions of all the variables; it also cites the source where longer definitions are available. Appendix B contains the cycle bases, that is, the average of a variable over the cycle, for each of the seven cycles since 1949. This allows the reader to observe absolute levels and to trace long-run trends, completely separate from business cycle influence. Appendix C presents the cycle relatives, averaged for all seven cycles from 1949 to 1982. Appendix D presents the cycle relatives for the average of four cycles from 1949 to 1970, because that is one significant period. Appendix E averages the cycle relatives for the three cycles from 1970 to 1982, because that period is significantly different from the previous period. Similarly, the growth rates per quarter are presented for all seven cycles (1949–1982) in Appendix F, for the four cycles of 1949–1970 in Appendix G, and for the three cycles of 1970–1982 in Appendix H. Not all variables are presented in every appendix, but only those pertinent to this book and mentioned in this book.

These appendixes are for reference throughout the book and are not designed to be read at once. Therefore, for the convenience of the reader, they are all located at the end of the book. Also, for the convenience of the reader, each appendix is arranged in order of the series numbers in the main source, cited in each appendix.

# CHAPTER 3

# History of the Business Cycle

JEAN B. SAY, a French economist writing in the early nineteenth century, declared the "law" that supply calls forth its own demand; that is, after any temporary disequilibrium, demand always adjusts to the level of supply so that the economy reaches equilibrium. Since demand adjusts to supply at *any* level of supply, it follows that if goods are supplied at the full employment level, the economy will adjust to a full employment equilibrium. Say's law implies that workers are never unemployed for any significant time as a result of lack of demand for labor, so most unemployment can be interpreted as "voluntary" by workers.

The ridiculous idea that millions of workers are voluntarily unemployed and that the economy is really at full employment equilibrium most of the time was an accepted part of orthodox economic wisdom from Say's time till the Great Depression of the 1930s—and still has many defenders. In the next chapter, the modern defenses of Say's law are examined, as well as the thorough refutation of Say's law by J. M. Keynes in the 1930s. This chapter considers the historical-institutional critique of Say's law, based on the approach of Wesley Mitchell. Mitchell contends—as in his definition of the business cycle cited in the previous chapter—that the business cycle takes place if, and only if, the institutions of a private enterprise capitalism are the dominant institutions. According to Mitchell, there is involuntary unemployment under capitalism.

Say's law denies that aggregate supply can be greater than aggregate demand (except temporarily). In the next chapter, we shall see that J. M. Keynes emphasized that the effective demand (demand in money terms) can be less than supply for a long time, causing a recession or depression. This chapter, therefore, concentrates on the historical conditions and institutions under which demand may be less than supply, causing a cyclical downturn. This does not mean that lack of demand is necessarily the only cause of cycles; that is a vital issue for later discussion and is not prejudged here.

Many economists, including Karl Marx and Thorstein Veblen (who was Mitchell's teacher) have pointed out that Say's law does hold true for earlier societies in which (1) production was for the self-use of the economic unit; (2) the motive of production was not to maximize individual profit; and (3) the very limited exchange that existed was conducted by barter. Say's law, however, does not hold true for a modern private enterprise capitalist economy, in which (1) production is for exchange in the market; (2) production is motivated by private profit; and (3) the economy is characterized by the general use of money and credit. Each of these conditions are considered in detail in this chapter, after which we examine the stages of evolution of the capitalist economy, the changes that have occurred in the business cycle in different stages and in some periods within stages of capitalism, and an empirical description of the cycle in three different periods of U.S. history.

## PRODUCTION FOR THE MARKET

It was characteristic of the private enterprise economy that was fully developed in England by the end of the eighteenth century that most production was solely directed toward its sale on the market. This was hardly ever true of earlier societies. In the most primitive societies, almost all productive activity was directed to production of food by mere gathering or growing of fruit and vegetables or hunting of animals by the collective unit of all the males and/or females of the tribe. Naturally, the produce was usually consumed in roughly equal proportions by these same tribal members or their families. Even at a later stage (characterized by agriculture and herding), production was for use, not sale; none of the Indian tribes of the Americas, not even the Aztecs, bought or sold land or produced crops to sell for a profit to others. In fact, "For the red man soil existed only in order to meet the necessities of life, and production, not profit, was the basis of his economy. . . . Unemployment was certainly never a problem in the Indian communities of early America" (Crow 1948, 54).

Since tribes handled most production collectively, there was little, if any, trade among its members. In fact, very little commerce was transacted between the most primitive tribes, and that was mostly limited to small and precious materials for their decorative or magical qualities. Even a relatively more advanced society, the Inca empire of South America, still was based on a self-sufficient economic unit consisting of a few families, called the ayllu, whose only external economic relation was the work-service tax owed to the state and paid in agricultural produce or work on government projects (see Crow 1948, 26–29). In fact, all over the world, for thousands of years, almost all economic systems—whether tribal or feudal—were based on relatively self-sufficient agricultural units.

In the Roman Empire there was a great deal of trade, but most of it was in luxury goods and did not affect the self-sufficiency of the basic agricultural unit, the slave-run plantation (although a lack of surplus could bring starvation to large numbers of city dwellers). As one author says, "[N]otwithstanding the phenomenal expansion of trade and industry the vast masses inside the Empire still continued to win their livelihood from the soil. Agriculture remained throughout antiquity the most usual most typical economic activity, and land the most important form of wealth" (Walbank 1956, 11–13). Rome did have unemployment among the urban laborers, most of whom were former peasants forced off the land by the competition of slavery. This was a long-run phenomenon caused by the complete lack of mass markets, not a cyclical breakdown of the market.

Feudal England lacked both extensive trade and towns because the primitive level of technology made the supply of large urban populations impossible and even greatly restricted trade between the villages. During most of the feudal period, England had very little trade with the rest of Europe. Of course, in the later medieval period, there were areas of more highly developed industrial production, such as Flanders and northern Italy, and even relatively backward England carried on a systematic wool trade with Flanders. Yet these were exceptions to the general rule of the feudal economy and may be considered early signs pointing to the beginning of the end of that economy.

During the Middle Ages, market institutions, as we know them today, were not well developed. If there happened to be surplus production from the slave or feudal estate, then it might be marketed in return for foreign luxury items for the lord of the estate, but it was not a matter of life and death for the economic unit. If the surplus found no market, the manor was still supplied with its necessities for that year and could and would continue the process of production for next year's needs.

Such economically self-sufficient societies could be disturbed only by those catastrophes that were more or less "external" to the economy, namely, the vicissitudes of nature (such as droughts, plagues, or floods) or the whims of human beings (such as government interference, war, or revolution). These phenomena could and did depress production (and bring about famines), both in various randomly spaced intervals and seasonally because of the special seasonal sensitivity of agriculture. Such economies could not, however, conceivably face the problem of lack of effective demand for all commodities, which is a serious frequent problem in market economics. The problem of lack of demand could not exist because the economic unit directly consumed most of the products of its own land and could do without trade altogether.

In the transitional period, in the England of the sixteenth, seventeenth, and eighteenth centuries, the majority of the people still lived on the land; but more and more products, both agricultural and industrial, were delivered to the marketplace. There was increasing long-run unemployment in this period because peasants were removed from agricultural production much more rapidly than employment grew in capitalist industry—but the unemployment was not cyclical.

By the end of the eighteenth century, the private enterprise system of production for the market embraced most of the economic activity. Production of commodities for the market was no longer a matter of accident as it had been, but was one of the most essential features of the private enterprise system. In the nineteenth century, one business entrepreneur might own a factory producing millions of shoes, but the whole family of the entrepreneur could consume only a few of these. The shoes had to be sold in order to buy other consumer goods for the entrepreneur's family, to pay wages to those working for the business, and to replace and expand the plant and equipment of the business.

In earlier economic systems, the self-sufficient economic unit—or the artisan producing a trickle of handmade items for known customers—could not possibly be troubled by lack of demand for its products. When almost all that was produced by the economic unit was consumed by it, lack of demand was not going to be a problem. But in the industrialized private enterprise system, the specialized businessperson produces only for the market and cannot continue production if there is no demand for his or her products in the market. This, then, is the first main institutional feature of the private enterprise economy of the late eighteenth century. It was one of three conditions making possible the beginning of large-scale, cyclical unemployment at that time.

## REGULAR USE OF MONEY

A second institutional feature that is necessary before there can be a deficiency of aggregate demand is the regular use of money in exchange, which takes the place of the barter system of exchanging goods for goods. Many economists have concentrated on this as the sole necessary condition for the possibility of a lack of effective demand, but that is because they hold that production for exchange in the market invariably accompanies the regular use of money in exchange. These two conditions might be presented in a single formal statement, but it is analytically useful to separate them.

Among the most primitive tribes, where there is very little trade, exchange is conducted by barter. In slightly more advanced societies, barter is still the only mode of exchange; but certain commodities, such as cows or horses, may be used as "money" in the sense that the value of all other commodities are calculated in terms of them. Only when there is a large volume of trade will a system begin to grow up more like that of the modern monetary economy, usually with a certain amount of precious metals becoming the known equivalent of certain amounts of all other commodities. At a still later period, the metals are stamped into coins, originally with the purpose of figuring amounts more conveniently and facilitating the exchange of goods.

The use of money, however, brings many new complications onto the economic scene. In the Roman Empire, for example, vast amounts of money were needed by the government to support wars of expansion, large standing armies, police and bureaucracy, and an unfavorable balance of trade (owing to the importing of luxuries from the East). The emperors were eventually forced to the expedient of debasing their coins by clipping or by contamination with baser metals. As the government debased the coins and as production declined in the later days of the empire, the amount that could be bought with the coins declined rapidly; in other words, a catastrophic inflation occurred.

In spite of the Romans' financial troubles and difficulties in the use of money, they were not confronted with the modern problem of "too many" commodities in the market relative to the money demand for them. Regular use of money was not enough, by itself, to usher in the menace of a lack of aggregate demand so long as most of the Roman economy was still contained in self-sufficient agricultural units. The luxury trade in the empire did suffer from the extreme inflation, but it was only one more affliction in addition to colonial wars, slave revolts, the extreme inefficiency of employing slave labor, and the Roman citizen's attitude that any participation in the work process was degrading (because work was only for slaves). Moreover, since most of the people still lived on the land, the relatively small amount of trade and commerce that did exist was not absolutely necessary to the continued functioning of most of the economy. This is not to deny that trade was essential to the preservation of the empire as a political unit and to the existence of higher culture in large urban centers, especially Rome. Rome was an importer of grain from Egypt and North Africa, as well as of wine and various fruits from Gaul, to mention only some of the more important imports. When this trade declined in the second century, the Roman cities suffered and also declined, but the agricultural units continued, though in new forms and on an even more self-sufficient basis.

With the breakup of the Roman Empire, trade suffered a considerable decline; in early feudalism the pattern was overwhelmingly that of the isolated, self-sufficient manor. Barter, therefore, grew in importance, and the use of money declined. On each manor, in return for the lord's "protection," the serf provided all the necessary articles of consumption and services needed by the lord, his family, and his retinue. In the later medieval period, however, technology began to improve, and industry and commerce slowly began to revive and reach new heights in Western Europe. The widespread trade of the later medieval period eventually led to the replacing of barter by a money economy; at the same time, as noted in the preceding section, production was increasingly designed for sale on the market rather than for use at home.

With the increased use of money, exchange in the market required the use of money as an intermediary. If the holder of money, for whatever reason, decided to hold it and abstain from using it for purchase, the demand for market commodities was lower than it otherwise would have been. Some goods available for sale on the market would remain unsold.

Most classical economists denied that the introduction of money into exchange could cause problems. For example, David Ricardo contended that "productions are always bought by productions, or by services; money is only the medium by which the exchange is effected" (Ricardo [1817] 1891, 275). It is true that one function of money is to facilitate the exchange of commodities, but it has other uses as well. In the modern economy the seller obtains only money for commodities. The seller may or may not use the money at a later time to buy other commodities; in the meantime, money may be used for the storage of value for future use. It is thus possible for a person to buy or sell without doing the opposite action at the same time. It is not always the case that all buyers will immediately use their money to buy what they want. There is, therefore, no inherent necessity in a money economy that sellers should find buyers for all commodities brought to market.

The problem is not an aggregate lack of money in the economy. While the poor, who wish to buy goods, have no money, the rich, who have money, may be reducing their spending. The chain of circulation may then be broken at any point at which the flow of money is slowed in its movement. The reduction of the flow of circulation, like the reduction of the volume of water flowing in a stream, by this means causes a slowdown in the movement of products. Although it is basically true that commodities are exchanged for commodities even after the introduction of money, the mere necessity of the money bridge makes all the difference in the world. If the bridge is absent, finished commodities may pile up in warehouses while potential consumers are unable to buy them. Only money can make a possible consumer into an actual buyer in the private enterprise system. Thus, the use of money makes possible the lack of aggregate effective, or monetary, demand for commodities, so it is a precondition of the business cycle.

An excess of supply in this economic system does not mean that everyone is fully satisfied. In every recession or depression, there are millions of poor people who would be happy to have more goods and services. Therefore, the problem is not overproduction of the total commodities of a society in the absolute sense that the supply is greater than what people want or desire; rather, the problem is that there may be "too many" commodities on the market relative to the monetary, or "effective," demand for them. The term "effective demand" simply means desire combined with money because desire or need without money has no effect under capitalism.

An additional problem in the sphere of money may arise from the use of tokens or paper money. The government may always cause some degree of inflation by merely having its printing presses start turning out more paper money. The economies of Europe, for example, were brought to their knees by the spectacular collapse of the French and English finance markets in the early eighteenth century. Excessive printing of paper money by these two governments resulted in a wild speculation in financial securities. The ensuing collapse destroyed numerous fortunes, escalated unemployment, and caused economic distress for nearly a decade.

An additional complication arises from the fact that money may merely be used as a unit of account for indebtedness—that is, in the form of credit. The use of credit intensifies all money problems because not only may a person sell something and not immediately purchase something else, but it is also possible to sell something and not receive the proceeds of the sale for some time. If Brown owes Smith, and Smith owes Johnson, and Johnson owes Martin, then a break anywhere along this chain of credit circulation will be disastrous for all the later parties in the chain. Moreover, the chain in the modern private enterprise economy is usually circular in nature, so that the reverberations reach the starting point and may begin to go around again. This does not, of course, explain why the chain should ever break in the first place.

It has been argued here that no problem of deficient effective demand was possible before money and credit institutions became the usual way of doing business. Does this mean that these institutions are sufficient to explain recessions and depressions? We know that money and credit existed in ancient Rome and during the sixteenth to eighteenth centuries in Western Europe; yet the financial disturbances of those times do not seem to have been the same sort of phenomenon as the modern type of economic downturn. It is true that after the development of money and credit, every catastrophic natural happening or violent political event might be reflected in a sudden distrust of monetary institutions and a panic in the financial markets. For example, when the English fleet was burned by the Dutch in 1667 and also in 1672 when Charles II stopped payments from the Exchequer, there were sudden runs on the London banks. In the eighteenth century, financial crises resulted from the Jacobite conspiracy in 1708, the bursting of the South Sea Bubble (a stock speculation) in 1720, the fighting with the Young Pretender in 1745, the aftermath of the Seven Years' War in 1763, and the disturbances caused by the American revolutionary war.

Wesley Mitchell comments, however, that these panics were unlike the modern business contractions in both cause and effect. First, they originated in "external" causes rather than in the endogenous mechanisms that operate (as we shall see) under capitalism. Second, they resulted in only limited depressions in a few trades. He concludes that the first truly general industrial depression of the modern type appeared as late as 1793 in England (Mitchell 1913, 583–84).

Distress in the financial sector has been a key causal factor in most depressions, but that is not always the case. Usually, the more serious downturns have involved one form of financial catastrophe or another. The contribution of the financial sector to economic distress will be reviewed in later chapters.

## PRODUCTION FOR PRIVATE PROFIT

Two necessary conditions have been examined—(1) production for the market and (2) the regular use of money—which must be present if a business contraction occurs in which demand fluctuates below the full employment level of supply. At least one more institutional condition is necessary before it can be said that a downturn may be caused by the fact that total demand is not equal to total supply in an economy. The third condition is the existence of private ownership of production facilities and production for private profit.

In an economy based on private ownership of individual competing units, the sum of their decisions to produce may not equal the sum of decisions by other individuals and businesses to spend—that is, to consume and invest. If the sum of the value of outputs is greater than the sum of the monetary, or effective, demand, then there is not enough revenue to cover the costs of production and an additional profit for the private entrepreneur. The criterion is decisive because if the private entrepreneur is not making a profit, the entrepreneur will reduce or discontinue production, machinery will stand idle, and many, if not all, of the workers of that enterprise will be unemployed.

No economists ever spent more time discussing the profit motive as the central motivation for production than did the classical economists. Yet, except in the case of Malthus, the fact that production might prove unprofitable does not often seem to have entered their discussions of business declines; therefore, they reached the conclusion of the impossibility of a contraction caused by lack of profitability in the private enterprise system. Actually, the possibility always exists that the production of commodities may outpace the demand for commodities, at least at a price sufficient to cover costs and also yield a profit.

As a tentative conclusion, precapitalist societies do not suffer from cyclical downturns due to lack of demand because they have limited exchange, the few exchanges are made by barter, and production is not primarily motivated by private profit. In the sixteenth and seventeenth centuries, market exchange became more extensive, and there was a gradual spread of the use of money; yet most production was not capitalist and was not focused on private profit. In this transitional period, use of money and credit did cause some random disruptions, but no systematic business cycle. The business cycle only emerged in England in the late eighteenth century, when the capitalist form became predominant. Under capitalism, most commodities were exchanged in the market (including labor power, which was bought and sold and could be left unemployed); private profit became the primary motivation of production (so there was no production if there was no expectation of profit); and, of course, the use of money and credit further expanded.

## The Spread of the Business Cycle

Wesley Mitchell argues that "the total number of past business cycles may well be less than a thousand. For business cycles are a phenomena peculiar to a certain form of economic organization which has been dominant even in Western Europe for less than two centuries, and for briefer periods in other regions" (Mitchell and Thorp 1926, 47).

The business cycle of capitalism appears to have made its first appearance in England—and then only at the end of the eighteenth century. The periods of economic crisis before that time were easily attributable to external or purely political events. It does appear that the British business cycle of the nineteenth century was an indigenous product of British economic development. The vast British trading network, however, reached most other countries in the world; therefore, in most other countries the cycle must have been partly a product of diffusion from England as well as of independent evolution. That does not mean, of course, that England has remained unaffected by the consequent development of other countries or that it is the country that is least influenced by present-day international events.

The business cycle is found in all capitalist countries, but the forms of the cycle are much influenced by international events and national peculiarities. There is a similar progression of cycle phases in country after country. Yet, no two cycles are exactly the same; they differ in cause, duration, industrial scope, intensity, and importance of various aspects and also in how rapidly they spread from one country to another. The most highly developed industrial countries, such as England, France, and Germany, have closely linked and coincident cycles. In the nineteenth century, however, the less developed and mainly agricultural countries, such as czarist Russia, Brazil, and China, diverged quite considerably from the international pattern (Mitchell and Thorp 1926, 93).

Wesley Mitchell found that the modern business cycle began in England in 1793; in the United States in 1796 (influenced by England); in France in 1847; in Germany in 1857; and during 1888 to 1891 in czarist Russia, Argentina, Brazil, Canada, South Africa, Australia, India, Japan, and China. After 1890, the business cycle assumed a truly international character with regard to major cycles. It also seems significant that there are no records of recurrent cycles in the less developed countries prior to that period, for these countries were mainly agricultural and did not have the capitalist institutions specified in the three conditions discussed earlier. After 1890, when the European economies came to dominate the rest of the capitalist world through colonization, trade, and investment, the cycle became more and more pronounced in the less developed countries. In the 1929 crash, every country in the world felt the impact and went into a depression period (excepting only the USSR). Again, in 1938, most countries suffered a relapse together. In Western Europe and Japan, recessions in the United States did not cause major downturns in the 1950s and 1960s. In the downturn of 1973 to 1975, however, these countries joined the U.S. economic contraction—and again in the period 1980 to 1982 all these countries joined the United States in a decline. In summary, the business cycle has spread as capitalist institutions have spread. Moreover, as capitalist economies intertwined, their business cycles became more synchronized.

## Stages in U.S. Capitalism

We shall see that the business cycle in the United States is not a static thing, but has changed dramatically. These changes in the business cycle reflected changes in the structure of U.S. capitalism. Originally, the United States was a colony, and its economy was dominated by England. Even after independence, British domination continued in a typical neocolonial pattern well into the nineteenth century.

The first stage of U.S. capitalism (in the early nineteenth century) resembled other underdeveloped economies, remaining dependent for investment and trade on England, being mainly agricultural, with underdeveloped small businesses, little government spending, underdeveloped organization of workers, an underdeveloped financial system, and no international power. The second stage of U.S. capitalism (late nineteenth and early twentieth centuries) was marked by the rise of monopoly power, in both industry and finance, with the relative decline of agriculture, and economic independence 'from England, but little U.S. international power. The third stage of U.S. capitalism, starting in the late 1930s, witnessed the rise of government power in the United States, both domestically and as the leading international power of the 1950s and 1960s. In the 1970s and 1980s, this stage continued, with respect to the importance of government and of the international sector, but the United States suffered a relative international decline, marked both by economic competition from Europe and Japan and by military defeat in Vietnam.

Now let us examine some of these trends in more detail. As noted above, in the first half of the nineteenth century the U.S. economy was still mainly agricultural, though with some commercial capital. Business was very small business, with strong competition in some industries, although regions were isolated from each other. The immature U.S. economy did not, for the most part, generate its own business cycles, but reacted to British business cycles with a time lag. After the Civil War, U.S. capitalism grew up, with many giant corporations and monopolies or oligopolies in many industries. Mergers came in waves, with a big wave from the late 1960s to the present. The impact of monopoly power on business cycles will be examined later.

Trade unions were fairly weak during most of U.S. history, but grew rapidly in the 1930s and 1940s because of labor militancy (due to the Great Depression), the friendly environment of the New Deal, and the full employment of World War II. Since the mid-1950s, however, union strength has waned because of hostile governments, the rise of the service sector, and the decline of the industrial sector. As a result, there has been a major, long-run fall in the percentage of unionized workers, reflected in a decline of union political and economic strength. Whereas one-third of U.S. workers were unionized in 1955, only about one-sixth are now unionized. Weak and declining union power is now a fact of life, though explanations for it differ widely. How the decline of unions has affected income distribution over the business cycle will be discussed in detail when the importance of income distribution is considered.

The U.S. banking and credit system was underdeveloped throughout the nineteenth century, with many financial crises and collapses resulting from its chaotic nature. After the 1907 financial panic, legislation was finally instituted leading to some control of the banking system by the Federal Reserve system. The 1920s were marked by much financial innovation and speculative expansion of credit, which helped set the stage for the collapse of 1929. During the 1930s, more controls and regulations were put into effect. The new regulations helped control finances during the war and the prosperous 1950s and 1960s. Striking new financial innovations along with deregulation led to a vastly overextended and vulnerable banking and credit system in the 1970s and 1980s, with some notable failures. Huge amounts of consumer debt, corporate debt, and government debt are another major fact of life in the modern U.S. economy; this book will emphasize their impact on the business cycle.

Except for war periods, there was very little government spending in the United States until the 1930s. As late as 1929, the U.S. government spent only 1 percent of GNP. Even in the 1930s, this rose to only 3 or 4 percent. During World War II, federal spending rose to 40 percent of GNP. Since World War II, federal spending has remained very high, with peaks during the Korean and Vietnam wars and in the Reagan years. Since state and local spending has also risen very rapidly, total government spending is now a large percentage of GNP. Revenue did not rise as rapidly, so government deficits are now very large (the government debt tripled in the Reagan years). Thus, after the model is outlined for the private sphere, the strong government impact on the business cycle will be discussed in detail.

Finally, after the end of British domination, the action of international influences on the U.S. economy remained relatively minor until after World War II. In the 1950s, the United States was the dominant world power in every respect, including production, trade, and investment. The U.S. impact on other countries was enormous, but others had seemingly little impact on the U.S. economy. By the 1970s, however, the U.S. economy was strongly affected by international relationships. For example, U.S. imports rose from 5.8 percent of GNP in 1949 to 11.4 percent in 1986. Moreover, the U.S. economy faced fierce foreign competition, even in its home market. By the 1980s, exports had risen, but imports rose even faster, and there was a huge trade deficit. The U.S. economy continues to make large investments abroad, but foreign investment in the United States is now very significant. Thus, the much higher level of international connections will be emphasized as another factor in the changes that have occurred in the U.S. business cycle.

These long-run structural changes have had several disturbing effects on U.S. capitalism since about 1970 (a number of these long-run trends are presented quantitatively in MacEwan [1989], and also in dramatic detail in Harrison and Bluestone [1988]). First, in the 1970s and 1980s, growth of productivity slowed considerably, with weak expansions and significant declines in recessions. Second, in the 1970s and 1980s the rate of unemployment rose in each recession to a higher rate than in the previous recession, so we can speak of a long-run trend toward higher unemployment in this period. Third, in the 1970s and 1980s, real hourly wages (taking inflation into account) actually declined; their average fell from $6.66 in 1980 to $6.32 in 1988. In this period, there were slight increases in real hourly wages in cyclical expansions and significant declines in cyclical contractions. Fourth, inequality of income distribution increased in the 1970s and 1980s, with the poor having declining real incomes since 1973, while the rich had rising real incomes. Fifth, inequality in wealth distribution also increased in the 1973 to 1989 period. The increased inequality of income was largely due to the increase of dividends, rent, and interest. The Gini index of income inequality declined from .376 in 1949 to .348 in 1968 (reflecting more equality), and then rose to .390 in 1986 (reflecting growing inequality [see Harrison and Bluestone 1988, 130]).

## LONG-RUN CHANGES AND REGULARITY IN THE BUSINESS CYCLE

The historical stages of capitalism, as well as the long-run trends within each stage, have greatly affected the business cycle. The misery of the Great Depression of the 1920s and 1930s was followed by a long period of war prosperity in the 1940s, with very mild recessions in the 1950s and 1960s. The 1970s and 1980s again witnessed severe contractions. The patterns or sequences of cyclical behavior in the 1970s and 1980s resembled the 1930s more than they did the 1950s and 1960s, although the severity of depressions in the 1970s and 1980s was nowhere near that of the Great Depression. Because business cycles are unique and change in each historical period, this book will usually consider the business cycle behavior of the 1920s and 1930s as quite distinct from later behavior, while the cyclical behavior in the period of the 1950s and 1960s will be considered as quite distinct from the 1970s and 1980s behavior.

On the other hand, while recognizing that each business cycle is unique, it is also worth emphasizing that the basic dynamics and pattern of the business cycle have persisted over a long time. Zarnowitz and Moore (1986) point out that the leading and lagging indicators have remained remarkably consistent in the last hundred years in the United States: "[T]he most notable feature of the record is the absence of major changes in the timing relationships among the group of indicators" (p. 571).

Furthermore, Klein and Moore (1985, 81) find that the sequence of turning points in the leading, coincident, and lagging indicators is much the same in all of the capitalist countries. Their finding is based on examination of six cycles in each of nine countries (United States, Canada, United Kingdom, West Germany, France, Italy, Belgium, the Netherlands, Sweden, and Japan). Thus, there is considerable evidence that the same type of internal mechanism of the business cycle exists in all capitalist countries at all stages of capitalism, though in very different and unique forms in each cycle.

## CYCLES IN THE U.S. ECONOMY

When a country is in its early stages of industrial development it is difficult to be independent of foreign influences. Likewise, when a country is small and unable to be self-sufficient, it is usually dependent on foreign supply and demand. In the beginning of the nineteenth century, the United States was immature industrially, and its main centers of commerce and industry were limited to the small area along its Atlantic coast. Therefore, the United States, at that period, was very susceptible to foreign influences on its economy, especially to the trade and investment of the United Kingdom. The basic direction of influence was surely from the rapidly developing industry of the United Kingdom outward to the less developed industry and commerce of the United States. When depressions developed in England, they often led to depressions in America because of the decline of American imports to England. In the few instances where the American decline began first, the reduction of British investment opportunities may have spread the depression to England.

Investment in the United States brought big profits, but had great risks attached to it and was subject to violent swings, according to the decisions of foreign investors. All the other features of the U.S. economy were also typical of a less developed country, including the following characteristics of that period. Two-thirds or more of all U.S. produce was agricultural. Most enterprises in the North and West, whether farm or handicraft, were one-person proprietorships. In the South, there were large slave plantations; there is no indication of internal generation of a business cycle under slavery, but Southern U.S. slavery was affected by business cycles in the rest of the world. Much work was done at home, and shop windows were often merely that part of the home that fronted on the street. There were few urban wage workers because there were few shops of more than one person (with perhaps an apprentice). Markets were limited to the local area. Most families in Northern agriculture were largely self-sufficient. There were large unclaimed and unexplored areas in the West. There was much barter, little use of money, and an undeveloped and inefficient banking system. By far the most important section of capital was engaged in commerce—and largely foreign commerce at that. Since it lacked the necessary conditions, the U.S. economy of the early period (at least until 1837) did not have internally generated cycles. (Material in this section is mainly from Lee [1955] and Mirowski [1985].)

In the period from 1837 to 1860, foreign influences were somewhat less important, and business cycles were partly the result of internal generation. If not dominant, however, foreign influences certainly played an often decisive part in U.S. development. For example, the British financial panic of 1847 led directly to the moderate U.S. depression of 1848.

The period from the Civil War to the end of the nineteenth century was the period in which the United States reached industrial maturity. By the end of that period, the corporate form of business was predominant; only a sixth of all output was agricultural; agriculture itself was more commercial and market-directed; the factory system with thousands of workers had replaced the small handicraft shops and the home production of almost all articles; the United States had a system of heavy industry, which was as complex and interrelated as any in the world; organized management faced a growing union movement; money had replaced barter in every aspect of the economy; markets were national or international in scope; the frontier had ended; and commerce provided only a small part of the national income. Since it now had the conditions of advanced capitalism, the U.S. economy generated its own cycles, but still interacted closely with Western European cycles.

In the United States in the twentieth century, foreign relations have dominated the domestic economy only in the major wars: World War I, World War II, the Korean War, and the Vietnam War. Otherwise, domestic internal mechanisms have dominated the U.S. business cycle, though military spending and international trade and investment have obviously played an increasingly significant role. Major declines in the U.S. economy, such as the Great Depression of the 1930s or the severe recessions of 1975 and 1982, have severely hurt the rest of the world. The mild recessions that the U.S. economy undergoes every three or four years do not have a major effect on most of the world, although they obviously hurt some specific trading partners. It should be noted that even "mild" recessions do increase human misery for millions of U.S. workers by involuntary idleness, drastic declines in income, and pessimism and alienation, which lead to higher rates of divorce, crime, and suicide.

Certainly, the most catastrophic economic event of the twentieth century has been the Great Depression. (For a detailed discussion of the causes of the Great Depression, see Devine [1983].) Although the Great Depression lasted throughout the 1930s in the common view, Geoffrey Moore (1983) analyzes more scientifically the decline from 1929 to 1933 as one unit (following Mitchell's definition) in terms of its duration, depth or amplitude, and scope. He finds that this decline lasted forty-three months (Moore 1983, 21). He finds that real GNP fell 33 percent, industrial production fell 53 percent, and nonfarm employment fell 32 percent, while unemployment increased by 22 percent (reaching the unprecedented official rate of 25 percent). The decline's scope was greater than that of any other in the twentieth century, with 100 percent of all industries declining.

Chandler (1970) tells the tale of this decline more graphically. He describes a complete collapse of the nation's banking system, a real estate market crash, a horrendous decline in national output, and a severe price deflation. The number of unemployed workers swelled from 1.5 million to 12.8 million. Wholesale prices fell over 30 percent in the same period. Investment dropped an amazing 88 percent. Although all industries declined, some key industries were devastated. Iron, lumber, and auto production fell 59 percent, 58 percent, and 65 percent respectively. Hardship was endemic.

There was a sluggish recovery between 1933 and 1937 even though the economy never recovered to the level achieved in 1929 during this period, and unemployment remained high. A second slump began in 1937. A full recovery was not to be experienced until World War II and the resulting military demand finally restored the economy.

After the enormous expansion of the U.S. economy during World War II, the late 1940s, the 1950s and the 1960s were characterized by moderate growth rates and four minor recessions. They were also characterized by two very large "limited" wars in Korea and Vietnam, which maintained a high level of military spending in the economy. The military spending led to a high rate of inflation in both wars. At the end of the Vietnam War, however, the inflation continued. It has continued ever since, increasing in expansions, but declining very slowly in contractions. In addition to continued inflation, the 1970s and early 1980s have been characterized by much lower growth rates, severe recessions, and higher rates of unemployment. The severe recession, or depression, of 1982 reduced inflation, but at the cost of 12 million unemployed, plus almost 2 million discouraged workers who gave up and no longer actively sought work, plus millions more involuntarily reduced to part-time work.

As noted in Chapter 2, Wesley Mitchell developed a method of dating business cycle peaks and troughs, which has been followed more or less by the National Bureau of Economic Research, and is now accepted by the U.S. Department of Commerce as official. The method, as applied at present, has many problems because it (1) is now applied mechanically with a computer program and (2) does not distinguish between minor recessions and major depressions. The official dates are given in Table 3.1. In spite of their many problems, these official dates are followed throughout this book because they are the most commonly accepted dates.

Table 3.1 shows that there have been thirty recessions, or depressions, in the United States since 1858. That is one contraction about every 4–5 years. But this calculation includes wartime cycles, which the table shows to be much longer than average peacetime cycles. If the wartime cycles are omitted, the average cycle is only 3–4 years long. More precisely, from 1945 to 1982, there have been eight cycles, with average expansions

TABLE 3.1

Business Cycle Expansions and Contractions in the United States, 1854–1981

| Business Cycle Reference Dates | | | Months of Expansion, Trough to Peak | Months of Contraction, Peak to Trough |
|---|---|---|---|---|
| Trough | Peak | Trough | | |
| Dec. 1854 | June 1857 | Dec. 1858 | 30 | 18 |
| Dec. 1858 | Oct. 1860 | June 1861 | 22 | 8 |
| June 1861 | Apr. 1865 | Dec. 1867 | <u>46</u> | 32 |
| Dec. 1867 | June 1869 | Dec. 1870 | 18 | 18 |
| Dec. 1870 | Oct. 1873 | Mar. 1879 | 34 | 65 |
| Mar. 1879 | Mar. 1982 | May 1885 | 36 | 38 |
| May 1885 | Mar. 1887 | Apr. 1888 | 22 | 13 |
| Apr. 1888 | July 1890 | May 1891 | 27 | 10 |
| May 1891 | Jan. 1893 | June 1894 | 20 | 17 |
| June 1894 | Dec. 1895 | June 1897 | 18 | 18 |
| June 1897 | June 1899 | Dec. 1900 | 24 | 18 |
| Dec. 1900 | Sept. 1902 | Aug. 1904 | 21 | 23 |
| Aug. 1904 | May 1907 | June 1908 | 33 | 13 |
| June 1908 | Jan. 1910 | Jan. 1912 | 19 | 24 |
| Jan. 1912 | Jan. 1913 | Dec. 1914 | 12 | 23 |
| Dec. 1914 | Aug. 1918 | Mar. 1919 | <u>44</u> | 7 |
| Mar. 1919 | Jan. 1920 | July 1921 | 10 | 18 |
| July 1921 | May 1923 | July 1924 | 22 | 14 |
| July 1924 | Oct. 1926 | Nov. 1927 | 27 | 13 |
| Nov. 1927 | Aug. 1929 | Mar. 1933 | 21 | 43 |
| Mar. 1933 | May 1937 | June 1938 | 50 | 13 |
| June 1938 | Feb. 1945 | Oct. 1945 | <u>80</u> | 8 |
| Oct. 1945 | Nov. 1948 | Oct. 1949 | 37 | 11 |
| Oct. 1949 | July 1953 | May 1954 | <u>45</u> | 10 |
| May 1954 | Aug. 1957 | Apr. 1958 | 39 | 8 |
| Apr. 1958 | Apr. 1960 | Feb. 1961 | 24 | 10 |
| Feb. 1961 | Dec. 1969 | Nov. 1970 | <u>106</u> | 11 |
| Nov. 1970 | Nov. 1973 | Mar. 1975 | 36 | 16 |
| Mar. 1975 | Jan. 1980 | July 1980 | 58 | 6 |
| July 1980 | July 1981 | Dec. 1982 | 12 | 17 |

Source: National Bureau of Economic Research, Inc., as reported in U.S. Department of Commerce, *Business Conditions Digest*.

Note: Underscored figures are the wartime expansions (Civil War, World War I, World War II, Korean War, and Vietnam War).

lasting forty-five months and average contractions lasting only eleven months. But these expansions also included some lengthy wars in two cycles, that is, the Korean and Vietnam wars. If those two war cycles are eliminated, then expansions averaged thirty-four months (or eleven quarters), while the contractions averaged only eleven months (or four quarters). Although contractions in this period were much shorter than expansions, this has not always been so. For example, in the fourteen peacetime cycles from 1854 to 1919, the average expansion was twenty-four months (or eight quarters), while the average contraction was also twenty-four months (or eight quarters).

## CONSUMPTION AND INVESTMENT IN THREE ERAS

We examine three very different periods of cyclical behavior in Table 3.2. The period 1921–1938 includes the Great Depression, so it has fairly large ups and downs; the 1949–1970 period reveals relatively mild cycles; and the 1970–1982 period again shows somewhat stronger fluctuations. Aside from the differences between the periods, what is most interesting are (1) the relative amplitudes among these series in each period and (2) the regularities that persist in all three periods.

Table 3.2 reveals that total consumption has much lower amplitudes than total investment in the Great Depression, and this is also repeated in the other two periods. There is, of course, a large body of literature on the consumption and investment functions, which discusses the reasons for the much greater fluctuation of investment, some of which is examined in later chapters.

Similarly, the Great Depression data reveal much larger amplitudes for durable consumer goods than for nondurable consumer goods—and that feature is also repeated in the later two periods. Of course, nondurable goods must be purchased more frequently, so it is impossible to postpone their purchase for long periods, as can be done with durables. Moreover, the Great Depression figures show much less fluctuation in consumer services than in consumer goods—also repeated in the later two periods. In this case, the reason for the lesser fluctuations in consumer services in all periods is related to the relatively strong secular trend toward expansion of the service industries. The upward growth trend of services has smothered the fluctuations in that area compared with production of goods up to this time.

Again, investment in equipment fluctuates more in all three periods than does investment in plant (nonresidential structures). That is not surprising since it is far easier to expand and decrease the stock of equipment than to expand or decrease plant—and investments in plant are

TABLE 3.2
Amplitudes of National Income Accounts: Expenditures

| | Average, 4 Cycles 1921–1938 | | Average, 4 Cycles 1949–1970 | | Average, 3 Cycles 1970–1982 | |
|---|---|---|---|---|---|---|
| | Expansion | Contraction | Expansion | Contraction | Expansion | Contraction |
| GNP (50) | 21.2 | −16.4 | 17.9 | −1.5 | 12.1 | −3.5 |
| Consumption | | | | | | |
| Total (231) | 15.0 | −9.9 | 16.6 | 1.0 | 10.4 | −0.7 |
| Nondurables (238) | 16.4 | −11.4 | 14.2 | 0.7 | 6.9 | −0.4 |
| Durables (233) | 31.0 | −27.0 | 24.1 | −5.9 | 20.8 | −5.0 |
| Services (239) | 14.4 | −6.4 | 18.0 | 2.9 | 10.7 | 2.1 |
| Investment | | | | | | |
| Gross Private Domestic (241) | 55.4 | −49.3 | 23.5 | −9.5 | 29.8 | −28.0 |
| Equipment (88) | 46.0 | −39.4 | 29.8 | −12.0 | 24.0 | −12.8 |
| Nonresidential structures (87) | 30.6 | −32.9 | 18.4 | −0.4 | 17.7 | −9.9 |
| Residential structures (89) | 33.9 | −22.0 | 6.9 | 3.0 | 16.9 | −18.4 |

Sources: Data for 1921–1938 are from Wesley Mitchell, *What Happens During Business Cycles* (New York: National Bureau of Economic Research, 1951). All data for the years 1949 to 1982 are from the *Business Conditions Digest*, published by the Bureau of Economic Analysis, U.S. Department of Commerce (Washington, D.C.: U.S. Government Printing Office).

Note: The numbers in parentheses indicate the series number from the *Business Conditions Digest*. These series are fully described by number in U.S. Department of Commerce, Bureau of Economic Analysis, *Handbook of Cyclical Indicators, A Supplement to the Business Conditions Digest*, 1984 edition (Washington, D.C.: U.S. Government Printing Office). Note that all expansion amplitudes are for stages 1 to 5 and all contraction amplitudes are for stages 5 to 9, except for total consumption in 1970–1982, which declined in stages 5 to 7.

more likely to have a longer time horizon since they must allow for a much longer construction period.

So far, we have noted regularities of the business cycle found to some degree in all cycles. What are the differences between the three periods? The main difference is that the first period, since it includes the Great Depression, has much more drastic declines than in the 1970s and 1980s, which in turn have more drastic declines than in the mild cycles of the 1950s and 1960s. Thus, the period 1921–1938 shows an average GNP decline in contractions of 16.4 percent, but GNP declines only 1.5 percent on the average in the 1949–1970 period, while declining an average of 3.5 percent in the 1970–1982 period. The same is true for most of the other consumption and investment variables.

In the 1920s and 1930s, total consumption declined in contractions, but consumption actually rose in the mild recessions of the 1950s and 1960s; consumption fell very slightly in the deeper contractions of the 1970s and 1980s. Consumer services declined in the contractions of the 1920s and 1930s, but continued to grow (at a slower pace) in the later two periods. Residential construction actually rose on the average in the four mild contractions of the 1950s and 1960s, but fell considerably in the average contraction of the other two periods.

CYCLICAL MOVEMENTS OF INCOME

As revealed in Table 3.3, in the 1920s and 1930s, employee compensation (all labor income, including wages and salaries) rises and falls more slowly than does total national income. Obviously, as a result, property income (all national income minus employee compensation, sometimes called unearned income) rises and falls more rapidly than national income. Within property income, corporate profits show, by far, the greatest declines in downturns. Net interest income has no cyclical decline, though its rate of growth declines; interest income reveals a secular upward trend stronger than the cyclical fluctuations.

In the 1950s and 1960s, the declines during contractions of all types of income are noticeably less than in the 1920s and 1930s. In fact, rental income—like interest income—rises rather than declines in these mild contraction periods. In the 1970s and 1980s, the contractions in each type of income are more severe than in the 1950s and 1960s, being double or triple in some cases. Rental income declines rather than rising, and interest income rises by only a fifth as much as in the 1950s and 1960s.

In the 1970s and 1980s, employee compensation fluctuates more slowly than does property income, and more slowly than all national income, just as it did in the 1920s and 1930s. Only in the somewhat unusual boom period of the 1950s and 1960s does employee compensation

TABLE 3.3
Cycle Amplitudes: Income

| | Average, 4 Cycles 1921–1938 | | Average, 4 Cycles 1949–1970 | | Average, 3 Cycles 1970–1982 | |
|---|---|---|---|---|---|---|
| | Expansion | Contraction | Expansion | Contraction | Expansion | Contraction |
| National income (220) | 22.5 | −17.6 | 18.7 | −2.5 | 12.5 | −4.8 |
| Employee compensation (280) | 19.8 | −13.0 | 22.7 | −1.9 | 10.5 | −2.2 |
| Proprietors' income[a] (282) | 8.7 | −6.1 | 3.9 | −0.5 | 9.8 | −11.1 |
| Rental income, with CCADJ (284) | 5.7 | −15.1 | 8.4 | 2.2 | −23.3 | −12.1 |
| Interest income (288) | 3.2 | 1.0 | 38.4 | 15.9 | 29.0 | 3.3 |
| Corporate profits before taxes[a] (286) | 168.8 | −174.6 | 18.8 | −16.2 | 23.2 | −27.5 |
| Property income (220–280) | 23.7 | −26.5 | 11.5 | −4.2 | 18.0 | −12.6 |

Sources: Same as Table 3.2.
Note: Same as Table 3.2.
[a] Because of inflation, the data for proprietors' income and corporate profits in the 1949–1982 period are given adjustments for inventory valuation (IVA) and capital consumption adjustment (CCADJ).

rise faster than property income and faster than all national income. Although the percentage differences appear to be small, the dollar amounts involved in each percentage point are very large, so it will be shown that consumer demand was affected by these shifts in income distribution. Thus, lack of consumer demand by the working class was a major problem in the 1920s and 1930s, was much less of a problem in the 1950s and 1960s, and again became a major problem in the 1970s and 1980s.

## UNEMPLOYMENT

Before comparing unemployment in the different periods, some warnings are in order on the meaning of the data. Throughout this book, unemployment is measured by the official unemployment data of the U.S. Department of Labor for the U.S. economy. But these official data have major biases. In fact, it should be emphasized that almost every official government series used in this book has various biases. The best discussion of how each is constructed, and what its biases are, may be found in an excellent and extremely useful book by Norman Frumkin (1987).

The unemployment data seriously understate the rate of unemployment in three ways. First, many workers get so discouraged when they are unemployed for a long time that they give up on active job hunting, though they still want a paid job. These "discouraged" workers should all be counted among the unemployed, but the official data do not count them as unemployed. Rather, they are categorized as not part of the labor force. Thus, unemployment is badly understated, and the underestimate becomes worse the longer the depression lasts (because the percentage of discouraged workers rises).

Second, some workers are "underemployed," that is, they are employed far below their level of qualifications. If a person has a Ph.D. in physics but can only find work as a gas station attendant, that is underemployment. Although it is easy to give anecdotes, this deficiency cannot be quantified and corrected because "underemployment" is very difficult to quantify.

Third, workers who are employed at any job for part-time work, even one hour a week, are counted in the official statistics as "employed." Yet many part-time workers are very anxious to have full-time work. Since they cannot find full-time work, they consider themselves to be partly unemployed. In fact, the average part-time worker works only half of a full-time schedule. Therefore, part-time workers who wish to work full-time should probably be counted, on the average, as half unemployed.

From 1970 to 1987, the whole employed work force grew by 39 percent, but the number of part-timers grew by 63 percent (U.S. Labor Department statistics reported by Russakoff and Skrzycki 1988, 1). In fact, the number of part-timers who want full-time jobs, but cannot get them, has risen from 2,446,000 in 1970 to 5,401,000 in 1987; this is a long-run trend because the part-time percentage usually grows in recessions and declines in expansions, but 1970 was a recession year and 1987 was in an expansion.

Why is there this trend? Because the part-time labor force

> is both expandable and expendable. Its ranks swell during periods of peak pro-
> duction and need, and these employees are the first to go in hard times, form-
> ing a sort of buffer around a core of better-paid, full-time workers. In the con-
> tinuing quest to enhance profits and meet global competition, this is now a
> favored tool for cutting labor costs and staying flexible.
>
> (Russakoff and Skrzycki 1988, 18)

Not only are part-time workers paid less and easier to fire, but they also normally receive no fringe benefits (now about 15 percent of wages).

In reading the unemployment data, one should also keep in mind that these are averages over a time period. But the percentage of the labor force that is unemployed at some time during the year is usually two and one-half times the percentage of unemployed for the whole year (see discussion in Magdoff and Sweezy 1987, 62). Thus, if 10 million people were unemployed on the average for the whole year 1982, we would expect that 25 million people (or two and one-half times 10 million) would be unemployed for one week or more sometime during that year.

For the period 1921–1938, we lack the detailed data now available on many aspects of unemployment, but Mitchell does present two comparable series. Table 3.4 shows factory employment and hours worked per week for all three periods. Both series vary pro-cyclically in all three periods, but the fluctuations are most powerful in the 1921–1939 period, weakest in the 1949–1970 period (especially in the contractions), and in between in the 1970–1982 period. The fact that hours and wages fluctuate as well as employment means that workers who remain on the job in a depression are still hurt by less wages per hour and less hours per week.

Data on some other characteristics of unemployment are available only since 1949. Table 3.5 and Figures 3.1 and 3.2 present averages for the seven cycles from 1949 to 1982. The data show the very large and systematic fluctuations in the unemployment rate, declining rapidly in every expansion and rising rapidly in every contraction.

Fluctuations, about the same or slightly larger than in total unemployment, are observed in claims for unemployment insurance. These two series in Table 3.5 reveal the reality of involuntary unemployment of millions of people in every cyclical contraction. An even clearer indicator of the involuntary nature of unemployment is the extraordinarily rapid

TABLE 3.4
Employment and Hours: Expansion and Contraction Amplitudes

| | Average, 4 Cycles 1921–1938 | | Average, 4 Cycles 1949–1970 | | Average, 3 Cycles 1970–1982 | |
|---|---|---|---|---|---|---|
| | Expansion | Contraction | Expansion | Contraction | Expansion | Contraction |
| Factory employment (#40) | 24.2 | −23.3 | 13.5 | −6.8 | 9.2 | −9.0 |
| Hours worked per week (#1) | 8.4 | −16.4 | 2.4 | −2.2 | 2.5 | −3.0 |

Sources: Same as Table 3.2.

TABLE 3.5
Unemployment, 1949–1982 (average amplitudes, 7 cycles)

|  | Expansion | Contraction |
|---|---|---|
| Unemployment rate (43) | − 42.7 | 48.9 |
| Claims for unemployment insurance (5) | − 43.8 | 53.9 |
| Help wanted ads/number of unemployed (60) | 73.9 | − 78.3 |
| Average number of weeks unemployed (91) | − 28.6 | 19.9 |
| Unemployment rate of persons unemployed 14 weeks and over (44) | − 71.1 | 83.8 |
| Average overtime hours (21) | 31.9 | − 28.0 |

*Sources*: Same as Table 3.2.

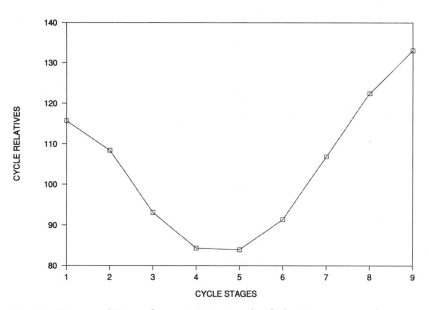

Fig. 3.1. Pattern of Unemployment Rate: Amplitude by Stage Averaged across Seven Cycles, 1949–1982 (from series 43, Appendix C)

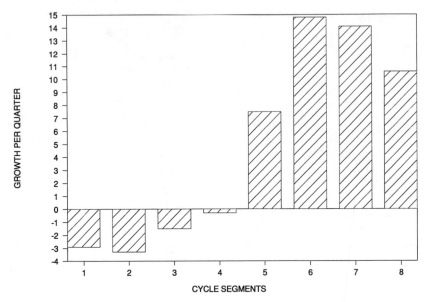

Fig. 3.2. Unemployment Rate: Growth by Segment Averaged across Seven Cycles, 1949–1982 (from series 43, Appendix F)

change in the ratio of help wanted ads to the number of unemployed, rising 74 percent in business expansions, but falling 78 percent in business contractions. Thus, at the very time when unemployment is rising, fewer and fewer jobs are available.

Table 3.5 also shows that the number of weeks people are out of work rises and falls countercyclically, that is, in the opposite direction from that of business activity over the cycle. This means that the unemployed are unemployed for much longer time periods in a recession or depression than in expansions. At the same time, the unemployment rate for those who remain unemployed a long time (fifteen weeks or more) rises dramatically in the average contraction (by 83 percent). Finally, those workers who remain on the job in a contraction are hurt in another way, by working less overtime hours, which means much less pay per hour since overtime pay is higher than regular pay.

CONCLUSION

Capitalism is characterized by economic crises, with recessions or depressions every few years. Previous societies did not suffer this type of crisis. Capitalism is vulnerable to cyclical crises because it has (1) production for the market, (2) production for private profit, and (3) use of money and credit. The U.S. economy has suffered recurrent cyclical crises, but their nature has changed as the structure of capitalism has changed. It is now characterized by (1) predominant monopoly power; (2) enormous use of credit by households, corporations, and government; (3) declining trade union strength; (4) vast influence by government; and (5) strong international competition. Trends in the 1970s and 1980s include weak growth of productivity, stagnant real wages, increasing income inequality, and severe recessions. Some major differences were found in the business cycles of three periods: the 1920s and 1930s included the Great Depression; the cycles of the 1950s and 1960s were very mild; and the cycles of the 1970s and 1980s were again more violent. There was relatively little involuntary unemployment in the 1950s and 1960s, but large amounts of it in the 1930s and again in the 1970s and 1980s.

The view expressed here of recurrent recessions and crises generated by capitalism is quite contrary to the prevailing neoclassical view that the system always adjusts to full employment equilibrium (so that recessions and depressions are all due to external shocks). Yet it is also opposed to the extreme view of some Marxists that the system is in one long crisis (some theorists date the crisis from World War I while others date it from the late 1960s). This chapter has shown that the concept of a continuous or long-run crisis has no particular empirical meaning, but that there are long-term trends resulting in different stages of capitalism—some of which are characterized by few problems and very mild downturns, others by worsening long-run problems (such as the government and trade deficits) and severe downturns (such as the crisis of 1982).

## FURTHER READING

A very interesting book on the history of the business cycle is Mirowski (1985). A useful, somewhat eclectic history of the Great Depression is Bernstein (1987). A useful collection of articles, with some historical aspects, has been edited by Philip Klein (1989b).

# CHAPTER 4

# Endogenous and Exogenous Cycle Theories

THIS CHAPTER provides an introduction to many theories of the business cycle. It does not attempt a rigorous presentation of each one because that is impossible in one chapter. The purpose is, rather, to introduce the reader to the alternative approaches to the cycle, to indicate those that will be considered in detail in later chapters, and to provide a framework of analysis for the rest of the book.

There is an immense gap between two types of business cycle theorists. As John Maynard Keynes put it, "What is it that makes the cleavage which divides us? On the one side are those who believe that the existing economic system is, in the long run, a self-adjusting system though with creaks and groans and jerks, outside interference and mistakes. . . . On the other side of the gulf are those who reject the idea that the existing economic system is, in any significant sense, self-adjusting" (quoted in Mirowski 1985, 46). Most of the classical and neoclassical economists believe that demand automatically adjusts to supply, that the system quickly returns to full employment equilibrium if there is no outside interference, and that all major downturns are exogenous, that is, due to external causes.

After investigating the classical and neoclassical theories of exogenous causes of the cycle, we turn to the "other side of the gulf." Post-Keynesians, Marxists, and institutionalists assert that the system does not self-adjust demand to supply, that the system does not necessarily return to equilibrium at full employment, and that recurrent cyclical downturns are primarily endogenous, that is, due to internal causes. There are, of course, important differences within each of these two groups, but there is a basic division between them.

## SAY'S LAW

The classical economists argued that the invisible hand of competition under capitalism produces a smoothly functioning system, always returning to equilibrium with an optimally functioning economy. In line with this view, in 1803, J. B. Say announced the law that "supply calls forth its own demand." In other words, if aggregate supply in the market increases, aggregate demand will also increase until a new equilibrium is reached at full employment. The system automatically adjusts to any change or external shock, so there can be no involuntary unemployment other than very temporarily. In the classical view, unemployment is caused by momentary frictions during adjustment or external barriers that do not allow the market system to function freely; otherwise, people are just voluntarily unemployed—that is, they prefer not to work at prevailing real wages.

This is not just an obsolete old theory, but has been revived and is currently an important, and perhaps dominant, theory among U.S. economists. As is shown later in this chapter, Say's law is now considered correct by monetarists, new classical economists, and supply-side economists. Let us see how this theory, which denies the possibility of cyclical depressions caused by lack of demand, has evolved.

J. B. Say and other classical economists (particularly James Mill and David Ricardo) argued that the act of production itself creates a level of income sufficient to purchase all that has been produced. The sum of all wages and salaries, rental income, interest income, and profit income will equal the value of all production. The aggregate value of income payments is identical to the value of all things produced for sale, so the income is sufficient to demand all that is supplied. Since whatever some save out of income will be loaned to others anxious to buy beyond their current income, Say believed that the total income would be used to buy the total production. Therefore, no matter how large the potential GNP is at full employment, market forces would ensure that all labor resources available for use would be employed.

J. B. Say admitted that an excess of a single product might be produced, but markets would correct that short-run difficulty. Such temporary maladjustments were sure to be corrected as soon as competition could force capital to switch from one industry to another. In a typical classical statement, Ricardo argued: "Too much of a particular commodity may be produced, which there may be said to be such a glut in the market as not to repay the capital expended on it; but this cannot be the case with all commodities" ([1817] 1891, 286).

The classical economists contended that savings (income not spent for consumption) would always find an outlet as investment because people would not forgo the yield offered by investment, which yield would be lost if one simply "hoarded" one's savings. A high level of savings is healthy and desirable for economic growth, since without high savings there could be no high investment. In sum, the classical economists saw no difficulties inherent in high levels of savings, only benefits.

The kernel of truth in Say's law is the platitude that a dollar's worth of production or supply generates a dollar's worth of income, or *potential* demand. Every purchase constitutes a sale; every sale means money in-

come to someone; and that income may be used for more purchases in
the next period. Ricardo wrote:

> No man produces but with a view to consume or sell, and he never sells but
> with an intention to purchase some other commodity which may be useful to
> him or which may contribute to future production. By purchasing them, he
> necessarily becomes either the consumer of his own goods, or the purchaser
> and consumer of the goods of some other person.         ([1817] 1891, 273)

In other words, the circulation of goods and money is circular: Business
produces and sells; it pays income to workers and capitalists; the income
is used to purchase consumer goods and producer goods from business;
and the process begins again. This is a correct description of circulation
when everything works perfectly, but it is not a proof that it works perfectly.

Ricardo correctly claimed the validity of what is today called "Say's
identity," that the value of production will always equal the value of income—but this could still be the case with a 50 percent unemployment
rate. Say's law claims not only that production creates an equal income
(always true by accounting definitions), but also that that income causes
an equal demand—and the latter proposition is not necessarily true.

## CRITIQUES AND DEFENSES OF SAY'S LAW

Assume that the capitalist system always tends to produce an equilibrium
of supply and demand at full employment. Then the only thing that can
cause a temporary disequilibrium is some external shock. From the time
that Say wrote in 1803, till the end of the classical period (about 1870),
Say's law was dominant. This dominance continued in the neoclassical
period (from about 1870 till the mid-1930s). After an interlude of Keynesian economics, Say's law has returned to dominance, prevailing from the
mid-1970s to the present. Since the dominant view is that the system
automatically reaches full employment equilibrium, the only acceptable
theories of depressions are theories of external shocks causing temporary
deviations from full employment.

The first famous exogenous (external shock) theory was Stanley Jevons's theory that business cycles are caused by sunspots. This peculiar
theory sounded less strange during the nineteenth century, when agriculture was more important. At that time, there were many theories that
periodic meteorological conditions (such as sunspots) caused bad weather
conditions, which caused trouble in agriculture, which caused business
cycles. Since the importance of agriculture has diminished, these theories have died away.

Marx ([1905] 1952) criticized Say's law on the ground that the classical economists were confusing capitalism with earlier systems (or an imaginary Robinson Crusoe island). Under feudalism (or on Crusoe's island), production was just for the use of an isolated group. Under capitalism, goods are sold in the market for money, and production continues only if profit is expected. Every sale brings in income (Say's identity), but that income may not be spent.

A similar criticism of Say's law was made by Wesley Mitchell (1913), who emphasized that business cycles appear only where there is capitalism because capitalism is a monetary economy. Production occurs only when profit is expected; lack of profit leads to unemployment under capitalism. In Chapter 3, the history of the business cycle was discussed, and it was shown that business cycles are indeed a creation of capitalism in which Say's law does not apply.

On the theoretical side, the criticisms were answered by an increasingly elegant defense of Say's law. Economists such as J. S. Mill, Alfred Marshall, Stanley Jevons, and Leon Walras emphasized that equilibrium is always restored, provided that prices, wages, and interest rates are flexible. A lack of demand causes business to lower prices, but this results in more demand and less supply, so that equilibrium is restored.

Then John Maynard Keynes (1936) attacked Say's law in a quite formal manner, using the style of argument and some of the tools familiar to neoclassical economists. Since the Great Depression had shown everyone that there was indeed a glut of goods and a deficiency of demand, causing 25 percent unemployment, Keynes was very persuasive. Finally, a majority of economists declared that Say's law was dead.

After World War II, however, a long period of prosperity in the 1950s and 1960s restored confidence in the capitalist system—and Say's law began a comeback. We discuss here the major classical/neoclassical arguments for Say's law, as they were made in the 1950s and 1960s, followed by the responses of two types of Keynesians.

## THREE ARGUMENTS FOR SAY'S LAW

First, suppose that the aggregate supply of commodities is temporarily greater than the aggregate demand. It is claimed that flexible prices under competition will quickly cure this imbalance. Under competitive conditions, the excess supply of output will automatically cause prices to drop. At the new, lower prices, demand will automatically rise to equal the supply. Since demand will adjust in that manner to any level of supply, that includes the full employment level of supply—so equilibrium may always be reached at the full employment level of supply.

Second, suppose that there is a temporary excess of savings (that is, income not spent for consumption) above investment demand. It is claimed that, under competition, flexible interest rates will quickly cure this imbalance. Under competitive conditions, the excess supply of savings will automatically cause interest rates to drop. At the new, lower, interest rates, many more investment opportunities will appear profitable. Therefore, investment demand will rise to equal the supply of savings. Again, the argument applies to the full employment level of supply of savings.

Third, suppose there is a temporary excess of labor supply over the demand for labor, causing temporary unemployment. It is claimed that, under competition, flexible wages will quickly cure this imbalance. Under competitive conditions in the labor market, the excess supply of labor (the unemployed) will automatically cause wages to decline. If wages fall, then workers will be able to produce more profit for capitalists. Therefore, at the new lower wages, capitalists will hire more workers until full employment is reached. This is defined to be full employment of those workers seeking jobs. Potential workers not employed are defined to be voluntarily unemployed or not in the labor force.

## NEOCLASSICAL-KEYNESIAN CRITIQUE OF SAY'S LAW

Most U.S. economists in the 1950s and 1960s agreed with what Paul Samuelson called the neoclassical-Keynesian synthesis. This synthesis argued that Say's law does not hold if there are certain barriers or rigidities in the economy, but that if the barriers are removed or are compensated for by government action, then Say's law and neoclassical competitive equilibrium will again prevail. They presented three arguments against the older position.

First, suppose that aggregate supply is greater than aggregate demand for all commodities. The neoclassical-Keynesians claimed that prices are relatively inflexible downward. Part of this rigidity may be oligopoly or monopoly power over the market. For whatever reason, if prices are not flexible downward and do not fall, then supply may remain above demand for a long time. Eventually, the excess supply in the form of increasing piles of unwanted inventories will cause a recession; that is, the quantity of goods produced may fall while the prices remain high. In this case, supply adjusts downward to demand, instead of demand adjusting upward to supply as envisioned by Say's law. Broadly speaking, the classical vision always adjusts demand upward to meet supply at the full employment level. The Keynesian vision adjusts supply downward to meet demand.

Second, suppose that savings are currently in excess of investment, causing the excess money to drop out of circulation, at least temporarily. Some neoclassical-Keynesians claimed that there may be a "liquidity trap," that is, a level below which the rate of interest may not fall. The interest rate stops falling because below a certain level, lenders expect the interest rate to rise again in the near future. Therefore, potential lenders (those with savings) may hold cash with a speculative motive because they believe that there will be higher interest rates in the future. This inflexible interest rate floor prevents investment demand from rising to meet savings.

Third, suppose there is an excess supply of labor over the demand for labor. Neoclassical-Keynesians claimed that wages may be inflexible downward. Wages may be rigid because of trade union strength, or because of minimum wage laws, or for other reasons. In this case, if wages do not fall, the demand for labor will remain below the supply, and involuntary unemployment will result.

In any of these cases, according to Samuelson's neoclassical-Keynesian synthesis, government action is required to restore equilibrium at full employment. If wages, prices, and interest rates are rigid, attempts should be made to remove barriers and to restore flexible prices, wages, and interest rates. So long as they are rigid, however, the government must stimulate the economy by fiscal and monetary means (to be discussed in detail later in this book).

## POST-KEYNESIAN CRITIQUE OF SAY'S LAW

The Post-Keynesians interpret Keynes in a more radical manner. The problem is not just rigidities, but cumulative processes that cause a lack of effective demand if prices and wages do decline, as well as problems of uncertainty in expectations that affect investment.

First, suppose there is excess aggregate supply of commodities, that is, a lack of effective demand. Suppose that all prices are flexible, and prices do drop. This does not solve the problem because it also means less revenue from the sale of the present supply of output. The lower revenue will result in lower aggregate income, which will again lower demand—so the process may be cumulative downward. In other words, one effect of lower prices would be to encourage demand out of a given income. But another, opposite effect will be a decline in aggregate income, which will also cause a decline in demand. Moreover, the decline in prices and incomes lowers the expectations of consumers and investors, causing a further decline in demand. Thus, flexible prices may become part of the problem. (Post-Keynesians also note that lower prices mean an increase in the real burden of debt, which increases bankruptcies in agriculture and industry.)

Second, suppose there is an excess of labor supply over demand, causing unemployment. Some Post-Keynesians (following one strand of

Keynes) point out that there may be a problem even if wages are flexible (contrary to the neoclassical view). Suppose wages are flexible and decline precipitously; this drastically reduces consumer demand. Since demand for labor is influenced by the demand for goods, this decline in consumer demand must tend to reduce the demand for workers. Of course, production is also influenced by the cost of labor, which is falling. But if the two factors (consumer demand and labor cost) are falling at the same pace, then the two effects cancel each other. Full employment equilibrium is not restored; rather, there may be a downward spiral.

How does the classical/neoclassical view overlook the fact that cutting wages leads to less aggregate demand? Part of the answer is that it concentrates only on each individual industry. If wages are cut in one industry, say, automobiles, then there may be no noticeable effect on the demand for automobiles. But if wages are cut in all industries, then aggregate demand certainly declines. The mistake of ignoring this aggregate effect has been called the fallacy of composition. This point was first made by Keynes and is supported by the Post-Keynesians, but usually ignored by the new classical economists.

Third, suppose there is an excess of savings over investment. If the expected rate of profit goes below zero, as it has in some depressions, then no positive interest rate can be low enough to induce investment. If insufficient demand causes expected losses, then why would any rational businessperson wish to borrow at any positive rate of interest? Keynes and the Post-Keynesians have emphasized that the uncertainty of future returns causes investors to react strongly to financial events. If the present rate of profit is rapidly declining, then investors may expect a negative future rate. In that case, no equilibrium of savings and investment may be possible at the present time.

## MONETARISM

There have been many monetary theories since at least the early nineteenth century (see the comprehensive survey in Haberler [1960, ch. 2]). These theories often argued that overoptimism led to a speculative bubble, followed by a financial crisis when banks refused to lend money (some of these theories are examined later when we deal with credit).

Monetarism differs from the earlier theories in that the villain is neither the private banking system nor the pessimism of lenders. Rather, monetarists see the government as the villain. In their view, the U.S. government first expands the money supply more than it should, and then it cuts it back more than it should. The monetarists believe that: "Given significant lags in wage and price adjustments, sequences of alternating phases of high and low growth rates in the quantity of money lead to corresponding fluctuations in aggregate demand and real economic activity . . ." (this summary of monetarism is given by Zarnowitz [1985, 547] in his excellent survey article on business cycle theories).

Milton Friedman (the founder of modern monetarism) and his followers argue that government should do nothing except increase the money supply at a steady rate equal to the growth rate of real gross national product. Government does not need to do anything else because the capitalist market economy is inherently stable; that is, demand automatically adjusts to supply. Thus, monetarism implicitly accepts Say's law. Business cycles are caused by exogenous shocks to the system by the government monetary authorities (who never learn, but repeat the same sequence of mistakes time after time because of political pressures).

## THE NEW CLASSICAL ECONOMISTS

The new classical economics reaches the old classical conclusions, but does so on the basis of more complex concepts—particularly, rational expectations and continuous market clearing. The older monetarists (such as Milton Friedman) assume "adaptive expectations" behavior, that is, that consumers and businesses slowly incorporate expectations into their behavior as they learn from the experience of recent events. Inflationary expectations, for example, are generated gradually, as the public begins to feel the impact of an existing inflation. Thus, government spending might stimulate output for a little while before the public learns that it is inflationary—after which prices rise so fast that in the long run output falls back to where it was. Thus, in this view, government spending gives no permanent stimulus to the economy, but does cause inflation.

Rational expectations monetarists (included in the new classical economists) argue instead that the public can rationally comprehend the likely impact of newly announced monetary and fiscal policies and will formulate their expectations immediately and correctly. For example, if the public knows that the Federal Reserve System has increased the money stock sharply, the public will immediately comprehend the inflationary consequences and will immediately and fully incorporate inflationary expectations into their behavior—consequently, prices will rise so rapidly that the new policy will have no effect on output and will generate no new employment.

Expectations operate through market behavior. All the relevant information that is known to buyers and sellers is reflected in the price. This price then clears the market efficiently, so there are no shortages or surpluses in the market. Since all citizens are rational and all-knowing, markets are basically competitive, and all prices are flexible, it follows that the economy automatically returns to a full employment equilibrium.

The new classical economists conclude "that any government intervention into the economy will be counter-productive" (Peterson 1987, 71). (Peterson's article offers a very clear explanation and critique of this view.)

The new classical economists incorporate Say's law, and they begin from individual preferences for leisure as a response to external shocks. Thus, Lucas (1986) writes: "To explain why people allocate time to . . . unemployment we need to know why they prefer it to all other activities" (p. 38). This implies that unemployment is voluntary.

These new classical theorists are often called equilibrium theorists because their whole approach is based on the notion that the economy rapidly adjusts to equilibrium after any change in conditions. (A typical example of this view is set forth in Black [1987].) If left to itself, with no external shocks or interference, the private capitalist economy would always be in equilibrium. This leads to such titles for their works as "An Equilibrium Model of the Business Cycle" (Lucas 1975), which would appear to be an oxymoron.

The equilibrium theory asserts that the market economy adjusts back to full employment equilibrium after random shocks, so that only the tools of equilibrium analysis are needed to understand business cycles. Lucas (1975) develops a theory of the business cycle only in the sense that it generates "serially correlated . . . movements in real output" (p. 1113), but these movements are created by exogenous shocks, not by internal features of capitalism: "The mechanism generating these movements involves unsystematic monetary-fiscal shocks . . ." (p. 1140). Thus, the initiating cause of cycles is not the capitalist system, but government mistakes (because government apparently does not have rational expectations, does not learn, and repeats its mistakes time after time). Individuals, on the other hand, are rational, but take time to learn about and process unannounced changes in monetary and fiscal policy.

Once a government mistake is felt, a cycle is propagated because "the effects . . . are distributed through time due to informational lags and an accelerator effect" (Lucas 1975, 1140). Consequently, the adjustment is not immediate, but takes some time, partly because people have imperfect information. In Lucas's model, "information is imperfect, not only in the sense that the future is unknown, but also in the sense that no agent is perfectly informed as to the current state of the economy" (p. 1113). Thus, businesspeople may think conditions are better than they are, so they overinvest or borrow excessively. Lucas notes that his theory is similar in some respects to the monetary overinvestment theories of the 1930s (see Haberler 1960).

Lucas's model is a rational expectations model in the sense that "the expectations of agents are rational, given the information available to them" (Lucas 1975, 1113). In fact, in this view people know all the implications of government policy (as predicted by monetarist theory). People make mistakes, these theorists hold, only because their information is imperfect, not because they lack understanding of neoclassical monetarist theory (which theory is obvious to any rational being, according to them). One such mistake—in their view—is the confusion between relative and general price changes, discussed below.

It is worth noting that the rational expectations approach is now a dominant form of neoclassical-Keynesian theory to the extent that it is assumed that "Keynesians" believe in rational expectations. For example, a critical review of Robert Eisner's allegedly old-fashioned Keynesianism asserts: "Modern Keynesian models assume that economic agents have rational expectations when setting money wages and prices" (Evans 1987, 1346). Aside from the erroneous view that all "modern" economists agree (so Eisner is not modern), note that the new classical economists make workers and capitalists disappear, speaking only of "economic agents."

Lucas's model is an equilibrium model in the sense that "prices and quantities at each point in time are determined in competitive equilibrium" (Lucas 1975, 1113). Of course, in one sense Lucas's new classical model is like most neoclassical-Keynesian models because both types are always in equilibrium at each point. Any model claiming to be Keynesian in any sense, however, may remain at an equilibrium with unemployment; the new classical models pass through times of unemployment equilibrium but eventually adjust back to full employment equilibrium. Lucas also assumes continuous competitive market clearing, whereas most neoclassical-Keynesian models assume rigidities caused by business or union monopoly power.

Zarnowitz comments that the objective of the new classical theorists "was to develop a general business-cycle theory in strict adherence to the basic principles of the analysis of economic equilibrium: consistent pursuit of self-interest by individuals and continuous clearing of all markets by relative prices" (Zarnowitz 1985, 552). Even some of their leading exponents have revealed "doubts about the explanatory value for business cycles of currently available equilibrium theories" (Barro 1980, 74).

The basic problem with the equilibrium approach is that it is unrealistic and misleading to think of the economy as being in continuous equilibrium. When we examine the business cycle, we find a period of rapid growth (with demand greater than supply), followed by crisis, and then a decline of output and employment (often with a financial panic)—none of which bears any relation to a continuous equilibrium. The equilibrium mode of thought has been part of the problem because it is a barrier to realistic analysis of the cycle. Lloyd Valentine (1987), author of one of the most widely used standard texts in the area, notes:

> Virtually all economic theory has been developed with the concept of equilibrium at its core. Movement or changes in any variables are viewed as returns to equilibrium . . . following some exogenous or outside change. It is very difficult to break out of this method of comparative statics to the kind of theory needed to explain the continuity of successive rises and falls in economic activity resulting in cyclical behavior. This has been one of the stumbling blocks to the development of a satisfactory theory of economic fluctuations. (p. 326)

Since the equilibrium theorists believe that the economy normally operates smoothly and always adjusts to a full employment equilibrium, they must contend that downturns are temporary and are due to external shocks (including policy "surprises"). Some of them see these shocks as mainly monetary and fiscal mistakes by government. Others refer to various other random shocks, such as higher oil prices imposed by OPEC rules, local wars that may disrupt supplies, bad harvests, unanticipated changes in tastes, or unanticipated changes in technology. One very abstract model of the "real business cycle" ignores the role of government and money, but merely assumes "random shocks to outputs of the many commodities, each of which can either be consumed or used as input in the production of any other commodity during each unit period" (Zarnowitz 1985, 567). The real business cycle theory associates most shocks with random technological change.

This real business cycle ("real" means nonmonetary) theory is the most fashionable theory at the moment among the new classical economists. There is a lengthy exposition of real business cycle theory in Barro (1989), a brief but very clear exposition in Plosser (1989), and an excellent critique in Mankiw (1989). The real business cycle theory claims that shocks are the cause of all cycles, that such shocks occur in all economies, and that therefore cycles are "natural." Since cycles are natural and part of every system, "[b]usiness cycle phenomena . . . are perfectly consistent with ideal economic efficiency" (Long and Plosser 1983, 43). It is a strange definition of efficiency that would allow us to call an economy in the midst of a deep depression an efficient economy. Like most neoclassical theories, the real business cycle theory is completely ahistorical since it suggests that all economies have cycles on the basis of theory rather than an extensive empirical survey (we saw in the previous chapter that some types of economies do not have business cycles of the modern type).

Since cycles are a "natural" phenomenon resulting from the shocks that are common to all economies, the real business cycle theorists conclude that nothing can be done about cyclical unemployment. If government takes any action, it will only make things worse (see Long and Plosser 1983, 68). This conservative conclusion follows from their imaginary ahistorical assumptions. (The description given here was heavily influenced by the outstanding critique of real business cycle theory by Klein [1989b]).

## SUPPLY-SIDE ECONOMICS

Supply-side economics was based on the idea (first drawn on a napkin by Arthur Laffer) that "productive activity is inversely related to taxation" (Peterson 1987, 71). If taxation is reduced, people will be willing to work harder and save more. The higher savings will automatically create higher investment because the higher output supplied will automatically create its own demand. As George Gilder (1981) writes, "The essential thesis of Say's law remains true. Supply creates demand. There can be no such thing as a general glut of goods" (p. 32).

Since there can never be a lack of demand, any problem must be caused by supply-side shocks. A typical supply-side shock would be a government tax increase.

Obviously, people are happier working if they are taxed less, but this theory goes much further. It argues as follows: First, lower taxes lead to more saving. Second, more saving leads to more investment. Third, more investment leads to more demand for workers, so there is less unemployment. Each of these three points has been denied or greatly qualified. Lower taxes on the rich may lead to more saving, but sometimes there is just an increase in luxury consumption. More saving does not lead to more investment unless there is an expectation of profit, which may be nonexistent in a recession situation. Finally, more investment may sometimes increase technology so much that only a few more workers are hired. (Supply-side economics is primarily a discussion of policy, not a theory of the business cycle. It is mentioned briefly here only because of its assumption of Say's law; we return in great detail to the policy issues in the last part of this book.)

## BLAMING THE VICTIM

Neoclassical economics stresses that the capitalist system always returns to full-employment equilibrium. Since the economic system is not responsible for cyclical unemployment, there is a strong tendency to blame government mistakes, or even to blame workers themselves (particularly union workers or women workers or young workers) for their unemployment. In his keynote speech to the American Economic Association, Alan Blinder (1988) attributed high European unemployment to the alleged fact that

[i]ntransigent trade unions and well-intentioned but unintelligent governments have erected a web of microeconomic barriers to full employment that both make labor more expensive and transform wages from variable into fixed costs. These include . . . high minimum wages, excessive severance pay, heavy fixed costs of employment, restrictions on hiring and firing, support for the closed union shop . . . heavy-handed work-place rules. (p. 2)

It would appear that the best policy to eliminate unemployment would be to abolish all unions, end all safety regulations, do away with minimum pay, and allow plants to be closed on an hour's notice. It is important to understand that these policy suggestions are not merely anti-worker bias, but stem from the basic neoclassical hypothesis that the system would work perfectly without interference.

In addition, the neoclassical approach begins with given individual preferences (as discussed in the next section), which provide a bias toward assuming that all or most unemployment is voluntary. Thus, many writers have speculated that the increase of women and young workers in the labor force may have increased unemployment rates because these workers are "prone to unemployment" (see Moore 1983, 163). Does being "prone" to unemployment mean that these groups voluntarily prefer unemployment or does it mean that they suffer discrimination that results in unemployment? The direction of cause and effect—and the policy implications—are quite different if one blames women and youth for their unemployment than if one blames employers. Of course, in an earlier period, similar arguments were made to blame black workers for their higher rates of unemployment, but more sensitivity to racist discrimination has now shifted the blame. Finally, there are many economists who speculate that higher unemployment compensation may mean a greater preference for voluntary unemployment—but the misery of unemployment (documented in Chapter 1 of this book) makes that argument implausible as an explanation for millions of unemployed in a recession.

The so-called search theory of unemployment is a related view that sees most unemployment as merely the voluntary movement of workers between jobs, hunting for higher pay. The search theory says that workers often have misinformation, leading them to believe that better jobs are available when that is not true, so workers voluntarily quit their present jobs to look for new ones (see Alchian 1969). Some advocates of this theory indicate that women and young people are most prone to leave one job voluntarily in search of a better one (see Perry 1970). This theory claims that when there are sudden economic changes, such as a recession, perfect information becomes more difficult to obtain, so this explains sudden surges in unemployment. Some search theorists claim that women and young people search longer for a new job because they have less information about the value of their labor, so it takes them longer to make an employment decision. Every empirical study from the U.S. Labor Department, however, shows that women and young people are less likely to leave a given job than adult men on the same job—the reason is that women and young people know that they have much less chance of finding a better job. Of course, people do not have perfect information, but, as documented in the previous chapter, in recessions millions of people are fired at the same time, so the assumption that they voluntarily leave their jobs is incorrect. Moreover, as documented in the last chapter, during recessions there are far fewer job advertisements per worker, so fewer jobs are actually available—and it is not merely a matter of poor information.

Another related theory says that there is a "natural" rate of unemployment. The natural rate of unemployment is defined as the rate that would exist in a labor market that has pure competition—that is, no labor unions and no government regulation. Thus, the "natural" rate of unemployment would include only (1) frictional unemployment (changing jobs or locations or both because of changing technology or preferences) and (2) search unemployment (voluntarily searching for a better job). Of course, this theory assumes that Say's law is correct and that there is no involuntary unemployment resulting from endogenous mechanisms in capitalism. If Say's law is incorrect, so is the natural rate theory (see the critique of this theory by Robert Cherry [1981]).

## NEOCLASSICAL MICROFOUNDATIONS OF NEOCLASSICAL-KEYNESIAN MACROECONOMICS

Neoclassical microeconomics begins with individual preferences determining demand, while production functions (output as a function of various inputs) determine supply. For each commodity, it shows how an equilibrium of supply and demand is reached through price adjustments: "The interdependent supply and demand curves, combined with the dynamic assumption that the system will move around until it reaches the set of prices that simultaneously has supply equal demand for all markets, is the Law of Supply and Demand that is beloved of writers of editorials and conventional textbooks" (Minsky 1986, 109). It is a short but fatal step from the microeconomic law of supply and demand to the macroeconomic law of supply and demand, that is, Say's law.

Hyman Minsky (1986) shows how this neoclassical microeconomic approach, with its emphasis on supply and demand equilibrium, biases standard neoclassical-Keynesian macroeconomics toward the full employment equilibrium theory, expressed in Say's law. Minsky argues that the neoclassical microeconomic description applies only to individual consumers with limited budgets in individual markets in an orderly economy. It does not apply to the problem of calculating new investments in an uncertain future macroeconomic environment, where the budget is made flexible by credit. In such an economy, investors may easily underestimate or overestimate the profitable amount of investment.

Furthermore, the application of the neoclassical approach to macroeconomics assumes that what is true in each market must be true in the aggregate, which may constitute a "fallacy of composition." As noted earlier, if wages (a supply cost) are lowered in a single market, this may have no significant effect on aggregate consumer demand, but if wages are lowered in all markets, then aggregate consumer demand is very much affected (these issues are discussed in a comprehensive critique of neoclassical microeconomics by John Weeks [1989]).

Moreover, neoclassical supply and demand analysis is conceptualized as barter in a village fair. But this assumption bears little resemblance to the modern monetary and credit economy. Frank Hahn (1983) spotlights this problem, when he writes: "The most serious challenge that the existence of money poses to the theorist is this: the best developed model of the economy cannot find room for it. The best developed model is, of course, the Arrow Debreu version of Walrasian general equilibrium" (p. 1). Even if money is acknowledged in the neoclassical model as a medium of exchange, credit and financial institutions are not: "In the neoclassical view, speculation, financing conditions, inherited financial obligations, and the fluctuating behavior of aggregate demand have nothing whatsoever to do with savings, investment, and interest rate determination" (Minsky 1986, 111). We shall see in later chapters that a credit economy may be fragile and vulnerable because optimistic investors may use credit to go far beyond what the objective situation warrants.

### EXOGENOUS SHOCKS AND ADJUSTMENT BARRIERS

Because neoclassical theory envisions the capitalist system as automatically and rapidly adjusting to equilibrium at full employment, we have noted that neoclassical economists attribute all downturns to exogenous shocks (such as bad harvests or government mistakes). Failure to return to equilibrium is seen as due to barriers to the working of the system, such as trade unions or minimum wage laws. The lack of acknowledgment of any internal dynamics causing upturns and downturns flies in the face of the facts that the same, regular sequence of events occurs in every business cycle.

The impossibility of a completely exogenous explanation is acknowledged by most of those who argue for a model of adjustment to equilibrium disturbed by random shocks. Thus, in his survey Zarnowitz (1985) concludes: "Equilibrium theorists recognize that the basic ingredients of their models are not sufficient to produce the persistent movements in output and employment which occur during the business cycle. However, they point out that random shocks to aggregate demand can be converted into persistent movements by suitable propagation mechanisms . . ." (p. 555). But these "propagation mechanisms" are exactly the lagging responses and other relationships that play a major role in the endogenous theories examined next.

In the new classical models, there are discussions of the lagging response to an increase in the money supply. An increase in the money supply in the expansion leads to rising prices. But capitalists are unaware that this is a general trend, so each thinks it is only a relative price increase attributable to more demand for his or her product. "This scenario . . . depends crucially on the confusion on the part of agents between relative and general price movements" (Lucas 1977, 22). The capitalists increase their production far beyond the objective demand because of the misinterpretation of the information. Eventually, when demand turns out to be less than expected, they realize their mistake and cut back production, setting off a recession. Thus, the leading exogenous theories place "a heavy explanatory burden on a single causal chain: Random monetary shocks induce price misperceptions which induce wrong production decisions" (Zarnowitz 1985, 552).

In fact, theories of random shocks to a basically stable economy appear to be much more acceptable to most economists whenever the economy does reasonably well and whenever the faith in private enterprise becomes a dominant view, as in the Reagan administration. In terms of factual content, however, "there is not much empirical validation that random shocks of all kinds play as large a role in business cycles as has been attributed to them in recent literature. The weight of exogenous policy factors [that is, government mistakes] too, seems more often than not overstated" (Zarnowitz 1985, 570).

Yet no serious endogenous or internal theory argues that external shocks have no influence on the economy. They sometimes do have a major influence, but the extent of the impact depends on the stage of the cycle. If a capitalist economy is undergoing a vigorous recovery in the early stages of expansion, then even quite strong outside shocks may have little negative effect. If, however, an economy has reached a very vulnerable stage of the internal cycle, then a fairly small external shock may set off a recession—and outside shocks during a recession may help make it a major depression.

There is also considerable confusion about what is external and what is internal. Economists use the term "exogenous factors" to mean those that are exogenous to the model or system they have described. Most of the theories in the rest of this chapter describe a cycle based mainly on the internal working of a private capitalist economy. But all of these theorists recognize that government plays a major role in capitalist economies— and some would argue that government actions are themselves to be explained endogenously by the conditions and interests of the capitalist economy. Similarly, the international actions of the multinational corporations are rooted in the individual economies from which they arise. Moreover, some theories consider technological innovations in industry as an exogenous factor, but technological innovations have clear internal causes. This is reflected in the fact that, no matter when an invention is made, most applications to industry come during the early expansion phase of the cycle, when the internal conditions of the economy are receptive to innovations. Thus, most internal theories easily incorporate technological innovation as part of their "internal" mechanism. Later chapters of this book will examine the systematic relations of government and international relationships to the business cycle.

## Conclusions and Policy Implications of Exogenous Theories

The dominant neoclassical, exogenous theories in this chapter conclude that (1) all unemployment is voluntary; (2) the capitalist system would always remain at full employment equilibrium without outside interference; and (3) all downturns are caused by outside interference, such as government policy mistakes, government laws (such as the minimum wage laws), and/or trade union actions. This theory is profoundly conservative because the policy implication is to do nothing, except to remove all government interference, as well as all trade unions from the economy. The assumptions of this theory are extremely unrealistic, but it is a useful tool for the preservation of the status quo.

Before leaving this brief exposition of exogenous cycle theories—intended only to highlight their main points rather than to give a comprehensive and balanced exposition—it may be helpful to note some further readings for those who wish a deeper knowledge of these theories. The best survey and best bibliography on modern exogenous theories is Zarnowitz (1985), while the best survey and bibliography of the earlier theories is Haberler (1960). A sympathetic survey and mathematical exposition of recent monetarist and equilibrium theories is in Mullineux (1984). The clearest exposition of Lucas's own view is in his article, "Understanding Business Cycles," reprinted in Lucas (1981). A brief, but very clear and very critical survey of theories is in Peterson (1987). The best collection of neoclassical empirical articles on the business cycle is the massive book edited by R. J. Gordon (1986). The natural rate of unemployment is clearly explained and refuted in Cherry (1981), while the entire evolution by which neoclassical economists have made involuntary unemployment magically disappear is traced in an excellent article by Lars Orsberg (1988).

## ENDOGENOUS THEORIES OF THE BUSINESS CYCLE

The endogenous theories help to answer two questions: Why is capitalism so unstable that it experiences recurrent recessions and depressions? Why are millions of workers involuntarily unemployed in each recession or depression? The rest of this book is mainly devoted to detailed consideration of the endogenous theories and supporting evidence, so the following sketches are merely intended as a brief overview of their basic ideas.

## DEMAND THEORIES: THE MULTIPLIER-ACCELERATOR THEORY

Although many economists contributed to this theory, it is mainly associated with the name of Paul Samuelson (1939). In his version, he emphasizes that consumption rises with income, but more slowly. The *multiplier* refers to the fact that any injection into the income stream (such as new investment) is respent over and over again for consumer goods and services, so the eventual total impact on spending may be several times the original injection. He also emphasizes that investment is determined by the change in demand. The proposition that it is not the level, but the change, in consumption that affects investment gives rise to the name of *accelerator* for this relationship. Since consumption is held to rise more and more slowly, while a slower growth of consumption is said to lead to an absolute decline of investment, this mechanism offers an endogenous theory of the business cycle. When this theory is considered at length later in this book, the multiplier and accelerator are expounded and criticized in detail.

## DEMAND THEORIES: UNDERCONSUMPTION

The underconsumptionists agree with Samuelson that slow growth of consumption causes a problem, leading to recessions and depressions. Most underconsumptionists, however, emphasize that the lack of consumer demand is caused by the maldistribution of income. All of them agree that a poor person will have a much higher ratio of consumption to income than will a rich person. It follows that if more income shifts to the rich, the average consumption out of income will decline, leading to an overall lack of demand.

Some underconsumptionists consider this to be a permanent problem, leading to long-run stagnation in the capitalist system, with each revival uncertain and due to unusual factors (such as innovations or wars). Other underconsumptionists, as we shall see in detail, argue that the problem worsens in each expansion of capitalism, leading to eventual crisis and depression. Liberal underconsumptionists (such as Hobson [1922]) view maldistribution as an aberration of the capitalist system, correctable by reform legislation. Marxist underconsumptionists (such as Sweezy [1942]) contend that income inequality is a necessary result of the class struggle under capitalism. For Marxists, the process begins with the struggle during production, which results in workers being exploited—and the ratio of exploitation always increases during an expansion (see Sweezy 1942).

## SUPPLY THEORIES: REAL OVERINVESTMENT

The so-called supply-side economics, discussed above, provides a purely exogenous view of recessions and depressions, holding them to be caused by mistaken government taxing policies. Totally different are the many theories explaining the business cycle in terms of endogenous supply factors. All of these theories have in common the view that profit rates are reduced by rising costs per unit, but they differ on the type of costs that are emphasized.

One interesting theory, seldom discussed in the literature, is the view that in an expansion, when there is a rapid pace of new investment, the attempted investment outruns the actual available raw materials. If raw material prices start rising much faster than the price of finished goods, then this reduces the profits of all capitalists producing finished goods. Analysts as different in approach as Frederick Hayek (1939) and Karl Marx ([1905] 1952) have identified this as a major factor in the business cycle. This theory is often related to an aspect of the accelerator relationship, whereby the demand for plant and equipment is a function of the change in consumer demand, while the demand for raw materials is a function of the change in the demand for plant and equipment. Thus a small change in consumer demand may lead to a large change in demand for raw materials.

## SUPPLY THEORIES: MONETARY OVERINVESTMENT

A large number of theories go under the general name of monetary overinvestment (see Haberler 1960, ch. 3). They range from exogenous theories of changes in the money supply to endogenous theories of rising interest rates or rising reliance on debt financing. A general expansion of production leads to optimistic expectations of future profits. Such optimism causes a huge increase in investments, some based on realistic predictions and some based on pure speculation. But the increase in investments very soon outruns the supply of profits available for reinvestment, so firms turn to credit. In the expansion, a higher and higher ratio of investment relies on credit. On the one hand, this means rising interest rates, as the demand for loans goes far beyond the previous supply of savings. Rising interest rates obviously lower profit rates of industrial capital, all other things being equal. Furthermore, the position of business becomes more precarious as the ratio of borrowed capital to equity capital rises. A small decline in demand may make it impossible to pay interest or even principal on many debts, leading to a financial panic and a deepening recession or depression.

## Supply Theories: The Reserve Army

Marx used the dramatic term "the reserve army of labor" to describe the unemployed. He emphasized that business may expand rapidly without raising wages so long as there is a large reserve of unemployed workers to be used as convenient. Marx also discussed the exceptional case in which the reserve army was completely depleted, after which wages might rise rapidly enough to cut into profits and cause a recession. Many modern Marxists (such as Boddy and Crotty [1975]) have developed this line of reasoning to argue that it is a normal occurrence in every business expansion. They note that at first a plentiful supply of unemployed workers holds down the wage rate. When an expansion nears its peak, however, the reserve army of unemployed almost disappears. Then workers gain in bargaining power, as there is less competition for jobs. Thus, eventually wage rates rise more rapidly than productivity, cutting into profits. This reduction of profits per unit leads to lower investment and a recession.

## Profit Squeeze (or the Nutcracker Effect) in Marx, Mitchell, Keynes, and Kalecki

The endogenous theories boil down to those emphasizing the limitations on demand versus those emphasizing rising costs. The term "profit squeeze" has been used in an illogical manner by supply-side theorists—for example, in the reserve army approach—to mean simply rising costs. This is not logical because it explains only how profit is "squeezed" from one side. But a thing cannot be squeezed from one side. If an orange is sitting on the floor and one pushes on it, it merely rolls along the floor. To squeeze an orange, one must find a way to squeeze it against something—otherwise it has as little meaning as one hand clapping. My conception of a profit squeeze is the closing of the jaws of a nutcracker. Leaving aside all metaphors, the problem with most demand theories has been that they ignore the cost side, while the problem with supply theories has been that they ignore the demand side. What must be explained in a coherent and consistent model of the business cycle is how the margin of profit is squeezed between the upper limit of demand-driven revenues and the lower limit of supply-driven costs.

That problem has been discussed in the works of the four giants of business cycle research who have inspired the approach of this book—Karl Marx, Wesley Mitchell, John M. Keynes, and Michal Kalecki. At this point, it is not possible to do justice to their full theories (which are discussed in several later chapters, where appropriate), but it is necessary to indicate the major ways in which they inspired the redefined profit squeeze theory discussed in this book.

Karl Marx provides one of the first explicit criticisms of Say's law in depth and portrays the instability of the capitalist system as one of the most important problems of economics. He states clearly the importance of both supply-side considerations (the production of profit by workers as well as the importance of capital costs) and demand-side considerations (the realization of profit by sales) in the determination of the profit rate. He emphasizes the importance of class conflict in the determination of wages—and he stresses how changes in wages will affect both consumer demand and production costs of capitalists. He points out how the class distribution of income will affect both consumption and investment. Marx discussed so many endogenous factors affecting the business cycle that one may trace almost any endogenous theory back to Marx, although he did not fully develop any of them, leaving merely many tantalizing comments—and a promise to develop a full theory of crises or business cycles in his later work (which he never did). Marx did discuss the conditions of smooth capitalist growth (see Appendix 4.1), but he showed that these conditions do not hold under capitalism for endogenous reasons.

Wesley Clair Mitchell wrote on the business cycle from 1913 till 1948 and produced the most important body of empirical data ever to bear on this subject, both in his own work and in the National Bureau of Economic Research (NBER), which he founded. Mitchell did not construct an explicit theoretical critique of Say's law, and usually did not mention it at all, but his entire work is an implicit rejection of Say's law, especially his historical finding that the business cycle is inherent in capitalist institutions and only in capitalist institutions. Mitchell's methodology pervades this book, both in its empirical research and to some extent in its theoretical aspects. Although Mitchell, like Marx, never spelled out a complete theory of the cycle, his empirical work is not at random, but is almost exclusively directed toward an explanation of profit behavior over the business cycle. His most extensive research is directed toward relative supply prices and costs over the cycle, but he also stresses that profit is equally determined by the need to sell products and considers, more briefly, the problems of consumer demand. Perhaps the most important part of Mitchell's methodology is his continual stress on the need to explain how recovery leads to prosperity, how prosperity leads to crisis, how crisis leads to depression, and how depression leads to a new recovery. This forced him, and anyone following his lead, to state a comprehensive theory of all the stages of the cycle and not just the crisis.

John Maynard Keynes, writing during the Great Depression, gave a rigorous theoretical critique of Say's law, which should have ended any further reference to that obsolete and peculiar notion—and he would have ended any serious reference to Say's law, except that it is an exceptionally useful tool to anyone wishing to defend the status quo. Say's law is a dividing line between orthodoxy and heterodoxy in economics:

> For the orthodox theorist the denial of Say's law (in whatever version happens to be dominant at the moment) is a sure sign of the heterodox theorist's confusion and incompetence. To the heterodox theorist the acceptance of Say's law is an instance of orthodoxy's blindness to reality, and fetishized attachment to absurd abstractions. (Foley 1983, 1)

Keynes was the preeminent theorist of the importance of demand in the macroeconomy. His analysis of the different components—consumption, investment, government, and net exports—is the basis for some of the organization of this book as well as its theoretical framework. Yet Keynes is well aware of the importance of costs when he considers the expected profit rate (the marginal efficiency of capital). He considers at length both wage costs and interest rates, adding a new financial dimension to the analysis. Keynes stressed that because wages have both cost and demand effects, neither higher wages nor lower wages are a panacea for a depression. His work on financial aspects of instability has been followed by the Post-Keynesians and is explored in this book in detail.

Michal Kalecki also wrote on the business cycle in the 1930s, at about the same time as Keynes. His work was parallel to Keynes in some ways, but mainly comes out of the Marxist tradition. Thus he takes the rejection of Say's law for granted and goes on to the positive construction of a business cycle model. His work is a paradigm for building a useful dynamic mathematical model of the business cycle and affects this author's theoretical work at a detailed level. Kalecki's equations make clear how investment affects profits as well as how profits affect investment. It is the interrelation and simultaneous impact of these two relations that Kalecki so beautifully reveals. Moreover, his profit determinants carefully include both the supply of funds and the demand for goods and services. He follows Marx in explicating the effect of class on income and on consumer demand, while at the same time considering in detail such cost elements as the interest rate.

## THE FRAMEWORK OF ANALYSIS

From these theorists, as well as the available econometric and other empirical studies, the following basic hypotheses emerge, which form the framework for testing and analysis in this book:

1. Investment is the key variable explaining cyclical ups and downs.
2. Investment is determined by expected profits.
3. Profits are a function of aggregate demand as well as a function of cost factors.
4. Demand may be conceptualized with Keynes as consumption, investment, government, and net exports.
5. Cost may be conceptualized with Marx as the cost of living labor power plus the cost of constant capital, which is plant, equipment, and raw materials.
6. U.S business contractions are primarily endogenous and are caused by limited demand combined with rising costs.
7. U.S. business expansions are primarily endogenous and are caused by falling costs combined with rising demand.
8. Other key considerations are the degree of monopoly, the financial system, international relationships, and governmental behavior.

## THE METHOD OF SUCCESSIVE APPROXIMATIONS

Everything on earth affects the business cycle. It is impossible, however, to present all of the major factors and relationships at once; attempts to do so only result in confusion because both the theory and the empirical results are too complex to be understood if they are presented all at once. The method of successive approximations is appropriate for this type of exposition; it says that one should begin from the simplest, least realistic models and most limited facts, and should then proceed to a realistic model becoming as complex as necessary (but no more so).

Thus, the systematic exposition following this chapter begins with consumption behavior (Chapter 5) and investment behavior (Chapter 6), followed by the multiplier-accelerator model (Chapter 7), which is built on the behavior of consumption and investment. Next, we introduce income distribution (Chapter 8), which helps to explain consumption and investment and is the basis for demand theories of the cycle (Chapter 9). The next chapter introduces the cost of plant, equipment, and raw materials

(Chapter 10), which—along with the chapter on income distribution—is the basis for the supply theories of the cycle (Chapter 11).

The supply and demand factors are combined to explain the empirical behavior of profits over the cycle (Chapter 12) and the profit squeeze theory (Chapter 13). This completes a theoretical structure and empirical survey largely limited to the private domestic sector, still ignoring the specific importance of monopoly and of financial institutions. The impact on the business cycle of financial institutions, money, and credit is explored in Chapter 14 in both its empirical and theoretical aspects. The impact of monopoly power on the business cycle is investigated in both its empirical and theoretical aspects in Chapter 15.

Next, we explore the fact that this is an interconnected world in which economies are anything but isolated (Chapter 16). Finally, the fact that government has an enormous influence on the business cycle is fully considered. After that we may at last synthesize all of the main factors in one analysis. This is followed by two chapters on policy, based on the analysis in all of the preceding chapters.

APPENDIX 4.1
MARX ON REPRODUCTION AND GROWTH

Marx's views on the "reproduction," or growth, of the economy form a useful framework on which several theories of the cycle have been built. Marx begins with a very simplified, abstract model of capitalism. Marx's concepts are translated here, as far as possible, into modern Keynesian symbols for the convenience of non-Marxist readers. (The same model in Marxist symbols appears in Sherman 1971). Thus, $X$ is gross national product, $Y$ is net national product, $GI$ is gross investment, $I$ is net investment, $C$ is consumption, $R$ is profit, $W$ is wages, and $M$ is material cost, that is, replacement cost of used-up raw materials, plant, and equipment. Each of these is used here to indicate the flow recorded during a year, *not* the stock of things at a given moment.

In Marx's terminology, "surplus value" is the name of all property income, that is, profit, rent, and interest. For this first approximation, I assume (as Marx did at first) no separate rent or interest payments. Thus, aggregate surplus value may be taken as being roughly identical with profits $(R)$. Marx's "constant capital" is the same as what is called here material cost $(M)$, that is, the replacement value or cost of used-up raw and semifinished materials (intermediate goods) plus the used-up or depreciated plant and equipment—the value of all these material objects is a constant, given by the previous labor put into them.

Crucial for Marx is the concept of "variable capital," represented here by wages $(W)$. It is variable in that living labor may produce a varying value *beyond* its wage payment. Various writers on Marx have caused confusion by interpreting his "variable capital" as an actual bundle of wage goods. This idea of a stock of consumer goods used to pay workers comes from the old wages fund doctrine. Although Marx explicitly attacked that particular idea, his terminology sometimes sounds like that view. Even in the nineteenth century, capitalists kept no such stock of goods or even a specific fund for wages. Today it is clear that they pay wages from their general credit (or demand deposits) at banks—and may merely put today's sales revenues into the bank to cover today's wage payments. Thus, a modern Marxist model may be stated consistently, provided that "variable capital" always refers to the *flow* of wages and salaries during a given period, not to a nonexistent stock of wage goods or a wage fund.

Marx showed that the value of gross national product ($X$) from the supply, or cost, side is composed of variable capital ($W$, wages) plus constant capital ($M$, material costs and depreciation) plus surplus value ($R$, profits):

$$X = W + R + M. \tag{4.1}$$

Notice that $X$ is larger than the Keynesian gross national product because $M$ includes not only replacement value of depreciated machinery, but also costs of intermediate material goods. Since this means adding the value of, say, wheat to bread, the same value is counted once in intermediate purchases and once as part of final goods. Thus, for the Keynesian purpose of measuring changes in total output, it seems that some goods are counted twice. For certain other problems, however, the concept is quite useful.

### Simple Reproduction (or Static Equilibrium)

Marx asked the question, What are the conditions under which an equilibrium supply and demand will be achieved? This long-run static equilibrium, which he called simple reproduction, implies that there is no expansion of capital and no net investment. Thus gross investment ($GI$) just equals replacement:

$$GI = M. \tag{4.2}$$

Since there is no net investment, this means that—if equilibrium is to be achieved—all the income of capitalists and workers must be exactly used up in buying consumer goods ($C$):

$$C = W + R. \tag{4.3}$$

Adding these together gives the equation of aggregate demand or gross national product:

$$X = C + GI = W + R + M, \tag{4.4}$$

which differs from Keynes's formulation only in that Marx's $X$, $GI$ and $M$ each include intermediate purchases as well as replacement of plant and equipment.

## Expanded Reproduction (or Dynamic Equilibrium)

Having stated the conditions for equilibrium in the simple case of a constant stock of capital, or no net investment, Marx then asked a more difficult question: What are the conditions of equilibrium when the economy is expanding year by year? In this case, some of capitalist profits must be used for net investment (Marx assumed that workers do not invest, but use all their income for consumption). Let $b$ represent the proportion of profits consumed by capitalists and $(1 - b)$ represent the invested proportion. For this purpose, Marx assumed that all income saved by not being consumed is invested, that is, that Say's law holds.

Then consumer demand is equal to workers' wages plus the consumed proportion of profits:

$$C = W + bR. \qquad (4.5)$$

Similarly, gross investment demand must equal replacement plus new net investment out of profits:

$$GI = M + (1 - b)R. \qquad (4.6)$$

Finally, by addition of consumer demand and gross investment, the value of the gross national product (including intermediate goods) is

$$X = W + M + bR + (1 - b)R = W + R + M. \qquad (4.7)$$

Equation (4.7) is the only consistent way of stating Marx's view: Its logical consistency is guaranteed by the fact that $b + (1 - b) = 1$, or 100 percent of $R$. Moreover, with this streamlined presentation of the reproduction schema, it is then very easy to state Marxist growth theory (which is implicit in the schema).

The scheme is somewhat simpler in net terms. If replacement is subtracted from both sides of equation (4.6), then net investment ($I$) is

$$I = (1 - b)R. \qquad (4.8)$$

Net national product ($Y$) is just consumption plus investment:

$$Y = C + I. \qquad (4.9)$$

Therefore, if we add equations (4.5) and (4.8), net national product is

$$Y = W + bR + (1 - b)R = W + R. \qquad (4.10)$$

We shall use these equations in the growth model.

*Growth Model*

In order to move from Marx's expanded reproduction schema (or national product accounting) to an explicit growth theory, it is necessary to date the variables, using $t$ as a given time period, $t - 1$ as the previous time period, and so forth. This model leaves aside the unnecessary complications of depreciation and intermediate goods; it deals solely in terms of the *net* national product $(Y)$ and *net* investment $(I)$.

Any growth model must determine the increase in national product. Marx saw the increase in net national product at any given time in a strict relationship to the amount of investment or increase in productive capacity. This proportional relation is represented here by the constant $k$, *small letters being used as constants throughout this appendix*. Thus, the change in output $(Y_t - Y_{t-1})$ equals investment $(I)$ times the proportional relation $(k)$:

$$\text{(capacity growth)} \qquad Y_t - Y_{t-1} = kI_{t-1}. \qquad (4.11)$$

The amount of investment, in turn, is the whole national income $(Y)$ minus consumption:

$$\text{(investment)} \qquad I_t = Y_t - C_t. \qquad (4.12)$$

Notice that equation 4.12 says that investment is assumed to be equal to nonconsumed income or to the saved proportion of profits (that is, [1 − b] R). Marx, of course, only assumed this version of Say's law as a first approximation. He clearly believes it to be *untrue* for capitalism, though valid for socialist growth.

Aggregate consumption, as explained earlier, equals the workers' consumption $(W)$ and the capitalists' consumption from profit $(bR)$:

$$\text{(consumption)} \qquad C_t = W_t + bR_t. \qquad (4.13)$$

Of course, national income remains divided into worker's income plus capitalist profits:

$$\text{(national income)} \qquad Y_t = W_t + R_t. \qquad (4.14)$$

Finally, it is assumed in the growth model that there is a given rate of exploitation, represented by the constant $w = W/Y$:

$$\text{(income distribution)} \qquad W_t = wY_t. \qquad (4.15)$$

Of course, this is a simplification because Marx, in his discussions of income distribution, predicted a long-run rising rate of exploitation under capitalism (or a declining $w$).

The Marxist growth model (with five equations and five variables) can be reduced to one equation in one variable, net national product, namely,

$$Y_t = [1 + k (1 - b) (1 - w)] Y_{t-1}. \tag{4.16}$$

This equation can be solved to show the path of net national product over time (in terms of an initial level zero, $Y_0$):

$$Y_t = [1 + k (1 - b) (1 - w)]^t Y_0. \tag{4.17}$$

It is perhaps simpler and clearer to translate this into the rate of growth of output, which is $Y_t - Y_{t-1}$ divided by $Y_{t-1}$. Then the rate of growth is

$$(Y_t - Y_{t-1})/Y_{t-1} = k (1 - b) (1 - w). \tag{4.18}$$

This equation shows that the rate of growth under capitalism may be increased if the marginal output of capital ($k$) is increased, if the wage share ($w$) is lowered, or if the capitalist consumption ratio ($b$) is lowered. This rule is true *provided* that all saving continues to be invested, as will *not* generally be the case under capitalism. Marx's point is that capitalism may grow at this rate if, but only if, the proportions postulated for expanded reproduction hold true. His cycle theories show why they do not hold true under capitalism.

## Static Input-Output

Marx not only dealt with aggregate equilibrium; he also used his reproduction schema to evolve a simple model of exchanges between the consumer and investment goods sectors. If Marx's model is disaggregated into investment and consumer departments, or sectors, then the value composition is repeated in each of the departments:

$$GI = W_i + R_i + M_i \tag{4.19}$$

and

$$C = W_c + R_c + M_c. \tag{4.20}$$

Here, $i$ refers to wages, replacement costs, and profits in the investment departments; while $c$ refers to the wages, replacement costs, and profits in the consumer goods department.

Under simple reproduction, or long-run equilibrium, it is assumed that there is only replacement of capital, with no net expansion of capital (or output). Therefore, the demand for the investment goods of department $i$ is simply for replacement investment (of depleted inventories of raw materials as well as depreciated machinery) in both departments:

$$GI = M_i + M_c. \tag{4.21}$$

The demand for the consumer goods of department $c$ is, then, equal to all the income received by both workers and capitalists in both departments (since it is assumed here that both workers and capitalists spend all their income on consumer goods):

$$C = W_i + W_c + R_i + R_c. \tag{4.22}$$

If we examine the equilibrium relations between departments, this analysis leads toward an input-output analysis of the kind developed by Leontief. All that is necessary is an extension of the model from two to a large number of departments or industries.

With two departments only, the equation of investment supply (equation 4.19) is set equal to the equation of investment demand (equation 4.20):

$$W_i + R_i + M_i = M_i + M_c, \tag{4.23}$$

and the equation of consumer supply (4.21) is set equal to the equation of consumer demand (4.22):

$$W_c + R_c + M_c = W_i + W_c + R_i + R_c. \tag{4.24}$$

These equations show all the conditions for equilibrium exchange within and between the departments.

The next step pursued by Marx is the elimination of all exchanges that are purely *within* one department (that is, canceling out like terms). Use of either equation 4.23 or equation 4.24 yields the same result:

$$M_c = W_i + R_i. \tag{4.25}$$

This equation describes the necessary exchanges between the two departments in simple reproduction. Department $i$ must supply and department $c$ must demand the amount of constant capital necessary to replace the depreciated capital of department $c$, that is, the amount $M_c$. On the other side, the workers and capitalists of department $i$ must demand from department $c$ a supply of consumer goods equal to their whole income; these are the amounts $W_i$ and $R_i$.

## Dynamic Input-Output

In the modern model of expanded reproduction, the supply equations in the aggregate and in each department can be represented exactly as in simple reproduction:

$$GI = W_i + R_i + M_i \tag{4.19}$$

and

$$C = W_c + R_c + M_c. \tag{4.20}$$

The difference comes on the demand side, where the spending of surplus value is divided into capitalist consumption and capitalist investment, assuming for the moment that all saving is invested. If $b$ is the proportion of surplus consumed by capitalists, while $(1 - b)$ is the saving or investment proportion, then consumer demand can be represented as

$$C = W_i + W_c + b(R_i + R_c), \tag{4.26}$$

and investment demand can be represented as

$$I = M_i + M_c + (1 - b)(R_i + R_c). \tag{4.27}$$

As Marx emphasized, the difference between equilibrium and growth is determined simply by the change in the composition of demand or use of the surplus (since in simple reproduction $[1 - b] = 0$).

It follows that the equilibrium input-output relations between the two departments (obtained by setting demand equal to supply, and simplifying the answer by elimination of intradepartment exchange) is

$$W_i + bR_i = M_c + (1 - b)R_c. \tag{4.28}$$

As is appropriate, this equation includes the result under simple reproduction (equation 4.17) as a special case in which $b = 1$ and $(1 - b) = 0$.

# PART TWO

# The Basic Model—Demand and Supply over the Cycle

# CHAPTER 5

# Consumption

THE BEHAVIOR of consumer demand is crucial to both the multiplier-accelerator theory and the underconsumptionist theories. Both assume that consumption rises more slowly than income. In addition, the underconsumptionist theories assume that consumption is strongly influenced by the distribution of income. It is, therefore, useful to begin the empirical investigation of the business cycle with the behavior of consumer demand.

## TYPES OF CONSUMPTION

Consumption is, by far, the largest category of aggregate demand. Year after year, consumption absorbs between 60 percent and 65 percent of total GNP. Over 90 percent of personal disposable income is absorbed by consumption. Obviously, the behavior of consumption will have considerable impact upon the behavior of aggregate demand.

In the national income accounts, consumption is divided into three categories: (1) consumer nondurable goods, (2) consumer durable goods, and (3) services. In 1982, the money spent on consumption was divided as follows: 12 percent for durable goods, 39 percent for nondurable goods, and 49 percent for services. Thus, the demand for services is now the most important category of consumption. Services have slowly grown in relative importance over the last thiry years at the expense of consumption of nondurable goods. The relative roles of these two categories have been almost exactly reversed since that time.

Despite the change in its composition, consumption as an aggregate category has been fairly stable. The ratio of consumption to GNP from 1952 to 1980 has never been below 61.5 percent and never above 64.5 percent. Furthermore, no trend is evident. Consumption changes slowly, but it is such a large category that a drop of only 1 percent in a given year will amount to a drop of over $20 billion in aggregate demand if it is not offset elsewhere.

Wesley Mitchell (1951, 1954) found that in the four cycles of 1921 to 1938, aggregate consumption rose 15 percent in expansions, but fell by only 10 percent in contractions; in Mitchell's terminology, the expansion amplitude was 15, while the contraction amplitude was 10. Disaggregating this wide category, he found that consumer perishables behave about the same way as does the aggregate, rising 16 percent in expansions and falling 11 percent in contractions. Consumer durables, however, react more strongly to the cycle (because consumers can postpone purchases), so they have much greater cyclical amplitudes, rising 31 percent in expansions, while falling 27 percent in contractions. Finally, he found that consumer services are much more stable, rising by 14 percent in expansions (representing an upward growth trend), but falling only 6 percent in contractions (showing resistance to declines). The full cycle amplitude, which adds the expansion and contraction amplitudes, is 58 percent for consumer durables, but only 21 percent for consumer services.

Obviously, the mix of types of consumption will affect cyclical amplitudes. One reason for milder fluctuations in consumption has been the trend to greater weight for services in consumption. Consumer services grew from 40 percent of all consumption in 1955 to 49 percent in 1982, a very significant increase in less than thirty years.

In the seven cycles from 1949 to 1982, aggregate consumption rose 14 percent in expansions, but consumption continued on the average to rise even in contractions, though by only 0.7 percent. Nondurable consumer goods, such as food and other perishables, behaved rather similarly, rising 11 percent in expansions, while remaining almost constant in contractions (actually rising by 0.2 percent). Consumer durables, such as automobiles, had much greater fluctuations, rising 21 percent in expansions and falling 5 percent in contractions, thus conforming rather well to the business cycle. Services, on the other hand, rose in expansions by 15 percent, but continued to rise in contractions by 3 percent. It appears that it was much less risky to invest in consumer services than in consumer durables in the United States in that period.

In Figures 5.1, 5.2, and 5.3, the different cycle patterns of the consumption components are shown in detail. As expected, consumer durables rose very rapidly in the average recovery phase, rose more and more slowly in the prosperity phase, fell rapidly in the crisis phase, and then fell more slowly in the depression phase. Nondurable consumer goods, however, rose throughout both the recovery and prosperity phases of expansion, then fell a bit in the crisis, but actually rose in the depression period. Finally, consumer services rose in every segment of the cycle, rising moderately in expansion and more slowly in contraction.

## KEYNES'S VIEW OF CONSUMPTION

Keynes saw a need for a description of the behavior of consumer demand in the aggregate. Previous neoclassical writers talked only about individual consumers because Say's law proved that aggregate demand was al-

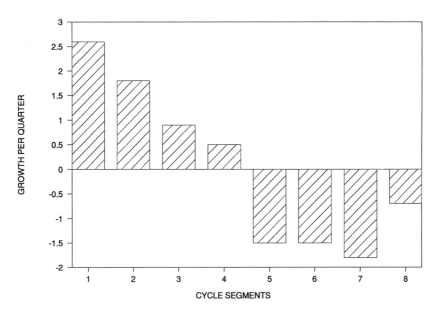

Fig. 5.1. Durable Consumer Goods: Growth by Segment Averaged across Seven Cycles, 1949–1982 (from series 233, Appendix F)

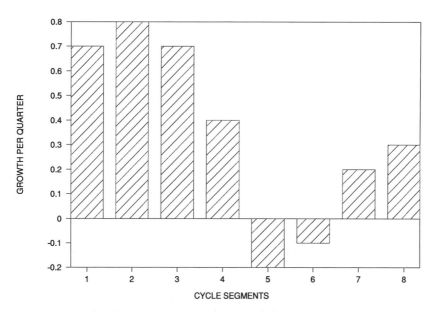

Fig. 5.2. Nondurable Consumer Goods: Growth by Segment Averaged across Seven Cycles, 1949–1982 (from series 238, Appendix F)

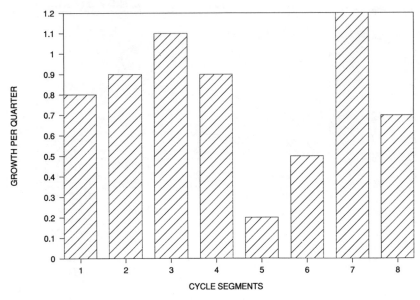

Fig. 5.3. Consumer Services: Growth by Segment Averaged across Seven Cycles, 1949–1982 (from series 239, Appendix F)

ways sufficient. When Keynes disproved Say's law, it became important for him to describe aggregate consumer behavior.

Keynes saw aggregate consumer behavior in terms of psychology. He stated the "fundamental psychological law" that "men are disposed, as a rule and on the average, to increase their consumption as their income increases, but not by as much as the increase in their income" (Keynes 1936, 96). He argued that people have a certain habitual consumption expenditure, or standard of living, out of a given level of income. If a person's income rises, he or she will—at first—continue the same standard of living, so the person will save more. That person will, however, soon adjust his or her consumption upward—so saving would still tend to rise somewhat faster than consumption in a business cycle expansion.

Since Keynes explained consumption in terms of psychological propensities, almost all economic textbooks today define the ratio of consumption to income as the average propensity to consume (APC). The ratio of additional consumption to additional income is called the marginal propensity to consume (MPC). As we shall see, it is not psychological propensities alone, but also many objective factors (such as the distribution of income) that determine the ratio of consumption to income. Moreover, the psychological propensities are by no means innate or eternally unchanging. The present psychological values of consumers are determined by the cultural environment, including family background, religion, education, and indoctrination by the advertising media. To call the result a purely psychological propensity is misleading. That terminology is used here only because it is so widespread, but there is always the implicit proviso that the propensity (APC or MPC) is socially conditioned and constrained by the objective facts.

The "Keynesian" consumption function is shown in beginning economics textbooks in its simplest form, with a constant marginal propensity to consume out of income. Keynes himself had a far more complex perspective, as indicated by his belief that the marginal propensity to consume (MPC) was likely to decline as income rises. In the textbook version of Keynes, it is also assumed that there is some minimum or autonomous consumption, so that people do not starve even at zero income. Because the theory begins with this minimum consumption, and then adds a constant MPC, it does reach the conclusion that the percentage of consumption to income must decline as we get further away from the minimum level (since consumption was greater than income at that low level). Thus, the usual presentation does reach the conclusion that the average propensity to consume must decline as income rises, but in a rather artificial manner of presentation. At any rate, both Keynes himself and the simplified presentations of Keynes do state clearly that the APC will fall as income rises in a cyclical expansion, while the APC will rise as income falls in a cyclical contraction.

The so-called Keynesian revolution generated a plethora of empirical research on consumption behavior. Cross-sectional studies of different families earning different levels of income in a given year confirmed the view that the average propensity to consume falls (and the average propensity to save rises) as the income level rises. Poor families had a very high APC, and wealthy families had a low APC (for a discussion of the early studies and their relation to later theories, see the excellent surveys by Mayer [1972] and Marglin [1984]).

The early studies of monthly or quarterly time-series data for aggregate consumption and income for relatively short time periods (that is, less than or equal to a whole business cycle) also seemed to confirm that the APC falls as income rises—whereas the APC rises when income falls. The important implication of these early Keynesian studies for business cycle theory was that in every business cycle expansion, consumption rises more slowly than income, with a growing gap between effective consumer demand and output.

These early results (which are confirmed again by the data presented in this chapter) all seemed to show that Keynes was exactly correct. This view hardened into the dogma that the average propensity to consume always declines as the absolute level of income rises. This simplistic dogma—which was far less careful and subtle than Keynes's own writing—has been called the absolute income theory and was affirmed with no limitations as to time or place.

Then long-run statistics for the United States became available, which used every ten-year average as one point or every business cycle as one point. In the long run, defined this way, the APC is very roughly constant (see the discussion of the literature in Green [1980]). Of course, Keynes was interested mainly in the short run, and he never predicted that the APC would fall decade after decade (nor has anyone else suggested such a theory). Moreover, it was later pointed out that there were many different factors operating together to produce the roughly constant long-run APC in the U.S. economy, and that England had a slightly falling long-run APC (there is an excellent discussion of this whole controversy in Green [1980]). Nevertheless, the importance of the long-run constant APC was used as a club to attack Keynes's whole theory on the assumption that he believed the simplest absolute income theory.

## RELATIVE INCOME THEORY

Three new theories arose as alternative views. One was the relative income theory of Duesenberry (1949). It had two versions, both compatible with Keynes's approach to consumption. One version stressed that consumer spending is always relative to past peak consumer spending because people persist in their old habits of spending even if their income drops; such "habit persistence" theories are discussed at length in Mayer (1972). The other version stresses that each consumer's spending is always relative to that of all other consumers. This version is similar to the institutionalist insight of Thorstein Veblen that people spend to keep up with their neighbors or to show off their wealth, which is spelled out by Veblen as the theory that people engage in "conspicuous consumption" of items such as fur coats or Cadillacs merely to impress others.

In either version, it is quite easy to explain a Keynesian falling APC in a short-run expansion but a constant APC over the long run (for example, if everyone's income rises together). While Duesenberry's theory saves the fundamental Keynesian framework, two other theories arose whose implications challenge Keynes fairly directly—though they pose the problem within the Keynesian framework, so they may be called neoclassical-Keynesian. These two theories are called the life cycle hypothesis and the permanent income hypothesis. They are still dominant, so they must be fully explained.

## THE LIFE CYCLE HYPOTHESIS

The life cycle hypothesis of Ando and Modigliani (1963) and Modigliani (1975b) explains the cross-sectional results by arguing that people's psychological propensity to save out of income is greater in the middle years of their lives than in the early and late years. Ando and Modigliani argue that at any point in time a higher than proportionate number of middle-aged people will be found in higher than average income brackets. At the same time, a higher than proportionate number of young and old will be found in lower than average income brackets.

In addition, the life cycle hypothesis explanation of both short-run and long-run aggregate time-series data hinges on the return of the pre-Keynesian assumption that consumption behavior is fundamentally determined by estimated total wealth, net worth, or present value. It also hinges on the belief that estimated total wealth differs from that of income over the cycle. Since estimated total wealth increases at the same rate as does total income in the long run and since consumption is a constant function of estimated total wealth, according to the life cycle hypothesis, consumption and income should increase at the same rate in the long run, making the propensity to consume roughly constant in long-run time series.

In the short run, the market value of wealth in property—and, therefore, the present value of income from property—falls less rapidly than does aggregate income during recessions (see Evans 1969, 37). Since consumption is based on the present value of income, holders of wealth in property will maintain their consumption and not let it fall as rapidly as their current labor income falls. Consequently, this is a factor tending to raise APC in business cycle contractions, while letting APC fall again to its long-run level in business cycle expansions. All the arguments and alleged facts in the life cycle hypothesis have been defended and attacked in numerous articles (see, for example, Modigliani 1975b; Buttrell-White 1978; Blinder 1976).

## THE PERMANENT INCOME HYPOTHESIS

The permanent income hypothesis of Milton Friedman explains the constancy of the ratio of consumption to income in the long-run time series as an accurate reflection of the "true" constancy of the relationship between estimates of *permanent income* and desired levels of *permanent consumption* (Friedman 1957). Permanent income is determined by total expected wealth during a person's lifetime. Friedman explains the apparent deviation from this relationship in the cross-sectional and short-run time-series data (in which the ratio of consumption to income falls as income rises) as a kind of statistical optical illusion in which the "true" behavioral relations between permanent consumption and permanent income are "disguised."

His reasoning is as follows. There is *transitory income*, which is defined as income received by accident or windfall in a single period. This transitory income will not affect our long-run estimate of permanent income. Yet the transitory income and *transitory consumption* (consumption out of transitory income) are inevitably measured as part of observed income and observed consumption. At any point in time, given the definition of transitory income, a higher than proportionate number of individuals with high transitory income will be found in high observed income brackets. Similarly, a higher than proportionate number of individuals with low transitory incomes will be found in low observed income brackets. Friedman assumes that the propensity to consume out of transitory income is less than the propensity to consume out of permanent income because people know they must return to their permanent level; consequently, the ratio of consumption to income would appear to decline as income rises in any cross-sectional study—but this is only an appearance because the ratio of permanent consumption to permanent income remains the same.

Similarly, since recession years are characterized by a lower than average ratio of transitory income to observed income whereas boom years have a higher than average ratio of transitory income to observed income, the ratio of consumption to income would appear to decline as income rises in the short-run business cycle expansion—again, this is only an appearance because the ratio of permanent consumption to permanent income remains constant. Of course, one cannot really measure some of these theoretical entities of Friedman, so there is no way to make a conclusive test to disprove the theory. Friedman's consumption function says that permanent consumption $(Cp)$ equals a constant $(k)$ times permanent income, where $k$ is constant in the short run, but changes slowly in the long run. It $(k)$ changes in response to changes in long-run interest rates; the utility functions of people, including their ages, family composition, and changing preferences; and the ratio $(w)$ of present physical assets to total wealth—but all of these factors change very slowly. Thus, over the long run there is very little change in the ratio of consumption to income (notice that the distribution of income is not among the factors affecting this ratio).

## EVALUATION OF NEOCLASSICAL-KEYNESIAN THEORIES

The life cycle and permanent income theories both emerged out of the attempts to test Keynesian theories, but they are distinctly neoclassical in their approach, so they are part of what Samuelson called the neoclassical-Keynesian synthesis—even though they reject some of Keynes's basic views. Both of the neoclassical-Keynesian theories still base themselves primarily on assumptions about psychological propensities to consume out of income; both of them see the fluctuations in the average propensity to consume as "a result of departures from the long-run average rate of growth of income" (Wonnacott 1974, 343–44). Much of the neoclassical-Keynesian literature thus explains the particular relationship of consumption and income over the short-run cycle mainly by the psychological preferences of all individuals. The clearest critique of these theories in both theory and empirical data appears in three excellent works by Mayer (1972), Marglin (1984), and Green (1984), all discussed below.

In these theories, the long-run preferences are modified by unexpected income fluctuations (see Rosen 1973), age, interest rates, or expected permanent wealth. All economists agree that there may also be effects by government tax policies or changes in exchange rates that affect imports (see, for example, Boskin 1978). One important issue is whether consumption is determined solely by a given, exogenous relation to income, or whether it may be affected by social influences, such as advertising and education, as argued by the institutionalists, for example, Galbraith (1967), and by socially determined habits, as in the relative income theory of Duesenberry (1949). An equally important issue is whether consumption may be affected by the socioeconomic factor of income distribution (discussed below).

The permanent income hypothesis and the life cycle hypothesis predict somewhat similar results (and in fact the same results are predicted by several nonneoclassical theories, as discussed below). Consumption is supposed to be a close function of the trend in income, staying at about 65 percent of the trend, but not a function of cyclical actual income. These hypotheses thus explain that the ratio of consumption to income (APC) declines during expansions and grows during contractions, but not because the APC rises or falls with income level; the reasoning has to do with the relationship of observed income to wealth or to permanent income.

In a detailed exposition and critique of the life cycle and permanent income empirical studies, Mayer (1972) concludes that the hypothesis that consumption is "strictly proportional" to permanent income "is definitely invalidated" as a factual statement by the empirical studies (p. 348). He also finds that the hypothesis that consumption is not correlated with transitory income is invalid. In a similar finding, he states: "The specific predictions of the narrow life cycle hypothesis have not performed well on these tests" (p. 350). On the other hand, he does find that these facts are not inconsistent with a looser version of the life cycle and permanent income hypotheses. In other words, these factors may influence consumption, but they are not the only influences. His final conclusion is that "the truth lies between the [Keynesian] measured income theories on the one hand and the full permanent income theory and the strict life cycle hypothesis on the other" (p. 352).

Marglin (1984) surveys the theories as well as the empirical studies for both the neoclassical and alternative views. He builds on Mayer's study, but warns: "Although the results [by Mayer] give little aid or comfort to the life-cycle view, they are not sufficiently strong to compel a believer to renounce the faith" (p. 394). In his own tests of alternative theories, Marglin (1984) finds: "It is not difficult to give examples of tests that superficially appear to support neoclassical saving theory, but that on closer examination turn out to support a nonneoclassical view equally well" (p. 393). Overall, his guarded conclusion is that none of the alternative consumption theories can be ruled out on the basis of econometric results alone.

A very careful study of the results of over 200 empirical studies by Green (1984) finds that there is no empirical support for choosing the life cycle hypothesis (LCH) or the permanent income hypothesis (PIH) over other theories: "[T]he tests of the LCH and PIH have failed to show their superiority over alternative theories on empiricist grounds" (p. 96). Green finds that these theories are accepted mainly because they fit so well with the basic assumptions of the neoclassical paradigm and strengthen its conclusions. The acceptance may be either conscious or unconscious by neoclassically trained economists. In terms of assumptions, they begin with individual preferences, taken as an external given fact. This supports the notion of consumer sovereignty, which is basic to the neoclassical view. By concentrating on individual preferences, they also rule out distinctions among the saving behavior of workers as a group, the saving behavior of capitalists as a group, and the saving behavior of corporations. Their view thus prohibits consideration of some of the main hypotheses of post-Keynesians, Marxists, and institutionalists, all of whom do concentrate on the differences in behavior among different groups and institutions (see, for example, Marglin 1984 and the literature cited therein). The neoclassical view thus provides a bias against macro policies for income redistribution from the rich to the poor.

In brief, most neoclassical-Keynesian theories—particularly the permanent income and life cycle hypotheses—lead to a very clear contradiction with one of Keynes's chief conclusions. Keynes argued that the average propensity to consume declines at higher income levels. Therefore, Keynes stressed that more inequality, that is, a higher proportion of income to the rich and a lower proportion to the poor, would tend to lower consumer demand. The implication is that if it is necessary to increase consumer demand to eliminate unemployment, then there should be greater equality of income.

The conservative neoclassical-Keynesians—such as Friedman—argue against Keynes's thesis, and their theories are designed in part to remove that thesis from the accepted "Keynesian" doctrine. For example, Alan Blinder (1975) argues thus:

In the early Post Keynesian days it was commonly assumed, presumably on the basis of Keynes' own intuition, . . . that equalization of the income distribution would increase consumption. With . . . the ascendancy of the Friedman (1957) and Modigliani and Brumberg (1954) models of consumer behavior, this view fell into disrepute in academic circles.          (pp. 447–48)

He states that the "modern," or Friedman, view "does not accord very well with intuition," especially the intuition of "those not schooled in macroeconomics" (Blinder 1975, 448). It is clear that, for Blinder, macroeconomics means only the viewpoint of neoclassical-Keynesians; it does not include the viewpoints of Keynes, the Post-Keynesians, or Marxists.

Whereas Keynes argued that the average propensity to consume falls at higher income levels, the two neoclassical-Keynesian theories discussed earlier all deny this basic finding. They argue that the short-run or cross-sectional results can be explained by other, temporary factors. It follows that a change in the distribution of income, in the eyes of these theorists, will not change the average propensity to consume (see Musgrove 1980). The policy implication is that a shift in income distribution from the poor to the rich, or from workers to capitalists, will not lower consumer demand, so it will not have a depressing effect. Similarly, redistribution from the rich to the poor, or from capitalists to workers, will not stimulate the economy.

Furthermore, Green (1984) points out that although the life cycle and permanent income theories were expounded at first as part of a neoclassical-Keynesian synthesis, their conclusions were used (as in the quote by Blinder above) to attack the basic views of Keynes himself as to the short-run, cyclical relation of the APC and national income. Moreover, the practical or policy importance of Keynes was to emphasize that government spending could have a multiplied effect on income through a high propensity to consume (this multiplier relation is considered in the next two chapters). But when the permanent income hypothesis assumed that the marginal propensity to consume out of transitory income was low or even zero, then the practical importance of government spending was undermined (which fits the general laissez-faire bias of neoclassical economics). Thus, Green concludes: "The reason why these theories survive, and why there are so many studies that use them, is to be found in the realm of ideology" (p. 96).

## THE CLASS INCOME HYPOTHESIS

Marx always stressed that class relationships under capitalism restrict consumer demand. He wrote that "the majority of the population, the working people, can only expand their consumption within very narrow limits" (Marx [1905] 1952, 492). Keynes emphasized that increasing inequality may widen the gap between income (or output) and consumer demand, saying: "Since I regard the individual propensity to consume as being (normally) such as to have a wider gap between income and consumption as income increases, it naturally follows that the collective propensity for a community as a whole may depend . . . on the distribution of incomes within it" (Keynes 1939, 129). Keynes was also quite explicit about the effect of an income shift from workers to capitalists. "The transfer from wage-earners to other factors is likely to diminish the propensity to consume" (Keynes 1936, 262).

Both Post-Keynesians and Marxists have argued that consumer demand is strongly affected by the distribution of income—see such theorists as Sidney Weintraub (1958), Michal Kalecki (1968), Eichner and Kregal (1975), Darity and Marrero (1981), Sawyer (1982), and Marglin (1984). The poor have high marginal propensities to consume, that is, a high ratio of additional consumption out of additional income. The rich have much lower marginal propensities to consume. Therefore, if the rich get a higher share of income and the poor a lower share than in the previous period, the marginal propensity to consume for the whole country will decline.

Capitalists, who receive profits from ownership of property and shares of corporate stocks, mostly have very high incomes. Even after consuming many luxuries, they are able to save and have a low propensity to consume. Workers, who earn wages and salaries from labor, have a much lower average income. Workers are, on the average, not able to save because they must consume all or almost all their income to meet basic needs.

The class income hypothesis stresses the lower marginal propensity to consume out of income from profits than out of labor income. This implies that a shift of income from workers to capitalists will cause a lower average propensity to consume for the whole society. A shift of income from capitalists to workers would raise the propensity to consume. For policy purposes, this means that policies (such as those of the Reagan administration in 1981) that shift income from the poor and workers to rich capitalists will restrict consumer demand.

The Post-Keynesians (such as Sawyer [1982]) contend that capitalists have higher savings ratios and lower consumption ratios than those of workers for two reasons. First, there is the usual argument that the low income of workers forces them to spend all of it merely to keep at the minimum socially acceptable standard of living (usually, today, with both husband and wife working at a paid job). Capitalists, on the other hand, have a high enough income that they may save if they wish to do so.

Second, not only do capitalists have higher savings above the socially necessary minimum, but their institutional situation forces them to invest. It is obvious that a small businessperson must keep on investing in order to continually expand capital to keep up with competitors because a small business must avoid being swallowed by competitors; he or she is under heavy pressure to invest for the survival of the business even if his or her income is low (see Sawyer 1982, 105; Fichtenbaum 1985, 237). On the other hand, in big business the decision for further investment is made by the corporation and only to a lesser extent by individual capitalists. Corporations pay out only part of profits as dividends to investors; the rest is retained by the corporation and used as savings for investment. As a potentially eternal institution, the corporation has an incentive to invest and expand as rapidly as possible—often contrary to the desire for immediate dividends on the part of many individual shareholders.

The important question is the needs of the corporate institution, not the needs or preferences of individuals, as usually assumed by neoclassical economists. Thus, Sawyer (1985) points out that "much of savings is made by firms in pursuit of their objectives (survival, profits, growth, etc.) with little reference to the utility of households who are the nominal owners of the firms" (p. 170). Marglin (1984, 432) emphasizes the importance of the impact of corporate decisions on consumption and saving when we examine reality. Thus, total private saving in the period 1952–1979 was found by him to be 9 percent of disposable income. But of that 9 percent, only 2.5 percent was household saving, while 3.8 percent was corporate saving and 2.7 percent was pension fund saving.

Since corporate saving—in the form of retained profits—is an institutional reality in modern capitalism, it is incorrect to ignore it when considering saving and investment. Yet most neoclassical studies look only at the personal income (or personal disposable, after-tax income) of capitalists and workers when studying consumption and saving tendencies—they exclude corporate and other institutional saving. This neoclassical approach results from its basic methodological bias in favor of starting all analyses with individual preference sets. On the contrary, a more realistic, more comprehensive theory must include all of the category of "national income," which includes (in addition to employee income) all of retained corporate profits, dividends, interest, and rental income of capitalists. In that appropriate framework, we shall see that it is quite clear that the capitalists' ratio of saving to income is higher than that of workers, while their ratio of consumption to income is lower than that of workers.

## WORKERS' AND CAPITALISTS' PROPENSITIES TO CONSUME

It is a well-documented fact that in most capitalist countries the spending for consumption is quite close in amount to the total wages paid out to workers. One survey of many countries over many years finds the ratio of consumption to total wages to be 1.03 in the United States, 1.04 in Canada, 1.00 in West Germany, 1.00 in the United Kingdom, 1.04 in Switzerland, 0.995 in the Netherlands, 0.98 in Denmark, and 1.04 in Finland (Heskel, Pinkham, and Robinson 1982, 66–77). These figures reflect the fact that most consumption is from worker's income. In countries where there is more equitable income distribution, workers' income is a larger part of total income, so consumption is smaller relative to workers' income. In Sweden, for example, where there is greater equality than in most capitalist countries, consumption is only 0.85 of workers' income. On the other hand, a high ratio of consumption to workers' income means that there is very unequal distribution of income because a small number of nonworkers have a large part of total consumption. Thus, countries with a high degree of inequality have high ratios of total consumption to total wages—for example, 1.88 in Mexico, 1.7 in all of Latin America, 1.6 in capitalist Asia, and 1.5 in Africa (though the data are not too trustworthy in many of these areas).

Moving beyond the simple point that consumption and workers' incomes are roughly of the same magnitude, there have been many attempts to estimate workers' propensity to consume as well as capitalists' propensity to consume. These studies cover different countries, cover different time periods, and use different econometric techniques, so the results are also quite different. One study looks at the APC (average propensity to consume, or ratio of consumption to income) while the rest look at MPC (marginal propensity to consume, or ratio of additional consumption to additional income). Some define workers' income as wages only, while others define it as all employee compensation, including salaries, bonuses, and fringe benefits. Some define capitalist income as personal profits only, while others define it as all property income, including interest, rents, and retained corporate profit.

With those warnings, the results of these studies may be considered. For the United States from 1929 to 1952, Klein and Goldberger (1955) find that the MPC out of labor income is 0.62, while the MPC out of property income is only 0.46. For the United States from 1948 to 1950, Milton Friedman (1957) finds that the APC out of labor income is 0.98, while the APC out of property income is only 0.77. For the Netherlands from 1947 to 1954, Lawrence Klein (1962) finds that the MPC out of labor income is 0.85, while the MPC out of property income is only 0.40. For the United Kingdom from 1960 to 1975, Murfin (1980) finds that the MPC out of labor income is 0.84, while the MPC out of property income is only 0.23. For the United States from 1949 to 1980, Sherman and Evans (1984) find an MPC of 0.99 out of labor income, but an MPC of only 0.13 out of property income. It should be emphasized that the lower estimates of MPC out of property income come from studies including all property income, including corporate retained earnings, net interest income, and rental income, as well as proprietors' income and dividends. The studies finding a much higher MPC from property income are concerned only with disposable personal income. There are many other studies, all finding a higher propensity to consume by labor than by property owners, reported in Burmeister and Taubman (1969), Holbrook and Stafford (1971), Modigliani and Steindel (1977), Steindel (1977), Arestis and Driver (1980), Marglin (1984), and Fichtenbaum (1985).

What all of these studies have in common is the finding that workers' spending from labor income (regardless of how it is defined) shows a higher propensity to consume than capitalists' spending from property income (regardless of how it is defined). The fact that so many investigators find the same general result for different times and places lends it some credibility.

An interesting and somewhat different approach by Fichtenbaum (1985) finds that consumption is a nonlinear function of the ratio of labor to nonlabor income (as well as being a function of total income). His results show that the marginal propensity to consume is a function of the ratio of labor to nonlabor income (note that the ratio of labor to nonlabor income moves the same way as does the labor share of total income). "Moreover, the results confirm the hypothesis that the MPC out of labor income is greater than the MPC out of property income" (Fichtenbaum 1985, 242). Fichtenbaum has successfully solved some of the earlier statistical estimation problems. So his findings support the commonsense view that the distribution of income between workers and capitalists does affect consumer demand.

## CONSUMPTION AND INCOME

Having established some facts about the relative propensities to consume of workers and capitalists, we may now turn to consideration of the cyclical behavior of the overall propensity to consume, and then to its relationship over the cycle to the class distribution of income.

### Average Propensity to Consume, 1921–1938

Wesley Mitchell (1951, 154–55) found that in the four cycles from 1921 to 1938, national income rose an average of 23 percent in expansions (its expansion amplitude), while total consumption rose only 15 percent. In the average contraction of that period, national income fell 18 percent (its contraction amplitude), while consumption fell only 10 percent (Mitchell 1951). Thus, national income rose faster than consumption in expansions, while income fell faster than consumption in contractions. In Keynesian

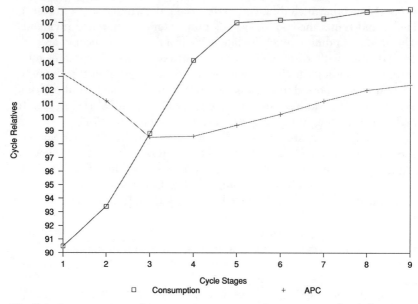

Fig. 5.4. Consumption and Average Propensity to Consume: Amplitude by Stage Averaged across Four Cycles, 1949–1970 (from series 231 and 231/220, Appendix D)

terminology, the average propensity to consume fell in expansions and rose in contractions.

### Average Propensity to Consume, 1949–1970

Figure 5.4 shows the average of the four mild cycles from 1949 to 1970 for consumption and APC. Real aggregate consumption rises throughout both the expansion and contraction phases, though consumption does rise more rapidly in the expansion than in the contraction. Since income mostly rose faster and fell faster, Figure 5.4 also shows that average propensity to consume is falling in the first half of expansion and rising throughout the contraction.

Figure 5.5 reflects consumer behavior in more detail in terms of its rate of growth in each segment of the cycle. Consumption rises in expansion, but at a slower and slower rate as the peak is approached. The rate of growth is much slower in the whole contraction, though there is no clear pattern of progression from segment to segment.

Real national income, represented in Figure 5.6, rises somewhat faster than does consumption in the recovery period. But, as is usual, it rises at a sharply declining rate in prosperity, so that its growth is about equal to

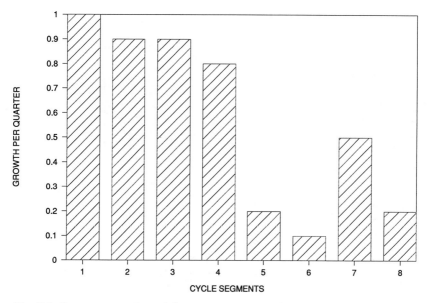

Fig. 5.5. Consumption: Growth by Segment Averaged across Four Cycles, 1949–1970 (from series 231, Appendix G)

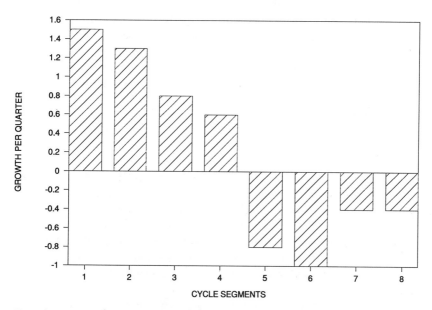

Fig. 5.6. National Income: Growth by Segment Averaged across Four Cycles, 1949–1970 (from series 220, Appendix G)

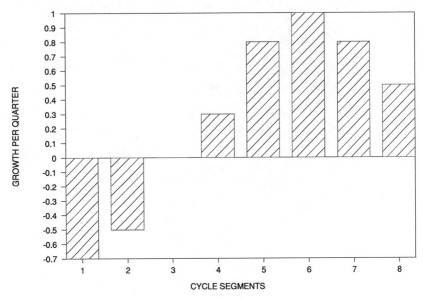

Fig. 5.7. Average Propensity to Consume: Growth by Segment Averaged across Four Cycles, 1949–1970 (from series 231/220, Appendix G)

that of consumption in the prosperity period. Throughout the contraction, in both crisis and depression periods, the real national income falls while real consumption continues to rise at a slow pace.

As a result, as shown in figure 5.7, in the period 1949 to 1970, the ratio of consumption to income (the average propensity to consume, or APC) falls significantly in the recovery phase, but rises very slightly in the prosperity phase of expansion. The average propensity to consume then rises throughout the contraction phase of the cycle.

### Average Propensity to Consume, 1970–1982

In the three more severe recessions and depressions of the 1970s and 1980s, the pattern of cyclical behavior of real aggregate consumption presents a picture (shown in Figure 5.8) between that of the 1920s and 1930s period and that of the 1950s and 1960s period. Consumption rises in the expansion, but then falls in the contraction, though the fall is very slight. The average propensity to consume presents a very clear pattern, with a decline throughout the expansion and a rise throughout the contraction.

In Figure 5.9, the rates of growth of consumption over the cycle are pictured in more detail. In the whole expansion, consumption rises. It rises most rapidly in the first segment of recovery, then more and more

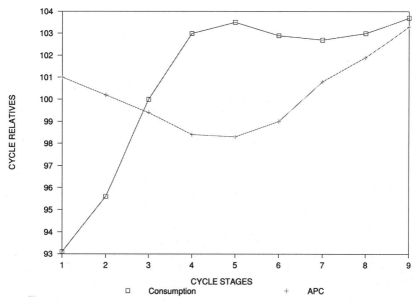

Fig. 5.8. Consumption and Average Propensity to Consume: Amplitude by Stage Averaged across Three Cycles, 1970–1982 (from series 231 and 231/220, Appendix E)

slowly until it is rising very slowly indeed in the "prosperity" phase just before the peak. In the crisis at the beginning of the cyclical contraction, consumption falls rapidly—so its decline is quite clear and is unlike the pattern in the mild recessions of the 1950s and 1960s, when real consumption never fell at all. Unlike its behavior in the 1920s and 1930s, however, consumption then revives and rises a little during the depression phase of the contraction, so that the severity of the contraction in consumption is much less than it was between the two wars.

In Figure 5.10, we note that real national income behaves as usual, both rising and declining at faster rates than consumption and at faster rates than it did in the 1950s and 1960s (the reader should note that, in order to show the higher rates, the vertical scale is more compressed than it is for consumption). As usual, national income rises more slowly in prosperity than it does in the initial recovery. Real national income declines in the crisis, as does consumption, but it also declines in the depression phase of contraction, so it is moving opposite to consumption in that phase. The reason, of course, is that consumers are managing to keep their consumption about stable in the face of falling national income through using up their savings and through going into debt, but also through government help.

Figure 5.11 pictures the rates of growth of the average propensity to

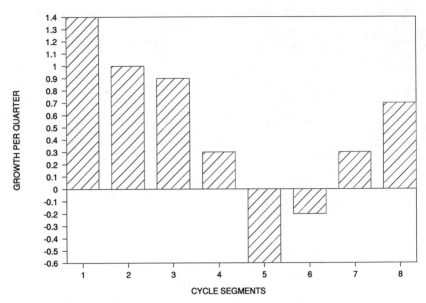

Fig. 5.9. Consumption: Growth by Segment Averaged across Three Cycles, 1970–1982 (from series 231, Appendix H)

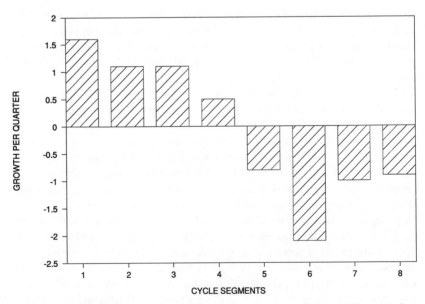

Fig. 5.10. National Income: Growth by Segment Averaged across Three Cycles, 1970–1982 (from series 220, Appendix H)

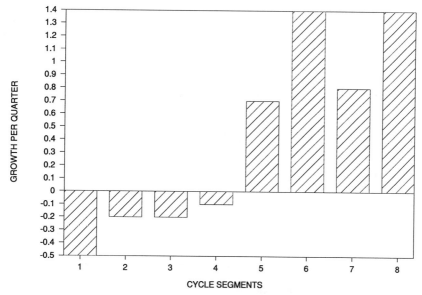

Fig. 5.11. Average Propensity to Consume: Growth by Segment Averaged across Three Cycles, 1970–1982 (from series 231/220, Appendix H)

consume in these three cycles, reflecting the differential between the greater fluctuations of national income and the lesser fluctuations of consumption. Thus, throughout the average expansion of this period, the average propensity to consume is declining, reflecting the greater rise of income than of consumption. Throughout the contraction, the average propensity to consume is rising, reflecting the greater decline of income than of consumption in the crisis—and the rise of consumption while income is still falling in the depression.

## PROPENSITY TO CONSUME AND LABOR SHARE

### Average Propensity to Consume and Labor Share, 1921–1938

In the four cycles from 1921 to 1938, national income rose by 23 percent in the average expansion, while employee compensation rose by only 20 percent (Mitchell 1951, 155). In the average contraction of that period, national income fell by 18 percent, while employee compensation fell by only 13 percent. If we call the ratio of employee compensation to national income the *labor share*, then we may say that the labor share drops in business expansions and rises in business contractions. As shown above, the average propensity to consume moved in the same cyclical pattern.

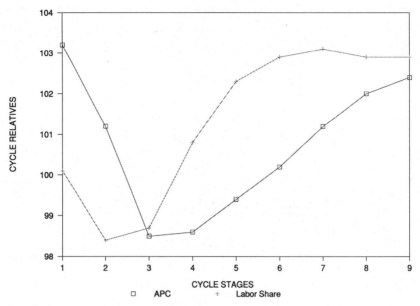

Fig. 5.12. Average Propensity to Consume and Labor Share: Amplitude by Stage Averaged across Four Cycles, 1949–1970 (from series 231/220 and 64, Appendix D; where labor share means the ratio of all labor income to national income)

### Average Propensity to Consume and Labor Share, 1949–1970

The observed relations between real national income and real aggregate consumption in more recent business cycles (from 1949 to 1970) are revealed in Figure 5.12. It should be emphasized that the behavior of the labor share in this period is very different from that in the later period (1970–1982) discussed below (also see Sherman 1986).

In the average of the four mild cycles of 1949 to 1970, the average propensity to consume (the ratio of consumption to income) falls during the first half of expansion, rises very slightly in the last half of expansion, and then rises throughout the contraction. The labor share moves in a way that is roughly similar, but it leads the average propensity to consume by a whole stage over much of the cycle. Both variables move downward in the recovery, or first half of expansion. Whereas the recovery phase shows declines in both variables, they both rise slightly in the prosperity phase, or last half of expansion, in the 1949–1970 period. Both move upward in the crisis phase of the contraction. In the last half of contraction, or depression phase, the propensity to consume continues upward, but the labor share is almost constant.

The labor share, like the APC, shows a rapid rate of decline in the first segment of recovery. In the whole prosperity period, it is already rising—while the APC starts to rise only in the last segment of prosperity. Both the APC and the labor share rise during the crisis phase. In the depression phase, we see that the labor share is roughly constant, while the APC continues to rise.

In these four cycles, the correlation between the APC and the labor share is not very close. The APC leads the cycle peak by a whole stage, while the labor share leads the cycle peak by two whole stages. It was this period that led to a rejuvenation of cost- or supply-type theories, emphasizing rising wages or falling productivity as the main cause of a decline in profits before the peak. Underconsumption theories seem to be partially refuted by the earlier turns of the labor share, long before the peak is reached. On the other hand, the fact that the labor share turns before the APC lends some credence to the labor share as a determinant of the APC. If the decline of the labor share in the recovery period does cause a decline in the average propensity to consume in that phase, part of the underconsumptionist theory is justified. We may also note that profit rates turned down very early in these cycles, so the causes for those profit downturns must be investigated at an equally early part of the business cycle. It is clear, however, that the rising labor share in the last half of prosperity was an important factor in these four cycles.

### Average Propensity to Consume and Labor Share, 1970–1982

In the average of the three severe cycles of the 1970 to 1982 period, the cycle pattern of both variables is quite different than in the previous period. A glance at Figure 5.13 shows that the movements of APC and the labor share are quite closely correlated in this period. Both the propensity to consume and the labor share fall in every segment of business expansion. Both the propensity to consume and the labor share rise in every segment of business contraction.

Both the labor share and the average propensity to consume fall most rapidly in the recovery phase of expansion, and then fall less rapidly in the prosperity phase of expansion. Both rise most rapidly in the crisis phase of contraction. This closely similar behavior gives some support to the hypothesis that the propensity to consume falls in expansion in large part because the labor share falls. The fall throughout the expansion provides support for the view that a low consumption ratio (caused by a low labor share) limits consumer demand at a crucial period of the cycle. Thus, the facts of the behavior of the APC and the labor share are much more encouraging for an underconsumptionist view—stressing lack of demand based on maldistribution of income—than in the previous two decades.

Econometric tests for the entire period from 1949 to 1988 show a strong correlation between the average propensity to consume and the

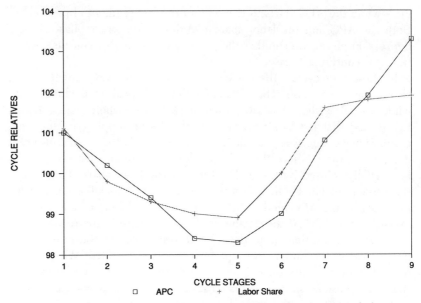

Fig. 5.13. Average Propensity to Consume and Labor Share: Amplitude by Stage Averaged across Three Cycles, 1970–1982 (from series 231/220 and 64, Appendix E)

labor share. The detailed results, presented in Appendix 5.1, show this regression relationship with a distributed time lag.

### CONSUMER CREDIT

In addition to total income and the distribution of income, a vital influence on consumer demand is the amount of consumer credit available and utilized. This factor is investigated in depth in Chapter 14, which examines credit of all types.

### GOVERNMENT

Governments usually add income (or reduce taxes) to stimulate consumer demand in contractions, while reducing support in expansions. We shall examine the details of this government activity in Chapter 17.

### INTERNATIONAL TRADE

As consumer incomes rise in expansions, some consumer demand flows overseas to pay for consumer imports to this country. As consumer incomes decline in contractions, less money flows overseas, and imports decline. Of course, payments for exports from this country add to consumer income. These transactions are detailed in Chapter 16.

## Conclusion

The works discussed in this chapter found that none of the major theories of consumption can be disproved by the empirical facts, but neither is any of them clearly proven by the facts to be the sole truth. The facts discovered in previous econometric research, as well as those presented here, are compatible with the class income theory stated here, though it has not been proven superior to the other theories. The class income theory says that consumer demand is influenced by the class distribution of income between workers' labor income and capitalists' property income—though it certainly does not deny the existence of other influences, such as total income.

The empirical evidence compatible with the class income theory includes the following findings: (1) There are higher propensities to consume out of labor income than out of property income. (2) The average propensity to consume declines in expansion and rises in contraction. (3) The average propensity to consume is significantly correlated to the labor share of national income. In the 1950s and 1960s, both the APC and the labor share declined in the recovery phase of the cycle, but began to rise long before the peak. In the 1970s and 1980s, both the APC and the labor share fell in most of the expansion and rose in most of the contraction.

The evidence of the 1950s and 1960s was used to cast doubt on a demand-side, or underconsumptionist, cycle theory because the labor share and APC were rising before the peak. The evidence probably does show that rising costs were more of a problem in the 1950s and 1960s than in most periods, but it does not prove that demand was not a problem even then. The profit rate—as we shall see—also declined very early in the expansion phase of those cycles, so the early negative influences by limited demand may have been a problem. The evidence of the 1970s and 1980s—that APC and the labor share move together downward for most of the expansion—gives support to demand-side cycle theories. We shall refer to this evidence again when discussing those theories.

## Appendix 5.1
### Time Lags

It is worth emphasizing that consumption is not an instantaneous function of anything, but operates with a time lag. The usual textbook "Keynesian" consumption function is given as a linear function with no time lag:

$$C = a + bY, \qquad (5.1)$$

where $C$ is aggregate real consumption, $a$ is a constant, $b$ is a constant representing the marginal propensity to consume, and $Y$ is income, usually real aggregate disposable personal income. To begin to approach reality, we must use a time lag:

$$C_t = a + bY_{t-1}, \tag{5.2}$$

where $t$ is a time period. In reality, however, the time lag is distributed over several past periods, with some influence on consumption from each, diminishing in effect as the time lengthens (see Sherman and Evans 1984, 154).

The simplest equation illustrating the class income hypothesis is

$$C_t = W_{t-1} + a + bR_{t-1}, \tag{5.3}$$

where $W$ is wages and all other types of labor income, while $R$ is profits and all other types of property income. Notice that it is assumed for simplicity that the coefficient of $W$ is 1, though that is not necessary for the theory to be true (it is only necessary that the coefficient of $W$ be greater than that of $R$). To estimate this equation properly, we should also include time lags distributed over several previous periods. But this equation cannot be estimated without a bias because $W$ and $R$ are not really independent of each other, since their total includes all income.

Another form of equation for the class income hypothesis could be the statement that consumption is a function of both income $(Y)$ and the labor share $(W/Y)$:

$$C_t = a + bY_{t-1} + c(W/Y)_{t-1}, \tag{5.4}$$

where $b$ is the effect of consumer spending for all income and $c$ is the positive effect of a greater labor share. Once again, if we were to estimate this equation, we would have to include time lags for several periods. This equation also would provide a biased estimate because $Y$ and $W/Y$ are not independent of each other (as will be shown in Chapter 8).

Finally, a third way to portray the class income hypothesis is to show that the average propensity to consume is a function of the labor share. An econometric test (using the ARMA method to correct autocorrelation) was run from the first quarter of 1949 to the first quarter of 1988. The data sources and definitions are given in Appendix A. The test correlated the average propensity to consume ($C/Y$, Consumption/National income, series #231/220 in Appendix A) to the labor share ($W/Y$, Labor income/National income, series #280/220 in Appendix A or series #64 in Appendix A). National income is used as the denominator for both ratios to show the full effect of property income and full effect of corporate saving. The result was

$$C/Y_t = 5.54 + .70W/Y_t + .37W/Y_{t-1} + .20W/Y_{t-2} \qquad (5.5)$$
$$(2.01) \quad (6.74) \qquad (3.13) \qquad (1.71)$$
$$CR^2 = .96 \qquad\qquad DW = 1.99,$$

where $CR$ is the correlation coefficient and $DW$ is the Durbin-Watson test (showing no significant autocorrelation in this case). The $t$-scores in parentheses indicate that there is a strong statistical significance to the relation between the propensity to consume and the labor share with no time lag, with a weaker significance for the influence from earlier periods. The evidence is consistent with the class income hypothesis. (Note that a statement that a variable is statistically significant in this book always means at the .01 level or better.)

# CHAPTER 6

# Investment: The Profit Hypothesis

INVESTMENT, or the accumulation of capital, is the heart of the capitalist economic system. Moreover, investment is the key variable in the business cycle. As will be seen below, investment fluctuates far more violently than does consumption, so it accounts for much of the increase of GNP in an expansion, but it also accounts for much of the decrease of GNP in a contraction. Keynes argued for the crucial importance of investment because a dollar spent on investment would have a multiplied effect on the economy through its responding on consumption. Marglin and Bhaduri (1990) write that in the Keynesian view, "investment demand is the centerpiece of the story, both because it is likely to be the most variable and elusive element of aggregate demand, and because of its direct role in the accumulation of capital."

Investment means a greater capacity to produce in the long run and more employment in the short run. It is important to stress this two-sided effect of investment. More investment is more demand for goods in the area of plant and equipment and inventories. The creation of these capital goods means more employment, which also means more income. On the other side, investment in new plant and equipment means the eventual supply to the market of a new flood of consumer goods.

## CONSUMPTION AND INVESTMENT

Even though consumption spending is much greater than investment spending, investment spending is the variable that explains more of the business cycle because investment rises and falls far more than does consumption.

As shown in Table 6.1, real investment has risen faster than has real consumption in the average expansion in all of the main periods in the last sixty years (and before that as well, as far as can be ascertained from the available data). Moreover, real investment has fallen much faster than has real consumption in the average contraction in all periods. According to Wesley Mitchell's data, shown in the first line of Table 6.1, investment fell drastically (50 percent) in the average contraction of the 1920s and 1930s, dominated by the Great Depression. Even in that period, aggregate consumption fell by only 16 percent—which is an enormous decline, but less than a third of the percentage decline in investment.

TABLE 6.1
Consumption and Investment

| Time Period | Expansion Amplitude | | Contraction Amplitude | |
| | Consumption | Investment | Consumption | Investment |
| --- | --- | --- | --- | --- |
| 1921–1938 | 21.2 | 55.4 | −16.4 | −49.3 |
| 1949–1982 | 13.9 | 26.2 | +0.7 | −17.4 |
| 1949–1970 | 16.6 | 23.5 | +1.0 | −9.5 |
| 1970–1982 | 10.4 | 29.8 | +0.2 | −28.0 |

Sources: Data for 1921 to 1938 from Wesley Mitchell, *What Happens During Business Cycles* (New York: National Bureau of Economic Research, 1951). Data for 1949 to 1982 from U.S. Department of Commerce, Bureau of Economic Analysis, *Handbook of Cyclical Indicators: Supplement to the Business Conditions Digest* (Washington, D.C.: U.S. Government Printing Office, 1984).

Note: Definitions: Consumption means real aggregate consumption. Investment means real gross private domestic investment.

By contrast with the era of the Great Depression, investment fell less than 10 percent in the mild recessions of the 1950s and 1960s, while consumption actually rose by 1 percent in the average contraction of that period as shown in Table 6.1. Thus, in the 1950s and 1960s, contraction meant contraction in investment, but not in consumption.

In the more severe contractions of the 1970s and early 1980s, investment again fell almost 30 percent on the average. Consumption was virtually stagnant in the contractions of the 1970s and early 1980s—though it did decline slightly in parts of the recessions of these periods—so the domestic, private sector decline of this period was due solely to the decline in investment. This behavior of consumption and investment is reflected in the data in Table 6.1 and is also pictured in Figure 6.1. Many investment theories, such as the accelerator theory discussed below, reflect in part this greater fluctuation of investment than of consumption. The importance of investment to the business cycle makes it imperative to have a reasonably accurate theory of investment; yet this is a very difficult area because so many factors affect investment. As a result, we shall find a wide variety of approaches.

THE PROFIT HYPOTHESIS

One of the most important institutional features of capitalism is the fact that output is produced in order to make a profit. Therefore, capitalists invest because they expect to make a profit. That expectation changes according to present and past conditions, including the past rate of profit

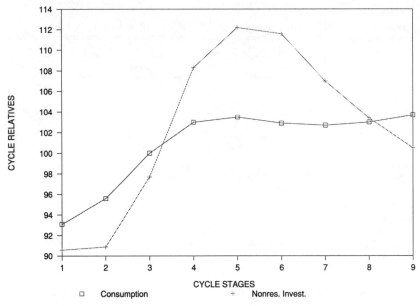

Fig. 6.1. Consumption and Nonresidential Investment: Amplitude by Stage Averaged across Three Cycles, 1970–1982 (from series 231 and 88, Appendix E)

and any factor that may affect the rate of profit. Factors affecting the rate of profit include (1) demand for goods and services, as evidenced by sales; (2) present and expected costs of labor, plant and equipment, and raw materials; and (3) the cost of credit, that is, the interest rate.

The hypothesis that investment is determined by the expected profit rate, within the limits of available funds, is noncontroversial only within a post-Keynesian, institutionalist, or Marxist framework. If we follow these approaches in rejecting Say's law, then planned investment may not equal saving. It is then necessary to specify how investors make their decisions within the institutions of capitalism. In that case, the decision to invest is based on expected profits, that is, the future flow of revenue minus the future flow of costs.

If, however, one begins by accepting Say's law within a neoclassical perspective, then the only issue is the determination of saving. It is assumed that investment will adjust to saving. The key decision in the neoclassical perspective is not investment based on expected profits, but whether to save or to consume. It is assumed that the rate of interest determines this decision and is based on the perception of the present utility of consumption versus the possible increased future utility from saving and investment.

By rejecting Say's law, we face the need to determine investment as the key to the business cycle. From that perspective, profit is important not only because it influences expectations, but also because actual investment is determined by the availability of funds. Available funds include corporate and individual profits, depreciation allowances, and credit from financial intermediaries of all types. In obtaining credit, past profit performance is one important indicator to creditors of the safety of a loan.

It is apparent and should be emphasized that profit plays a dual role. On the one hand, profit performance motivates the investor by affecting expectations of profits. On the other hand, profit is one of the sources of available funds for investment: "Today's profits are, on the one hand, a primary source for the accumulation of business capital. Tomorrow's profits, on the other hand, are the lure which attracts business" (Marglin and Bhaduri [1990]). Both the favorable expectation and the available funds are necessary for investment.

To say that profit and profit expectations determine investment, however, is only to begin the task. Since almost everything affects profits, economists have spent much time and effort trying to pinpoint the most important elements affecting profits and, consequently, investment. In this chapter, we begin by analyzing the role of competition, the issues of expectations and uncertainty, demand factors, and cost factors. Since demand is one of the factors affecting profits, and since investment is one component of aggregate demand, the relationship between profit and investment is reciprocal, with each influencing the other. Additional factors affecting profits and investment are so important and complex as to deserve separate chapters. These include (1) availability and cost of credit; (2) existence of monopoly power; (3) government; and (4) international relationships.

## COMPETITION

The enormous influence of monopoly power on profit and investment is discussed in Chapter 15 (also see the excellent analysis by Sawyer [1982, ch. 3]). Here, however, the fundamental point is that in any capitalist economy, investment is made not only to take advantage of new situations involving the prospect of profit, but also in response to the actual or perceived moves of competitors. When IBM decides to market a new computer, all other computer producers must consider whether or not they will respond. To the degree that there is real competition in an industry, they are not only motivated but forced to respond. This competitive pressure to invest is not separate from the profit motive, but is basic to survival in order to make a profit. Corporations that worry about short-run profits, while ignoring the need for innovation and investment in order to make profits over the long run, find themselves facing problems down the road. In the unusually soft and easy environment of the 1950s and 1960s, many U.S. firms did ignore the long-run need to innovate, and as a result they were later overtaken by Japanese and European competitors (and many U.S. firms continue that practice today).

## EXPECTATIONS AND UNCERTAINTY

Keynes gave considerable emphasis to the role of expectations in explaining economic performance and in explaining the recurrent crises that affect capitalist market economies. His use of the expression "animal spirits" to describe the formation of expectations is perhaps unfortunate because the use of this term has occasionally engendered undeserved ridicule. In the use of it, Keynes simply meant that the guesses that are made about the economic future are the consequence not only of reason, but also of intuition, emotions, peer pressure, and other imprecise forces. Because this is so, expectations about the future returns from investment decisions might be inaccurate—perhaps grossly so. Various world political and economic events may occasionally generate unjustified pessimism or optimism.

Consider, for example, the situation in the late 1920s. There is considerable evidence that until 1929 the public mood was very optimistic—probably unreasonably optimistic (see Galbraith 1972). Investors imagined that all of their investment projects were likely to yield very lucrative returns. Such expectations generated an overly optimistic investment schedule. Likewise, many consumers felt very secure, believing that they would keep their jobs and perhaps even experience a robust rise in their standard of living. Thus, their own consumption may have been at artificially high levels, maintained by credit.

Then in the autumn of 1929 the stock market crashed, a dramatic event that ushered in a chain of economic calamities. This shocking event burst the optimistic bubble and replaced it with confusion, fear, and gloomy pessimism. Such a sharp change in expectations could and did severely affect the supply of funds, the expectation of profits, and investment.

Keynes and the Post-Keynesians have also emphasized the related factor of uncertainty. Keynes makes the distinction between risk and uncertainty (see Davidson 1978; see also Weintraub 1978). When considering risk, some economists wish to impute a certain known probability distribution to future events and, indeed, speak of the "expected value" and measures of dispersion of certain variables in the future. Often, it is thought that a reliable estimate of the probability distribution of future events—such as next year's investment—can be obtained by using accepted techniques in statistical inference on the basis of time-series data.

In effect, one employing such techniques would be using the statistical past to predict the statistical future. One can calculate the risk of losing at roulette by statistical technique. According to Keynes, however, uncertainty cannot be estimated by conventional statistical techniques. Because human beings are so complicated, enigmatic, and emotional, their future behavior is difficult or impossible to predict. Decisions that involve costs today (such as investment) in pursuit of uncertain future rewards are made in this uncertain and sensitive environment. The upshot is that investment decisions are quite unstable and very sensitive to even fairly small changes in the environment.

From the discussion of expectations in an uncertain world, the conclusion is drawn that any objective changes in the economy upward or downward will have a much larger effect on investment decisions than would otherwise be predicted. This does not mean that one cannot understand the course of events. By hindsight, it is possible to trace the objective changes that led to the major shift in expectations. Thus it is vital to emphasize that the stock market crash of 1929—and the resulting changes in expectations—did not come out of the clear sky, but were the results of changes in real, objectively measurable factors. For example, profit rates turned down some months before the 1929 crash. Thus, after the fact, we can see that future expectations were based on past happenings, but (1) the reactions went far beyond what the statistics would have predicted, and (2) consequently could not have been predictable in detail. At each cyclical turning point, if we can explain the actual movements of profits, then the drastic shifts in expectations can also be explained. Let us now turn to explanations of the actual changes in profits and, consequently, investment.

## DEMAND AND SALES

If there were no expectation of future demand for a product, then it would be expected that investment would result in a loss. As a result, even if capital were easily available, there would be no investment in this case. This Keynesian view contradicts Say's law and contradicts the notion that more saving is always good for the capitalist economy.

In his well-known article on the business cycle, Paul Samuelson (1939) argued that the level of investment is a function of the change in consumer demand (a theory called the accelerator, which is explained in the next chapter). Later versions of the theory emphasized that it is not just the change in consumer demand but the change in all types of demand that affects investment. (For the early Keynesian investment models, see Meyer and Kuh 1957.)

The first simple models of the relation of investment to the change in output demand were long ago replaced by far more complex ones (see the survey by Jorgenson 1971). The simplest models have been replaced by models (called flexible accelerator models) in which the optimal capital stock is viewed as a function of many previous changes in output, rather than merely a function of the most recent change. Considerable attention has been focused on the most appropriate set of time lags for such a flexible investment function. As in the case of consumption, it is generally agreed that some type of distributed lag structure over many periods is required. Different views of the most appropriate form of time lag structure range from geometrically declining weights to many more complex forms (see Solow 1960; De Leeuw 1962; and Evans 1969).

In the same famous article, Samuelson (1939) made use of the concept of the multiplier. The multiplier concept says that when there is a new investment into the economy, it will raise national income by a multiple of the amount of the new investment. That will happen because the money from the new investment becomes income for people, such as secretaries or construction workers, who respend it for consumer goods and services. Those receiving the additional money spent for new consumption will themselves respend it, and so forth. Thus, over time, the initial money spent for investment will have a multiplied effect on income. The multiplier theory will be discussed in detail in the next chapter, but it is mentioned here because it stresses the important impact of investment on the economy. Samuelson's genius was combining these two concepts—the multiplier and the accelerator—into a single, simple explanation of the cycle, discussed in the next chapter.

## Cost Theories of Investment

In addition to demand for goods and services, the capitalist's profit is affected by the costs of producing that output. Many modern econometric approaches to investment have attempted to combine complex accelerator (demand) theories with theories of the cost of capital. The earlier accelerator theories emphasize output demanded and the level of capital stock, which are assumed to affect profit expectations. Other theories, however, emphasize those variables that affect the marginal cost of funds, including variables showing the interest rate and the rate of corporate cash flow.

The "user cost of capital," along with the effect of changes in output demanded, is emphasized by Jorgenson and Hall (1963) and by Grilliches and Wallace (1965). Such theories heavily stress the interest rate and the availability of funds to corporations, variables that were downplayed in the early years of the Keynesian revolution, when all eyes were focused on effective demand. Since the 1960s, however, almost all sophisticated investment theories have emphasized the cost side as well as the demand side.

It should be stressed that there is no necessary conflict among demand, cost, and profit explanations of investment. The Jorgenson model of investment discusses the importance of changes in output demanded, but also emphasizes cost factors. Jorgenson synthesizes both revenue and cost factors in the notion that the firm maximizes profits. Since profits equal revenue minus costs, the profit variable encompasses both demand and cost factors. In Jorgenson's model, the revenue side of profits is represented not only by the change in output demanded, but also by the price of output. The cost side of profits is represented in Jorgenson's model by the cost of capital, which includes all related costs, such as the cost of electricity to run machines.

A number of theories have emphasized not only direct costs of capital, but also the availability of money and credit to the firm. Thus, there have been studies of the importance of total profits available for reinvestment, interest rates, cash flow, debt-asset ratio of corporations, and other measures of the liquidity of corporations (see, for example, Wood 1975; and Evans 1969). These issues are discussed in detail in Chapter 14, which examines money and credit.

Another variety of cost-side theories of investment deals with the costs of raw materials. Many of these theories have become prominent again since the oil shortages of the 1970s. Such theories are discussed in detail in Chapter 10.

Finally, cost-side theories of profits and investment include those that concentrate on the cost of wages. Industrial capitalists buy labor power as well as raw materials, plant and equipment, and borrowed capital. Empirical studies of these variables are presented in Chapter 8. Theories focusing on the high cost of wages—and its presumed negative effect on profits and investment—are discussed in Chapter 11.

## PROFIT STUDIES

Since demand and cost are both elements in profits, it is not surprising that many economists directly consider profits rather than the constituents of profits, in relation to investment. Robert Eisner (1978) conducted an extensive empirical study of both demand (as reflected in sales) and of total profits. He found that investment is "clearly related . . . closely to current and past sales and profits" (p. 171). Many other studies have found a close correlation of investment and profits in time-series data (see the works cited in Eisner [1978]).

Some comprehensive studies have found that present and previous total profits do affect investment (see, for example, Eisner 1978; and Wood

1975). The "profit" affecting investment may be defined to include corporate profits, noncorporate profits, rental income, and the interest income of financial capitalists—in other words, all property income. In addition to studies of profit, some have found a significant effect of the rate of profit on investment (see, for example, Sherman and Stanback 1962). Another study has found a statistically significant effect on investment by both total profits and the rate of profits (Sherman and Evans 1984, 173). Using quarterly data from 1949 to 1980, the study found that investment had a statistically significant positive relation to total profit with a two-quarter time lag, as well as a statistically significant positive relation to the rate of profit on capital with a three-quarter time lag.

## TYPES OF INVESTMENT

Investment is not a homogeneous category, but a group of several different categories, which perform differently over the cycle. These include (1) spending for equipment, (2) spending to construct nonresidential structures, such as factories, (3) spending to construct residential structures, and (4) spending to increase inventories. Inventory investment differs enough from the other three categories (all of which are fixed investment) that it is best left for a later section. Table 6.2 indicates the cyclical behavior of the first three categories in real terms, giving their expansion and contraction amplitudes.

The table, based on Wesley Mitchell's data, reveals the behavior of these investment components in three very different periods of U.S. capitalism. In the average of the four cycles from 1921 to 1938, equipment had the greatest expansion and contraction amplitudes. That is the case because capitalists can react fairly quickly to changes in profit expectations by ordering more or less equipment.

Mitchell's data indicate that factory construction, called nonresidential structures, has a somewhat smaller cyclical amplitude than that of equipment—though still very large in that period. The lower fluctuation in spending on factories than on equipment is due to the fact that building a factory takes much more planning and preparation, so decisionmaking has a longer time horizon than for purchases of equipment. Once a new factory is started, it is not desirable to stop construction in the middle. Therefore, cyclical fluctuations in spending on plant tend to be less than those on equipment.

Because of the severity of the Great Depression, even housing (residential structures) had a very significant decline in the average contraction from 1921 to 1938, though much less than that of plant or equipment. We shall see below that housing is often much less correlated with the business cycle than the other categories of investment.

TABLE 6.2
Types of Investment

|  | *Expansion* | *Contraction* |
|---|---|---|
| PART A. Average Amplitudes, 4 Cycles, 1921–1938 | | |
| Equipment (88) | 46.0 | − 39.4 |
| Nonresidential structures (87) | 30.6 | − 32.9 |
| Residential structures (89) | 33.9 | − 22.0 |
| PART B. Average Amplitudes, 4 Cycles, 1949–1970 | | |
| Equipment (88) | 29.8 | − 12.0 |
| Nonresidential structures (87) | 18.4 | − 0.4 |
| Residential structures (89) | 6.9 | + 3.0 |
| PART C. Average Amplitudes, 3 Cycles, 1970–1982 | | |
| Equipment (88) | 24.0 | − 12.8 |
| Nonresidential structures (87) | 17.7 | − 9.9 |
| Residential structures (89) | 16.8 | − 18.4 |

*Sources*: Same as Table 6.1.

*Notes*: Definitions: All variables in real terms. Series numbers in parentheses: #88 is gross private nonresidential fixed investment in producers' durable equipment; #87 is gross private nonresidential fixed investment in structures; #89 is gross private residential fixed investment.

As shown in Table 6.2, in the mild cycles of 1949 to 1970, the cycle amplitudes of all three categories were much less than in the earlier period. In fact, factory construction had only the slightest decline, while housing actually rose in the average contraction. In the three more severe cycles of 1970 to 1982, all three categories of investment again conformed to the business cycle, rising considerably in expansions and falling considerably in contractions, but with smaller fluctuations than in the 1920s and 1930s.

Residential structures, in fact, should be in a different category; they are not productive investments, but are more like durable consumption. There is also some indication that construction has a different and longer (fifteen-year) cycle. Investigation of residential construction cycles was pioneered by Simon Kuznets ([1932] 1967), with other excellent studies by Long (1939), Guttentag (1961), Gottlieb (1963), and Arcela and Metzler (1973). At any rate, residential construction tends to be much more irregular with respect to the official (NBER–Department of Commerce) business cycle dates than the other categories of investment. Al-

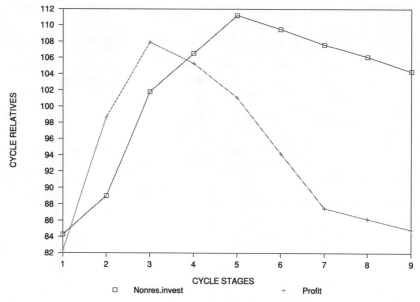

Fig. 6.2. Corporate Profit before Taxes and Nonresidential Investment: Amplitude by Stage Averaged across Four Cycles, 1949–1970 (from series 286 and 88, Appendix D)

though, as shown in Table 6.2, spending on residential structures conformed to the business cycle during the more severe recessions and depressions of the 1921–1938 and 1970–1982 periods, during the milder contractions of the 1949–1970 period, residential construction (like consumption) actually rose a little from peak to trough—and it also began to decline before the peak. For these reasons, empirical exploration of investment in the next part of this chapter is limited to nonresidential investment.

## INVESTMENT, PROFITS, AND PROFIT RATES, 1949–1970

Corporate profits fluctuate in a strong, procyclical fashion. Wesley Mitchell (1951, 324) found that in the average of the four cycles of 1921 to 1938, corporate profits rose 169 percent in expansions and fell 175 percent in contractions. Of course, profitability affects not only investment, but also survival. In the sixteen business cycles from 1879 to 1938, business failures fell by 62 percent in expansions and rose by 58 percent in contractions (Mitchell 1951, 321).

Figure 6.2 compares investment (all real fixed nonresidential investment, including both plant and equipment) with total real corporate profit after taxes. In addition to the exclusion of residential construction from investment, this figure includes only fixed investment because inventory investment is discussed fully in a later section of this chapter. Corporate profit is taken before taxes to see its performance before government taxation, but the impact of taxation is discussed in the chapter on government behavior.

Figure 6.2 reveals that in this period investment and profit behave fairly similarly, but with a time lag. Investment, as always, conforms closely to the cycle, rising throughout the expansion and falling throughout the contraction. Profit, however, leads the cycle, reaching its peak in stage 3, and then declining. This behavior fits most theories, since most theories do predict that the effect of profit on investment will have a time lag.

Figures 6.3, 6.4, and 6.5 picture the behavior of investment, profit, and profit rates in greater detail, showing their rates of growth in each segment. The profit rate is given solely for manufacturing because reliable quarterly data are available only for that sector; the data state the ratio of profit before tax to stockholders' equity capital.

Figure 6.3 indicates that investment exactly follows the business cycle in the 1949–1970 period, conforming to the cycle as a coincident indicator. Figure 6.4 shows the level of corporate profit leading the cycle in the average expansion by declining in the prosperity phase (the last half of expansion), declining most rapidly just after the peak in the crisis phase, and then declining again more slowly in the depression phase.

Figure 6.5 discloses the same behavior in the rate of profit, particularly the decline in the prosperity phase before the peak. The decline in profit rates reduces expectations and therefore limits investment. As a result, the rate of growth of investment declines in the prosperity phase, though investment is still growing. In general, during the cycles from 1949 to 1970, few indicators of income or financial viability expanded past the recovery phase into the "prosperity" phase. The prosperity phase (or last half of expansion) was an expansion only in direct production activities. In activities governed by the profit rate, such as new investment, a sluggish growth continued to the peak, followed by a comparatively gentle and mild downturn, not marked by any spectacular financial collapse.

## INVESTMENT, PROFITS, AND PROFIT RATES, 1970–1982

For the 1970 to 1982 period, Figure 6.6 reveals a somewhat different picture. Total corporate profit continued to rise to the middle of the prosperity period, declining only slightly in the last segment of expansion. Although investment began the expansion with an unusually weak recovery, the continued rise of profits caused investment also to rise at a strong pace throughout the rest of the expansion. Profit and investment both declined in the whole contraction more rapidly than in the 1949–1970

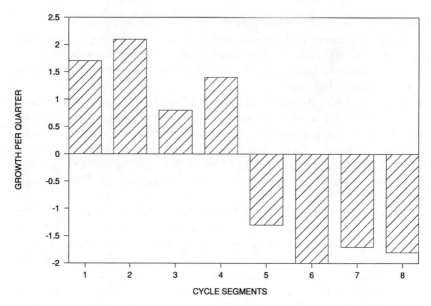

Fig. 6.3. Nonresidential Investment: Growth by Segment Averaged across Four Cycles, 1949–1970 (from series 88, Appendix G)

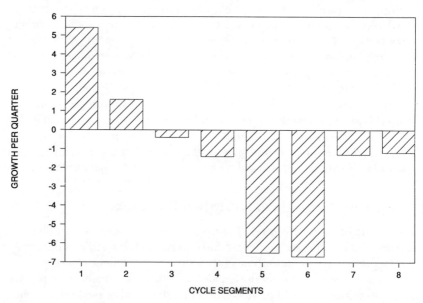

Fig. 6.4. Corporate Profit before Taxes: Growth by Segment Averaged across Four Cycles, 1949–1970 (from series 286, Appendix G)

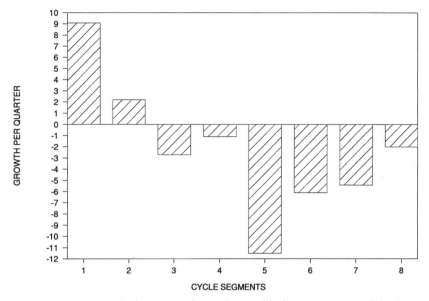

Fig. 6.5. Corporate Profit Rate as Share of Capital before Taxes: Growth by Segment Averaged across Four Cycles, 1949–1970 (from series A, Appendix G)

era, reflecting the greater severity of business cycles in the 1970–1982 era.

Figures 6.7, 6.8, and 6.9 allow us to compare investment, profits, and profit rates in more detail for the 1970–1982 era. Investment rises only slightly in the first segment of recovery, but then rises at a significant rate for the rest of expansion. Investment falls only slightly in the first segment of the crisis phase, but then falls at a significant rate for the rest of the contraction. On the average over all known business cycles, investment rises in every segment of expansion and falls in every segment of contraction. Therefore, as a stylized fact, it is best to think of investment as simply conforming to the business cycle, usually with slower growth just before the peak. (Of course, new orders for plant and equipment normally lead actual investment expenditures by a considerable time, so new orders often lead at cycle turns; see Appendixes D and E for specific data.)

Figure 6.8 makes the lead of profit quite clear. Its highest growth rate is in the first segment of recovery, as usual, followed by declining growth rates in the rest of recovery and early prosperity. In the last segment of prosperity, there is a slight absolute decline before the cycle peak, which is the usual behavior of this leading indicator. In the contraction, profits decline at varying rates in all segments.

Finally, Figure 6.9 portrays a pattern of profit rate behavior very sim-

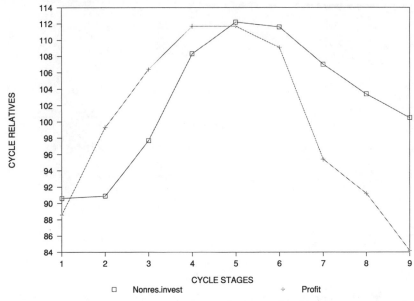

Fig. 6.6. Corporate Profit before Taxes and Nonresidential Investment: Amplitude by Stage Averaged across Three Cycles, 1970–1982 (from series 286 and 88, Appendix E)

ilar to that of total profits, except that the lead is still more clearly marked. The profit rate rises in the recovery and early prosperity phases, but falls significantly in the last segment of prosperity. It then continues to fall throughout the contraction phase.

In all the data for both periods, in spite of considerable differences in amplitude and timing, the overall pattern remains the same: First, the profit rate rises rapidly, but then it declines in late expansion as one of the earliest indicators of the coming contraction. Soon thereafter, the total profits decline, though not quite as strongly. The decline in the profit rate removes the motivation for more investment, since it leads to pessimistic expectations for the future. The decline in total profits means a reduction in the main internal source of funds for investment. When these two effects are combined, after a time lag for information spread and new decisionmaking, actual investment declines at the cycle peak and the contraction is under way.

## TIME LAGS IN THE INVESTMENT PROCESS

It is also useful to compare investment and profits in each of the seven cycles with respect to their time lags or leads, as well as their cyclical

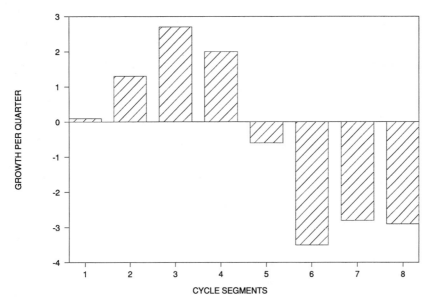

Fig. 6.7. Nonresidential Investment: Growth by Segment Averaged across Three Cycles, 1970–1982 (from series 88, Appendix H)

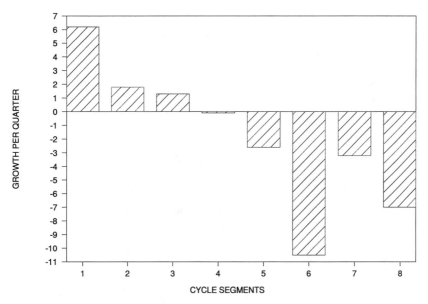

Fig. 6.8. Corporate Profit before Taxes: Growth by Segment Averaged across Three Cycles, 1970–1982 (from series 286, Appendix H)

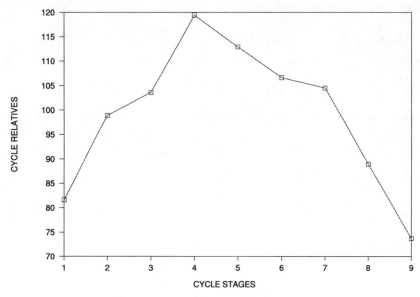

Fig. 6.9. Corporate Profit Rate as Share of Capital before Taxes: Amplitude by Stage Averaged across Three Cycles, 1970–1982 (from series A, Appendix E)

amplitudes. Table 6.3 highlights the most important statistics. This table makes clear that investment turns at the cycle peak and trough, but profit normally leads investment. On the average in these seven cycles profit peaks in stage 3 and reaches a trough in stage 8. The amount of lead time, however, is quite unpredictable because there is a wide variation, so any quantified prediction of investment from profit turns is going to be very rough and untrustworthy.

The table also shows that the cyclical amplitudes of profit and investment are often in the same range. Investment fluctuates far more than does any other spending component of GNP. One reason for that violent fluctuation of investment is that corporate profit and profit rates fluctuate even more than investment does. The average expansion amplitude of investment (25 percent) is almost as great as the amplitude of profit (29 percent), but the contraction amplitude of investment (−9 percent) is much less than that of profit (−30 percent).

## Timing in Different Industries

There is a statistically significant correlation among aggregate investment, aggregate profits, and aggregate profit rates (see Sherman and Evans 1984, 173; also see the excellent econometric work by Crotty and

TABLE 6.3
Investment and Profit: Timing and Amplitude

| Cycle | Timing | | | | Amplitude | | | |
| | Peak Stage | | Trough Stage | | Expansion | | Contraction | |
| | Invest. | Profit | Invest. | Profit | Invest. | Profit | Invest. | Profit |
|---|---|---|---|---|---|---|---|---|
| 1949–1954 | 5 | 2 | 9 | 7 | 25.5 | 20.2 | −3.5 | −30.0 |
| 1954–1958 | 5 | 3 | 9 | 8 | 17.6 | 25.2 | −13.6 | −33.0 |
| 1958–1961 | 5 | 3 | 9 | 9 | 12.1 | 29.2 | −4.0 | −19.2 |
| 1961–1970 | 5 | 4 | 9 | 9 | 52.4 | 40.4 | −5.5 | −27.1 |
| 1970–1975 | 5 | 5 | 9 | 9 | 22.9 | 37.0 | −13.8 | −26.3 |
| 1975–1980 | 5 | 4 | 9 | 7 | 33.4 | 46.4 | −8.1 | −26.5 |
| 1980–1982 | 5 | 3 | 9 | 9 | 8.6 | 0.9 | −13.3 | −49.8 |
| Average | 5 | 3.5 | 9 | 8.3 | 24.6 | 28.5 | −8.8 | −30.1 |

Sources: Same as Table 6.1.

Note: Definitions: Investment means real, nonresidential fixed investment. Profit means corporate profit before taxes. "Expansion amplitude" is the specific cycle amplitude, that is, from the specific initial trough stage to the specific peak stage of that variable. "Contraction amplitude" is the specific peak stage to the specific final trough of that variable.

Goldstein [1988]). But no simple aggregate function can explain investment very fully and accurately. One reason is that there are vast differences in timing in each industry. All industries do not have rising profits (or profit rates) to the same point, nor do all industries have rising investment in the entire expansion and falling investment in the entire contraction. Most business activity expands and declines with different timing in different industries. In his study of 794 different indicators of economic activity over the business cycle, Mitchell (1951) discovered: "During the four stages of expansion, 74, 77, 78, and 69 percent of all series characteristically rise; during the four stages of contraction, 68, 77, 76, and 63 percent characteristically fall" (p. 76).

The same phenomenon is exhibited by sales, profits, profit rates, and investment according to the diffusion indexes published by the U.S. Department of Commerce in the *Business Conditions Digest*. A diffusion index simply measures the percentage of industries with a rise in some indicator, such as profits. For example, a value of 69 in a diffusion index of profits means that 69 percent of the industries have rising profits. Examination of such diffusion indexes indicates that the percentage of industries with rising sales or rising profits rises in the early and mid-expansion, but then the percentage with rising sales or rising profits declines even while the aggregate sales or profits are still rising (see, for example, Hickman 1959, 535). Thus, the economy does not fall apart all at once with no prior sign (as in the story of the one-horse shay); there are advance signs for those who can read them, though they are not regular enough for simple predictions.

Though the timing is very different, the sequence of events in every expansion is approximately the same in most industries. Total sales rise rapidly in recovery, and then rise more slowly in prosperity, while the diffusion index of sales starts to fall. In late prosperity, both the profit margin on sales and the profit rate on capital begin to decline, which is an early warning signal of recession or depression. Soon thereafter, total profits begin to fall in most industries. Still later, new capital appropriations for expansion by businesses, the first indication of new investment decisions, begin to decline. Finally, at the business cycle peak, total sales and net investment begin an absolute decline. This sequence of events is repeated in the contraction in reverse. (The facts in this paragraph are from Sherman and Stanback [1962]).

Another reason why aggregate investment functions are unsatisfactory is the fact that the time lags are lengthy and they change in different cycles. On the average, total profits lead investment by one to two quarters whereas profit rates lead investment by two to three quarters. But some important differences may be observed between the period of 1949 to 1970 and the period of 1970 to 1982. In the rapid growth of the 1950s and the 1960s, recovery of investment was strong, and contractions were mild. In the 1970s and 1980s, recoveries of investment in early expansion were weaker, and the declines in investment and profits in contractions were much steeper.

Nevertheless, in spite of all of these complications, all the data indicate that profits do influence net investment. This bears out the pioneering work by Michal Kalecki ([1935] 1968), which has been followed by most Post-Keynesians and Marxists in its emphasis on the role of profits and profit rates. Profit, in turn, is shaped by demand factors, such as the change in output demanded, but it is also shaped by cost factors, such as raw material prices and interest rates on credit, which we will discuss later.

INVENTORY INVESTMENT

The discussion has so far been built on the behavior of investment as if all investment were solely in equipment and factory construction. Aggregate nonresidential investment is actually composed of the increase in plant construction, the increase in equipment, and the increase in inventories. Inventories include stocks of raw materials, semifinished goods in process, and finished goods ready for sale.

Changes in inventory investment play a very important role in most business cycles. For example, in the five business cycles from 1919 through 1938, the average change in inventory investment accounted for 23 percent of the average rise in gross national product in expansions and 48 percent of the decline in gross national product in contractions. In the same period, changes in construction and producers' durable equipment together accounted for an average of only 21 percent of the rise and 37 percent of the decline (see the pioneering study by Abromowitz [1950, 5]). In the postwar period, changes in inventories again constituted very large percentages of the cyclical changes in gross national product (see the excellent studies by Stanback [1963] and Blinder and Holtz-Eakin [1986]). In the mild cycles of the 1950s and 1960s, so much of the expansions and contractions was accounted for by the change in inventory investment that the cycle theories of that era tended to focus exclusively on inventories, leaving aside plant and equipment.

If the longer and more severe, or "major," depressions and expansions are examined, it appears that much of the decline or rise is in investment in plant and equipment. When the shorter, less severe, "minor" recessions and expansions are examined, however, most of the decline or rise is in inventory investment. For the five cycles from 1919 through 1938, considering the whole expansion or the whole contraction as one cycle phase, Abromowitz found that in cycle phases lasting eight months to a year, the change in inventory investment was 96 percent of the change in gross national product. In that same period, in cycle phases of 1.5 to 2.5 years, the change in inventory investment was 47 percent of the change in gross national product. Yet in cycle phases lasting 3.75 to 4.17 years, the change in inventory was only 19 percent of the change in gross national product (see Abromowitz 1950, 481–82).

For the period since World War II, the same phenomena are observed. Shorter cycle phases show more importance for inventory investment, whereas changes over longer cycle phases show more importance for changes in plant and equipment investment (see Stanback 1963, 6). It seems that the adjustment of inventories to cyclical changes in production is more rapid than that of plant and equipment, though the latter must make a very large adjustment if the phase lasts long enough.

What is the cyclical behavior of inventories? Most theories predict that during the expansion phase, inventory investment will increase to meet the demand. A glance at Figure 6.10 reveals that inventory investment does tend to be procyclical, rising in the expansion and falling in the contraction. Why does inventory investment rise in the expansion? The main reason is that in the expansion phase, demand is greater than sup-

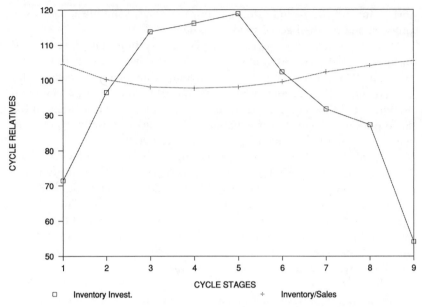

Fig. 6.10. Inventory Investment and Inventory/Sales Ratio: Amplitude by Stage
Averaged across Three Cycles, 1970–1982 (from series 30 and 77, Appendix E)

ply; sales increase faster than inventories. The greater rise in demand is
reflected in the fact that the ratio of inventories to sales declines in the
recovery period. Figure 6.10 shows that the ratio of inventory to sales is
countercyclical, tending to fall in expansions and rise in contractions. The
more rapid rise of demand than of supply uses up inventories, causing
the ratio of inventories on hand to sales to decline. At the same time, the
greater demand also motivates a high level of inventory investment (as
noted above) in order to return to the desired ratio of inventory to sales.

Of course, inventory investment is not determined by a purely mechanical relationship to the change in sales. The real issue is always the
expectation of profits. For one thing, prices are rising in the expansion
phase of the cycle; as a result, holding inventories provides the possibility
of more profit by selling the goods at an enhanced value. Therefore, some
inventories will be acquired on a purely speculative motive. There is also
a time lag between the change in sales and the acquiring of inventories.
Consequently, inventory investment continues approximately up to the
peak of the cycle.

Figure 6.11 shows in more detail that net inventory investment, the
change in business inventories, rises very rapidly in the recovery phase
of expansion. Capitalist entrepreneurs are very optimistic in this period,
so they rapidly increase their inventories of goods on hand—including

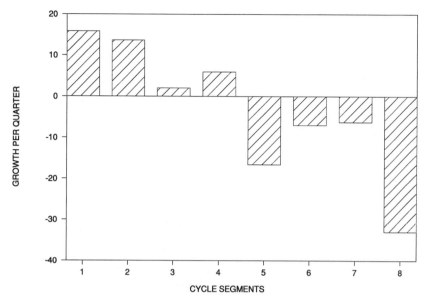

Fig. 6.11. Inventory Investment: Growth by Segment Averaged across Three Cycles, 1970–1982 (from series 30, Appendix H)

raw materials for more production and finished goods for more sales. In the later prosperity phase of expansion, capitalists are more cautious in their purchases of inventories because demand growth is slowing. Therefore, there are sometimes declines as well as increases of inventory investment in the prosperity phase of expansion. In the entire contraction phase, on the other hand, as shown in Figure 6.11, inventory investment declines rapidly because capitalists are very pessimistic about future sales.

These movements of inventory investment are mirrored in the ratio of inventories to sales, recorded in Figure 6.12. In the recovery from recession, during the early part of the expansion, sales are booming, so inventories fall behind. Therefore, the ratio of inventories to sales falls in the early expansion. As the expansion progresses, sales growth slows down, while inventories continue to grow. Consequently, the ratio of inventories to sales rises to its desired level (or slightly beyond the desired level). In the contraction, the ratio of inventories to sales rises fairly rapidly and goes way beyond the desired level. The reason is that even though inventory investment has a very rapid decline, sales fall even faster. Thus, the rising ratio of inventories to sales in the recession is a sure symptom of economic illness.

In the first part of the contraction, the amount of inventory investment

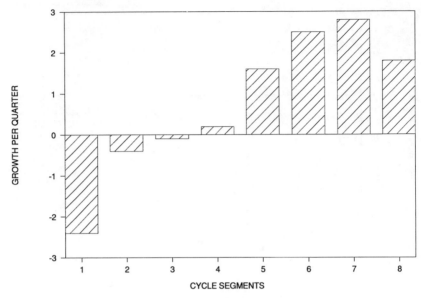

Fig. 6.12. Inventory/Sales Ratio: Growth by Segment Averaged across Three Cycles, 1970–1982 (from series 77, Appendix H)

declines rapidly as a result of falling sales, but inventory investment is still positive. There is no planned inventory investment at this point. There is, however, unplanned inventory investment because goods already produced cannot be sold and pile up. In the period from 1945 to 1961, the quarterly data indicate that inventories continued to rise for one to eight months after each cycle peak (see Stanback 1963, 17). In the last half of the contraction, inventory investment continues to decline and it becomes negative, so there is a big decline in the amount of inventories on hand. Yet, as shown earlier, the amount of sales declines even faster, so the ratio of inventory to sales keeps rising.

It may be noted that, whether or not interest rates affect investment in plant and equipment, they seem to have no effect on inventory investment. A 1981 study says: "We find no strong, systematic influence of real interest rates on inventory investment . . . the conventional literature . . . has consistently failed to uncover an influence of interest rates on inventory investment" (Maccini and Rossana 1981, 21).

There are those who argue that overstocked inventories at the end of expansion are an independent factor causing part of the decline and, in fact, in short, or "minor," cycles, may be the sole factor causing decline (see Metzler 1941, 1947). Since investments both in inventories and in plant and equipment show a significant decline at about the same time, however, we may suspect that many of the same factors cause the decline of both categories of investment. To some extent, inventory investment—like other investment—may be affected by the declining profits and profit rates in the last segment of prosperity.

Less profits mean both less funds with which to purchase inventories and less optimistic expectations for the use of inventories. To some extent also, the decline in the increase of sales will eventually affect inventory investment. There is, however, a very considerable time lag before increased production allows the adjustment of inventories to approach the desired ratio to sales. Furthermore, the beginnings of price decline (or reduction of inflation to a lower level) after the peak will cause a dramatic decline in the speculative motive for holding inventories. Finally, when sales do begin an absolute decline, planned inventory investment is pushed downward till it is quite negative.

Both Marx and Keynes argue that the length of time necessary to reduce inventories to their desired level is an important factor in determining the duration of the depression (see Marx 1909, 576–77; Keynes 1936, 317). Yet this does not mean that inventory investment in the recovery increases for some reason different from that for other investment. It seems better to consider inventory investment as reacting to most of the same factors as do plant and equipment investment, with the actual role of inventories being greater the shorter the cycle, and the role of plant and equipment being greater the longer the cycle. Of course, all contractions—and especially the shorter ones—would be much less severe if there were no contractions in inventory investment.

## DEPRECIATION AND REPLACEMENT

So far it has been assumed that the income allotted to the depreciation allowance is always exactly balanced by the spending on replacement investment. Yet we have advanced no reason, other than initial simplicity of exposition, for accepting this assumption. The importance of this assumption lies in the fact that depreciation is a very large part of gross investment. For example, depreciation was 63 percent of gross expenditures on construction and producers' durables during the period of 1919 to 1928 (see Gordon 1952, 293). In this section, therefore, the differences in the movements of depreciation and replacement investment are considered.

In fact, in any unplanned economy, there must be continuous small random differences between depreciation and replacement. An excess of depreciation allowance over replacement spending means more funds are available for net investment. Of course, this greater amount of funds saved may or may not be invested. If the excess funds are not invested, there will be a decrease in demand. If, on the contrary, replacement spending is greater than depreciation allowances, this will increase total demand.

We must also recognize that in practice it is difficult to distinguish between replacement and net investment. Much investment takes the guise of replacement of old capital by new capital that has been improved by innovations. If investment consists of a new innovation, can it be rightly considered a mere replacement?

In each business cycle expansion, a great deal of replacement is hurried into place long before the old capital has fully depreciated. Thus, in expansion, because of optimistic expectations, replacement investment tends to rise rapidly regardless of physical depreciation. The contrary is true in each recession or depression: There is no desire to maintain a high level of output, so many "necessary" replacements are postponed. Thus, in contractions there is a decline of replacement investment even if depreciation remains constant. Therefore, the very strong cyclical behavior of gross investment is partly due to the cyclical fluctuation of net investment in new plant, equipment, and inventories; but it is also partly due to the cyclical fluctuation of replacement investment. Unfortunately, there are no available aggregate data to separate net investment and replacement except by the false assumption that replacement equals depreciation.

Depreciation, on the other hand, proceeds serenely, changing little in business cycle expansions and contractions (except by changes in the law). In an expansion, this source of saving falls behind replacement investment. In a recession or depression, this source of saving may be far greater than the replacement investment in this period. In fact, since depreciation is related to aggregate capital accumulated in many previous years, it declines only very slightly, except in very long depressions. For example, in the four cycles from 1921 to 1938, depreciation of all business capital fell an average of only 0.5 percent during the contractions, and even that drop was largely due to the weight of the Great Depression (Mitchell 1951, 142).

In the period of 1949 to 1980, depreciation in constant dollars rose at almost the same pace in recessions as in expansions (see Sherman and Evans 1984, 174). There was simply no cyclical pattern to depreciation, but a mostly smooth increase. If replacement investment was rushed in expansions and postponed in contractions, then actual replacement spending was greater than depreciation in expansions and much less than depreciation in contractions.

Most new investment is made during expansions, so the average time of purchase of capital will be somewhere during the expansion phase; the average machine will wear out some fixed time after that date. Suppose that expansion lasts five years and that the contraction lasts another five years. If the average machine is bought in the third year of expansion and lasts ten years, then the spending for its replacement will not take place until the next expansion period. On these assumptions the process of replacement intensifies the business cycle because replacement spending exceeds depreciation saving in each expansion, while depreciation saving exceeds replacement spending in each contraction (see Einarsen 1938).

Both Marx (1907, 211) and Keynes (1936, 317) observed that the duration of the depression may depend to some extent on the lifetime of machinery since when machinery begins to wear out, some of the funds of the corporation may begin to be used for replacement investment. Following this view, R. A. Gordon (1952, 291) finds the length of cycles influenced by the fact that spending on new construction has declined in relation to spending on new producers' durables, from over 300 percent in the nineteenth century to about 80 percent in the 1946–1950 period. Since producers' durables have a shorter lifetime than that of construction, this would lead us to expect shorter and more frequent cycles.

There are, however, many reasons why replacement "needs" may be far from a mechanical function of previous investment. In addition to all the technical factors, there is the fact that firms are as strongly influenced by their expectations when making replacements as when making net investments. Even such apparently technical factors as the life span of the machinery become quite flexible when the very standard of scrapping is influenced by business expectations. Accordingly, after a depression begins, firms hold back on replacement; but when a period of prosperity seems to be already under way, they may spend for replacement much sooner than necessary.

If a business cycle is to result purely from periodic replacement, then the useful economic life of capital goods must be a fixed time and must be "external" to other business conditions. If this is not so, then most replacement investment must be only a secondary factor intensifying cycle movements in either direction. J. S. Bain (1939, 79–88) shows that the economic lifetime of a machine is a function not merely of its physical wear and tear, but also of rates of obsolescence and available replacements, scrap values, operating and maintenance costs, and rates of interest. Moreover, both the present and expected values of each of these factors are important, and each is systematically influenced by the changing business expectations over the cycle. Therefore, replacement is often postponed as not "needed" until recovery, at which time the economic life of the machine is quickly found to be finished.

The conclusion is that the need for physical replacement, called forth at the end of a lengthy depression, probably has an effect on the duration of a contraction, but it is not a simple relationship. Depreciation allowances have grown at a roughly unchanging rate. Replacement investment, on the contrary, appears to move as an effect of the business cycle, speeding up in expansion and slowing or declining in contraction. Therefore, the cyclical fluctuations of replacement investment do intensify cyclical swings. In other words, replacement investment is moved to expand and decline by most of the factors affecting net investment, but probably somewhat more mildly.

## TENTATIVE CONCLUSIONS ON INVESTMENT

In spite of all the complications and qualifications, we may conclude that the profit hypothesis is consistent with the known facts. In other words, investment is associated with profit rate expectations and total profits available for reinvestment. In an econometric test, expected profit rates and available funds may be represented by previous profit rates and previous total profits, with a long time lag. Of course, the available facts are also consistent with the positive influence of demand factors and the negative influence of cost factors (including credit cost and availability), both of which are reflected in profits. Each of the factors affecting profits, and therefore investment, are discussed separately in later chapters.

## APPENDIX 6.1
### INVESTMENT EQUATIONS

The simplest demand-oriented equation for investment says that

$$I_t = v\,(C_{t-1} - C_{t-2}). \tag{6.1}$$

Here $I$ is real investment, $C$ is real consumption, and $v$ is the accelerator coefficient, relating investment to the change in consumer output demanded. A slightly more sophisticated equation substitutes total demand $(Y)$ for consumption:

$$I_t = v\,(Y_{t-1} - Y_{t-2}). \tag{6.2}$$

A still more sophisticated demand-oriented equation will consider investment to be the result of the change in output at several previous periods:

$$I_t = f\,(Y_{t-1}, Y_{t-2}, Y_{t-3} \ldots Y_{t-n}). \tag{6.3}$$

Many such distributed lag functions have been estimated econometrically (see, for example, Jorgenson 1971).

The profit hypothesis may be stated as the relation of investment to profits and profit rates in many previous periods:

$$I_t = f\,(R_{t-1}, R_{t-2} \ldots R_{t-n};\ R/K_{t-1}, R/K_{t-2} \ldots R/K_{t-n}). \tag{6.4}$$

Here $R$ is total profit, $K$ is total capital, and $R/K$ is the rate of profit on capital.

The relationships of investment, profits, and profit rates were tested by the author econometrically, using the official government sources and series as listed and defined in Appendix A for the period from the first quarter of 1949 to the first quarter of 1988.

First, real nonresidential investment ($I$, series #86) was regressed on real total corporate profit before taxes ($R$, series #286) with the result (using the ARMA method) that

$$I_t = 404.6 + .23R_t + .12R_{t-1} + .14R_{t-2} \qquad (6.5)$$
$$(4.96) \quad (5.49) \quad (2.90) \quad\quad (3.41)$$
$$CR^2 = .98 \qquad\qquad DW = 2.00.$$

Here $CR$ is the correlation coefficient and $DW$ is the Durbin-Watson test. There is a high correlation (and no significant autocorrelation) when investment is regressed on profits with a distributed time lag. According to the $t$-scores (in parentheses) there is a strong relationship with no time lag, but some significant relationship with time lags of one and two quarters.

Second, real nonresidential investment ($I$, series #86) was regressed on the ratio of profit before taxes to stockholders' equity capital ($R/K$, series #A). The result (using the ARMA method) was

$$I_t = 708.8 + 1.19R/K_t + 1.01R/K_{t-1} + .67R/K_{t-2} + .67R/K_{t-3}(6.6)$$
$$(5.54) \qquad (5.86) \qquad\quad (5.16) \qquad\quad (3.50) \qquad\quad (3.45)$$
$$CR^2 = .99 \qquad\qquad\qquad DW = 1.98.$$

Investment appears to be correlated with the profit rate (with no significant autocorrelation). There is a significant relationship of investment to the profit rate for several previous periods, with a declining strength as we go back in time (at the .01 confidence level or better, according to the $t$-scores).

Finally, investment can be correlated to both profits and profit rates in a multiple regression, but one should remember that the results are biased by the fact that profits and profit rates are not independent of each other. With that qualification in mind, real nonresidential investment ($I$, series #86) was regressed on real corporate profits before taxes ($R$, series #286) and on the ratio of profits before taxes to stockholders' equity capital ($R/K$, series #A) with the result (using the ARMA method) that

$$I_t = 365.5 + .26R_t + .57R/K_{t-1} + .68R/K_{t-2} \qquad (6.7)$$
$$(6.01) \quad (6.13) \quad (2.91) \qquad\quad (3.60)$$
$$CR^2 = .99 \qquad\qquad DW = 2.00.$$

Investment has a statistically significant correlation (at the .01 confidence level or better) with both total profits and profit rates. The relation of investment with profit rates is strongest with a two-quarter time lag.

# CHAPTER 7

# The Multiplier-Accelerator Model

THE MULTIPLIER and the accelerator relationships each offer brilliant insights into cyclical behavior, while Samuelson's (1939) synthesis of these two relationships into one theory was an outstanding achievement. This chapter examines each of these relations, as well as their implications and limitations, because they constitute the best introduction to formal cycle theory. Their limitations are to some extent the limitations of all cycle models. Their original statement is very simple, clear, and forceful—but leaves out many of the complex aspects of economic reality. Each limitation has been overcome in more complex and realistic models, but the end result is neither clear nor very forceful. Simplicity versus reality is the trade-off in all such models.

## THE ACCELERATOR RELATION

The most popular theory of investment, called the accelerator relation, says that investment demand is derived from the change in output demanded. The accelerator relation has a long history in economics; it has played a major role in cycle theories by Albert Aftalion, Mentor Bickerdike, T. N. Carver, A. C. Pigou, J. M. Clarke, Roy Harrod, Alvin Hansen, Paul Samuelson, and John Hicks. (For the early history of the accelerator, see Haberler [1960, ch. 3].)

The basis for this theory is the truism that, in the long run, if technology remains unchanged, then increased demand can be met only by more capital investment. In fact, if there is an unchanging technology, then the ratio of capital (plant and equipment) required to output produced must be constant. That constant is called the accelerator, so the accelerator coefficient may be defined as the ratio of new investment to the change in output.

What is the systematic reasoning that links investment to a change in output? With a given technology, a factory needs a certain amount of capital equipment to produce a given output. Assume that there is an increase in demand for a factory owner's products, so that the owner wishes to increase the factory's output beyond the present capacity. If the technology stays the same, capital equipment must be increased in proportion to the increase in output demanded. Therefore, the factory owner's demand for new capital (net investment) bears a precise relation to the increase in output.

This reasoning may be extended to the determination of net investment in the whole economy. At a given level of technology, aggregate output can be increased only in proportion to a certain increase in aggregate capital. Therefore, the demand for an increase in capital (net investment) is in some fixed ratio to the decision to increase output. That ratio is by definition the accelerator. Thus, in general, we may say that

$$\text{change in Capital} = \text{Accelerator} \times \text{change in Output.} \qquad (7.1)$$

*Capital* is defined as the value of productive facilities. But the expenditure to increase productive facilities is defined as *net investment*. Thus, we may write:

$$\text{Net investment} = \text{Accelerator} \times \text{change in Output.} \qquad (7.2)$$

Similarly, we could say that the accelerator equals net investment divided by the change in output. It should be remembered that this theory claims that the accelerator ratio is some precise and roughly constant number.

In the United States, yearly output runs at about one-third of the value of all capital. Thus it may be assumed that roughly three units of new capital are required to add one unit to national product. The accelerator coefficient would then be roughly equal to 3.

As an example, the output of shoes may be related to the net investment in new shoe machinery. According to the accelerator theory, more demand for shoes will eventually mean more demand for new shoe machinery. But if demand for shoes remains the same, there should be no further investment in shoe machinery. If demand for shoes actually declines, then the accelerator theory would predict negative net investment. Negative net investment (or disinvestment) occurs when old shoe machinery is allowed to wear out but is not replaced.

One point that is still ambiguous in this exposition is whether "output demanded" means just consumer demand or the demand for all commodities, including producer goods. In his famous article, Samuelson (1939) defined output demanded to mean only output demanded by consumers. In the above example, shoes are a consumer good, but the demand for shoes generates a demand for shoe machinery, which is an investment or producer good.

Consumer demand is a very important part of aggregate demand, but it is not the only demand that generates new investment. Suppose a capitalist produces shoe machines. If the capitalist expects an increase in the demand for shoe machinery, then he or she must increase his/her own investment in machines that make shoe machinery. Therefore, the more

TABLE 7.1
Example of the Accelerator in Shoe Production

| Time Period | Output of Shoes | Shoe Machinery | Interval | Change in Output | Change in Shoe Machinery (Net Investment) |
|---|---|---|---|---|---|
| 1 | $100 | $300 | | | |
| | | | 1 to 2 | $10 | $30 |
| 2 | 110 | 330 | | | |
| | | | 2 to 3 | 20 | 60 |
| 3 | 130 | 390 | | | |
| | | | 3 to 4 | 5 | 15 |
| 4 | 135 | 405 | | | |
| | | | 4 to 5 | 0 | 0 |
| 5 | 135 | 405 | | | |
| | | | 5 to 6 | −5 | −15 |
| 6 | 130 | 390 | | | |
| | | | 6 to 7 | −20 | −60 |
| 7 | 110 | 330 | | | |
| | | | 7 to 8 | −10 | −30 |
| 8 | 100 | 300 | | | |

*Note*: The accelerator is assumed to be 3; that is, $3 of new capital is required to produce $1 of new output per year. Figures for output of shoe machinery are chosen arbitrarily.

general formulation is that the accelerator measures the ratio of new investment to the change in aggregate demand, not just in consumer demand. Of course, since the demand for consumer goods is several times larger than the demand for producer goods, consumer demand will have a greater weight in the relationship.

If the value of the accelerator is known, then we can predict exactly how much new investment will result from any increase in desired output. Table 7.1 assumes some arbitrary changes in the output of shoes to see what will happen to net investment in shoe machinery at some fixed accelerator (it is assumed that the accelerator is fixed at 3).

Although the movements of shoe production are arbitrarily chosen, the rest of the table follows by assumption and definition. Thus, from period 1 to period 2, it is assumed that shoe production rises by $10. But because $3 of capital is required to produce $1 of output, capital must rise by $30, that is, net investment is predicted to be $30. In the next interval, a larger rise of $20 in shoe production causes a level of $60 of net investment. On the other hand, from period 3 to period 4 a smaller rise of $5 in shoe production causes a decline in net investment, to only $15. In the next interval, there is no change in shoe production, so there is no net investment. Finally, in the interval from period 5 to period 6, shoe production declines by $5, so net investment in shoe machinery is a negative $15, or $15 of disinvestment. Throughout, we note that the level of net investment (the change in capital) is related to the *change* in output.

This fact, that the accelerator theory predicts net investment to be a function of the change in output demanded, has attracted the attention of many cycle theorists. Suppose that demand grows rapidly, which causes a certain high level of investment. If the rate of growth of demand slows, then the level of investment must decline. But an actual decline in investment will cause a recession or depression (because less investment means less employment, which means less demand, and so forth). Thus, a theory may explain business cycle downturns, assuming the accelerator principle is correct, merely by showing why aggregate demand will slow its growth, and it is not necessary to prove that aggregate demand will decline before investment declines.

### LIMITATIONS AND QUALIFICATIONS OF THE ACCELERATOR

The investment process is very complex, so the accelerator has many qualifications and limitations. First the accelerator does not operate instantaneously, but with a time lag. Suppose demand increases from one period to the next. There will be a time lag before new investment ensues for several reasons. It takes time for the information to be known and recorded. It takes time for concrete plans to be made for new investment. It takes time to borrow new financial capital. It takes time to actually spend money to build a new factory. For all of these reasons, most careful theories assume a time lag.

In formal terms, suppose that $v$ is called the accelerator coefficient, that $I$ is investment, and that $Y$ is the amount of aggregate output demanded. In order to show the time lag, let $t$ be the present time period, let $t - 1$ be the previous time period, and so forth. The change in output demanded affecting this period's investment occurred from $t - 1$ to $t - 2$. Then,

Investment = Accelerator (change in Output, lagged),

expressed as

$$I_t = v\,(Y_{t-1} - Y_{t-2}). \tag{7.3}$$

This equation shows a time lag of one period from the change in output demanded to the change in investment. In reality, however, the investment response to changes in output demanded exhibits a changing time lag over the cycle, so no fixed time lag is really appropriate.

Second, the accelerator coefficient itself changes over the cycle because of changes in business expectations as to profits. There is no simple technical relationship between demand and investment in the short-run time horizon of the business cycle, but a changing relationship based on changing expectations.

Third, the unused capacity at the beginning of expansion would first have to be put into use before a capitalist would add to it—for example, if half a factory is idle, no capitalist will rush out to build a new factory just because demand rises a little. So the accelerator will be lower in the recovery phase of the cycle than at the cycle peak.

Fourth, at the peak of profitability capitalists may desire rapid expansion (based not just on current demand, but on speculative expectations), but expansion of investment has the physical limit of the total capacity of the economy to produce more plant and equipment. Thus, there is a ceiling to the investment predicted by the accelerator (see the detailed discussion in Hicks [1950]).

Fifth, in a severe depression all capitalists may wish to sell their excess capital. One capitalist can sell excess capital to another. In the aggregate, however, the only way to reduce capital is to let it depreciate and not be replaced. So the limit of reduction of capital is the amount of wear and tear or depreciation suffered in that time period. In other words, the level of depreciation in a given year sets a maximum limit to the amount of disinvestment in that year. Thus there is a floor to the disinvestment predicted by the accelerator (see the detailed discussion in Hicks [1950]).

Sixth, the accelerator investment function deals only with demand and omits the cost variables. In particular, it omits inflation in labor costs, raw material costs, and the cost of borrowing. If all of these variables are considered seriously, then we must go back to a function based on total profits and the rate of profits. Other variables determining net investment, but omitted to this point are the degree of monopoly, the amount of government activity, and the amount of net exports; these are explored in later chapters.

Neoclassical economists have used more and more sophisticated and complex accelerator functions to meet some of these criticisms (see, for example, Jorgenson, 1971). But other neoclassical studies have questioned the accelerator theory's validity and emphasized the need to consider other variables, such as monetary variables (see, for example, Gordon and Veitch 1986) or profits (see Eisner 1978). One may conclude that the accelerator is a powerful tool, but requires many qualifications, as well as the consideration of other variables, if a complete investment function is desired.

## THE INVESTMENT MULTIPLIER

Some economists believe that Keynes's most important conceptual contribution to macroeconomics is the consumption function and that the most important analytic tool to come out of the Keynesian analysis of consumption is the multiplier. The multiplier expresses the relation between the initial increase (or decrease) in one of the components of aggregate demand and the total increase (or decrease) in national income caused by it. The initial spending change may come from any one of the components of aggregate demand. For example, the *investment multiplier* is the ratio of additional income to new investment, while the *government multiplier* is the ratio of additional income to new government spending.

Obviously, it is vital that government policymakers know how any change in spending, whether in direct government spending or in private investment encouraged by government spending, will affect national income. The question as to how government spending will affect national income first received considerable attention during the 1930s, when New Deal politicians in the United States debated ways of combating the depression. In England in that period, these questions were debated by a group at Cambridge, including Keynes. The multiplier concept was first rigorously worked out by R. F. Kahn, then a student of Keynes.

In precise terms, the investment multiplier may be defined as the ratio of change in national income to change in investment. This is more than a definition; there is alleged to be a causal relationship running from change in investment spending to change in income. Change in investment usually causes a larger change in aggregate income because the money spent on investment is only the direct effect. Often more important is the indirect effect that the new income will be respent by its recipients for additional consumption—this is the main point of the multiplier.

Assume that during a period with some unemployment a firm decides to construct a large new factory. This sudden increase in investment spending will increase the incomes of the contractors who supply the necessary machinery and materials and will provide jobs and wages for previously unemployed workers. Now assume that the initial increase in investment spending and income is $1,000. The recipients of this income will immediately respend most of it for consumer goods, which will result in new income for businesspeople and workers in the consumer goods industries. These income recipients will, in turn, spend much of their new income on more consumer goods. Exactly how much additional spending occurs in each round will depend on the marginal propensity to consume of the income recipients. But, according to this theory, it is already clear that any additional consumer spending must mean that the total income generated will be something more than the original $1,000 of investment spending.

The easiest way to see how the multiplier is supposed to work is to study a numerical example. In the example in Table 7.2, only some initial

TABLE 7.2
How the Multiplier Works

| Number of Rounds of Spending | Increase in Investment | Increase in Consumption | Increase in National Income | Increase in Saving |
|---|---|---|---|---|
| 0 | $1,000 | — | $1,000 | — |
| 1 | 0 | $800 | 800 | $200 |
| 2 | 0 | 640 | 640 | 160 |
| 3 | 0 | 512 | 512 | 128 |
| 4 | 0 | 410 | 410 | 102 |
| 5 | 0 | 328 | 328 | 82 |
| 6 | 0 | 262 | — | 66 |
| — | 0 | — | — | — |
| — | — | — | — | — |
| — | — | — | — | — |
| — | — | — | — | — |
| — | — | — | — | — |
| — | — | — | — | — |
| Infinite number of rounds of spending | $1,000 total increase in investment | $4,000 total increase in consumption | $5,000 total increase in national income | $1,000 total increase in saving |

Note: Assumptions: 1. Suppose an increase in investment of $1,000. 2. Also suppose a marginal propensity to consume of 4/5, or 80 percent.

change in investment and a certain marginal propensity to consume need be assumed; $1,000 dollars of investment becomes $1,000 of income when it is spent. It is assumed that 80 percent, or $800, of that income is respent on consumption, or the marginal propensity to consume is 0.80. As a result, another $800 of national income goes to other individuals. They will then spend 80 percent, or $640 of that income, and so it goes. In the first round, 20 percent, or $200, leaks out into saving, and in the second round, 20 percent of the remaining income, or $160, leaks out into saving. The process ends only when the last $1 of the increased income is saved. At that point, the whole $1,000 of investment has been saved, but there already have been many rounds of consumption spending in between. In this example the total of all the rounds of consumption spending (or respending) will eventually approach $4,000, and national income will approach a level that is $5,000 higher than before.

The new investment may be pictured as a one-time expenditure or it may be conceptualized as a permanent increase in the level of investment. If the $1,000 increase in investment is considered as a one-time injection of new spending, then the totals at the bottom of Table 7.2 represent only temporary additions to consumption, saving, and national income. After these one-time increases are realized, however, total spending will eventually return to its original level. But if the $1,000 increase is a new, stepped-up rate of investment spending that continues through several subsequent periods, the totals represent the rise from the old, lower levels to the new, higher levels of spending flows, which will persist in each future period.

From this description of how the multiplier works, it should be clear that if less is saved out of each increment to income, then each increment to consumption spending will be larger. In other words, if the marginal propensity to consume rises, the subsequent increases in consumption and income will be larger.

The multiplier formula is just a shortcut for finding where the process of Table 7.2 ends without repeating the calculation a great many times. The formula can be derived with only one crucial assumption. By definition, the investment multiplier is

$$\text{Multiplier} = \text{change in Income/change in Investment.} \qquad (7.4)$$

The crucial assumption in the multiplier theory is that there is movement from one equilibrium to another equilibrium position. Therefore, at the end of the process, the theory assumes that the change in saving must equal the change in investment. Substituting saving for investment, the result is

$$\text{Multiplier} = \text{change in Income/change in Saving.} \qquad (7.5)$$

By simple mathematical manipulation,

$$\text{Multiplier} = 1/(\text{change in Saving/change in Income}). \qquad (7.6)$$

But the ratio, the change in saving to the change in income, is simply the marginal propensity to save (MPS). Therefore, the formula to remember is just

$$\text{Multiplier} = 1/\text{MPS.} \qquad (7.7)$$

Notice that the marginal propensities to save (MPS) and consume (MPC) always add up to exactly 1.0, so we could also write

$$\text{Multiplier} = 1/(1 - \text{MPC}). \qquad (7.8)$$

The theory says that total increase in income equals increase in investment times the multiplier. In the example in Table 7.2, the increase in
investment is $1,000. The marginal propensity to consume is 4/5, so the
MPS is 1/5. The multiplier must equal 1 divided by 1/5, which is 5. So it
may be calculated that

$$\text{total increase in Income} = \$1,000 \times 5 = \$5,000. \qquad (7.9)$$

This demonstrates how the multiplier is used to find the end result of
investment spending.

Of course, if the multiplier is reduced, then the investment spending
has less effect. At one extreme, if the multiplier is just 1, the change in
income is just equal to the change in investment. At the other extreme,
if the multiplier approaches infinity, any small change in investment will
cause an infinite change in income.

The value of the multiplier is controlled by the marginal propensity to
consume (MPC). If MPC falls, so does the multiplier (because less is respent out of each increase in income). If the MPC is only 1/2, then the
multiplier is only 2. If the MPC is zero, so that everything is saved and
there is no respending of the initial income, then the multiplier is 1, that
is, the final result just equals the initial income. But if all income is immediately respent for consumption, so that the MPC is 1, then the multiplier will be infinity if the process is instantaneous.

### Qualifications and Limitations of the Multiplier

There are some obvious qualifications that must be kept in mind when
the multiplier theory is used. First, it assumes that the economy is in
equilibrium, and that saving always equals investment. This is certainly
not true in the business cycle, since planned investment is usually
greater than planned saving in expansions, while planned investment is
usually less than planned saving in contractions.

Second, a time lag must be included because it takes a certain amount
of time before income received is respent for consumption and still more
time before the second and third and later rounds of respending may
occur. If the time lag happens to be more than one period, then a more
complicated multiplier will be needed to get a realistic value for the
change in income for one year. If the time lag is variable, there is no easy
answer.

Third, it has been assumed that MPC remains constant until the process is completed. In reality, MPC does change and is affected by many
psychological and institutional factors. For example, the accumulated
savings of World War II greatly increased the propensity to consume in
the immediate postwar years.

Moreover, saving is not the only leakage from the income stream. Higher or lower taxes will also change MPC out of national income. Furthermore, if purchases of imports (such as Volkswagens) increase, there will be a leakage from domestic consumer spending. Thus, the domestic MPC may change too often to permit accurate prediction of the multiplier for more than a few months in the future. This international leakage has become very important in the present period, and it will be discussed in detail in Chapter 16.

Fourth, the multiplier formula assumes that investment will remain the same while consumption and national income are expanding rapidly. Obviously, the simple multiplier theory cannot be used if further changes in investment are to be considered. Yet the accelerator assures us that when aggregate income increases, there will be further increases in investment.

For all of these reasons, the conclusion is that whereas the multiplier is a helpful explanatory device, the simplest multiplier formula cannot be relied on for an exact estimate. Various more realistic multiplier models can obtain better predictions, but they are also more complex and difficult to understand.

## THE MULTIPLIER-ACCELERATOR MODEL

The simplest Keynesian model, by Samuelson (1939), is called the multiplier-accelerator model, because it combines these two principles. There are just three relationships in this simple demand model.

First, *if there is equilibrium*, then total income or output ($Y$) will just equal aggregate demand. Leaving aside government demand and net export demand for the moment, the aggregate demand may be defined to be consumption demand ($C$) plus investment demand ($I$). Therefore, at each equilibrium point,

Output supplied = Consumption + Investment,

expressed as

$$Y_t = C_t + I_t. \tag{7.10}$$

Here $t$ is a time period, such as one quarter. This equation shows what happens at each point where there is equilibrium—but there is disequilibrium between these points as supply adjusts to demand. Remember that Keynes rejected Say's law, which says that demand always adjusts to supply. Thus, this equation means the contrary assertion: that supply will adjust to demand—so if demand is below full employment, the output will also be below the full employment level. The equation shows the path taken by demand at each point where supply has adjusted to it—but that equilibrium may be below full employment, and frequently is in Samuelson's model. In reality in the business cycle, during expansions demand tends to be above supply, while in contractions demand tends to be below supply.

Second, Samuelson adopts his consumption function from Keynes, who describes consumer behavior on the basis of the alleged psychological propensities of consumers. His assumption is that consumption does rise and fall with income but psychologically determined behavior usually causes consumption to rise and fall more slowly than does income. The simplest way to portray this Keynesian hypothesis is to assume that aggregate consumption is equal to some minimum level of consumption plus a constant proportion of the aggregate income. Since there is a time lag, it is assumed that consumption is a function of the aggregate income of the previous time period:

Consumption = constant + percentage of Income, lagged,

expressed as

$$C_t = a + bY_{t-1}, \tag{7.11}$$

where $a$ and $b$ are constants (as are all small letters used in equations in this chapter), and where $t - 1$ is the previous time period.

In this equation, the marginal propensity to consume is shown by the constant $b$. Although the MPC is assumed to be constant (which is an oversimplification), note that there is also assumed to be a minimum level of consumption, $a$, regardless of income. Therefore, as income rises in an expansion, consumption adds a constant percentage of income, but it is always added to the same constant minimum—so the average propensity to consume (the ratio of all consumption to all income) must fall. Similarly, if income falls in a cyclical downturn, the minimum level becomes a larger part of consumption, so the average propensity to consume rises. Clearly this picture faithfully follows the psychological laws assumed by Keynes.

Because this consumption function is based on a constant MPC, it is easy to calculate the multiplier in this model—it equals $1/(1 - \text{MPC})$. Thus Samuelson's second equation builds the investment multiplier into the system. The multiplier works through this consumption function by controlling the rate of respending of income.

Third, Samuelson puts the accelerator principle into his model. He assumes that new investment is a function of the change in consumer demand, with a time lag. This relationship is explored later, but here we may make use of the more usual statement that new investment is a function of the change in aggregate output demanded ($Y$), not just consumer demand. Remembering that there is a time lag before the increase in output demanded affects new investment, the relationship is

Investment = accelerator × (change in Output, lagged),

expressed as

$$I_t = v\,(Y_{t-1} - Y_{t-2}), \tag{7.12}$$

where $v$ is a constant coefficient called the accelerator. As stated earlier, this relationship means that if the growth of output slows down, then investment will actually decline. In this model, the growth of output demanded does slow down because of the consumption function, as we shall see below.

Perhaps the easiest way to see how this model works is to examine a numerical example. Table 7.3 pictures the multiplier-accelerator model over time, showing how we can start from a few simple assumptions and then follow the path of the economy as it moves. The table assumes arbitrarily that national income is expanding from \$996 billion in the first period to \$1,000 billion in the second period. Starting with such an expansion, what happens next? The table assumes a consumption function (like equation 7.11) in which consumption is always equal to \$96 billion plus 90 percent of the previous period's income. The \$96 billion is the constant minimum level of consumption, arbitrarily chosen in this case. Finally, it is assumed that net investment is always just equal to the previous change in output demanded; thus, the form is that of equation 7.12, but we are assuming that the accelerator just happens to equal 1.

On these very simple assumptions, when income is at \$1,000 billion, consumption in the next period will be \$96 billion plus 90 percent of \$1,000 billion, which equals \$996 billion. On the investment side, when output rises from \$996 to \$1,000 billion, an accelerator equal to 1 predicts that the change (+ \$4 billion) will be equaled by new investment (+ \$4 billion). Since consumption is \$996 billion and investment is \$4 billion, the output supplied in equilibrium must be \$1,000 billion in period 3. These calculations can be repeated for each period to obtain all the values in the table. Notice that national income is constant from period 2 to period 3, so net investment is zero in period 4. This causes a decline in national income and begins a recession phase. The recession phase continues for ten periods, and then a new expansion begins as net investment again becomes positive.

## How the Multiplier-Accelerator Model Works

The model has been shown in equations and in a numerical example; now it must be explained verbally in order to answer the four questions always

TABLE 7.3
Example of Multiplier-Accelerator Model

| Time Period | Consumption | National Income | Net Investment |
|---|---|---|---|
| 1 | | $ 996 ⎤ | |
| 2 | | 1,000 ⎦ | |
| 3 | $996 ← | 1,000 | → $4 |
| 4 | 996 | 996 | 0 |
| 5 | 992 | 988 | −4 |
| 6 | 985 | 977 | −8 |
| 7 | 975 | 965 | −11 |
| 8 | 964 | 952 | −12 |
| 9 | 953 | 940 | −13 |
| 10 | 942 | 930 | −12 |
| 11 | 933 | 923 | −10 |
| 12 | 927 | 920 | −7 |
| 13 | 928 | 925 | −3 |
| 14 | 928 | 933 | 5 |
| 15 | 936 | 944 | 8 |
| 16 | 945 | 956 | 11 |
| 17 | 957 | 969 | 12 |
| 18 | 969 | 982 | 13 |
| 19 | 978 | 991 | 13 |
| 20 | 987 | 996 | 9 |
| 21 | 992 | 1,000 | 8 |

Note: Assumptions: Income is assumed to be $996 in period 1 and $1,000 in period 2. It is also assumed that the constant, $a$, or minimum level of consumption is $96. The marginal propensity to consume, $b$, is .90. The accelerator, $v$, is 1. All figures are in billions. Figures are not exact due to rounding. The arrows indicate the direction of influence by one variable upon another.

asked of business cycle models: (1) What causes the cumulative process of expansion? (2) What causes the expansion to end and a downturn to begin? (3) What causes the cumulative process of contraction? (4) What causes the downturn to end and recovery to begin? (This discussion assumes parameters such that the cycles are roughly regular, but in Appendix 7.1, we will consider cases in which cycles get more and more explosive or else die away to nothing.)

### The Cumulative Process of Expansion

When expansion begins (as in period 14 of Table 7.3), what causes it to continue? The answer, of course, is the multiplier and the accelerator acting together. A small increase in investment leads, through the multiplier effect of increased consumer spending, to a larger increase in national income. The increase in national income leads, through the accelerator, to a certain amount of new net investment. The new investment leads to more consumer spending, which leads to more national income, which leads to more investment, and so forth. This model does an excellent job of depicting that cumulative process of expansion.

### The Causes of the Downturn

Why does a cumulative expansion ever lead to a downturn? As expansion goes on, the consumption function dictates that the increases of consumption become less and less. Since consumption is by far the largest element of national income or output, this means a declining growth of output. The result—via the accelerator—is that sooner or later net investment must decline. This decline of net investment sets off a recession. (This process is illustrated numerically in Table 7.3.)

### The Cumulative Process of Decline

Why does the decline in net investment cause a downturn to continue for some time? The decline in net investment leads, via the multiplier process of reduced consumer spending, to less national income. The lower national income leads, via the accelerator, to less net investment. The lower investment causes less income, which leads to less consumption, which leads to declining output, which leads to less investment, and so forth.

### The Causes of Recovery

Once there is a cumulative process of downturn, how does the economy ever recover? Consumers reduce their consumption by less than their income is reduced. As consumer demand falls more and more slowly, so does national output, until the accelerator eventually causes net investment to stop falling and have a slight rise. The very slight rise in net investment means more employment and income and, through the multiplier process of consumer spending, a greater rise in national income. Thus the recovery begins. (Again, the process is illustrated numerically in Table 7.3.)

### CONCLUSION

The multiplier is an useful tool of analysis, provided we remember its limitations and qualifications, some of which may be removed in more complex models. Similarly, the accelerator is a powerful tool of understanding, so long as its limitations and qualifications are kept in mind. When the multiplier and accelerator are combined, as Samuelson did in 1939, the result is a simple model of the business cycle that offers some very important insights. Even with all the qualifications in more realistic models, these insights remain valid. The model is especially helpful in understanding the cumulative processes of the economy once an expansion or contraction begins. It is somewhat less persuasive in the story that it tells about the causes of the cyclical turns because it is so abstract. Nevertheless, Samuelson's pioneering effort remains an outstanding contribution to economic knowledge.

Of course, later theories have criticized the weaknesses of the multiplier-accelerator mechanism and have substituted more sophisticated functions to cure each of these weaknesses. Nevertheless, most of the later models have built on and benefited from the knowledge of the multiplier-accelerator model. These models will be examined in the rest of Part Two.

## Appendix 7.1
### Formalizing the Multiplier-Accelerator Model

This appendix presents a formal, or mathematical, model of the multiplier-accelerator model. To understand why that may be useful, but also what its limitations are, it is necessary to consider the uses and abuses of mathematics in economics.

### The Uses and Abuses of Mathematics

Mathematics is only a tool, but it can be a powerful one (two excellent discussions of the uses and abuses of mathematics in economics are by Mirowski [1986] and by Ruccio [1988]). Before the use of mathematical models of the business cycle became widespread, some theorists wrote underdetermined theories, that is, they used more variables than they gave explanatory relations, so some key variables were left unexplained. On the other hand, some nonmathematical theories gave two or three explanations for the same variable's behavior, so they were overdetermined and in that sense internally inconsistent. One virtue of a mathematical model is that the reader can tell at a glance whether the number of variables equals the number of behavioral equations. Thus a mathematical model should normally be consistent and logical, though not necessarily true.

Another virtue of simple mathematical models is that they may offer a clear illustration or reflection of a theory. If one understands the language of mathematics, a model may clarify and illuminate complex relationships.

In spite of the fact that mathematics can be a useful tool, many economists have been worried that it is often misused. Alfred Marshall and J. M. Keynes were both expert mathematicians, but neither used much math in their theories and both had a healthy skepticism about its use in economics (see Turner 1989). Institutionalists, such as Robert Heilbroner and John K. Galbraith, have expressed dismay over the abuse of mathematics in economics (see, for example, Heilbroner 1989, and Galbraith 1989). Wassily Leontief (1985), who won a Nobel prize for his work in mathematical economics, wrote: "Uncritical enthusiasm for mathematical formulation tends often to conceal the ephemeral substantive content of the argument behind the formidable front of algebraic signs" (p. 272).

What exactly are the alleged abuses of mathematics in economics? First, symbols are sometimes written without careful explanation of the concepts and arguments involved. Second, in order to make the model manageable in mathematics, oversimplified and extremely unrealistic assumptions are often used. Third, in order to find problems that can be easily quantified, there is a tendency to choose trivial problems, not relevant to the difficult and complex issues facing the world today. Fourth, mathematics must assume given relationships between variables in order to calculate the value of parameters; yet, in reality, not only do the values change, but even the relationships change over time—nothing is frozen in economics, and every relation is specific to a particular historical period. Finally, because of these problems, our most complex and elegant mathematical models are often irrelevant to real world economic problems.

### Equations of the Multiplier-Accelerator Model

With these limitations in mind, let us explore the three equations of the multiplier-accelerator model, defining output, consumption, and investment. Output supplied is expressed as consumption plus investment, or

$$Y_t = C_t + I_t. \tag{7.13}$$

Consumption is expressed as a constant plus the percentage of national income, lagged, or

$$C_t = a + bY_{t-1}. \tag{7.14}$$

Investment is expressed as the accelerator times the change in output, lagged, or

$$I_t = v\,(Y_{t-1} - Y_{t-2}). \tag{7.15}$$

If we substitute 7.14 and 7.15 into 7.13, and collect the terms, the result is

$$Y_t = a + (b + v)Y_{t-1} - vY_{t-2}. \tag{7.16}$$

Equation 7.16 is called a reduced-form equation because it is all in terms of the single variable $Y$. This equation is a second-order difference equation because it has two time lags or differences. Solving a difference equation means being able to state the time path of the variable (national income) in terms of its initial values, called initial conditions. If there are two time lags, as in a second-order equation, then two initial values of national income must be given, from which we can derive the rest of its time path. For this reason, the numerical example in Table 7.3 assumed that two initial values of national income were known.

Begin the solution by ignoring the constant ($a$) in order to obtain the simplest case of a homogeneous equation. To get a standardized form, let $A = b + v$ and let $B = v$. Then,

$$Y_t - AY_{t-1} + BY_{t-2} = 0. \tag{7.17}$$

Next, consider a constant, $Q$, such that

$$Q^2 - QA + B = 0. \tag{7.18}$$

This is a simple quadratic equation. From high school algebra, remember that the quadratic formula says:

$$Q = A \pm \sqrt{(A^2 - 4B)/2.} \tag{7.19}$$

When the quantity under the square root sign ($A^2 - 4B$) is negative, the solution will fluctuate in a cycle (it is a trigonometric function, which oscillates as the angle goes around the circle). In other words, according to the mathematical solution to this equation, there will be cyclical fluctuations in the time path of national income if the parameters are in a certain range, namely, if $A^2$ is less than $4B$. If, however, $A^2$ is greater than $4B$, there will be no fluctuations, but will be constant growth (it is also mathematically possible to have constant decline).

In the range in which there are fluctuations, if $B = 1$, then the fluctuations are of constant magnitude, producing a regular cycle. If $B$ is less than 1, then the cycle is damped, that is, the amplitudes become smaller and smaller till the cycle converges toward some constant value. If $B$ is greater than 1, then the cycle is explosive, that is, the fluctuations become larger and larger. In this particular simple model, the accelerator equals $B$, so the fluctuations will be regular, damped, or explosive depending on the value of the accelerator. For that reason, in the numerical example in Table 7.3, it was assumed that $v = 1$ in order to obtain regular fluctuations.

Note that only the values of the parameters $A$ and $B$ affect the cyclical fluctuations. If the constant, $a$, is included in the equation, then it only affects the level around which fluctuations will occur.

## Damped and Explosive Cycles

As noted in the previous section, the coefficient $B$ (which is equal to the accelerator, $v$, in this model) must equal exactly 1 if cycles are to be constant in amplitude. If $B$ is less than 1, then cycle amplitudes get greater and greater until the economy explodes. Since the business cycle has not disappeared and the economy has not exploded, it appears that the cycle and the economy exist only because—by some cosmic miracle—this coefficient happens to equal exactly 1. Something must be wrong with the assumptions or with the reasoning.

There are several possible solutions. One suggestion is that there is a damped solution to the business cycle equation, but there are exogenous shocks that keep it going. There is a considerable literature on whether the shocks could be purely random, their nature, and so forth. But this view approaches the erroneous neoclassical view that the cycle is due to purely random accidents.

Another solution assumes that the endogenous system is explosive, but that there are so-called floors and ceilings holding it within bounds at every turning point (see Hicks 1950). Hicks cites empirical studies showing that if we use the most commonly estimated values, the multiplier-accelerator model produces explosive cycles. The ceiling is usually described as the limit of physical production at the full-capacity level, which could increase only very slowly over a long time. The floor is usually described as the fact that capital can be disinvested only up to the amount of depreciation. In other words, the largest decline that can occur in aggregate capital in one year is the amount of wear and tear of capital.

One problem with this floor-and-ceiling solution is that the capitalist economy at the peak of the cycle seldom reaches full capacity. Another problem is that disinvestment has seldom, if ever, reached the limit of depreciation. In other words, the economy hardly ever comes near the possible floors and ceilings in the actual, historical business cycle.

Another possibility is that the functions mentioned here have longer time lags than supposed, that is, that they are influenced by a number of past periods. The result would be a difference equation with many time lags, that is, a higher-order equation. Such an equation allows for a more complex solution, with cycles and growth in a wide range of parameters.

Finally, it has been assumed that all the relations are linear, but that is not true. There are nonlinear relations, for example, involving $Y^2$ and

$Y^3$. Nonlinear equations can also generate cycles and growth over a wide range of parameters.

In summary, the mathematical form of the simplest multiplier-accelerator model is based on unrealistic assumptions. Yet a much more complex mathematical form would greatly reduce its usefulness as a tool of understanding. In later chapters, we shall explore some models that have somewhat more realistic assumptions, but still keep this simple mathematical form—but the reader should remain skeptical of this simple form.

# CHAPTER 8

# Income Distribution:
# The Utilization-Unemployment Hypothesis

THE DISTRIBUTION of income is of extreme importance to many business cycle theories. "Income distribution" here does not mean the range of individual incomes, but the functional distribution between economic classes. The main distinction used here is between labor income, which goes to wage and salary workers, versus property income, which goes to capitalists, financiers, and landlords.

In theories stressing lack of effective demand—such as the underconsumption theory—a key claim is that income distribution shifts from workers' wages to capitalist profit in every business cycle expansion. On the contrary, in theories emphasizing costs of the supply of labor—such as the reserve army theory—a key claim is that income distribution shifts from capitalist profits to working-class wages in every business cycle expansion. To help evaluate and resolve these conflicting views, the main point of this chapter is to describe and explain the behavior of functional income distribution over the business cycle. The chapter begins by exploring the major theories, and then turns to the empirical facts to see how well the theories conform to the facts.

## FRAMEWORK AND DEFINITIONS

This chapter makes use of the official U.S. national income categories, keeping in mind their weaknesses (see Chapter 3). All variables are in real terms, that is, constant dollars. Let labor income ($W$) be defined to include all employee compensation, namely, wage income, salary income, fringe benefits, bonuses, and commissions. Let property income ($R$) be defined to be all the rest of national income, namely, corporate profits, noncorporate profits, rent, and interest. Then, of course, the national income ($Y$) equals labor income plus property income:

$$Y = W + R. \qquad (8.1)$$

The labor share—which is also sometimes called the wage share because its most important component is wages—is defined as the ratio of labor income to all national income ($W/Y$). The property share—which is also sometimes called the profit share because its most important component is profit—is defined as the ratio of property income to all national income $(R/Y)$. It also follows that the labor share $(W/Y)$ plus the property share $(R/Y)$ equal 1:

$$W/Y + R/Y = 1. \tag{8.2}$$

Thus, if either the wage share or the profit share is known, so is the other one. Note that national income is used throughout this chapter rather than other measures of output or income because national income includes corporate profit, which is definitely part of the property share.

A third way of measuring income distribution between classes is what Marx called the rate of exploitation, which—in its closest equivalent in national income terms—is property income divided by labor income, or the ratio of $R$ to $W$. The rate of exploitation, by this definition, also equals the property share divided by the labor share:

$$R/W = (R/Y)/(W/Y). \tag{8.3}$$

From equations 8.2 and 8.3, if the labor share or the property share is known, then the rate of exploitation is known. Therefore, income distribution by class may be described here by any of these three ratios. The labor share is used most of the time because that is the most convenient context for discussing hourly wages and productivity, but the movements of the rate of exploitation and the property share are clearly implied. Any statement about the labor share $(W/Y)$ can be restated in terms of the property share $(R/Y)$ or the rate of exploitation $(R/W)$.

If real wages $(W)$, which are the numerator of the labor share, are divided by the number of hours of labor expended in the entire economy $(N)$, the result is $W/N$, which equals the real hourly wage. If real national income or output $(Y)$, which is the denominator of the labor share, is divided by the number of hours of labor expended in the entire economy, the result is $Y/N$, which equals productivity, or product per labor hour. Then, if we divide both the numerator and denominator of the labor share by the hours of labor, the result is $(W/N)/(Y/N)$, which equals the labor share. In other words, the labor share equals the average real hourly wage divided by average productivity per labor hour. In symbols,

$$W/Y = (W/N)/(Y/N). \tag{8.4}$$

Let us consider the fact that the income share of workers is equal to the average real hourly wage divided by the average productivity of labor. Obviously, the labor share rises if the hourly wage rises, while it falls if the hourly wage falls, all other things being constant. The labor share falls if productivity rises, but it rises if productivity falls, all other things being constant. Throughout the discussion of the labor share, an attempt will be made to explain not only its movements, but also the movements of its two components: (1) real hourly wages, and (2) the product per labor hour.

The term "productivity," or "labor productivity," used in this chapter just means the total product (real national income) divided by the number of hours of labor; it is an average product/labor ratio. Its changes may reflect not only changes in the amount of labor, but also changes in the quality of labor, changes in capital, changes in technology, or changes in the availability of natural resources—in short, anything that affects output or employment. To avoid confusion, remember that this is very different from the often-used term "marginal productivity of labor," which measures the additional output of additional labor, but with all other factors held constant. The simpler average product/labor ratio, with other factors changing, is more useful for the present analysis.

## Determinants of the Labor Share

The labor share is directly dependent on the real hourly wage and on productivity. What determines these components of the labor share? The real hourly wage $(W/N)$ is determined by industrial conflict between capitalists and workers, within the framework of capitalist relations of production, under certain economic conditions. It is easy to give a reasonable list of the demand and supply conditions—but which to emphasize is extremely controversial. The conditions under which the wage bargain is struck include: (1) the demand for labor, which is a function of the demand for products, given a certain level of technology; (2) the supply of labor, which is a function of population and the labor participation rate; (3) the excess supply of labor, reflected in the unemployment rate; (4) the worker's fallback position if fired, depending on such things as the level of unemployment compensation and welfare provisions; (5) the power of labor unions, reflected in percentages of unionization especially in key firms and industries; (6) the degree of business monopoly power over prices and wages; (7) the power and tactics of the capitalist government, including recognition of unions and enforcement of fixed labor contracts for a given period of time; and (8) international events, such as wars or international shifts of economic power.

The productivity of labor is affected by industrial conflict in a fight over speedup by the capitalists versus slowdown by the workers. The conditions influencing the outcome of this struggle include the same eight conditions that influence the real hourly wage. In addition, however, labor productivity is also affected by at least three other factors. In the long run, (9) productivity is very much influenced by technological change. In the short run, (10) the productivity of both machinery and labor will differ at different levels of capacity utilization. Finally, (11) productivity is in part constituted by the amount of effort per hour (the intensity of labor), which is a result of class conflict between capitalists and workers (see Bowles and Gintis 1981; also see Weisskopf, Bowles, and Gordon 1983).

Most economists would agree that all these factors have some effect; the highly controversial issue is, which ones should be emphasized? We shall examine four hypotheses emphasizing different factors: (1) the wage lag hypothesis; (2) the overhead labor hypothesis; (3) the reserve army hypothesis, and (4) the utilization-unemployment hypothesis.

## The Wage Lag Hypothesis

Does the labor share increase or decrease in cyclical expansions? Does the labor share increase or decrease in cyclical contractions? What happens to labor productivity and real hourly wages over the cycle? Why do the labor share, productivity, and real wages behave as they do?

One theory, often espoused by trade unionists and underconsumptionists, may be called the wage lag theory (see, for example, Sweezy 1942; Baran and Sweezy 1966; and Foster 1987). It contends that in every expansion the labor share falls because wages lag behind national income, but that the labor share rises in every contraction because wages also lag in the decline. The basic wage lag argument is that—because of the institutions and relations of capitalism—it is more difficult for the working class to expand its real wages to keep up with increasing production, based on rising productivity, than to maintain its real wages in the face of falling production.

The wage lag theory argues that cyclical changes in income distribution are dominated by the simple institutional fact that the capitalist employer owns the product. If, as is always true in expansions, there is increasing productivity, then the employer automatically owns the increased product. To continue to obtain the same share of the increased revenue as they had before the increase in production, workers must struggle and bargain and play catch-up. It is thus not surprising that in an expanding economy the share going to wages normally declines. On the other hand, in a contraction the capitalist owns a declining product. If workers can hold on to their old wage level, they may receive a rising share of a falling product.

The institutions of capitalism also conspire in more specific ways to hold back real wage increases in expansion, while making it more difficult to lower wages in contraction. First, wage bargains by organized workers are fixed for a set period. When there are both rapid price increases and rapid productivity increases, organized workers must always struggle at the end of a two- or three-year contract just to maintain their percentage share. The same two- or three-year contracts prevent any rapid decline in money wages in a contraction. Second, the media often attack wage increases, especially if they go beyond the workers' share of price and productivity increases. The media are far more reluctant to attack workers for preventing wage cuts. Third, public opinion also tends to support workers in resisting wage cuts or speedup, but does not support fights to increase real wages faster than profits or fights to slow productivity. This public opinion is, of course, influenced by the media. Fourth, the capitalist state often enters the battle against workers' efforts to raise real wages faster than productivity is rising and strongly opposes efforts to lower productivity. Yet even the capitalist state finds it very difficult to attack workers openly when it is clear that they are merely resisting wage cuts or speedup.

According to this hypothesis, productivity rises rapidly in expansion and declines rapidly in contraction. Wage lag theorists seem to argue two points to explain productivity behavior. First, technology improves in the expansion because of new research and innovations. In the contraction, on the contrary, there is little research and almost no innovation. This reasoning is at least partially correct, but it does not account for the rapidity of the rise in early expansion (when innovations are just beginning to be built), nor does it account for actual declines in productivity in contractions.

Second, some argue that in the expansion, factories are used closer to their optimal designed capacity, whereas in contraction operation is far below that level. For example, mass production assembly lines can only work at a certain level. Therefore, labor costs per unit may fall in much of expansion as the optimal minimum cost level is approached, but may rise in contraction as production goes below that level. Again, there is something to this explanation. Yet many empirical studies have found that costs are constant in a wide range in the short run, so one may be skeptical as to its quantitative importance as an explanation of productivity changes.

In summary, the wage lag hypothesis contends that the workings of capitalist relations are such that during expansions marked by the rise of demand, reflected in rising capacity utilization, productivity rises faster than hourly wages do, so the share of labor declines. In business contractions, marked by declining demand, reflected in falling capacity utilization, capitalist relationships cause productivity to fall faster than wages do, so the share of labor rises.

## THE OVERHEAD LABOR THESIS

Overhead labor includes workers such as bookkeepers, maintenance people, clerical help, lawyers, accountants, engineers, and security staff—all people who are needed all the time and are not hired or fired in direct proportion to the amount of production. The overhead labor thesis argues that in the early expansion employers do not need to hire new overhead workers because the need for these types of workers does not rise directly in proportion to increases in output. Since output and capacity utilization are rising very rapidly, while employment is not expanding as rapidly, measured productivity rises rapidly.

In the last half of expansion, capitalists do have to begin hiring more overhead workers as well as production line workers to meet the increased needs of a greatly expanded production. Yet the growth rates of output and capacity utilization are declining, so measured productivity growth slows.

The overhead labor theory argues that in the crisis or early contraction phase, capitalists are lowering production. They fire a proportionate number of production line workers. They cannot, however, fire a proportionate number of overhead workers because the need for these types of workers does not decline directly as output falls. Since output is declining, while the total number of workers does not decline as much, the measured (or apparent) product per worker declines. Therefore, less profit is made per worker, counting both production line and overhead workers, so the labor share rises in contraction while falling in expansion (see Steindl 1952; and Weisskopf 1979). In the depths of the contraction, employers do start firing large numbers of all types of workers, so measured productivity becomes constant or even rises again.

The overhead labor hypothesis says that productivity rises as capacity utilization rises, and falls as capacity utilization falls. Therefore, all other things being equal, the labor share declines as capacity utilization rises; that is, the labor share is a negative function of capacity utilization. Since the wage lag hypothesis also maintains that the labor share is a negative function of capacity utilization, the overhead labor thesis tends to support the wage lag view of income distribution behavior.

This area has posed a problem for neoclassical economics because neoclassical economics assumes in theory that, all other things being equal, rising output and employment should mean a declining marginal productivity of labor, reflected in falling real wages. On the other hand, in a contraction falling output should mean rising productivity of labor, and hence rising real wages. This real wage should move countercyclically—and real marginal cost should move countercyclically. (Even John M. Keynes [1936] followed this widespread view, but when it was criticized in 1939, he was perfectly willing to drop the idea, [see Costrell 1981–1982, 287].)

Unfortunately for any simple version of neoclassical theory, many empirical studies have found that real wages do not move countercyclically, but procyclically (for a review of the literature, see Geary and Kennan [1982]). Because real wages are actually falling in each contraction, an interesting empirical study of prices and marginal labor costs over the cycle concludes that "this evidence . . . is . . . inconsistent with the view that wage stickiness is an important cause of the business cycle" (Bils 1987, 854). Not only do real wages move procyclically, but productivity is also strongly procyclical (a result that Costrell [1981–1982, 277] uses to challenge the whole theory of short-run marginal productivity). This cyclical behavior of wages and productivity has led to the overhead labor theory as one way of explaining the apparent anomaly.

Since labor productivity falls in a contraction (when a textbook neoclassical theory would expect it to rise), many neoclassical economists have considered the possibility that some costs of firing workers may prevent firms from adjusting their demand for labor as expected (beginning with the pioneering study by Walter Oi [1962]). Thus, Charles Schultze (1964) observes that since employers may have spent money to train skilled workers, they do not wish to fire them if they perceive a brief decline. Hence, labor is hoarded, as employers do not fire skilled workers proportionately in a contraction, but then employers will also not need to hire a proportionate number of skilled workers in an expansion. This pattern would explain why recorded productivity per worker might decline in a contraction and rise in an expansion. Schultze uses this hypothesis to explain why the share of labor income rises in a contraction of capacity utilization and falls in an expansion of capacity utilization. Schultze found a negative correlation between capacity utilization and the labor share, which he thought was based on his hypothesis about skilled labor hoarding.

The most thorough investigation of this issue was done in an outstanding article by Frank Munley (1981). He finds, as have other investigators, that *capacity utilization negatively influences the labor share*. But he also divides workers into salaried (overhead) labor and wage (production line) workers. He finds that lower capacity utilization results in the firing of a proportionate number of production line workers, but very few salaried, overhead workers. Therefore, productivity, labor income, and the labor share are affected mainly by the ratio of overhead workers to production. The change in the ratio of overhead workers to output is determined by changes in capacity utilization, which is a function of effective demand. Thus, Munley's findings on the overhead labor thesis are compatible with a more general wage lag theory; the overhead labor theory may, in fact, be viewed as a better way of explaining the procyclical behavior of productivity, which is crucial to the wage lag theory.

## THE RESERVE ARMY HYPOTHESIS

The reserve army hypothesis asserts that the labor share rises in the last half of expansion, while it falls in the last half of contraction (see Boddy and Crotty 1975; see also Gordon, Weisskopf, and Bowles 1987). The reason given is that the decline of the reserve army of the unemployed puts labor in a better bargaining position.

The argument of this thesis may be spelled out as follows. As output rises, employment rises. With a given labor force and a given technology, this means that the unemployment rate must decline. As this occurs, labor militancy rises. Workers are willing to take more chances and to back up demands by strikes, and this gives them more bargaining power. At the same time, employers know that there is a smaller reserve army of unemployed available to replace striking workers, so they are less likely to resist workers' demands. Therefore, the greater power and militancy of labor pushes wages upward.

The bargaining issues are not just wages but also productivity. Capitalists always wish to increase the intensity of work by speeding up the labor process, while workers wish to reduce the intensity of work and resist speedup. Workers may also resist new technology if it would replace workers with machines. Thus, according to this theory, near the peak of expansion when worker bargaining power is very strong, productivity growth may be stopped. Conversely, in a business contraction, unemployment reduces workers' bargaining power, so productivity is assumed to rise. One study by a reserve army theorist concludes: "The principal empirical findings are that increases in the general level of unemployment enhance productivity growth" (Rebitzer 1987, 627).

The argument that more unemployment weakens workers' power while less unemployment strengthens workers' power has also been supported in an article by Schor and Bowles (1987). They contend that more unemployment increases the cost to workers of losing a job and consequently makes workers less militant and less willing to strike. They state: "[W]hen the cost of job loss is high, it is more difficult for workers to win strikes, and they are therefore less likely to strike" (p. 584).

According to this theory, when the economy expands toward full employment, the result of higher wages and constant or declining productivity is a rising labor share. Thus, the labor share rises every time business output and employment expand toward full employment. When unemployment has risen sufficiently in a depression, there will be lower wages and rising productivity, so the labor share will fall.

Someone reading the reserve army hypothesis for the first time might expect the labor share to rise for the entire expansion period and fall for the entire contraction period. This is not true because the labor share always falls in the recovery phase of expansion and always rises in the crisis phase of contraction according to all studies. The sophisticated formulation of the reserve army theory (see Boddy and Crotty 1975; see also Gordon, Weisskopf, and Bowles 1987) emphasizes only that the labor share rises in the prosperity phase, the latter part of expansion before the peak. Presumably, for symmetry and internal consistency, the theory would require that the labor share fall again in the latter part of contraction before the trough. The sophisticated reserve army theorists are quite willing to admit that the labor share falls in early expansion and rises in early contraction. They postulate a lag effect. The reserve army theorists postulate a long time lag between changes in unemployment and changes in the wage share—due to a time lag in changes in labor militancy.

If lower unemployment brings more militancy and a higher labor share, why does the labor share fall in the first half of expansion? If higher unemployment brings less militancy and a lower labor share, why does the labor share rise in the first half of contraction? The answer from the reserve army theorists is that there is a subjective time lag after the peak before worker militancy declines, as well as a subjective time lag after the trough before worker militancy rises again. In other words, workers remember the high unemployment levels in the first half of expansion, so they act cautiously. In the first half of contraction, workers still act militantly until unemployment reduces worker resistance. Reserve army proponents would also accept some of the arguments of the wage lag theorists showing objective reasons for a time lag, particularly fixed wage contracts. Thus, the reserve army hypothesis explains the labor share by unemployment with a long time lag. (For a complete cycle theory based on the reserve army hypothesis, see Chapter 11.)

## THE UTILIZATION-UNEMPLOYMENT HYPOTHESIS

Whereas the reserve army hypothesis states that the labor share is explained by unemployment, the wage lag and overhead labor hypotheses explain it ultimately in terms of changes in capacity utilization (or output). The utilization-unemployment hypothesis accepts parts of both theses. It assumes that capacity utilization affects the labor share—through overhead labor, class conflict, and capitalist institutions—with no time lag. But it also assumes that the labor share is affected in the opposite direction by unemployment with a time lag. To argue either one without the other is considered in this viewpoint to be inadequate and incomplete.

In the recovery phase, rising capacity utilization leads to rapid rises in productivity, but much slower increases in wage rates. The decline in unemployment has no immediate effect. Therefore, the labor share declines.

In the prosperity phase, capacity utilization rises much more slowly, so it has less effect on increases in productivity. At the same time, there are slow wage increases due to the increase of demand for labor. Unemployment falls further and begins to cause pressures for higher wages and less productivity growth. The result is that the labor share is relatively stagnant, usually falling a little, but sometimes rising a little.

In the crisis phase, capacity utilization falls, and pressures develop for a rising labor share through slowly declining wages and rapidly declining productivity. Rising unemployment as yet has no effect.

In the depression phase, capacity utilization falls very slowly, with some pressure for further productivity decline and wage decline tending to cause more increase in the labor share. But unemployment now exerts its pressure—with a time lag—toward a decline in the labor share. The result is a fairly stagnant labor share, usually rising slightly, but sometimes falling slightly.

## PRESENT U.S. INCOME AND WEALTH DISTRIBUTION

Before turning to cyclical changes in the distribution of income, let us examine personal income distribution in terms of quintiles of U.S. households (a quintile is each 20 percent, or one fifth, of households; data is from the Census Bureau, analyzed in an excellent article by Amott [1989]). In 1986, according to the usual official measure of income, the lowest quintile had only 4 percent of U.S. income, the second quintile had 10 percent, the middle had 16 percent, and the fourth had 24 percent, while the highest quintile had 46 percent. In other words, the top 20 percent of U.S. households had almost as much income as the bottom 80 percent—a clear measure of severe inequality.

The usual measure, however, understates the inequality because it excludes capital gains, which go mostly to the rich. It also includes government transfer payments, which are not part of the private economic system. The Census Bureau has published a new measure, called private sector income, which includes capital gains, but excludes transfer payments from government. In 1986, the private sector income was distributed as follows: just 1 percent for the lowest quintile, 8 percent for the second, 15 percent for the middle, 24 percent for the fourth, and 52 percent for the highest quintile. In other words, private sector income is even more unequally distributed than the usual measure indicates, with the top 20 percent of U.S. households actually holding more income than the bottom 80 percent.

There is also evidence over time that the average American has gotten poorer in the last decade or so. For all families (in constant 1985 dollars), the median family income rose by 43 percent in the thirteen years from 1960 to 1973. But a peak in median income was reached in 1973. The real median family income fell by 5 percent in the twelve years from 1973 to 1985 (U.S. Bureau of the Census 1986). At the same time, the rich continued to get richer in the latter period, though not as rapidly as in the former period. For example, families in the 5th percentile from the top (that is, the 95th percentile of income) had their income grow by 48 percent in the 1960–1973 period, but it continued to grow—though by only 7 percent—in the 1973–1985 period. (An outstanding, comprehensive book on income and wealth is Winnick [1989]; also see the excellent article by Kloby [1987].)

If income per year is unequally distributed, total accumulated U.S. wealth is even more so. In 1983, the richest 10 percent of U.S. families had 72 percent of U.S. wealth. The superrich, that is, the top 0.5 percent of families, had 35 percent of all wealth by themselves (Winnick 1989). The only type of wealth distributed to a large number of families was home ownership. In fact, if we exclude the value of home ownership, the superrich had 45 percent of U.S. wealth, while the top 10 percent of families had 83 percent of the wealth. In terms of the types of wealth, the superrich owned 36 percent of real estate (excluding private homes), 47 percent of corporate stock, 44 percent of all types of bonds, and 58 percent of all business assets (including corporations, unincorporated business, farms, and professional practices). At the same time, the richest 10 percent of families owned 78 percent of real estate, 89 percent of corporate stock, 90 percent of bonds, and 94 percent of business assets.

What is the share of labor income and what is the share of property income? Since the top 10 percent of families have 94 percent of all business assets and most other property, most business or property income goes to this top 10 percent. The bottom 90 percent of the population by income size, on the contrary, have almost exclusively labor income. On the average, in the period from 1949 through 1982, those people earning labor income (that is, all employee compensation) earned 70 percent of all national income. The richest 10 percent, with unearned or property income, received 30 percent of all national income (calculated from U.S. Department of Commerce, Bureau of Economic Analysis 1984, series #64).

## PROBLEMS WITH MEASURING PROFITS, WAGES, AND PRODUCTIVITY

The biases present in the official definition of national product were discussed in Chapter 3 (also see Frumkin 1987). The biases are greater when it comes to dividing the product or income between all labor income and all property income. In the first place, the Internal Revenue Service always finds more illegal nonreporting of profits than of wages. For example, it is estimated that 58 percent of all rent and interest income is not reported (see Kloby 1987, 3). This does not necessarily mean that workers are more honest than capitalists. The U.S. tax system makes it much easier to hide property income (which is not withheld at the source) than to hide labor income (part of which is withheld for taxes before it is even paid).

Second, there are very few legal tax loopholes available for labor income. The law is filled with legal tax loopholes for property incomes of both individuals and businesses. For this reason, corporate taxes are a steadily decreasing percentage of the whole revenue. To note all the legal loopholes would require a long book (see Perlo 1976). The loopholes were reduced in the Tax Reform Act of 1986 (which also drastically reduced progressivity of tax rates), but very large loopholes remain.

On the other hand, labor income, or what is officially called "employee compensation," is greatly overstated. It includes managerial salaries. Many managers' salaries actually contain large amounts of profits in disguise as labor salaries. As salaries, they can then be counted as corporate "costs." Moreover, employee compensation includes "fringe benefits," which also disguise much profit income to executives. Most of these executive payments are really profits, so they should not be counted as labor income.

After eliminating just a few of these biases, one careful study found that there has been no change in the labor share in the last thirty years. The labor share was 0.68 in 1948 and was 0.69 in 1977, which is quite different than the upward trend in the official data (see Bowles and Gintis 1982, 71).

Finally, since more and more self-employed petty entrepreneurs and small farmers are going bankrupt and becoming workers, the percentage of people earning wages and salaries keeps going up. A correction should also be made for this change in calculating the labor share because it goes to a larger and larger percentage of the people. This is a major change over a long period because the percentage of wage and salary earners (excluding managers) rose from 20 percent in 1780 to well over 80 percent in 1970.

There have been many attempts at careful correction of the official national income accounts to derive a more unbiased set of categories from a prolabor view (see, for example, Perlo 1976), but these studies are considered controversial by most economists. The official national income categories are used here only because they are (1) readily available, (2) familiar to most economists, and (3) biased against prolabor conclusions. Therefore, when one can use these data and still come to prolabor policy conclusions, these conclusions are more persuasive.

The bias is strongest in absolute comparisons at a given time. For example, the ratio of property income to national income stated earlier would be much higher than in the official statistics if we corrected for all the biases mentioned earlier. In data on long-run trends, however, there may be much less bias because in a comparison of the growth of two things, there will be a bias in the trend only if there is an increase in the bias over time. Unfortunately, in this area there is some evidence of that. For example, managers are growing in numbers, and their salaries are increasing by leaps and bounds, with a good number of managerial salaries now over $1 million a year. For this reason, it is necessary to be extremely cautious about presenting trend data.

Finally, data on purely cyclical fluctuations of the labor share will be biased only if there is a systematic increase in bias at certain points in the cycle. By testing many different definitions, one finds very little change in cyclical results. Thus the bias seems least in the data used most in this book.

Another category of data that are very unreliable and biased are the data on productivity, the ratio of product to labor hours. Many writers have pointed out that productivity has a roughly defined meaning for manufacturing output, but is ambiguous for other sectors. For example, how is the "productivity" of a lawyer defined? Since the usual definitions give a lower growth rate of productivity in the service sectors than in manufacturing, a shift to services may mean less apparent growth of productivity. This shift is occurring, so it may explain some of the apparently lower productivity growth rates of recent years. On the other hand, this shift from manufacturing to services has been occurring continuously for some time. Therefore, the purely cyclical pattern of productivity should not be much affected by it, though the absolute levels of productivity growth may be affected by it.

These warnings about biases in the data will not be repeated, but the reader should maintain a healthy skepticism about the data in both long-run and cyclical contexts.

## CYCLICAL CHANGES IN INCOME DISTRIBUTION, 1921–1938

Wesley Mitchell (1951) had much less data than are available today, but he does present a few suggestive figures on income distribution for the average of the four cycles between 1921 and 1938 (these figures are mostly dominated by the cycle of the Great Depression). For the average expansion of these four cycles, national income rose by 22.5 percent of its average cycle base, whereas total employee compensation rose only 19.8 percent. Therefore, the labor share $(W/Y)$ declined in the average expansion of the 1920s and the 1930s. The decline in the labor share is also reflected more dramatically in the fact that in the average expansion phase of the same four cycles, net profits of all U.S. corporations rose 199.2 percent.

In the average contraction phase of these four cycles, national income fell by 17.6 percent of its cycle average, whereas total wages fell by only 13.0 percent. Therefore, the labor share $(W/Y)$ rose in the average contraction of the 1920s and the 1930s. Again, the rise in the wage share in the average contraction is emphasized by the fact that net profits of all U.S. corporations fell 174.6 percent.

The fact that the labor share was countercyclical in the 1920s and 1930s led many economists, particularly those sympathetic to the labor movement, to endorse the wage lag theory. The wage lag theory is an important component of underconsumptionism, as we shall see, so many of these economists also supported the underconsumptionist viewpoint.

## LONG-RUN CHANGES FROM 1949–1970 TO 1970–1982

After the Great Depression, the economy was dramatically altered by World War II, during which unemployment vanished, unions grew, and demand expanded. Before examining cyclical patterns in the 1949–1982 period, it is useful to summarize the relevant changes that occurred in the structure of the U.S. economy from the 1949–1970 period to the 1970–1982 period. First, monopoly power continued to grow, particularly with the wave of conglomerate mergers beginning in the late 1960s. Second, trade unions were strong and growing until the mid-1950s, but have suffered a steady decline since then. Third, financial regulations and strong liquidity meant a fairly safe money and credit system in the 1949–1970 period, but deregulation and new financial innovations led to high debt ratios and increased bankruptcies in the severe cycles of the 1970–1982 period. Fourth, government military spending remained high after World War II in the 1949–1970 period. It has grown even larger in the 1970–1982 period, but has declined as a percentage of GNP. Fifth, the U.S. economy dominated international trade and investment in the 1950s, but was meeting stiff competition and was suffering trade deficits by the 1970–1982 period.

These structural changes reduced the demand for U.S. goods and for U.S. labor, so they resulted in performance changes: (1) There was a declining growth rate of productivity in expansions and actual declines in contractions in the 1970–1982 period. The decline in productivity growth was primarily due to the fact that more severe downturns caused less investment, which reduced technological change embodied in that investment (for a different view, see Weisskopf, Bowles, and Gordon, [1983]). (2) There were much higher rates of unemployment in the 1970–1982 period. (3) The 1970–1982 period witnessed much lower rates of capacity utilization in contractions. (4) Real weekly wages rose steadily in the 1949–1970 period, but had a declining trend in the 1970–1982 period. (5) There were generally more severe contractions in the 1970–1982 period. (6) Effective demand was not a severe problem in 1949–1970, but became the major problem in 1970–1982.

This last fact, the greater deficiency of effective demand in the 1970–

1982 period, was documented in detail in an article by this author (Sherman, 1986) and independently in an important article by Henley (1987b). It was found that consumer demand and capitalist problems of realization were far less important in the mild crises of the earlier period, 1949–1970, than in the more severe crises of the later period, 1970–1982. Henley noted that previous research had found demand and realization problems not too important from 1949 to the early 1970s, but he concludes that in the two "cycles from 1975 to 1982 we have found that . . . all the secular decline in the rate of profit is explained by a deterioration in realization conditions, indicative of the general conditions of recession experienced by the U.S. economy at the time" (Henley 1987b, 328).

Henley also separated the share of labor (all employee compensation) in income into three parts: the income share of wage (production line) workers, the income share of salaried workers (whom he identifies as overhead workers, though the two categories are far from identical), and the share of supplemental labor costs (fringe benefits). His important contribution shows a secular decline in the wage share, but a secular rise in the salary share as well as the share of fringe benefits (1987b, 318). His cyclical data indicate that the cyclical pattern of the whole labor share moves with and is dominated by the wage share, but that the salary share and fringe benefit shares move differently, being dominated by their upward trends (1987b, 324). Henley's data are annual, so while we may trust the trend conclusions, the lack of quarterly data make the cyclical conclusions less reliable. Because of the lack of quarterly data on salary share and fringe benefits (which are necessary for a credible cyclical analysis), the analysis here will be limited to the total labor share, that is, the ratio of all employee compensation to national income.

## CYCLICAL PATTERN OF LABOR INCOME AND LABOR SHARE, 1949–1970

The pattern of income distribution—between labor and property income—changes systematically over the business cycle. The pattern, however, was quite different in the mild cycles of the 1949–1970 period and the severe cycles of the 1970–1982 period. Figure 8.1 shows the pattern for the earlier period. Note that all variables in this chapter are in real terms, that is, constant dollars.

Real labor income is procyclical, though not very strongly so. It may be considered as the average employee compensation times the number of employees. As we shall see, both the average employee compensation (per hour, week, month, or year) and the amount of employment rise in the expansion and fall in the contraction. It is worth noting, however, that both national income and labor income tend to rise at a slower and slower rate of growth in the expansion.

In the 1949–1970 period, the share of labor (its ratio to national in-

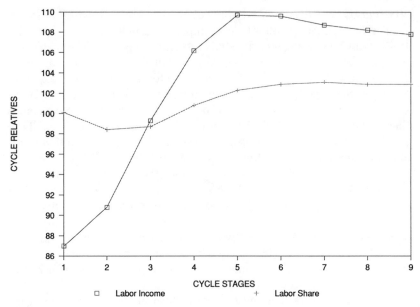

Fig. 8.1. Labor Income and Labor Share: Amplitude by Stage Averaged across Four Cycles, 1949–1970 (from series 280 and 64, Appendix D)

come) fell significantly only in the first segment of expansion. In this period, there was a long-run trend toward a higher labor share, according to the official data (which badly need adjustment, as shown earlier). Thus, in most of the expansion, labor income rose faster than did national income, while in most of the contraction, labor income fell more slowly than did national income. To the extent that the trend was real—and not mere distortion of data—some of the trend itself was probably caused by the very mild cyclical downturns and low unemployment, which gave labor a stronger bargaining position.

The fact that the labor share declined only in early expansion but rose throughout the last half of expansion during the 1949–1970 period gave rise to the resurgence of the reserve army hypothesis of the labor share behavior. This support for its main hypothesis led to a number of articles supporting the reserve army cyclical theory. It also brought criticism of the wage lag hypothesis and the underconsumptionist cycle theory.

## WAGES AND PRODUCTIVITY, 1949–1970

The share of labor in the final product represents a cost to the capitalist, reducing the property share. That cost ($W/Y$) is determined, by definition, by hourly wages ($W/N$) divided by productivity ($Y/N$). Higher hourly

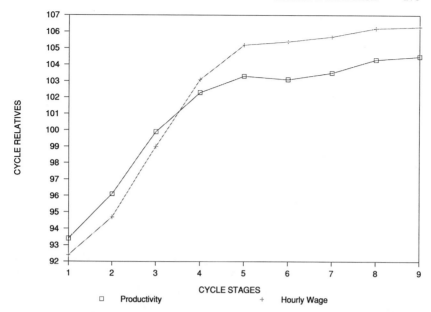

Fig. 8.2. Hourly Wages and Productivity: Amplitude by Stage Averaged across Four Cycles, 1949–1970 (from series 346 and 358, Appendix D, where productivity means ouput per labor hour)

wages obviously mean more cost per unit, but lower productivity also means more cost. There will be less cost to the capitalist if hourly wages are reduced or if the productivity of labor is increased. Figure 8.2 explores the cyclical behavior of productivity and hourly wages for the 1949–1970 period.

Productivity, that is, real product per hour for all nonfarm business, rose in this period throughout the average expansion. It rose rapidly in the recovery from depression, and then more and more slowly. Since the downturns were very mild, productivity turned down only in the first segment of contraction, and then slowly rose again.

The mildness of these contractions was emphasized still more by the real hourly wage. The real hourly wage rose very rapidly in the first segment of recovery, and then more and more slowly over the whole cycle—but never declined.

It may also be noted that labor's hours worked increased throughout the expansion and decreased throughout the contraction. The number of hours worked usually leads the cycle because it is easier to cut back on hours than to fire workers, just as it is easier to increase hours than to hire more workers. For more on the leads and lags of hours and employment, see Moore (1983, 70) and Bernanke and Powell (1986, 586).

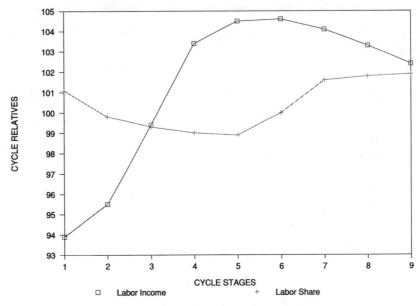

Fig. 8.3. Labor Income and Labor Share: Amplitude by Stage Averaged across Three Cycles, 1970–1982 (from series 280 and 64, Appendix E)

In the 1949–1970 period in the first segment of recovery, both productivity and hourly wages rose rapidly, but productivity rose faster—partly because there was still a large reserve of labor and partly because better use of overhead workers increased production per person. Therefore, the share of labor declined.

In that period in the rest of the expansion, both wages and productivity rose more slowly, but wages rose a little faster, so labor's share crept up. In the first segment of contraction, productivity declined while hourly wages were still rising slightly, so the labor share rose significantly. In the rest of the contraction the movements were fairly small and mostly canceled one another out, so there was little change in the labor share.

## LABOR INCOME AND LABOR SHARE, 1970–1982

The story is rather different for the more severe downturns of the 1970–1982 period. The cyclical patterns of labor income and the labor share in this period are shown in Figure 8.3. Real labor income was clearly procyclical, rising in expansions, but falling throughout the more severe contractions of this period. On the other hand, the labor share generally moved countercyclically, falling in most of business expansion and rising in most of business contraction. These facts strongly support the wage lag

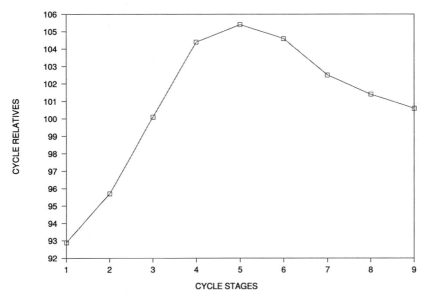

Fig. 8.4. National Income: Amplitude by Stage Averaged across Three Cycles, 1970–1982 (from series 220, Appendix E)

hypothesis, since wages lagged behind profits in most of the cycle. These facts have brought new support to the underconsumptionist theory, since the falling labor share in expansion tends to mean less consumer demand.

Now let us examine some of the underlying series in greater detail. Figure 8.4 reveals that national income behaved exactly as one would predict; it rose—although more and more slowly—throughout expansion; then it fell throughout contraction. Figure 8.5 shows that labor income rose throughout the expansion, but that it rose significantly more slowly than did national income, which is shown in Figure 8.4. In this particular period, labor income lagged a little, so that it still rose very slightly in the first segment of contraction; after that, it fell during the whole contraction. Property income is pictured in Figure 8.6. Property income rose far more rapidly than did labor income during the expansion, but also fell more rapidly than did labor income in the whole contraction (note that the scales are different in the two graphs).

Since labor income rose more slowly than did national income in expansion, the labor share, shown in Figure 8.7, fell in the average expansion. On the other hand, since labor income also fell more slowly than did national income, the labor share necessarily rose during the average contraction. Notice, however, that the sharpest rise of the labor share was in the crisis phase of contraction, while the sharpest decline of the

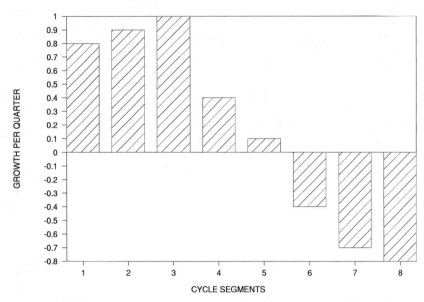

Fig. 8.5. Labor Income: Growth by Segment Averaged across Three Cycles, 1970–1982 (from series 280, Appendix H)

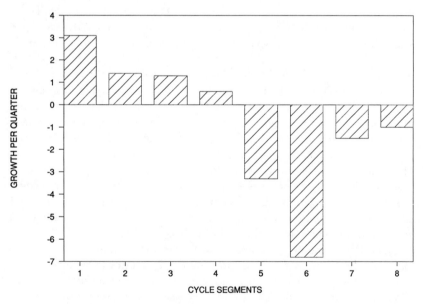

Fig. 8.6. Property Income: Growth by Segment Averaged across Three Cycles, 1970–1982 (from series 220 − 280, Appendix H)

labor share occurred during the first segment of recovery. During prosperity, the labor share continued to decline, but very slowly. During depression, the labor share continued to rise, but very slowly.

Naturally, as shown in Figure 8.8, the behavior of the property share was exactly the opposite of that of the labor share. The property share (and the rate of exploitation) rose rapidly in recovery, and then rose more slowly in prosperity. In the crisis phase, the property share (and the rate of exploitation) fell rapidly—but one should keep in mind that this was after the peak, so it was a result of the crisis, not an initiating cause of it. Then, in depression, the property share continued to fall slightly. The rise of the property share in expansion and its fall in contraction tend to confirm the wage lag theory.

## WAGES AND PRODUCTIVITY, 1970–1982

Recall that the labor share is affected positively by higher hourly wages. The labor share is affected negatively by higher productivity—because the fruits of this higher product of labor automatically go to the capitalist receivers of profits. As shown in Figure 8.9, real hourly wages rose more slowly than did real product per hour in most of the expansion phase. Both series led the cycle peak in this period, but hourly wages turned down more rapidly than did productivity in late prosperity, so the labor share continued to fall in that phase. On the other hand, productivity fell more rapidly than did hourly wages in most of the contraction, so the labor share rose in this phase.

Figure 8.10 depicts real hourly wages in more detail over the cycle. In the 1970–1982 period, real hourly wages rose in expansion, but more and more slowly—a normal sort of pattern. It is unusual to find real hourly wages falling before the cycle peak; that occurred in this period because nominal wages were unable to keep up with inflation. Hourly wages continued to fall in the first segment of the crisis phase. The fact that real hourly wages showed a clear and significant rate of decline in two segments of the cycle reflects the severity of these downturns—and shows how different these cycles were from the mild cycles of the 1950s and 1960s. Real hourly wages did return to positive growth in the depression phase of the cycle, so these downturns were nowhere near as severe as in the Great Depression of the 1930s, when real hourly wages declined for several years.

As shown in Figure 8.11, productivity rose very rapidly in the recovery phase of the cycle, as is usual in most recorded cycles. In the prosperity phase, productivity continued an anemic rise for one segment, followed by a slight decline—reflecting the long-run weakness of productivity growth in this period. In the crisis phase, productivity declined very sig-

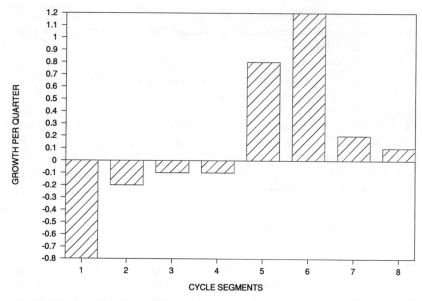

Fig. 8.7. Labor Share: Growth by Segment Averaged across Three Cycles, 1970–1982 (from series 64, Appendix H)

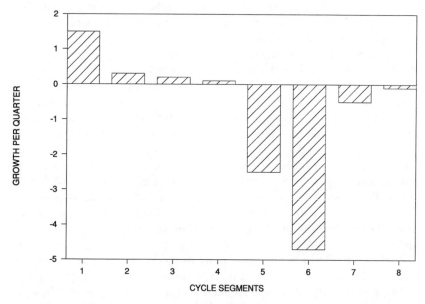

Fig. 8.8. Property Share: Growth by Segment Averaged across Three Cycles, 1970–1982 (from series [220 − 280] /220, Appendix H)

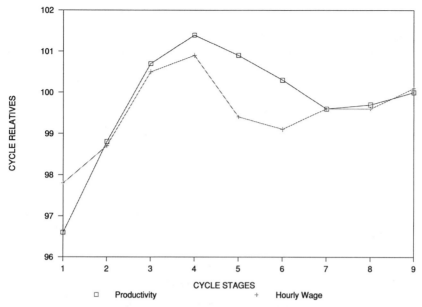

Fig. 8.9. Hourly Wages and Productivity: Amplitude by Stage Averaged across Three Cycles, 1970–1982 (from series 346 and 358, Appendix E)

nificantly, again reflecting the greater severity of these cyclical downturns compared with the previous period. In the depression phase, productivity showed a slight recovery. We see once again how the behavior of hourly wages and productivity adds up to the behavior of the labor share.

The clearest and most consistent cyclical behavior is portrayed in Figure 8.12, concerning the number of hours worked by workers each week. This variable grew during the whole expansion, while it declined during the whole contraction. The real hourly wage is nothing but total wages (or labor income) divided by the number of hours worked. Productivity is nothing but real output divided by the number of hours worked. In expansion, hours worked increase, but total wages and total product usually increase faster. In contraction, hours worked decrease, but wages and output usually decrease faster.

## UNEMPLOYMENT AND CAPACITY UTILIZATION

What determines the cyclical behavior of the labor share (and its components, hourly wages and productivity)? The reserve army hypothesis puts the strongest emphasis on the effect of higher employment or lower employment on labor's bargaining position. On the other hand, the wage

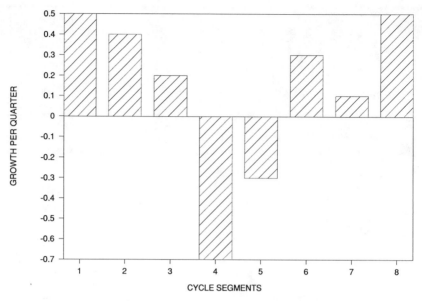

Fig. 8.10. Hourly Wages: Growth by Segment Averaged across Three Cycles, 1970–1982 (from series 346, Appendix E)

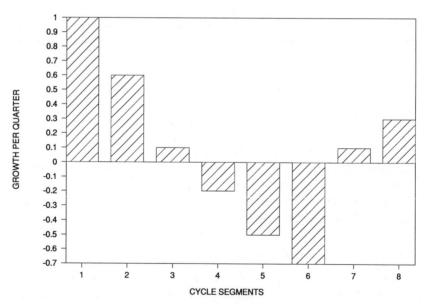

Fig. 8.11. Productivity: Growth by Segment Averaged across Three Cycles, 1970–1982 (from series 358, Appendix H)

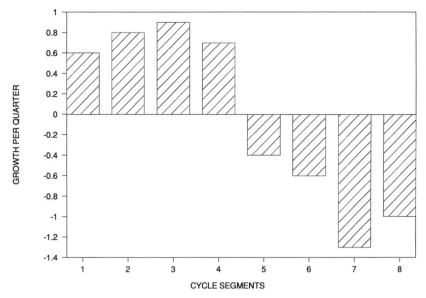

Fig. 8.12. Hours Worked: Growth by Segment Averaged across Three Cycles, 1970–1982 (from series 48, Appendix H)

lag hypothesis contends that institutional factors prevent wages from moving as fast as productivity does when capacity utilization rises or falls. Finally, we saw that the overhead labor hypothesis expects measured productivity to rise or fall faster than wages do because of the hesitation to fire overhead labor in contractions and lack of need to hire more overhead labor in expansions. The reserve army hypothesis implies an inverse link between labor share and unemployment, while the wage lag and overhead labor hypotheses imply an inverse link between labor share and capacity utilization.

*Long-Run Trends*

As a background, let us examine the long-run trends of unemployment and capacity utilization. There has been a long-run trend toward higher unemployment levels and lower capacity utilization levels. The unemployment rate averaged 4.8 percent in the four cycles of 1949 to 1970, but rose to 7.0 percent in the three cycles of 1970 to 1982 (see Appendix B). The capacity utilization rate declined from an average 83 percent in the first four cycles to 79 percent in the last three cycles (see Appendix B). Looking at the more recent cycles in more detail, the average unemployment rate rose as follows: 4.7 percent (1961–1970 cycle); 5.7 per-

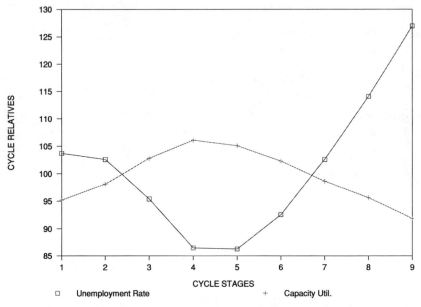

Fig. 8.13. Unemployment Rate and Capacity Utilization: Amplitude by Stage Averaged across Three Cycles, 1970–1982 (from series 43 and 82, Appendix E)

cent (1970–1975 cycle); 7.0 percent (1975–1980 cycle); and 8.4 percent (1980–1982 cycle). At the same time, the capacity utilization rate fell as follows: 85 percent (1961–1970 cycle); 82 percent (1970–1975 cycle); 80 percent (1975–1980 cycle); and 75 percent (1980–1982 cycle). Of course, these rates have changed in the expansion of 1983–1989, but one can draw no long-run conclusions until that whole cycle is completed.

### Cyclical Behavior

Turning from long-run trends to the business cycle, Figure 8.13 shows the cyclical performance of unemployment and capacity utilization for the 1970–1982 period. We see that unemployment fell—as it always does—during the entire expansion, while unemployment rose—as it always does—during the entire contraction. Capacity utilization moves in the opposite direction. Capacity utilization rose in most of the expansion, falling slightly just before the peak, while it fell throughout the entire contraction. Aside from the slight lead at the peak, this is the normal behavior of capacity utilization in all cycles.

Figure 8.14 reveals in detail that in the average expansion of the 1970–1982 period, the unemployment rate fell during the whole expansion phase—but it fell very slowly. In the contraction phase, the unemployment rate rose with startling speed. Of course, the fact that unemploy-

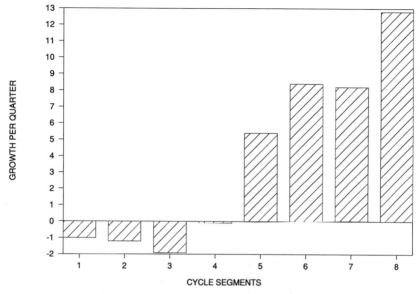

Fig. 8.14. Unemployment Rate: Amplitude by Stage Averaged across Three Cycles, 1970–1982 (from series 43, Appendix H)

ment fell so slowly in expansions while rising so rapidly in contractions merely reflects the long-run trend in this period toward rising unemployment.

Finally, Figure 8.15 portrays capacity utilization, which rose in the first three segments of expansion, but at a slower and slower rate, thus revealing the weakening of demand factors. In the last segment of expansion, capacity utilization actually declined a little, reflecting an unusually drastic further decline in demand and a falling profit rate. In the entire contraction, capacity utilization declined rapidly, reflecting an absolute decline of demand. The fact that capacity utilization was rising rather slowly in expansion, while falling rapidly in contraction again dramatically reflects the long-run trend toward less capacity utilization in this period.

In the average of the three cycles of 1970–1982, (1) the labor share fell in expansions and rose in contractions; (2) productivity rose faster than did wage rates in expansions and fell faster than did wage rates in contractions; and (3) capacity utilization rose in expansions and fell in contractions; while (4) unemployment fell in expansions and rose in contractions. These basic facts appear to support the wage lag and overhead labor hypotheses, but appear to contradict the reserve army hypothesis. But before drawing conclusions, we should turn to the econometric evidence.

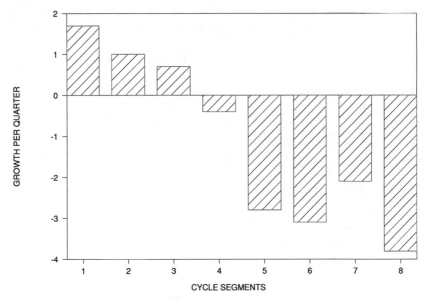

Fig. 8.15. Capacity Utilization: Growth by Segment Averaged across Three Cycles, 1970–1982 (from series 82, Appendix H)

### Econometric Evidence

The econometric evidence covering the entire period is presented in detail in Appendix 8.1, but may be summarized here. If we look separately at the relation of the labor share to capacity utilization, there does appear to be a significant negative relation, as predicted by the wage lag and overhead labor hypotheses. If we look separately at the relation of the labor share to unemployment, the relationship is positive with no time lag and not significant with time lags, so it appears to contradict the reserve army hypothesis. But it is incorrect to look at these two factors separately because they operate simultaneously. If we examine the relationship of the labor share to both capacity utilization and to unemployment, then we find that there is a significant negative correlation of the labor share to capacity utilization with no time lag, but there is also a significant negative correlation of the labor share to unemployment with a long time lag—as predicted by the utilization-unemployment hypothesis.

In other words, it appears most likely is that we have not one, but two main factors affecting cyclical behavior of the labor share: both capacity utilization and unemployment. They push the labor share in opposite directions, so the question is which is strongest at each point and what time lags operate. Capacity utilization is the stronger effect, and unemployment operates with a long time lag. It is useful to clarify the relationship of the variables at each point in the cycle (see the next section).

Finally, it is worth noting that capacity utilization has a strong positive relationship to national income, while unemployment has a strong negative relationship to national income. These two facts are well known and noncontroversial, but help round out our knowledge in this area.

## EXPLANATION OF CYCLICAL MOVEMENTS OF LABOR SHARE BY CYCLE PHASE

Given this theoretical approach and the above facts, we can now explain the movements of the labor share, real hourly wages, and productivity over the cycle in relation to the influence of unemployment and capacity utilization.

### Recovery (Early Expansion)

In the recovery phase, when output and capacity utilization are rising rapidly, productivity also rises rapidly—partly because of improving technology, partly because of more optimal use of capacity as more workers are added, and mostly because overhead workers can be more fully utilized. The rise in productivity is greater than the rise in real hourly wages, so the labor share declines.

Why do real hourly wages rise more slowly than does productivity in spite of the increase in demand for labor? Part of the answer to the slowness of growth of real wages is the fact that unemployment is still high and the memories of the previous recession are still very sharp. A second reason may be that although workers' share of output is falling, they are more aware of the pleasant fact of rising wages. Third, under capitalist institutions, wage contracts are fixed at the old levels. It takes time before the next bargaining period is reached. Until there are changes forced through bargaining, all of the increase in product automatically goes to the capitalist employer because the employer owns the product under capitalism. Fourth, prices are rising, so it is extra difficult to raise real wages. Fifth, the government, the media, and "public opinion" are all opposed to further wage increases when wages (and prices) are rising.

### Prosperity (Late Expansion)

In the last half of the average expansion, productivity increases very little, but real wages are also sluggish. As a result, the labor share is virtually stagnant; it rose a little in the cycles of the 1950s and 1960s, but fell a little in the cycles of the 1970s and early 1980s.

Real wages are sluggish toward the end of expansion partly because demand for products, and hence for labor, has slowed their rate of growth. The increase of consumer demand is limited, and the increase of investment demand is limited. Yet unemployment is declining, so workers' bargaining power improves—thus, real wages do usually continue to rise in this phase (but severe inflation will tend to lower real hourly wages even before the peak).

Productivity increase is also slowed (and sometimes begins to decline) for several reasons. First, falling unemployment means a better bargaining position for labor, more militancy, and more strikes—so speedup is prevented and the rise of productivity is limited. Second, overhead workers are now fully utilized, so there are no more easy gains from this source. Finally, as Wesley Mitchell noted in all of his books, thousands of new, small, and inexperienced firms come crowding into the market at this point. Their entry undoubtedly does lower average productivity.

### Crisis (Early Contraction)

In the early stages of the downturn, employment remains fairly high. Employers are hoarding some skilled labor and all overhead labor. Therefore, measured productivity declines very rapidly (even though technology is not running backward).

At the same time, fixed labor contracts prevent any rapid decline in hourly wages. Moreover, the government, the media, and "public opinion" are much more sympathetic to labor's resistance to wage cuts than they were to higher wages.

In summary, as output and capacity utilization decline, wage rates decline very slowly while productivity rapidly declines. These facts explains the rising share of labor in national income during the crisis phase of contraction.

### Depression (Late Contraction)

By late contraction, employers fire every possible worker who is not absolutely essential—even some of the overhead workers. Therefore, measured product per worker hour may finally rise again at the cycle trough.

At the same time, rapidly rising unemployment worsens the bargaining power of workers, lowers their militancy, and reduces the number of strikes. Therefore, real hourly wages usually fall in this phase.

As a result of rising or stable productivity and lower real wages, the labor share stops rising and may even decline at the end of the contraction.

## SUMMARY

In mild business cycles, such as those in the 1950s and 1960s, (1) the labor share declines in early expansion, but rises slightly in late expansion, and then rises further in contractions; (2) productivity rises more rapidly than do wage rates in early expansion, but rises slightly more slowly than do wage rates in late expansion, and rises more slowly than do wage rates throughout the contraction; and (3) capacity utilization is procyclical, while unemployment is countercyclical. In more severe business cycles, such as those in the 1920s and 1930s or the 1970s and early 1980s, (1) the labor share falls throughout most of expansion and rises throughout most of contraction; (2) wage rates rise more slowly than does productivity during expansion, but wage rates also fall more slowly during contraction; and (3) capacity utilization is strongly procyclical, while unemployment is strongly countercyclical.

Over the entire period, (1) the labor share is negatively correlated to capacity utilization with no time lag and is negatively correlated to unemployment with a time lag; (2) capacity utilization is correlated to real national income; and (3) unemployment is negatively correlated to real national income.

## CONCLUSIONS

Since the labor share and unemployment usually move in the same direction at a given time, the direct comparison (with no time lag) does not give much support to the reserve army hypothesis, but it is *not* inconsistent with a lagged reserve army hypothesis. The econometric findings do indicate that unemployment influences the labor share negatively with a time lag.

Since the labor share usually moves opposite to capacity utilization (while productivity usually moves with capacity utilization), there is obvious support for the wage lag and overhead labor hypotheses—but there were some times during the expansions of the 1950s and 1960s when wages did not seem to lag behind profits.

The evidence is consistent with the utilization-unemployment hypothesis, which says that the labor share is negatively influenced both by capacity utilization and by unemployment, the latter with a long time lag.

## Further Considerations

Before reaching any final conclusions as to the implications of these findings for business cycle theories, some further discussion is necessary. Chapter 9 considers in more detail the role of the labor share in demand-side theories, such as underconsumptionism; while Chapter 11 examines the role of the labor share in the supply-side theories, such as the reserve army theory. Chapter 10 examines nonlabor costs to understand their relative importance.

Chapter 12 considers the behavior of profit rates in more detail to see the relation of the leads and lags in the labor share to the leads and lags of profit rates. To understand the reasons for a downturn, what is important is *not* what happens just before the peak of output and investment, but what happens just before the peak in the profit rate. Once profit expectations begin to decline, the cyclical downturn is inevitable because output and investment will decline with a time lag.

## Appendix 8.1
## Models of the Labor Share

A brief formalization of the hypotheses presented in this chapter would be as follows. The wage lag and overhead labor hypotheses emphasize that the labor share $(W/Y)$ is a function $(f^1)$ of capacity utilization $(Z/Y,$ where $Z$ is the possible output at optimum utilization):

$$W/Y_t = f^1(Z/Y_t). \tag{8.5}$$

The reserve army hypothesis emphasizes that the labor share is a function $(f^2)$ of unemployment $(U)$ with a time lag $(g)$:

$$W/Y_t = f^2(U_{t-g}). \tag{8.6}$$

The utilization-unemployment hypothesis, however, contends that the labor share is influenced by both capacity utilization and by unemployment, pulling in different directions. Thus, according to this view, it is more reasonable to combine the two factors into one equation. That equation states that the labor share is a function of both capacity utilization (with no measurable time lag) and of unemployment (with a long time lag):

$$W/Y_t = f^1(Z/Y_t) + f^2(U_{t-g}). \tag{8.7}$$

Econometric tests using data from the sources indicated in Appendix A were made from the first quarter of 1949 to the first quarter of 1988. (Autocorrelation was corrected in all regressions by the ARMA method, based on the correction suggested by Cochrane and Orcutt [1949].) The results of a simple regression of the labor share (W/Y, series #64) on the capacity utilization ratio (Z/Y, series #82), with all rates expressed as percentages, were as follows:

$$W/Y_t = 81.0 - 0.10(Z/Y_t) \qquad (8.8)$$
$$(46.6) \quad (-5.6)$$
$$CR^2 = 0.97 \quad DW = 1.99.$$

Here the figures in parentheses are $t$-statistics, showing a high level of statistical significance of the regression coefficients. $CR^2$ is the correlation coefficient squared, and $DW$ is the Durbin-Watson coefficient, showing almost no autocorrelation in this case. It does appear that the labor share is highly and negatively correlated with capacity utilization, but this result could be misleading until we add the unemployment factor in a multiple regression.

A multiple regression attempts to explain the labor share with both capacity utilization and with the unemployment rate (series #43):

$$W/Y_t = 82.7 - 0.11Z/Y_t - 0.28U_{t-3} \qquad (8.9)$$
$$(43.1) \quad (-6.54) \quad (-3.38)$$
$$CR^2 = 0.97 \quad DW = 1.99.$$

The $t$-statistics indicate that the regression coefficients are statistically significant. There is a high correlation and no significant autocorrelation. Thus, it appears that the labor share is negatively correlated with capacity utilization, but also is negatively correlated with unemployment with a time lag.

Of course, this does not prove cause and effect. Moreover, the high correlation in the main merely reflects the fact that most economic variables conform to the business cycle, so they move together procyclically (or move inversely if one is countercyclical). One must also remember the biases in the data that make it suspect, as well as the various statistical problems in such time data (such as the fact that capacity utilization and unemployment are not really independent of each other). At any rate, the evidence is at least compatible with the hypotheses suggested here (though it may also be compatible with other hypotheses).

Much less controversial is the hypothesis that unemployment is closely related to real national income (Y, series #220):

$$U_t = 62.5 - 0.01Y_t \qquad (8.10)$$
$$(8.7) \quad (-11.5)$$
$$CR^2 = 0.97 \quad DW = 1.99.$$

Unemployment has a significant negative correlation with real national income.

Similarly, it is obvious that capacity utilization is closely related to real national income:

$$Z/Y_t = -179.1 + 0.05Y_t \qquad (8.11)$$
$$(-5.7) \qquad (12.2)$$
$$CR^2 = 0.93 \qquad DW = 2.00.$$

Capacity utilization has a significant positive correlation with real national income.

# CHAPTER 9

# Demand-Side Theories:
# The Underconsumption Hypothesis

MANY THEORISTS have contended that the main problems of capitalist downturns are caused by the lack of consumer demand. The most famous of these theories are the group called underconsumption theories. These theories have been advocated by both mainstream economists and by socialist or Marxist economists—the two groups approach these theories differently, so those differences must be spelled out. Furthermore, most underconsumption theories have not been business cycle theories at all, but theories of long-run stagnation—these stagnation theories must also be distinguished from business cycle theories.

## NONSOCIALIST UNDERCONSUMPTIONIST LONG-RUN STAGNATION THEORIES

All underconsumptionist long-run stagnation theories—whether socialist or nonsocialist—include, by definition and tradition, two main components. First, the most important shared belief is that insufficient consumer demand for goods and services is the main cause of depression and unemployment. Second, it is believed that this lack of consumer demand is a problem for the economy at all times, so the usual status of the economy would be stagnation. Certain external, or exogenous, events, such as wars or new inventions, may pull the economy upward for a while in some of these theories, but it will eventually come back to stagnation. Other than these two beliefs—that the problem is lack of consumer demand and that it results in stagnation—long-run underconsumptionist theories differ in various ways. (Underconsumptionist long-run stagnation theories are discussed in a comprehensive, but hostile, history by Bleany [1976].)

There have been many nonsocialist underconsumptionist theories, ranging from the earliest beginnings with Lord Lauderdale and the Reverend Thomas Malthus in the early nineteenth century to the later theories of W. T. Foster and W. Catchings in the 1930s (see Haberler [1960, ch. 5] for a careful but unsympathetic discussion of these theories). In many of these theories the emphasis was that on the one hand, industry turns out an increasing flood of commodities, while on the other hand, some people save part of their income. As a result, consumer demand does not keep up with the flood of commodities, there is a pileup of unsold goods, and production is cut. Less production leads to unemployment, which means still less income and less consumer demand.

Among the classical economists, Malthus was almost unique in having an underconsumption theory. From his conservative viewpoint he recommended that society maintain a class of parasites, who would consume but not produce. He felt that the landlord class fitted this solution because they were magnificent at the art of consuming without producing anything.

Since the problem, according to underconsumptionists, was lack of demand and too much saving, their view ran exactly contrary to the usual classical view that more saving is always good for the economy. While most classical economists recommended more saving for economic growth, some underconsumptionists recommended that everyone be forced to respend all of their income rapidly.

Another form of underconsumption theory was popular with liberal reformers, such as John Hobson (1922), a writer whose liberal discussion of imperialism was the factual basis for much of Lenin's work on that subject. Hobson stressed that the cause of deficient consumer demand is not a general tendency toward too much saving, but a lack of demand by the poor. He demonstrated that there was a maldistribution of income, with a few rich people having much income, but a large mass of poor people having little income. Most wage workers, he said, are poorly paid, so their income and consumption are very limited. On the other hand, the rich have incomes that are far above their consumption needs, so they save most of their income. There is a lack of consumer demand because those that have large amounts of income do not need more consumption, while those who are poor have the need, but not the income.

Hobson's solution was a more equal distribution of income. Trade unions often agree with Hobson. At least, they tend to argue that the way out of any recession or depression is higher wages and more unemployment benefits, so that workers will have more money to spend on consumption.

In the 1930s, when the U.S. economy suffered ten mostly depressed years, theories of underconsumption and stagnation naturally became very popular. Alvin Hansen, who was a president of the American Economic Association, held an underconsumptionist long-run stagnation theory (see Hansen 1964). He argued that stagnation was held off before the Great Depression by certain unique historical factors, including the U.S. expansion on its frontier, rapid population growth, and rapid technological innovation—such as railroads, the automobile, and electricity (Hansen's theory and similar ones are discussed in R. A. Gordon 1961).

## SOCIALIST UNDERCONSUMPTIONIST LONG-RUN STAGNATION THEORIES

Early socialist writers, such as Sismondi ([1815] 1946) or Rodbertus (1898), argued that the exploitation of workers led to a lack of consumer buying power. They claimed that the worker is not paid his or her "full product" but is limited to a subsistence wage. Therefore, as production expands, the workers' share in national income must decline. As a result, consumer demand must inevitably decline relative to production. A crisis of overproduction must follow, leading to economic stagnation (all of the earlier socialist writing on underconsumption is reviewed in detail in Sweezy [1942]).

Stagnation theories based on the underconsumptionist hypothesis were amplified by many later Marxists, such as the brilliant Rosa Luxemburg (discussed thoroughly and sympathetically in Sweezy [1942]). Luxemburg argued that the exploitation of workers and the consequent lack of consumer demand must lead to long-run stagnation. The only reason that underconsumption has not yet led to a state of complete stagnation has been the global expansion of capitalism. In Luxemburg's theory, capitalists expand their markets by expanding their colonial and neocolonial empires. When all of the world is conquered by capitalism, economic stagnation must inevitably result.

A series of powerful Marxist works, in which underconsumptionism was one theme in an overall theory of long-run stagnation, were written by Paul Sweezy (1942), Paul Baran (1957), and Baran and Sweezy (1966). More recently, Marxist stagnation and underconsumption theory has been clearly and strongly restated by Szymanski (1974) and by J. B. Foster (1985, 1987). Within the framework of a Marxist long-run stagnation and underconsumption theory, Sweezy and Baran made some incisive and impressive contributions to economics, still worthwhile reading today. They argued "that the normal state of the monopoly capitalist economy is stagnation" (1966, 108). The economy tends to stagnate because of lack of demand, but the system sometimes prevents stagnation by making wasteful expenditures. Some of these expenditures are private waste, such as advertising and planned obsolescence—one example of planned obsolescence is designing an automobile so that it falls apart after a certain number of years. Others of these expenditures are public waste, such as military spending financed by a government deficit. Sometimes the economy revives for a while for one of two main reasons. First, there may be new technological innovations that expand the economy through entrepreneurial greed for some time (Sweezy was a student of Schumpeter and this idea follows a theme of Schumpeter's). Second, the economy is stimulated by major wars, such as World War II, the Korean War, or the Vietnam War.

## CRITICISMS OF UNDERCONSUMPTIONIST LONG-RUN STAGNATION THEORIES

There have been many criticisms of the underconsumptionist stagnation view from right, left, and center. Haberler (1960) comments: "The under-consumption theory is a theory of the crisis and depression rather than a theory of the cycle" (p. 119). In other words, the long-run underconsumption theory explains why capitalism declines into stagnation; but it has no endogenous explanation of why capitalism should ever recover.

If Marxists simply predict the decline of capitalism at all times—or discuss a "general crisis" as always existing—it does not help them to understand the reality of capitalism, nor does it give them popular credibility. It is easy to observe in the United States that there has been a great deal of prosperity and some periods of rapid expansion, even though crises and mass unemployment do occur frequently—and even though a part of the population does not participate much in the apparent prosperity. To constantly assert that the U.S. economy is in a continuing condition of crisis or decline does not help the Marxist understanding of the capitalist economy. Marx himself stressed that, as opposed to long-run crises of continuous decline or permanent crises in capitalism, a temporary period of "overabundance of capital, overproduction, crisis, is something different. There are no permanent crises" (Marx [1905] 1952, 373). Some Marxist writers seem to worry that if one cannot prove that capitalism is inevitably falling apart day after day, there is no hope for socialism. Yet even the revolutionary Lenin criticized the view that capitalism is in a permanent crisis (otherwise known as the sky is falling hypothesis); he said: "There is nothing more stupid than to deduce from the contradictions of capitalism its impossibility, its unprogressive character, etc.—that is flight from an unpleasant but undoubted reality into the cloud world of romantic fantasies" (quoted in Sweezy 1942, 185). Surely, it is enough of a critique of a system to point out that it goes through periods of mass unemployment of labor and widespread underutilization of capacity on a cyclical basis.

Another criticism of the underconsumptionist long-run stagnation theory is the argument that lack of consumer demand by itself is not a sufficient condition for a downturn. Haberler (1960) argues, as have many other critics, that even if consumer demand declines, "there is always an equilibrium position possible with full employment" (p. 125). He is referring to the fact that demand for producers' goods for investment may always fill any gap between total output and consumer demand. Marx also demonstrated in his reproduction schema in volume 2 of *Capital* that it is possible for capitalism to expand with full employment—but he did enumerate the difficult conditions that must be fulfilled for that to happen. For an equilibrium to exist, it must be the case that the total demand for output of both consumer goods and investor goods just equals the aggregate output and that they are in the correct proportions.

The basic criticism of the early, crude type of underconsumptionist theory is that it lacked a theory of investment. Although Keynes shares the underconsumptionist worries over the lack of demand, his theory is distinguished by the focus of attention on investment. He notes that there will be equilibrium if all of nonconsumed income, that is, saving, is equal to investment plans. It is only if a theory can show that the total demand by both consumers and investors is insufficient to purchase all of the supply on the market at present prices that a theory can explain a downturn by a demand-oriented theory. In that respect Samuelson (1939) did have a complete theory, as opposed to incomplete theories that talk only about insufficient consumer demand.

Marxist underconsumptionists had long been saying that capitalism in the private sector (that is, leaving aside military spending) cannot just build more factories to produce more factories and so forth. In other words, private investment, it was asserted, cannot grow to fill any gap left by consumption. But why? In fact, it always happens that for some time during every expansion, investment is growing faster than consumption. The accelerator principle does explain why that happens, as a function of rising growth of consumption. At first, this faster growth of investment is no problem, but is rather the engine of prosperity, because the savings are invested to produce output and employment. Even if consumer demand then becomes stagnant, it is technically possible for the increased flow of goods all to be in the form of investment goods (plant and equipment), which are designed to produce more plant and equipment.

What an underconsumptionist investment function must explain is why this makes no economic sense, primarily because capitalists will not invest if their expectation is for a lack of demand in the near future when the new goods are produced. Sweezy (1942) began to solve this problem for underconsumptionists when he examined the role of the accelerator. The accelerator principle does explain why investment must decline when aggregate demand slows down—and it may be emphasized that consumer demand is the largest part of aggregate demand. This defense of underconsumptionism is stated forcefully by John B. Foster (1987), who writes:

> Any continual plowing back of profits into investment would mean that the means of production . . . would expand very much faster than the articles of consumption. . . . This, in fact, is the basic pattern of every accumulation boom. But it is a self-annihilating process. Sooner or later . . . the means of

production are built up to such a prodigious extent that a social disproportionality develops between the capacity to produce and the corresponding demand. A crisis of overaccumulation rooted in overexploitation occurs. (p. 61)

Foster's disproportionality thesis could be translated into the action of the accelerator principle, which limits investment when aggregate demand is limited. Of course, many criticisms of the accelerator were noted in Chapter 7, so what is really required is an adequate investment explanation, which may include the accelerator as one part of the explanation. At any rate, the early underconsumptionists were rightly accused of having an incomplete theory as long as they did not explain the path of investment as well as consumption.

The final criticism of the underconsumptionist long-run stagnation theory is the fact that profit expectations are not limited merely by demand, but also by cost considerations. In criticizing early underconsumptionists, Marx pointed out that the problem of the capitalist's making a profit has two stages. First, the capitalist must have the workers create a product with profit embodied in it by keeping costs low enough—including the costs of labor, the costs of raw materials, and the costs of plant and equipment (depreciation). Second, after such a profitable product has been created, it must be sold in order to realize the profit. The underconsumptionists tend to overlook the cost side of the problem.

This issue becomes apparent when some underconsumptionists argue that higher wages will resolve a crisis or prevent a depression. The problem is that higher wages not only create more demand (as both Keynes and Marx emphasized), but also mean higher costs per unit. Therefore, in Marx's terms, higher wages allow more realization of profit, but allow less production of profit. What each capitalist really wants is lower wages in his or her own plant, but also generation of higher purchasing power, which may require higher wages throughout the rest of the economy.

## MARX AND UNDERCONSUMPTION

The fact that Marx criticized the earlier simplistic underconsumption theories has been interpreted by some Marxists to mean that Marx opposed all theories focusing on lack of consumer demand or on lack of effective demand in general. In recent decades, a number of Marxists have made strident attacks on all demand or underconsumption theories. Some Marxists deny that there could be anything Marxist about any theory that concentrates on lack of effective demand. These Marxists, such as Shaikh (1978), seem to be worried that exclusive attention to this problem may lead to neglect of other problems that he considers more fundamental (see Chapter 11). Robert Cherry (1980) even makes the assertion that

"Marx believed that deficient demand would not create fundamental problems for capitalist societies" (p. 331).

Yet Marx stated his views on the importance of effective demand very clearly on many occasions. He wrote: "The ultimate cause of all real crises always remains the poverty and restricted consumption of the masses" (1909, vol. 3: 568). Marx argued that capitalist expansions are brought to an end by the limits imposed on consumption by the class structure:

> The epochs in which capitalist production exerts all its forces are always periods of overproduction, because the forces of production can never be utilized beyond the point at which surplus value can be not only produced but realized; but the sale of commodities, the realization of the . . . surplus value, is limited not only by the consumption requirements of society in general, but by the consumption requirements of a society in which the great majority are poor and must always remain poor. (1903, vol. 2: 363n)

It was Marx, not Keynes, who first systematically dissected Say's law by showing that lack of effective demand can cause mass unemployment in capitalism. It was Marx, not Keynes, who first demonstrated in his famous reproductive schema that dynamic equilibrium is possible in capitalism if, and only if, effective demand grows at a certain rate. It was Marx, not Keynes, who first showed that capitalists face not one, but two problems: (1) the problem of producing profit and (2) the problem of realizing profit.

It appears that Marx, unlike some of his followers, had a fairly balanced view that criticized some naive underconsumptionist formulations, but did emphasize the basic importance of the lack of demand. Certainly, for Marx, capitalist downturns are based, in part at least, on problems of realization of profit due to lack of demand (see the models of simple and expanded reproduction in volume 2 of Marx's *Capital* [1903])—though Marx also considered very different types of problems, which will be discussed in Chapter 11.

## KEYNES AND UNDERCONSUMPTION

John Maynard Keynes refers to the underconsumptionists only in passing as part of the underground in the economics profession. Yet he did more to emphasize the importance of the deficiency of effective demand than did any other human being. Keynes destroyed Say's law in a more rigorous fashion than did Marx. He analyzed the reasons for a growing gap between consumer demand and national income in an expansion.

Keynes's framework for exploring problems of effective demand is different from that of the early underconsumptionists in that it puts consumer demand and investment on the same footing with respect to aggregate demand. In Keynes's framework it is impossible to speak as if lack of consumer demand alone—without specifying investment—is sufficient to explain a downturn. (Keynes, of course, also considered government demand and net export demand, but these are ignored for simplicity in this chapter.)

Keynes's contributions on effective demand, the role of consumption, and the importance of income distribution have been expanded and formalized by the Post-Keynesians, who follow Keynes in these three important aspects of business cycle research (see any issue of the *Journal of Post-Keynesian Economics*). Many Post-Keynesians have also incorporated the insights of Michal Kalecki, who combined some aspects of Keynesian and Marxist approaches, though he first wrote independently before Keynes had elaborated his views on these points.

## AN UNDERCONSUMPTIONIST (OR REALIZATION OR DEMAND-SIDE) BUSINESS CYCLE THEORY

Underconsumptionist theories are often assumed to be stagnationist by definition. It is perfectly possible, however, to present a business cycle theory from an underconsumptionist perspective that presents a logically complete view of the cycle. If one does not wish to call it underconsumptionist, then a Post-Keynesian could call it a theory of effective demand, while a Marxist could call it a theory of profit realization.

A demand-side or profit realization or underconsumptionist theory of the business cycle may be stated within the framework of Marx's reproduction schema or in the framework of Keynes's aggregate relationships, on which the U.S. national income accounts are based. Marx's framework can be translated into the Keynesian-based U.S. national income accounting schema as follows. First, Marx used two sectors of production, consumer goods and producer goods, which must equal the demand for those two sectors if there is to be an equilibrium. Keynes would say that it is a condition of equilibrium that the total output supplied (the real national income) equal the aggregate consumer spending plus the aggregate investment spending. In terms of the Keynesian-based national income accounts,

$$\text{National income } (Y) = \text{Consumption } (C) + \text{Investment } (I). \quad (9.1)$$

Second, Marx divides the national income into surplus value (profit, rent, and interest), and the value of variable capital (wages, salaries, and benefits). Keynes would say that income is divided into a stream going to recipients of labor income (wages, salaries, and benefits) and a stream going to recipients of property income (profit, rent, and interest). In terms of the Keynesian-based national income accounts,

National income $(Y)$ = Property income $(R)$ + Labor income $(W)$.

$$(9.2)$$

Note that in the national income accounts, labor income is called employee compensation, while property income is all income that is not employee compensation.

This framework portrays the supply and demand for the two sectors as well as the aggregate property income and aggregate labor income paid out by both sectors. Keynes normally discussed aggregate income, rather than treating labor and property income separately, but he was acutely aware of the importance of the distribution of income. The distinction between labor and property income is crucial in most underconsumptionist models and is incorporated in most Post-Keynesian theories (see the survey in Eichner and Kregal [1975]).

*The Consumption Function*

Obviously, an underconsumptionist theory must have a clearly defined consumption function. The basic thrust of such a consumption function is that consumer demand is influenced not only by the amount of national income, but also by the distribution of national income between labor and property owners.

Anther way to say the same thing is to assert that the propensity to consume is a positive function of the labor share. When the labor share rises, so that workers have a larger share of national income, the ratio of consumption to national income will also rise. When the labor share falls, so that property owners have a larger share of national income, the ratio of consumption to national income will also fall. In Keynesian terms, both the average and marginal propensities to consume are positively influenced by the labor share. In Chapter 5 it was shown that the evidence is consistent with this hypothesis.

A third way to say the same thing—and probably the simplest way to think about it—is to assert that consumer demand includes all of labor income plus some percentage of property income. In other words, wage workers spend all of their income for consumer goods, but capitalists spend only a portion of their income for consumption (and remember that property income includes corporate retained income, none of which is used for consumption). Also remember that there is a time lag between the receipt of income and its expenditure. Thus, we may say that

Consumption $(C)$ = part of Property income $(R)$, lagged
+ all of Labor income $(W)$, lagged. $\qquad (9.3)$

It should be noted that this formulation—in which all of wages are consumed—is an oversimplification because the percentage of wages consumed is sometimes somewhat below 100 percent by the usual accounting (see evidence in Chapter 5). A consumption function of this type was
used in 1935 in the pioneering work of Michal Kalecki (see Kalecki 1968,
53; also see discussion in Sawyer [1985b, ch. 4]).

In fact, all wages need not be spent for consumption to support the
underconsumptionist thesis. It is only necessary that the marginal propensity to consume out of labor income should be significantly higher
than the marginal propensity to consume out of property income. This
fact was confirmed by almost all the empirical investigations reported in
Chapter 5. It was also shown in Chapter 5 that the evidence is compatible
with the hypothesis that the average propensity to consume is a positive
function of the labor share. In that case, with a given amount of national
income, consumer demand will be greater if income is shifted from property income to labor income. Consumer demand will be less, however, if
income is shifted from labor income to property income. We must examine the distribution function to find out what does happen to the
shares of labor and property income according to this theory.

## The Distribution Function

In the Marxist view, the struggle in the production process over distribution of income between capital and labor reflects the exploitation of
labor under capitalist relations of production. That must be the starting
point for any Marxist theory. What is important here, however, is the
cyclical movement of the shares of income of capital and labor. This issue
was explored in detail in Chapter 8. The important finding from an underconsumptionist point of view is that the profit share (and the rate of
exploitation) generally rises throughout the expansion and falls throughout the contraction. Of course, this means that the labor share generally
falls throughout the expansion and rises throughout the contraction. This
finding is quite compatible with Marxist, Post-Keynesian, and institutionalist ways of looking at the economy. (On institutionalist macroeconomics, see the survey in Dugger [1989].)

The underconsumptionists usually rely on the wage lag hypothesis,
giving all of the reasons that capitalist institutions hold back wages from
rising as rapidly as profits in a capitalist expansion. These reasons were
spelled out in great detail in Chapter 8 and need not be repeated in detail
here. The real wage rises in expansions and falls in contractions, but national income and profits rise and fall more rapidly. The conclusion is that
the labor share falls throughout the expansion, while it rises throughout
the contraction.

It was found in Chapter 8 that the labor share is a negative function of the ratio of capacity utilization, which is obviously consistent with the fact that capacity utilization is strongly procyclical while the labor share is countercyclical. But capacity utilization also marches in step with real national income to a large extent. When income and output are rising, more capacity is utilized. Thus we could also say that the labor share is a negative function of real national income. A rising national income is usually accompanied by a falling labor share, while declining national income is usually accompanied by a rising labor share.

The simplest possible representation of this relationship is to show the labor share as a constant minimum (the long-run subsistence wage?) plus some fixed percentage of real national income:

$$\text{Labor income } (W) = \text{constant} + \text{percentage of} \\ \text{National income } (Y). \tag{9.4}$$

As national income rises, labor income rises, but it rises more slowly. As national income falls in a contraction, labor income falls, but it falls more slowly. On these assumptions, the labor share $(W/Y)$ is countercyclical—because the ratio of labor income to national income falls in expansions and rises in contractions. Since the property share must always move in the opposite direction to the labor share (because they are dividing one pie between them), the property share $(R/Y)$ must be procyclical. A similar distribution function was first used in 1935 by Kalecki (see Kalecki 1968, 40; also see discussion in Sawyer [1985b, ch. 2]).

The countercyclical behavior of the labor share is important to underconsumptionists because it affects the amount of consumer demand. A falling labor share in the expansion has a negative effect on consumer demand, while a rising labor share in the contraction will have a positive effect on consumer demand.

## The Investment Function

An underconsumptionist business cycle theory may make use of the simplest version of the accelerator. It says that net investment is a function of the previous change in aggregate demand. Specifically,

$$\text{Investment } (I) = \text{Accelerator } (v) \\ \times \text{ change in National income } (Y). \tag{9.5}$$

Given this relationship, as was shown in chapter 7, when national income begins to rise more slowly, net investment will actually decline. Net investment is thus the catalyst for a cyclical downturn (or a cyclical upturn) in this underconsumptionist business cycle model. Unlike the long-run stagnation models, this cyclical model makes the investment function one of the key foundations of its theory.

Of course, the largest component of national output is consumer goods and services. The decline in the growth of national output or income, therefore, is based mainly on the decline in the growth of consumer demand. But the decline in consumer demand affects the cycle mainly through its effect on investment, via the accelerator.

The earliest underconsumptionist theories based the accelerator not on changes in aggregate demand, as in most modern models, but on changes in consumer demand, as in Samuelson's (1939) original model. Using this formulation, a decline in the rate of growth of consumer demand leads to an absolute decline in net investment, which leads to a recession or depression. While this formulation is appropriate to an underconsumptionist model, it cannot be upheld because it leaves out the significant effect of the investment goods industries themselves on investment. In other words, the demand for machinery originates not only in industries producing consumer goods, but also in industries producing producers' goods—even machines need other machines to produce them. The underconsumption model works perfectly well if investment is based on aggregate demand because consumption is by far the largest part of aggregate demand.

One last way to look at the investment process is in terms of the profit rate, as discussed in detail in Chapter 6. It is perfectly possible in an underconsumptionist model to assume that net investment is a function of the change in the profit rate or the change in total profits, or both. An investment function based on both profits and the profit rate was first explored in formal terms in 1935 in an important contribution by Kalecki (see Kalecki 1968, ch. 9; also see Sawyer 1985b, ch. 3).

The theory must then explain how the profit rate is determined. In an underconsumptionist model the emphasis is on the realization of profit through the demand for products (ignoring costs of production). Thus, it would be necessary to assume that the profit rate is itself a function of the aggregate demand. This formulation might be a more elegant way to state the model because it emphasizes the role of the profit, and its dependence on realization through adequate demand. A simpler underconsumptionist model, using the usual accelerator, does not explicitly consider profit, except in its role as consumer demand by profit recipients. But the simpler models and the more elegant underconsumptionist models do operate in about the same way.

## OPERATION OF THE UNDERCONSUMPTIONIST CYCLE MODEL

We must ask the usual questions as to the causes of expansion, downturns, contraction, and recovery in this theory (using the simple version stated in equations 9.1 to 9.5).

*What Are the Causes of Cumulative Expansion?*

As recovery begins, national income is rising, including both property income and labor income. The rising national income causes more consumer spending, leading to more output demanded. As output demanded rises, this leads—through the accelerator principle—to more net investment. The new investment means more employment and income (both wages and profits), which leads to increased spending on consumption and—through the multiplier—to a further rise in national income. Thus, this model makes use of a multiplier-accelerator interaction as the cause of a cumulative expansion. The basic difference from Samuelson's model is that the increase in income is separated into property income and labor income, which have different impacts.

*What Are the Causes of the Downturn?*

As the expansion continues, the rising output is accompanied by a declining labor share. The reasons include the continued unemployment in the early expansion, the fact that wage bargains are usually fixed for some time period, the fact that capitalists automatically own any increased product due to higher productivity, and the fact that productivity does rise in expansion. In this picture of the economy, the distribution function says that during expansion income does indeed shift from labor to property income.

The consumption function in the underconsumptionist model says that consumption depends, not only on total national income, but on how it is divided between labor and property income. In other words, rising real wages lead to higher levels of consumption. But in the average expansion real wages rise more slowly than do real profits, so the marginal propensity to consume falls. Labor income has a much higher propensity to consume than does property income. If the marginal propensity to consume falls, it follows that if national income were constant, consumption would shrink. In fact, in the expansion, national income is growing, so both labor income and property income are growing, even though property income is growing faster. Therefore, the combined result of the behavior of the distribution function and the consumption function is that consumer demand grows, but more and more slowly because of the shifting income distribution.

The slower growth of consumer demand is reflected in a slower growth of aggregate demand. The accelerator principle says that when aggregate output demanded grows more slowly, net investment will decline absolutely. This decline of net investment means less income and employment, so a contraction begins.

## What Causes the Cumulative Downturn?

The decline in net investment causes—through the negative effect of the multiplier process on consumer spending—a greater decline in national income (with declines in both property income and labor income. The fall in national income causes—through the accelerator principle—a still further decline in net investment. As this process repeats itself, a cumulative decline results.

## What Causes the Recovery?

As the decline continues, labor income falls more slowly than does property income (for all the same reasons that it rises more slowly in expansion, but in reverse). The consequent rise in the labor share raises the marginal propensity to consume. The higher marginal propensity to consume helps stop the decline in aggregate consumption and in aggregate output demanded. The slower decline in aggregate output demanded leads eventually to a small increase in net investment. This sets off the recovery and a cumulative expansion ensues.

### EVALUATION OF THE UNDERCONSUMPTIONIST CYCLE THEORY

The underconsumptionist cycle theory produces a model that is complete and consistent within itself. Moreover, none of its assumptions are inconsistent with the evidence presented in Chapters 5, 6, and 8. This is an important achievement.

The model also overcomes some of the alleged weaknesses of the long-run stagnation theories of underconsumption. First, unlike the stagnation models, it fully explains the recovery and expansion process as well as the downturn and contraction. Second, unlike some of the earlier stagnation models, it does have a clear and coherent investment function. It can explain a downturn not merely in terms of a lack of consumer demand, but in terms of a lack of aggregate demand, combining the behavior of consumption and investment.

The remaining weakness of the underconsumption model, however, is the fact that it leaves out of consideration all of the evidence concerning the cyclical behavior of costs. It says nothing about labor costs, raw material costs, or interest costs. Yet this is a severe limitation. The theory alleges that consumer demand is limited because income shifts from labor to property income. That shift means lower demand, but it also means lower costs per unit. Admitting that the lower demand will mean problems in realizing the profits, it nevertheless does not consider the fact that investment demand might be raised by the lower costs per unit.

Finally, this model is complete in the logical sense that it tells a consistent story, but it is very incomplete in the sense that it leaves out some very important aspects of reality. These important variables are brought into theoretical consideration in this book as follows: Money and credit are discussed in Chapter 14; the impact of monopoly power is considered in Chapter 15; international relationships are explored in Chapter 16; and government behavior is analyzed in Chapter 17. Each of these variables has a group of economists who contend that macroeconomic analysis should concentrate on that variable. Indeed, no model is complete without consideration of all of these variables. Yet no theory can discuss everything in the world at once, so it is better to approach our complex reality by beginning with a simple abstract model and gradually adding to it in successive approximations. Such abstraction is necessary and legitimate as long as one remembers that the model is not complete until all of the important variables, such as the finance system and the international economy, are fully considered.

APPENDIX 9.1
FORMALIZING THE UNDERCONSUMPTION CYCLE MODEL

A simple, basic version of the underconsumption model will be presented, followed by a somewhat more complex and elegant version. In both cases, the model is restricted to the private domestic economy, so government activity and net exports are omitted. All variables are in real terms.

*A Basic Underconsumption Model*

This model consists of five relationships, the first two being identities or definitions. First, as a condition of equilibrium, it is necessary that the output supplied (which is equivalent to the real national income) equal the consumer demand plus the investment demand:

National income = Consumption + Investment,

expressed as

$$Y_t = C_t + I_t, \tag{9.6}$$

where $C$ is real consumption, $Y$ is real national income, $I$ is real investment, and $t$ is a time period.

Second, following a post-Keynesian or Marxist approach, the national income must be divided into wage and profits, or more precisely, into labor income and property income:

National income = Property income + Labor income,

expressed as

$$Y_t = R_t + W_t, \tag{9.7}$$

where $R$ is property income (mostly profits) and $W$ is labor income (mostly wages).

Third, turning to behavioral assumptions, it is supposed that labor income rises and falls more slowly than national income:

Labor income = constant + percentage of National income,

expressed as

$$W_t = w + gY_t, \tag{9.8}$$

where $c$ and $g$ are constants and $g$ is between zero and 1.

Fourth, another behavioral assumption is that consumption is determined by spending out of property income and out of labor income and that the former has a much lower marginal propensity to consume than the latter. For simplicity, it is assumed that all labor income is consumed. Thus,

Consumption = constant + part of Profits, lagged
+ all of Wages, lagged,

expressed as

$$C_t = a + bR_{t-1} + W_{t-1}, \tag{9.9}$$

where $a$ and $b$ are constants and $b$ is between zero and 1.

Fifth and last, the behavior of investment is assumed to be determined by the accelerator principle:

Investment = Accelerator × change in National income,

expressed as

$$I_t = v(Y_{t-1} - Y_{t-2}), \tag{9.10}$$

where $v$ is the accelerator coefficient.

By successive substitutions, this set of five equations and five variables can be reduced to one equation in one variable. That reduced-form equation is

$$Y_t = H + AY_{t-1} - BY_{t-2}, \tag{9.11}$$

where $H = a + w - bw$, $A = b - bg + g + v$, and $B = v$. There will be cycles if $A^2$ is less than $4B$. The cycles will be of constant amplitude if $B = 1$, damped if $B$ is less than 1, and explosive if $B$ is greater than 1.

*A More Elegant Underconsumptionist Model*

Once again, the model begins with the equilibrium condition that

National income = Consumption + Investment,

expressed as

$$Y_t = C_t + I_t. \tag{9.6}$$

Second, the consumption function may be rewritten to say explicitly that it includes the influence of both the level of national income and the functional distribution of income, reflected in the labor share:

$$C_t = a + bY_{t-1} + c(W/Y)_{t-1}, \tag{9.12}$$

where $a$, $b$, and $c$ are constants. Consumption increases with a higher level of national income, but also with a higher labor share.

Third, the labor share may be specified to be a negative function of the national income:

$$W/Y_t = w - gY_t, \tag{9.13}$$

where $g$ and $w$ are constants. The labor share falls as national income rises, but rises when national income falls.

Fourth, investment is a function of the change in the profit rate:

$$I_t = v(R/K_{t-1} - R/K_{t-2}), \tag{9.14}$$

where $v$ is a constant. Investment responds to changes in the rate of profit.

Fifth, the rate of profit is assumed to be a function of the aggregate output demanded:

$$R/K_t = rY_t, \tag{9.15}$$

where $r$ is a constant.

This model has five variables and five equations. By successive substitutions, it may be reduced to one equation in one variable. In terms of national income, the reduced form equation is

$$Y_t = H + AY_{t-1} - BY_{t-2}, \tag{9.16}$$

where $H = a + cw$, $A = b - cg + rv$, and $B = rv$. There will be cycles if $A^2$ is less than $4B$. The cycles will be of constant amplitude if $B = 1$, damped if $B$ is less than 1, and explosive if $B$ is greater than 1.

# CHAPTER 10

# Cost of Plant, Equipment, and Raw Materials

MANY THEORISTS, from completely different viewpoints, have argued that a key factor in the business cycle may be that capitalist profits are hurt in the expansion phase by disproportionate rises in the prices of capital goods, that is, plant, equipment, and raw materials. In the contraction phase, on the other hand, profits are helped by disproportionate declines in the price of capital goods. This chapter notes very briefly the theoretical approaches to this subject (which are discussed at length in the next chapter), and then discusses the empirical findings in this area.

## THEORETICAL VIEWS OF CAPITAL COSTS OVER THE CYCLE

One of the first to discuss the cyclical behavior of capital costs was Marx. He stated that in the expansion phase just before the peak, the rapid increase of investment leads to rising costs of capital goods, lowering profit margins (see Marx [1905] 1952, 371; also discussed in detail in Chapter 11 of this book). Many neoclassical economists of the group called nonmonetary overinvestment theorists put a similar stress on this factor of the business cycle; the most important such theorist was Hayek (see Haberler 1960, ch. 3; also discussed in detail in Chapter 11 of this book). In addition to the obvious point that a boom in investment tends to raise prices of capital goods, many of these theorists stressed the importance of the accelerator principle. Because of the operation of that principle, demand for plant and equipment rises faster than does demand for consumer goods, while demand for raw materials rises most rapidly of all.

## PREVIOUS EMPIRICAL STUDIES OF DIFFERENTIAL PRICE CHANGES

All of the books of Wesley Mitchell (for example, 1913, 1951) have discussed the different rates of change in various prices as a cause of the business cycle. Mitchell points out that in the recovery phase of the cycle the prices of raw materials remain fairly low at first because there are large stocks of them in reserve, left over from the recession. By the prosperity phase of expansion, however, these reserves are exhausted, so the costs of raw materials rise rapidly. Mitchell notes that these rapidly rising costs cut into profit margins because they rise faster than output prices.

This negative effect, however, is somewhat balanced by the fact that the wages of production labor and the salaries of overhead labor lag behind output costs, so workers continue to be a source of increasing profit: "For, while the prices of raw materials and wares bought for resale usually, and the prices of bank loans often, rise faster than selling prices; the prices of labor lag far behind, and prices that make up supplementary (overhead) costs are mainly stereotyped for a time by old agreements concerning salaries, leases, and bonds" (Mitchell 1941, 152–53).

In other words, by the middle of expansion, rising raw material prices and rising interest rates have become negative factors for business profits, but the lag of wages and overhead costs still increases profits. Mitchell gives several reasons why output prices do not rise as rapidly as do raw material costs: (1) public regulation of some prices; (2) long-term contracts for purchases by retailers; and (3) the possibility that the vast new supply of goods in the expansion may outrun the consumer demand (but Mitchell says he does not yet have sufficient evidence on this last point).

A considerable number of Mitchell's followers at the National Bureau of Economic Research (NBER) have conducted empirical research in this area (most of these studies are listed in Moore [1983, 175]; see also the detailed study by Thor Hultgren [1965]). The fascinating NBER study by Ruth Mack (1956) finds that prices of shoes fluctuate less than does the price of leather, which fluctuates less than does the price of hides. Geoffrey Moore (1962), long associated with the NBER, surveyed the existing empirical studies of costs and profit margins and concluded: "Of course, like the two blades of the proverbial scissors, both prices and costs determine margins, but costs have generally been the widely moving element accounting for the leads in margins" (p. 11). It is clear that costs play a major role in the cycle, but it is very controversial as to whether demand or costs play the larger role—and it depends to some extent on which period we are discussing.

The best historical study is the NBER report by Frederick Mills (1946), who investigated the cyclical pattern of different categories of prices averaged over many business cycles (from three to twenty cycles), all ending in 1938. He provides data on the prices of twenty-two consumer goods, prices of forty-eight producers' goods (excluding raw materials), and prices of thirty-two raw materials. He found that during the average expansion the price of consumer goods rose 12 percent (as a percentage of the cycle base), the price of plant and equipment rose 21 percent, and the price of raw materials rose 23 percent and that during the average contraction the price of consumer goods fell 18 percent, the price of plant and equipment fell 25 percent, and the price of raw materials fell 26 percent. Thus, the cyclical price fluctuations of consumer goods were least strong, price fluctuations of plant and equipment were in the middle, and prices of raw materials fluctuated the most.

The main explanation for this price behavior by most writers is a combination of accelerated demand with much less fluctuation of supply. In the accelerator theory, a rapid rate of growth of demand for goods and services results in a greater percentage growth of demand for raw materials and other producer's goods—because it is a derived demand based on the change, rather than the level of output of consumer goods. Similarly, when the demand for finished goods and services declines in contraction, the demand for raw materials and other producer goods declines even more rapidly (because of the accelerator).

During the expansion, the supply of raw materials is much harder to expand than the supply of finished goods. Increasing the production of shoes can be done far more quickly than can increasing production of cattle hides, since cattle take a certain number of years to grow. As a result, in each expansion, the quantity of raw materials rises more slowly than does the quantity of finished goods, while the price of raw materials rises more rapidly than does the price of finished goods. (Since a certain amount of raw materials is required for a given output of finished goods, the slower rise in raw materials production means depletion of raw material inventories and a "rationing" effect resulting from higher prices and may eventually mean shortages of raw materials in some periods of rapid expansion.) Similarly, in a depression the flow of manufactured goods may be quickly reduced, but raw materials such as industrial crops already planted cannot be cut so fast. Thus, in a depression, the quantity of raw materials usually declines less than that of finished goods, while the price of raw materials usually declines more than that of finished goods.

The data of Wesley Mitchell (1951, 312–21) indicate the same conclusions. In the average expansion of the four cycles from 1921 to 1938, the price of finished goods rose only 8.6 percent, while the price of raw materials rose 16.0 percent. In the average contraction of the same four cycles, the price of finished goods fell 13.0 percent, but the price of raw materials fell 21.9 percent.

## CYCLICAL PRICE MOVEMENTS, 1949–1970

The picture of differential price movements is very different after World War II because of the existence of inflation in much of the period. In most cases we are talking about rates of growth of prices continuing in the contraction phases as well as the expansion phases. For various reasons, there is also little difference between the cyclical patterns of consumer goods prices and plant and equipment prices in the period since

World War II. There continue to be striking differences between consumer goods prices and raw materials prices, so it is these differences that we will examine (keeping in mind that whatever we say about consumer goods prices is fairly similar to what could be said about plant and equipment prices). Thus, all finished goods prices move together in the same inflationary pattern, while raw material goods prices move differently.

In the 1949–1970 period, that is, the 1950s and 1960s, the consumer price index mostly kept rising. It rose 10.8 percent in the average expansion, but continued to rise by 2.4 percent in the average business contraction. Contrariwise, the price index of crude materials showed practically no change in this entire period—or, rather, its many ups and downs did not conform to the business cycle, and there was no long-run trend. Thus, in the average expansion, the price index of crude materials changed only − 0.2 percent, while in the average contraction it changed only 0.1 percent (all data in this section and the next section refer to series #320 and #331 in U.S. Department of Commerce 1984).

Why did raw material prices remain unchanged for this lengthy period? Because it is a central issue, the literature on development is full of discussions of this question—with some economists alleging that it was the power of imperialism that kept the price of raw materials from rising to reflect the general world inflation. Many other conditions of supply and demand (beyond the scope of this book) also have been considered. The long-run implication, of course, was that the terms of trade were moving against the raw material commodities of the Third World—and in favor of the finished goods of the industrialized capitalist countries.

What were the cyclical implications for U.S. business? Since most raw materials were imported, in the expansions, the rise of finished goods prices combined with the lack of change in raw material prices meant that the profits of U.S. firms were increased. In the contractions, the rise of finished goods prices combined with the lack of change of raw material prices again meant that the profits of U.S. firms were increased. Thus, in contrast to cycles in previous eras, the differential movements of raw material prices and finished goods prices were a positive factor for U.S. business throughout the business cycle.

## CYCLICAL PRICE MOVEMENTS, 1970–1982

A very different picture is revealed in the 1970–1982 period, in which the theories and facts of earlier periods again became relevant, with Marx and Hayek again providing models of excellent prediction. The only difference from the cycles of the 1920s and 1930s as to cyclical pattern is that this was a period of even greater inflation than in the 1950s and

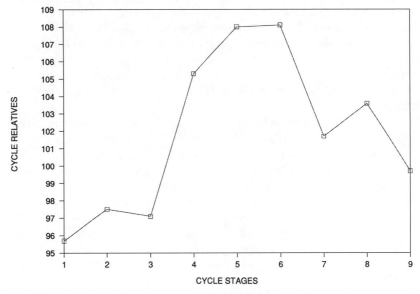

Fig. 10.1 Crude Prices/Consumer Prices Ratio: Amplitude by Stage Averaged across Three Cycles, 1970–1982 (from series 331/320, Appendix E)

1960s. Nevertheless, after allowing for inflation the differential price movements are those predicted by theory.

In the whole period, 1970–1982, the consumer price index rose during cyclical expansions an average of 21.8 percent, while the price index of crude materials actually rose by an average of 37.8 percent. Thus, in the average expansion phase, the aggregate profits of U.S. business were reduced by the greater rise in raw material prices, mostly imported from abroad.

In the average contraction of the 1970–1982 period, the consumer price index continued to rise by 9.2 percent, while the price index of crude materials rose only 1.0 percent. Thus, in the average contraction phase, the aggregate profits of U.S. firms were helped greatly by the lack of change in raw material prices, mostly imported from abroad.

The differential price movements are presented in Figure 10.1. This graph shows clearly that the ratio of crude material prices to consumer goods prices rises rapidly in the average expansion, but falls quite considerably in the average contraction. More precisely, the ratio of crude material prices to consumer prices rose by 0.72 percent per quarter in the average expansion, while falling by 1.51 percent per quarter in the average contraction.

The different movements of this ratio over the cycle in the two periods can also be investigated through a simple econometric test (shown in Appendix 10.1). The ratio of capacity utilization is strongly procyclical and may be assumed to reflect forces of demand in the business cycle. In the 1950s and 1960s, there is no significant relationship between the ratio of crude material prices to consumer prices and the ratio of capacity utilization. In the 1970s and 1980s, on the other hand, there is a strong and significant positive relation between the ratio of crude material prices to consumer prices and the ratio of capacity utilization.

## CONCLUSIONS

Except for the period of the 1950s and 1960s, raw material prices rose much faster than did finished goods prices in the average expansion. In the average business contraction, however, raw material prices fell much faster (or rose much less) than did finished goods prices. This meant that, except for the period of the 1950s and 1960s, profits of U.S. firms were hurt by this differential price movement in expansions, but were helped by it in contractions. The theoretical implications of this fact for supply-side cycle theories are discussed in the next chapter.

## APPENDIX 10.1
## FORMAL ECONOMETRICS EXPLAINING THE RATIO OF RAW MATERIALS PRICES TO FINISHED GOODS PRICES

The ratio of raw materials prices ($M$) to all finished goods prices ($P$) is procyclical in most periods. It may therefore be explained as a function of the ratio of capacity utilization—or the ratio of actual output ($Y$) to potential output at full capacity ($Z$)—which is strongly procyclical in all eras and periods of capitalist history. In equation form,

$$M/P_t = f(Y_t/Z_t), \qquad (10.1)$$

where the ratio of raw material to consumer prices is a positive function of the ratio of capacity utilization.

The data used here are defined in Appendix A, with all data being quarterly and expressed as rates. The ratio of raw materials prices ($M$, series #331) to the consumer price index ($P$, series #320) was regressed against the ratio of capacity utilization ($Y/Z$, series #82) for the two different periods discussed in the text. The results for the period from 1953 to 1970 are

$$M/P_t = 89.2 + 0.06Y/Z_t \qquad (10.2)$$
$$(9.4) \qquad (0.7)$$
$$CR^2 = 0.97 \quad DW = 1.60.$$

Although there appears to be high correlation, there is significant auto-correlation, even though the ARMA method of correcting for autocorrelation was used, so the correlation must not be trusted. Moreover, the *t*-statistics shows that the regression coefficient for capacity utilization is not statistically significant.

If we use the same data source, with all data again being quarterly and expressed as rates, the results for the period from 1970 through 1988 are

$$M/P_t = 37.1 + 0.78Y/Z_t \qquad (10.3)$$
$$(1.4) \qquad (3.0)$$
$$CR_2 = 0.92 \quad DW = 1.99.$$

In this period, there is still quite a high correlation, but now there is no significant autocorrelation. Moreover, the *t*-statistic for capacity utilization is now statistically significant at the .01 confidence level.

The econometric conclusion is that there was no significant correlation between the ratio of raw material prices to consumer prices and the ratio of capacity utilization in the 1950s and 1960s, but there was a statistically significant correlation in the 1970s and 1980s (when both were procyclical).

# CHAPTER 11

# Overinvestment and Reserve Army
# Theories of the Business Cycle:
# A Walk on the Supply Side

MANY DIFFERENT THEORIES of business cycles emphasize supply-side problems, the production process, the cost of production, or excess consumption and overinvestment—rather than the problems of effective demand, underconsumption, and excess saving emphasized in Chapter 9. First, the most popular supply-side theory is the view that too high a rate of taxation will dry up savings and also make people less willing to work. These theories have come to be called supply-side theories in recent decades, but they are only one type of supply-side argument (and they are not mainly cyclical theories). They were presented among the exogenous theories considered in Chapter 3, and similar arguments will be encountered when government policy is discussed in Chapter 18, but this type of theory is not discussed here because this chapter is limited to the private economy, not the role of government.

Second, also concerned with the supply side of the economy are most of the theories known as monetary overinvestment theories, monetary theories, or monetarism. But these theories all relate to money, interest rates, credit, and the financial system, so they will be discussed in detail in Chapter 14, which is on that subject.

Third, there is a long-run Marxist stagnation view called the organic composition of capital theory. Since it is not a cycle theory, it is not discussed in this book. There is an enormous literature on this theory; see, for example, Shaikh (1978), Yaffe (1973), Fine and Harris (1976), Bell (1977), and Weisskopf (1978).

Fourth, there is an important set of theories that may be called nonmonetary overinvestment theories; most of them argue that the problem is the high cost of plant, equipment, and raw materials, but some are concerned with falling output/capital ratios in the boom (the most interesting in recent years is that of Devine [1987]). These theories are discussed here. (All theorists mentioned in this chapter without an exact citation are discussed in Haberler [1960, ch. 3] in his discussion of overinvestment theories.)

Fifth, economists concerned with size and concentration, beginning with Wesley Mitchell, have noted that the entrance of more small, inexperienced firms in a boom may lower capital productivity, but that issue is left for the discussion of the cyclical effect of monopoly and competition in Chapter 15.

Sixth, there is the reserve army theory, which is concerned with the rising cost of labor as full employment is approached. We shall explore both long-run and short-run variants of the reserve army theory in this chapter.

## MARX ON CYCLICAL BEHAVIOR OF SHORT-RUN CAPITAL COSTS

Karl Marx discussed the rising price of capital goods as a normal occurrence in expansions:

> The . . . phenomenon (and this as a rule proceeds crises) can occur if the production of surplus value [profit] takes place at a very rapid rate, and its retransformation into productive capital so increases the demand for all the elements of the latter that real production cannot keep pace, and consequently there is a rise in the prices of all the commodities which enter into the formation of capital. (Marx [1905] 1952, 371)

Not only does Marx point to the rising cost of capital goods in an expansion, but he also shows how a fall in the price of capital goods is an important component of the adjustment process of capitalism in the depression. Marx describes this process in a very colorful manner:

> The principal work of destruction would show its most dire effects in a slaughtering of the values of capitals. . . . One portion of the commodities on the market can complete the process of circulation and reproduction only by an immense contraction of its prices. . . . The depreciation of the elements of constant capital [plant, equipment, and raw materials] itself would be another factor tending to raise the average rate of profit. . . . And in this way the cycle would be run once more. (Marx 1909, 297–99)

The falling costs of capital goods in the depression reduce total cost per unit for capitalists, raise the rate of profit for finished goods, and help cause a recovery.

A somewhat similar theory is put forth by Michal Kalecki (1968, ch. 1; also see Sawyer 1985b, ch. 2), who paid much attention to the relations between the price of final output and the price of capital goods, particularly raw materials, over the cycle. He contends that the greater price fluctuation of capital goods causes profit problems for most capitalists.

## NONMONETARY OVERINVESTMENT THEORY

Many economists, mostly quite conservative and anti-Marxist, have (like Marx) investigated how capital costs rise and fall in the business cycle;

these theorists include Spiethoff, Cassel, Tugan-Baranowski, and, in some respects, Hayek and Schumpeter (see Haberler 1960, ch. 3). All of them see the cycle as mainly one of the rise and fall of capital investment. Many such theorists refer to the fact that investment rises and falls more rapidly than consumption; some refer specifically to the accelerator principle. They emphasize that the demand for investment funds outruns the supply of saving, so that there is a "shortage of capital." They are concerned that there is too much consumption and not enough saving—exactly the opposite of Keynes and the underconsumptionists, but very much like the classical economists. The decline of the economy is attributed to rising prices of capital goods and/or higher interest rates and/or falling productivity of capital, leading to lower industrial profits.

Recovery in many of these theories depends on technological innovation. The greatest theorist of the cyclical impact of technology is Schumpeter (1939). Following Marx, he discusses in great detail the revolutionary nature of new innovations. He emphasizes the role of entrepreneurs in introducing these innovations and how, once a recovery is begun on the basis of some important new innovation, many other entrepreneurs crowd into the field to expand production and take advantage of the profit opportunities. Such an effect is undoubtedly important. The problem, however, is that Schumpeter offers no independent reason why such innovations should be cyclical in nature. He does a wonderful job of describing their spread, but that is after recovery has begun, not the cause of it. Entrepreneurs are usually very hesitant to introduce new innovations in a recession or depression because of the lack of a market. Thus, many later economists would accept Schumpeter's emphasis on technology, not only in the long run, as is obvious to everyone, but also in the business cycle—yet not as the cause of the cycle itself.

## HAYEK'S THEORY OF CAPITAL COSTS

All of those economists known as nonmonetary overinvestment theorists have argued that an "excessive" amount of investment in a business cycle expansion will mean that the demand for plant, equipment, and raw materials will outrun supply (for a survey, see Haberler [1960, ch. 3]). The excess demand raises the cost of purchasing these goods. Suppose that the price of the product made with this investment is constant or rises very slowly. The overinvestment theorists all assume that the price of finished goods rises more slowly than does their costs. In this case, the margin of profit per unit must fall, setting off a depression. Other nonmonetary overinvestment theorists are concerned that too close an approach to capacity limitations may cause chaotic supply conditions, some shortages, and a general lowering of the physical productivity of capital (see the provocative argument by Devine [1987, 275]).

The most important overinvestment theorist, Frederick Hayek (1939), pictures production as being ordered in a series of stages; each stage feeds the next one and is part of the cost of the next stage. Production of raw materials may be considered to be the first or earliest stage. The raw materials are then used, at a certain cost per unit, to produce plant and equipment in the second stage. The plant and equipment plus more raw materials—all called producers' goods or capital goods—are used to produce consumer goods in the third stage.

According to Hayek, in every expansion, the rising demand for consumer goods generates an even greater percentage increase in demand for plant and equipment. The fact that the demand for these capital goods, that is, investment, is more than proportionate to the increased demand for consumer goods is explained by the accelerator principle (discussed in Chapter 7). The large demand for plant and equipment in the second stage generates an even stronger demand (by a further accelerator) for raw materials.

The theory predicts that as a result of these pressures in expansions the price of consumer goods will rise least, the price of plant and equipment will rise more, and the price of raw materials will rise most. Hayek argues that the higher costs coming from the earlier stages eventually reduce profit margins in the later stages, thus causing a contraction.

In each contraction the accelerator works in reverse, causing a small decline in the output of consumer goods to be reflected in a much larger decline in investment in plant and equipment. Therefore, the price of plant and equipment must fall more than does the price of consumer goods. Because of a further accelerator, the demand for raw materials falls even faster than does the demand for plant and equipment. In addition, it takes time to reduce the supply of raw materials from agricultural operations (because planning must take place so far in advance). With a more rapid fall in demand and a slower fall in supply, the price of raw materials must fall much faster than does the price of finished goods. Hayek argues that the declining costs help stabilize profit margins at some point in the contraction—and this sets the stage for economic recovery.

Hayek's theory is pre-Keynesian, so it is impossible to express it exclusively in Keynesian aggregates; a model of it requires some disaggregation. The national income accounts do not include raw materials, but only the value of finished goods, which is supposed to include raw materials. Thus, a formal model of Hayek's theory would have to disaggregate the economy into a consumer sector, capital goods sector, and raw materials sector.

A more important problem is that Keynesian national income accounting includes an aggregate profit. Suppose raw material prices rise. All other things remaining constant, the profits of capitalists in consumer goods and plant and equipment production must decline. But the profits of capitalists in raw material production must rise an equal amount. In that case, it would appear that aggregate profits will remain constant.

Those stressing the importance of raw material prices may answer this argument in one of two ways. Hayek argues that demand for raw materials is strictly derived from demand for finished goods. If lower profit rates lead to an expected decline in production of finished goods, then the demand for raw materials and the expected profit in raw materials will decline. This will lead to a reduction of raw material production, regardless of the present profit in raw materials. Thus a downturn beginning in finished goods will quickly spread to raw materials. This argument has an important grain of truth, but it is a difficult theory to test because it uses a disaggregated model of the economy, that is, a division of the model into the three sectors of consumer goods and services, plant and equipment, and raw materials. Thus, the argument may be correct, but it has not yet been proven.

The second argument is much simpler. Suppose the economy of some one country imports all of its raw materials. Then rising raw material prices in the rest of the world will have a clear negative effect on profits in that country. For example, a high proportion of raw materials used in the United States comes from foreign sources. If the price of raw materials rises faster than does that of finished goods, then the profit rates of U.S. capitalists relying on imports of raw materials will be hurt. Thus, it appears that the disproportionate rise or decline of raw material prices (such as oil prices) could affect U.S. aggregate profits. These issues of international trade are discussed further in Chapter 16.

## AN OVERINVESTMENT MODEL OF THE CYCLE

We may utilize the main features of the various nonmonetary overinvestment theories to state a simple model of the business cycle—insofar as possible in the spirit in which they were written, but in terms of the usual national income accounting.

Leaving aside foreign and government demand, the condition of equilibrium is that output supplied equals consumer demand plus investment demand:

$$\text{National income } (Y) = \text{Consumption } (C) + \text{Investment } (I), \quad (11.1)$$

where supply adjusts to demand in each period, but demand may not equal the full employment level of supply.

## The Consumption Function

We must now explain the path of consumption and of investment over the cycle. The overinvestment theorists assume that there is no lack of consumer demand, so it may be simply assumed to be a constant proportion of income:

$$\text{Consumption } (C) = \text{a constant} \times \text{National income } (Y). \quad (11.2)$$

Since consumption clearly has no deficiency, we may turn to investment as the key variable.

## The Investment Function

All of the overinvestment theorists think in terms of the margin of profit above costs. It may therefore be assumed that the amount of new net investment is a function of the rate of profit:

$$\text{Investment } (I) = \text{function of change in rate of profit.} \quad (11.3)$$

A rising rate of profit inspires confidence in the future and causes net investment. A falling rate of profit makes entrepreneurs worry and prevents new net investment.

## Definition of Profit Rate

The profit rate on capital can be thought of as the property or profit share of output times the ratio of output to capital:

$$\begin{aligned} \text{Profit rate } (R/K) = {} & \text{Property share } (R/Y) \\ & \times \text{Output/Capital } (Y/K). \end{aligned} \quad (11.4)$$

This is an identity, true by definition. It is, however, a very useful definition for this theory because it separates out the distribution of income between labor and property owners as one component, while making a separate component of the ratio of output to capital. The output to capital ratio depends on both the physical product of capital (with labor) and the cost of capital goods, including plant, equipment, and raw materials. (It should be noted that this definition leaves out the degree of capacity utilization, reflecting demand, but these theories do not emphasize demand.)

## The Distribution Function

The overinvestment theories are not directly concerned with the distribution of income between labor and property; at least, that is not where they concentrate their attention. Therefore, we may simply assume that both the labor share and the property share remain constant proportions of the total output:

$$\text{Property share } (R/Y) = \text{a constant } (k). \tag{11.5}$$

This assumption means that the distribution of income plays no important role in this model.

### The Cost Function

Finally we come to the active, crucial part of the model. The ratio of output to capital reflects both physical quantities and relative prices. The output may be divided into quantity of output ($Q^y$) and price of finished output ($P^y$). Similarly, the capital may be divided into the quantity of capital goods ($Q^k$) and the price of capital goods ($P^k$). The physical ratio of the quantity of output to the quantity of capital is governed in the long run by technology. But this is a short-run cycle model in which we may hold technology to be more or less constant. The physical ratio could decline if production were pushed beyond the optimum level of capacity utilization, as some overinvestment theorists have assumed, but there is no good evidence for this. Others have speculated that the physical ratio of output to capital may be lowered before the peak of expansion by the entrance of large numbers of small, inexperienced firms.

The main thrust of Hayek's model, however, is that the ratio of finished output prices to the prices of capital goods (including plant, equipment, and raw materials) must decline as the expansion continues. In Chapter 10, it was found that this assumption is indeed true. In many previous cycles, consumer goods prices fluctuated less than did all capital goods prices. At present, the prices of plant and equipment fluctuate about the same as consumer prices do. But the price of raw materials still fluctuates much more than do consumer prices, so it may be asserted that all capital goods prices fluctuate more than do all finished goods prices. It follows that the ratio of output prices to capital goods prices will fall in expansions as output is rising—and will rise in contractions as output is falling. This rise in an important price/cost ratio is considered of vital importance in these theories.

Some overinvestment theorists assert that the physical ratio of output to capital declines in expansions, while others assert that the price ratio of output to capital declines in an expansion. Both versions of overinvestment theory give us reason to believe that the ratio of the dollar value of output (revenue) to the dollar value of capital (cost of all producer goods) will decline as output expands and will rise as output declines:

$$\text{Output/Capital } (Y/K) = \text{negative function of Output level.} \tag{11.6}$$

As this ratio declines in an expansion, the rising cost per unit will lower the profit rate, which causes less investment, causing a recession or depression.

## OPERATION OF THE OVERINVESTMENT THEORY

Let us ask the usual questions to see how this theory explains the business cycle.

### How Is the Downturn Explained?

In this model, a rising rate of profit leads to greater investment. The new investment leads to more output. But as the level of output rises, the ratio of output prices to capital goods prices declines—and perhaps also as full capacity is approached, the physical output to capital ratio may decline. At any rate the revenue from output does not rise as rapidly as does the cost of capital goods for new investment. Therefore, all other things being equal, the rate of profit rises more slowly and eventually declines. The stagnant or declining rate of profit leads to a decline in investment. The decline in investment lowers output and income, so a recession or depression ensues.

### How Is the Recovery Explained?

The falling rate of profit causes less investment, which leads to less output. As the contraction progresses, however, the cost of capital goods (at least raw material costs) falls faster than do the prices of finished output. The physical output to capital ratio may also rise when the economy retreats from its capacity ceiling and when the most inefficient firms go bankrupt in the depression. Therefore, the revenue from output does not decline as rapidly as does the cost of capital goods. Eventually, the rate of profit declines very slowly or starts to rise. The better profit expectations cause a recovery of investment, which leads to greater output and employment.

## EVALUATION OF THE OVERINVESTMENT THEORY

Nonmonetary overinvestment theories have added to our understanding of the business cycle by the attention paid to price/cost ratios. The ratios of prices to costs, involving a microeconomic perspective, were not often investigated in the peak period of Keynesian economics, but they are an important part of the story.

On the other hand, theories such as Hayek's do not consider other types of costs, such as labor costs. Above all, they do not consider problems of demand, without which one cannot understand the business cycle. Thus, such theories are a useful part of the whole, but they are incomplete by themselves.

## MARX ON THE RESERVE ARMY OF LABOR

Marx not only recognized the possibility that high costs of capital goods could cut into profit rates, but also recognized the possibility that high costs of wages could lower profit rates. Marx argued that it is the usual case that the unemployed, whom he called the reserve army of labor, hold down wages because capitalists can always use these reserves during expansions. He also stated, however, that there are some extraordinary historical episodes in very rapid capitalist expansions that may lead to a depletion of the reserve army and a shortage of labor, resulting in higher wages. Marx wrote: "If the quantity of unpaid labor supplied by the working class [i.e., profits], and accumulated by the capitalist class [i.e., investment], increases so rapidly that its conversion into capital requires an extraordinary addition to paid labor, then wages rise, and all other circumstances remaining equal, the unpaid labor diminishes in proportion" (1903, vol. 1: 620).

Marx argued that in unusual periods, such as the late nineteenth century railway building boom in the United States, higher wages may lower the rate of profit and cause stagnation. Marx wrote this statement in the context of long-run changes' resulting in a very unusual situation, but some Marxists have interpreted it as support for a short-run theory alleging higher wages in every expansion. Marx emphasized, however, that in most eras wages usually rise more slowly than total product or profits: "The falling tendency of the rate of profit is accompanied by a rising tendency of the . . . rate of exploitation. Nothing is more absurd, for this reason, than to explain a fall in the rate of profit by a rise in the rate of wages, although there may be exceptional cases when this may apply" (1909, vol. 3: 281). Thus, Marx argues that in most eras, wages usually lag behind profits, but in a few extraordinary cases the reserve army is depleted, so wages may rise faster than output in those few cases. Marx emphasized long-run tendencies in this case, not cyclical movements. In the following sections that distinction is made as rigorously as possible.

## A RESERVE ARMY THEORY OF LONG-RUN STAGNATION

In the 1950s and 1960s in England there was relatively high employment and quite strong trade unions. In this context, Glyn and Sutcliffe (1972) argued that in this period the reserve army of labor was almost gone, while trade unions were extremely influential, both in the economy and in the labor governments. As a result, they argued, the strength of labor was strong and rising. The strength of labor was great enough to overcome capitalist resistance and raise wages faster than productivity. Therefore, the share of labor in the national product was continually rising. This rising share going to labor meant a declining profit share and a long-run falling rate of profit.

Whether or not their analysis was correct for that period, the election of Margaret Thatcher initiated a long period of weakness of labor, in which no such cause could be given for Britain's economic problems. Moreover, it is very clear that this was a theory of long-run stagnation of the British economy, not a theory of the business cycle, so it does not explain the phenomena with which this book is concerned (though it may be important background to those phenomena, if it is correct).

Such theories of stagnation caused by high wages are not new to England. In 1732 it was argued in the House of Commons: "It is now a universal complaint in the Country that the high Wages given to Workmen is the Chief Cause of the Decay of our Trade and Manufacturers; our Business then is, to take all the Measures we can think of, to enable our Workmen to work for less Wages than they do at present" (quoted in Mirowski 1986, 15).

## A RESERVE ARMY CYCLE THEORY

Boddy and Crotty (1975) argued a reserve army theory, not of an unusual era as Marx did, nor as an explanation of long-run stagnation as Glyn and Sutcliffe did, but as an explanation of the business cycle (also see the discussion of long-run and cyclical issues in Gordon, Weisskopf, and Bowles, [1987]). They argued that in every expansion, the increasing output leads to increasing employment, which slowly reduces the reserve army of unemployed workers. As full employment approaches, there is a greater demand for labor relative to the supply. This causes the bargaining power of labor to improve. Moreover, as workers eventually come to realize their increased strength, they become more militant.

As was shown in Chapter 8, that militancy is reflected in the fact that the number of strikes rises in expansion and declines in contraction. As a result of their increased strength, workers are able to obtain higher wage rates. They are also able to prevent further speedup of work—thus reducing the growth of productivity.

For these reasons, the labor share will rise toward the end of expansion. For a more detailed statement of the reserve army hypothesis about the behavior of the labor share, see Chapter 8. Chapter 8, however, discussed only this central hypothesis and did not put it in the context of a full theory of the business cycle. Here, a full business cycle theory is explained, with the reserve army hypothesis as one of its main hypotheses.

The rising labor share means a decline in the profit share. All other things being equal (such as demand's remaining constant), a decline in the profit share of the product causes a lower rate of profit. Finally, the reduced rate of profit lowers expectations for future profits. This causes a fall in investment, setting off a recession or depression.

In the crisis phase or early contraction, wages remain high as a result of labor strength and militancy, while productivity is held down. Thus the profit share falls further, the rate of profit is further reduced, and the contraction worsens.

Eventually, however, the rising unemployment causes the strength and militancy of labor to disappear. In the last half of the recession or depression phase, the weakened labor movement cannot prevent falling wages and rising productivity. This means that the share of profits begins to rise once more, so the profit rate rises. The rising expectations of profit lead to new investment, and an economic recovery begins.

It is important to emphasize that at the beginning of the recovery, unemployment remains very high, so labor remains very weak. Thus the profit share continues to rise in the recovery as productivity grows, but wages are sluggish. Only after the recovery has gone on for a long time does unemployment drop low enough that, with a time lag, labor begins to regain its strength. Thus it is only in the last half of expansion that the share of labor begins to rise once more, setting off the same cycle again.

## A MODEL OF THE RESERVE ARMY THEORY

What are the main relationships and assumptions of this theory? As part of its framework, we make the usual assumption that, in equilibrium, real national income equals real consumption plus real investment (see equation 11.1). This theory also distinguishes between labor and property income, so we may stress that these two shares of national income equal the whole thing:

$$\text{Labor share } (W/Y) + \text{Property share } (R/Y) = 1. \qquad (11.7)$$

Thus if we specify the labor share, we know the property share—which equals 1 minus the labor share.

### The Consumption Function

We must now explain the path of consumption over the cycle. As in the previous model, however, reserve army theorists assume that there is no lack of consumer demand, so it may be simply assumed to be a constant proportion of income. When income rises, it is assumed that demand rises at the same rate. Repeating the same relationship as in the previous model:

$$\text{Consumption } (C) = \text{a constant} \times \text{National income } (Y). \quad (11.2)$$

Since consumption clearly has no deficiency, we may turn to investment as the key variable.

### The Investment Function

Also as in the previous model, we may assume that investment is a function of the change in the profit rate:

$$\text{Investment } (I) = \text{function of change in rate of profit.} \quad (11.3)$$

A rising rate of profit inspires confidence in the future and causes net investment.

### Definition of Profit Rate

As in the previous model, the profit rate on capital can be thought of as the property or profit share of output times the ratio of output to capital:

$$\text{Profit rate } (R/K) = \text{Property share } (R/Y) \\ \times \text{Output/Capital } (Y/K). \quad (11.4)$$

This definition is very useful for this theory because it separates out the distribution of income between labor and property owners as one component, while making a separate component of the ratio of output to capital. Unlike the previous model, the output/capital ratio is not important to the reserve army theorists, but the distribution of income between labor and property income is the most crucial issue for them.

### The Capital Cost Function

The ratio of output to capital plays no explicit role in this model, so it may be assumed to be constant:

$$\text{Output/Capital } (Y/K) = \text{constant } (k). \quad (11.8)$$

Having outlined the less important—but logically necessary—parts of the model, we may now turn to the most vital part of this model.

## The Distribution Function

The reserve army hypothesis says that the labor share rises in the last part of expansion and falls in the last part of contraction. The labor share behaves that way because it is governed by the level of unemployment, with a time lag:

Labor share $(W/Y)$ = negative function of Unemployment $(U)$.

$$(11.9)$$

It is a negative function because greater unemployment weakens labor, which causes a decline in the labor share—whereas lower unemployment strengthens labor and consequently produces a higher labor share. Also note that the property share is always equal to 1 minus the labor share; thus, when the labor share is rising, the property share must fall, and vice versa.

## The Unemployment Function

In this theory, the labor share is a function of unemployment, so we must explain what determines unemployment. The simplest answer is that unemployment and employment are related to the level of output, all other things being equal:

Unemployment $(U)$ = negative function of National income.

$$(11.10)$$

Employment is a positive function of real national income, or output, so unemployment must react negatively to output; that is to say, higher output will lower unemployment.

### OPERATION OF THE RESERVE ARMY MODEL

How are these relationships put together? How can we explain why the business cycle exists according to this model?

## What Causes a Downturn?

When expansion first begins, unemployment is high, so the labor share is low and falling. This means more profits for investors, leading to still more investment. The investment creates more jobs; there is more income, more consumption, and less unemployment.

As the expansion progresses, unemployment continues to drop. Workers and unions find that jobs are easier to get, and they witness rising profits. Eventually, the lower unemployment rates give workers more bargaining strength, workers become more militant, and the share of labor rises. The rising labor share in the last half of expansion means a lower profit share, causing a lower rate of profit. The lower rate of profit reduces expectations. When investors have lower expectations, they invest less, and this leads to a recession or depression.

## What Causes a Recovery?

In the contraction, falling output leads to rising unemployment. As unemployment rises, it slowly undermines the strength of labor and its bargaining power. Workers are not able to keep their real wages from falling. Workers are forced to work harder, so productivity rises. Eventually, by the last half of the contraction, the share of labor in the national product begins to fall. But a falling share of labor means a rising share of profits and other property returns. The higher rate of profit leads to rising expectations, an increase in investment, and an eventual economic recovery.

## EVALUATION OF THE RESERVE ARMY CYCLE THEORY

The reserve army theory does emphasize some important facts. The rate of unemployment does fall in the expansion phase of all business cycles. Wage costs are the largest single element of costs, so higher wages may significantly increase unit costs. Moreover, as discussed in Chapter 8, the econometric evidence is compatible with the view that lower unemployment—with a long time lag—does lead to higher wages and less growth of productivity. This, in turn, leads to a rising labor share. The time lag is very long, so unemployment normally, in most cycle phases, moves in the same direction as does the labor share, not in the contrary direction, as some simplistic interpretations of this theory seem to think. Critics may argue that with a long enough time lag anything is connected in the business cycle, but it is a fact that the negative relationship of unemployment and the wage share (with a time lag) is statistically significant.

A more telling criticism of the reserve army theory is that the labor share begins to rise only after the profit rate begins to fall in an expansion (this was true even in the 1950s and 1960s). The rise in the labor share may thus be seen as an effect of the falling profit rate rather than a cause of it, let alone the only cause of it. In other words, it is true that wage costs are rising before the profit rate reaches its peak, but they are usually rising less rapidly than profit, so the *share* of labor is falling until profit reaches its peak. Only when the level of profit begins to fall does the labor share begin to rise.

Moreover, what the reserve army theory neglects is the fact that total profits (and the rate of profit) are affected by factors other than the cost of labor. For example, if the cost of labor stays the same but the cost of raw materials rises, then the profit rate of a firm using those raw materials will decline. There is also the fundamental fact that cost is not the only thing determining profits. Profits are determined by revenue minus costs. Thus if total cost remains the same, profit may still decline if revenue declines. How much revenue a firm earns depends on demand for its products. Therefore if aggregate demand declines, then—even if costs stay the same—aggregate profits will decline because some goods will remain unsold and/or some capacity will remain unused.

The basic criticism of all supply- or cost-oriented cycle theories is that profit behavior cannot be understood without considering demand as well as cost. The next chapter will examine the cyclical behavior of profits and profit rates in the light of both demand and cost factors. A theory based on both demand and cost factors will be presented in Chapter 13.

APPENDIX 11.1
FORMALIZATION OF THE OVERINVESTMENT AND RESERVE ARMY
    MODELS

This appendix uses the analysis developed in this chapter to produce, first, an overinvestment model and, second, a reserve army cycle model.

*The Overinvestment Cycle Model*

The nonmonetary overinvestment model (leaving aside government and foreign trade) is as follows:

$$\text{Income} = \text{Consumption} + \text{Investment,}$$

expressed as

$$Y_t = C_t + I_t. \tag{11.11}$$

Consumption does not play an important role in this theory, so it is assumed that consumption has a constant ratio to income:

$$C_t = bY_{t-1}. \tag{11.12}$$

Investment is a function of the change in the profit rate $(R/K)$:

$$I_t = r + p(R/K_{t-1} - R/K_{t-2}). \tag{11.13}$$

The profit rate may be defined as the profit share $(R/Y)$ times the output-capital ratio $(Y/K)$:

$$R/K = (R/Y)(Y/K). \tag{11.14}$$

But the distribution of income between labor and property owners is not important for this model, so the property share is assumed to be constant:

$$R/Y = k. \tag{11.15}$$

Finally, and most important, it is assumed that—mainly because of movements in relative prices—the ratio of output to capital will decline as the expansion progresses, while rising in business contractions:

$$Y/K_t = a - cY_t. \tag{11.16}$$

These six equations and six variables can be reduced to one equation in one variable, namely, national income. By successive substitutions, the result is

$$Y_t = H + AY_{t-1} + BY_{t-2}, \tag{11.17}$$

where $H = r$, $A = b - pkc$, and $B = pkc$. There will be cycles if $A^2$ is less than $4B$. The cycles will be of constant amplitude if $B$ equals 1, damped if $B$ is less than 1, and explosive if $B$ is greater than 1.

## The Reserve Army Cycle Model

The reserve army model is as follows (leaving aside government and foreign trade):

$$\text{Income} = \text{Consumption} + \text{Investment},$$

expressed as

$$Y_t = C_t + I_t, \tag{11.11}$$

and

$$\text{Income} = \text{Property income} + \text{Labor income},$$

expressed as

$$Y_t = R_t + W_t, \tag{11.18}$$

from which it follows that $R/Y = 1 - W/Y$. Thus, if the labor share is explained, so is the property share.

Consumption does not play an important role in this theory, so it is assumed that consumption has a constant ratio to income:

$$C_t = bY_{t-1}. \tag{11.12}$$

Investment is a function of the change in the profit rate $(R/K)$. When the profit rate grows more rapidly, investment rises:

$$I_t = r + p(R/K_{t-1} - R/K_{t-2}). \tag{11.13}$$

The profit rate may be defined as the profit share $(R/Y)$ times the output-capital ratio $(Y/K)$:

$$R/K = (R/Y)(Y/K). \tag{11.14}$$

But the output-capital ratio plays no important role in this model, so it is assumed to be constant:

$$(Y/K)_t = k. \tag{11.19}$$

The key relationship in this theory is that the labor share is a function of unemployment $(U)$ with a time lag:

$$(W/Y)_t = a - gU_{t-1}. \tag{11.20}$$

Finally, unemployment rises when real income falls and vice versa:

$$Ut = n - hYt. \tag{11.21}$$

Thus, unemployment is a negative function of output, falling when output rises and rising when output falls.

There are eight variables and eight independent equations in this model. By a series of substitutions, we obtain the following reduced-form equation in terms of national income:

$$Y_t = H + AY_{t-1} + BY_{t-2}, \tag{11.17}$$

where $H = r$, $A = b - pkgh$, and $B = pkgh$. This equation will produce cycles in the range where $A^2$ is less than $4B$. This proves that it is possible to have a logically coherent supply-side, reserve army theory of the business cycle; but it says nothing about the realism of the assumptions.

# CHAPTER 12

# Profits and Profit Rates

THIS CHAPTER EXPLORES the behavior of total profits and profit rates over the business cycle, establishing the empirical base for a cycle theory centered on profits in the next chapter. Profits are important to cycle theory because of their close relationship to investment, which is the immediate cause of recessions or recoveries.

The main hypothesis of this chapter is that the profit rate is strongly procyclical, contrary to some popular misconceptions. One subsidiary hypothesis is that there is no significant long-run trend to the profit rate, contrary to some theories. Another subsidiary hypothesis is that the profit rate leads at the turning points of the business cycle. Contrary to Weisskopf's (1979) data (discussed below), the lead is not always a long one, but is sometimes very brief. It is also argued that these movements of profits are best explained by both the demand factors and the supply factors, contrary to those theories that concentrate on just one or the other.

Each of these empirical issues affects our understanding of the business cycle and the credibility of various cycle theories. For example, the fact that there is no significant long-run trend to profit rates deals a severe blow to the theory that long-run technological changes cause an inevitable decline in the profit rate and that this causes or helps to cause cyclical downturns.

If it were true that the profit rate is countercyclical, this would be a severe blow to demand-side theories, which assume a rising profit rate in expansions as a key part of their argument. It would also boost a simplistic supply-side theory that costs rise in expansions, leading quickly to falling profit rates. The data show clearly, however, that profit rates are strongly procyclical—which supports demand-side theories and negates simplistic versions of supply-side theories. On the other hand, profit rates do lead in the cycle, which means that one must explain why profit declines before output does and, conversely, why profit rises before output does—thus implying that one must consider cost as well as demand factors.

Why are profits important to the capitalist business cycle? All theories of the endogenous business cycle begin with the fact that the wide fluctuations of investment constitute the proximate cause of business expansions and contractions. But profit expectations determine capitalist investment. In other words, investment is the crucial variable for understanding the business cycle. But profits and profit rates are the keys to understanding investment.

As Keynes emphasized, investment is based on the expectation of profits in the future when the investment produces products for the market. But that merely poses the question of what causes our expectations to change. If expectations changed on the basis of purely random whims, we could not construct a helpful theory. Fortunately, there is quite a bit of scientific evidence on the systematic formation of expectations.

Klein and Moore (1985) conducted an extensive review of existing survey data on actual profits and profit expectations; they also considered the actual quantitative measures of past profits. They found that "the survey data of expected profits turn with few exceptions after the turn in both the actual profits survey and the quantitative data" (p. 254). In fact, they found a time lag of three to four months between the actual turns in profits and the turns in profit expectations. Thus, we may conclude that capitalist expectations of a rise or fall in profits are based on recent increases or decreases in actual profits with a time lag.

It is important to distinguish two different ways in which actual profits affect investment. First, profit expectations are the motivation for investment, but profit expectations are mainly based on past profits. Here, it appears to be not just total profits, but primarily the rate of profit on investment (or sales) that influences capitalists because investors consider profit relative to investment (or sales). Long-run decisions are affected by the return on investment, while short-run decisions to invest (such as inventory investment or rapid addition of new equipment) are influenced more by the recent returns on sales.

Second, motivation to invest means little unless the capital funds are available. Funds for investment depend on previous total profits as well as on credit—but availability of credit is also based in part on the internal profitability of the firm. Thus total profit is important as well as profit rates.

In fact, in the real world total capital changes very slowly, while profits change very rapidly. Thus changes in the profit rate mostly reflect changes in total profits, and almost always move in the same direction, except that profit rates sometimes turn down before total profits because capital is slowly increasing.

## DEFINITIONS AND BIASES IN PROFIT DATA

Much profit data come from the Internal Revenue Service, so they are affected by accounting conventions and by changing tax laws, neither of which are based on any economic theory. Because of the tax laws, there is naturally an attempt by capitalists to hide as much profit as possible and also to take advantage of tax loopholes as much as possible. All of this results in underreporting of profits and—to the extent that changes in tax laws have allowed it—an underestimation of the trend in the profit share and the rate of profit (see, for example, Perlo 1976).

For long-run analysis, the denominator of the profit rate should be capital, but that is even more difficult to calculate empirically (with no quarterly data) and is quite problematic as to theoretical meaning. In the short run, sales can be used as the denominator rather than capital because that is the ratio that probably influences more cyclical decisions. There are also difficult decisions on inclusion and exclusion, for example, profit before taxes or after taxes. These decisions on definitions depend on the problem under investigation. Fortunately, the cyclical behavior—as opposed to long-run trends—in profits and profit rates is very similar for a wide variety of definitions (see below; also see Sherman 1968, ch. 1).

Finally, one could certainly argue that it would be useful to investigate profit rate trends for the nonfinancial sector or for the whole economy. The investigation here is limited to the manufacturing, mining, and trade sector because (1) it is still an important sector, and (2) there are quarterly data on profit/capital in manufacturing, mining, and trade, but there are no quarterly data for the whole nonfinancial sector or the whole economy. Cyclical analysis must be done with quarterly data, so it is best to be consistent.

## LONG-RUN PROFIT RATE TRENDS

The official data for the rate of profit on stockholders' equity capital in all of U.S. manufacturing, mining, and trade from 1933 to 1982 are shown in Table 12.1 and Figure 12.1. Sometimes, beginning graduate students in economics will make the mistake of calculating a supposed long-run trend from the peak of one cycle to the trough of another. For example, they may start from a peak profit rate period in 1965 or 1966 and go to the trough in 1975 or 1982. Such calculations show a spurious downward trend. To correct that mistake, just one average is presented for each whole cycle (based on quarterly cycle dates from 1949 to 1982).

These statistics reveal no long-run trend in the rate of profit in the past ten cycles (for similar data on the United Kingdom, see King [1975]). Of course, one can find a "trend" by taking an appropriate period. From the depths of the Great Depression (1933–1938) to the Korean War, there is a clear upward trend. From the Korean War till the early 1960s (1958–1961 cycle), there is a downward trend. These trends, however, prove little except that profit rates tend to rise in wars (and were obscenely high in the Korean War).

TABLE 12.1
Trends in Profit Rates, 1933–1982 (average for each cycle)

| Cycle | Profit before Taxes to Equity Capital | Profit after Taxes to Equity Capital |
|---|---|---|
| 1933–1938 | 3.8% | — |
| 1938–1945 | 16.2 | — |
| 1945–1949 | 17.8 | — |
| 1949–1954 | 24.3 | 11.6% |
| 1954–1958 | 21.0 | 10.9 |
| 1958–1961 | 17.3 | 9.3 |
| 1961–1970 | 19.3 | 11.2 |
| 1970–1975 | 19.4 | 11.5 |
| 1975–1980 | 22.9 | 14.2 |
| 1980–1982 | 18.3 | 11.9 |

Source: Data for 1933–1949 from U.S. Internal Revenue Service, Statistics of Income, Corporate Income Tax Returns (Washington, D.C.: U.S. Government Printing Office, 1935–1955). Data for 1949–1982 from Bureau of Census, U.S. Department of Commerce, *Quarterly Financial Report on Manufacturing, Mining, and Trade Corporations* (Washington, D.C.: U.S. Government Printing Office, 1949–1983).

Note: Definition: Rate of profit to stockholders' equity as a percent in all U.S. Manufacturing, Mining, and Trade.

There is also a large body of literature using other definitions and adjustments to the official data in order to correct for biases in measuring profit rates. Certainly, an extreme enough change in definition can produce a profit rate trend, but that is beyond the scope of this book. It will be seen below that the cyclical pattern in profit rates is affected very little by changes in definition (even when the different definitions do change the absolute level or the long-run trend).

## WEISSKOPF'S ANALYSIS OF THE RATE OF PROFIT

Thomas Weisskopf (1979) used a new, innovative framework for analyzing the rate of profit; within that framework, he conducted an empirical analysis of the components of the profit rate. Let $R$ be profit; let $Y$ be national income; and let $K$ be capital. By definition, the rate of profit may be written as the profit share of income $(R/Y)$ times the ratio of output to capital $(Y/K)$:

$$R/K = (R/Y)(Y/K). \tag{12.1}$$

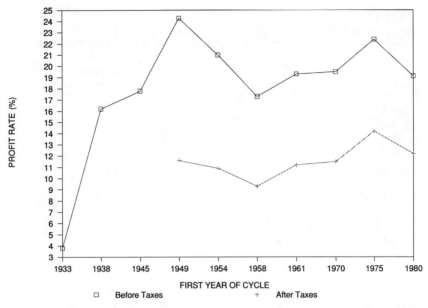

Fig. 12.1. Trend in Corporate Profit Rate as Share of Capital before Taxes and after Taxes, 1933–1980 (from Table 12.1)

This framework emphasizes that a higher share of profit (and lower share of labor) will raise the rate of profit—a formulation important to theories emphasizing the cost of labor. It also emphasizes that more product per unit of capital will raise the rate of profit—an important consideration for those worried about the long-run effect of technology on the rate of profit.

In looking at business cycles, Weisskopf recognized that actual output ($Y$) hardly ever equals the potential output ($Z$), which might be produced at full utilization of capacity. The ratio between actual output and potential full-capacity output is defined as the capacity utilization ratio, or $Y/Z$. By definition, the rate of profit may be written as the profit share ($R/Y$) times the capacity utilization ratio ($Y/Z$) times the ratio of potential full-capacity output to capital ($Z/K$):

$$R/K = (R/Y)\,(Y/Z)\,(Z/K). \tag{12.2}$$

This definition is very useful because it distinguishes three different factors, each of which is important in different theories. The profit share plays a major role in many supply-side theories (especially the reserve army theory). Capacity utilization reflects demand, so it represents demand-side theories, according to Weisskopf. The ratio of potential output to capital plays a role in long-run theories, but is also claimed to be important in some cyclical overinvestment theories. Any macroeconomic change, such as rising aggregate wages, can be traced through its effect on each of these three factors.

When Weisskopf examines the empirical data (mostly for the 1950s and 1960s) within this framework, his most important findings are as follows: First, in early expansion, the most important influence on the rising profit rate is the rapid rise in capacity utilization. Second, in late expansion, the most important influence on the profit rate is falling unemployment, which raises the wage share and lowers the profit share. Third, in early contraction, the most important influence on the profit rate is the falling capacity utilization ratio. Fourth, in late contraction, the most important influence on the profit rate is rising unemployment, which lowers the wage share and raises the profit share. Thus, Weisskopf finds demand factors important in the first two-thirds of expansion and contraction, but supply factors more important in late expansion and late contraction. He strongly implies that the supply factors are the main cause of the downturn and upturn.

Weisskopf's interesting article has generated an economic upsurge in the handicraft production of articles criticizing his article from various points of view (see Munley 1981; Hahnel and Sherman 1982a, 1982b; Moseley 1985; and Henley 1987b). Munley's article criticizes the empirical methodology in great detail. Henley extends the data through 1982 and—while noting the influence of supply—finds that the dominant influence is demand throughout the cycles of the 1970s and early 1980s.

This book (in this chapter and previous chapters) agrees with Weisskopf's empirical data for the 1950s and 1960s, while disagreeing with his theoretical conclusions (for reasons explained below). It agrees with Henley, however, on the empirical data for the 1970s and 1980s. Further comparisons are made after examination of the data.

CYCLICAL BEHAVIOR OF TOTAL PROPERTY INCOME AND CORPORATE PROFITS, 1949–1970

The mild cycles of the 1949–1970 period produce the picture of property income and total profits shown in Figure 12.2. Note that all variables in this chapter are in real terms, having been converted to constant dollars in the government data or by the author. Total property income and total profits do behave in a normal procyclical pattern. What is unusual is the pattern of extreme leads. Property income rises more and more slowly for the first three segments of expansion (being almost constant in the third segment), and then declines for the rest of the cycle. Corporate profit, however, rises for only the first half of expansion (two segments), and then declines at various rates for the rest of the cycle. This long lead correlates with other long leads in the 1949–1970 period noted in previ-

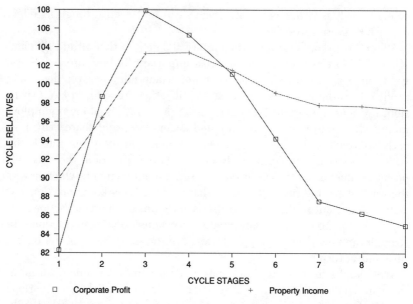

Fig. 12.2. Property Income and Corporate Profit before Taxes: Amplitude by Stage Averaged across Four Cycles, 1949–1970 (from series 220 − 280 and 286, Appendix D)

ous chapters, such as the long leads of the property shares and labor shares.

The total property income continues to rise a little longer than do corporate profits—and does not fall as rapidly in the business contraction—because of the fact that the other components of property income mostly continue to grow throughout the whole cycle in this era. These other components are rental income, interest income, and individual proprietors' income, all of which had a long-run growth trend in this period (the details are shown in Appendix G). In spite of these growing components, the cyclical fluctuations of corporate profits still give a procyclical nature to total property income. The most important point, however, is the long lead time of corporate profits at the cycle peak, the implication of which is discussed below.

### CYCLICAL BEHAVIOR OF CORPORATE PROFITS AND TOTAL PROPERTY INCOME, 1970–1982

In the more violent cycles of the 1970–1982 period, the various components of property income conform much more closely to a procyclical

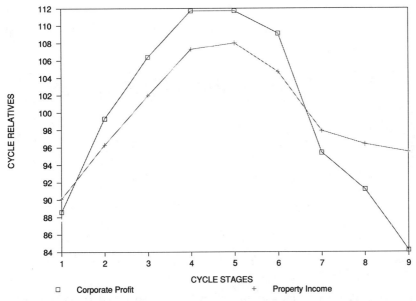

Fig. 12.3. Property Income and Corporate Profit before Taxes: Amplitude by Stage Averaged across Three Cycles, 1970–1982 (from series 220 − 280 and 286, Appendix E)

pattern, and the lead times of corporate profits are shorter. Figure 12.3 shows these patterns of corporate profit and total property income.

In this period, total property income is procyclical and coincident with the cycle. Corporate profit is procyclical and leads the peak, but only by one stage—a much shorter lead than in the previous period. The implication, as discussed below, is that in the earlier era, the explanation of the downturn in profits must be sought much earlier in the cycle than in the later period. It will be shown below that this makes a major difference in our evaluation of different business cycle theories.

## OTHER COMPONENTS OF PROPERTY INCOME, 1970–1982

In addition to corporate profits, we have noted that total property income includes rental income, interest income, and individual proprietors' income. The cyclical behavior of each of these for the last three cycles, 1970–1982, is depicted in Figures 12.4, 12.5, and 12.6. While most series discussed in this book are quite cyclical in nature, none of these three conform very well to the cycle, though they are more procyclical in the severe cycles of the 1970–1982 era than in the mild cycles of the 1949–1970 era (when they mostly show only growth).

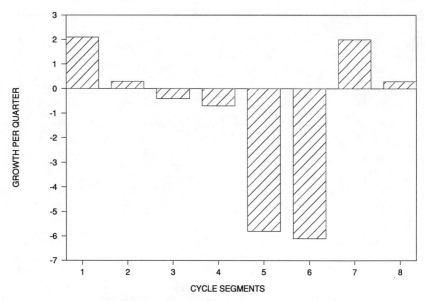

Fig. 12.4. Proprietors' Income: Growth by Segment Averaged across Three Cycles, 1970–1982 (from series 282, Appendix H)

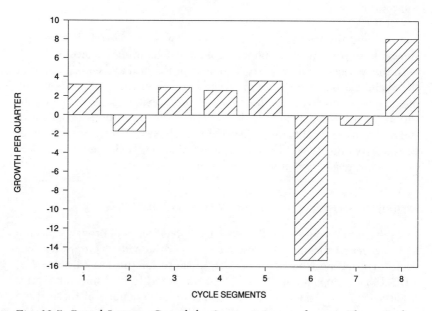

Fig. 12.5. Rental Income: Growth by Segment Averaged across Three Cycles, 1970–1982 (from series 284, Appendix H)

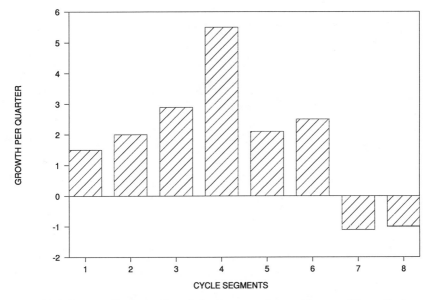

Fig. 12.6. Interest Income: Growth by Segment Averaged across Three Cycles, 1970–1982 (from series 288, Appendix H)

Proprietors' income leads the cycle by two stages, both at the peak and at the trough, but it is procyclical in the first half of expansion and the first half of contraction. Rental income is more procyclical than in the previous period, since it does rise in three of the four expansion stages and falls in two of the contraction stages, but it still conforms poorly to the cycle on the whole. Interest income rises for most of the cycle, reflecting a continued growth trend, but it does fall for the last half of contraction, the depression phase of the cycle.

## CYCLICAL BEHAVIOR OF PROFIT RATES, 1949–1970

The rate of profit is also a leading cycle indicator, turning about the same time as does profit; total profit usually dominates movements of the profit rate because profit moves much faster and more strongly than does capital or sales. Figure 12.7 presents the cyclical pattern of the profit rates on sales and on capital for the period 1949–1970 (both variables being before taxes). This figure reflects two facts: (1) The profit rate is procyclical, and (2) the profit rate leads at the cycle peak. In this period, the profit rate lead at the cycle peak is about two whole segments, a very long lead.

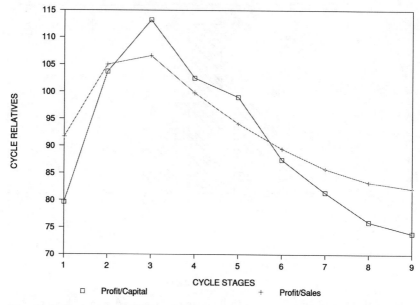

Fig. 12.7. Corporate Profit Rate before Taxes as Share of Capital and as Share of Sales: Amplitude by Stage Averaged across Four Cycles, 1949–1970 (from series A and B, Appendix D)

## CYCLICAL BEHAVIOR OF PROFIT RATES, 1970–1982

Figure 12.8 presents the cyclical pattern of the profit rates on sales and on capital for the period 1970–1982 (both variables being before taxes). This figure reflects two obvious facts: (1) The profit rate is strongly pro-cyclical in this era, and (2) the profit rate leads the cycle. In this period, the profit rate lead is only one segment (a fairly brief segment in these cycles), much shorter than the lead was in the 1949–1970 period.

One can argue about whether it is more useful to investigate the profit rate on capital or the profit rate on sales. Most investments in plant and equipment are determined by the expected profit rate on capital, so that is very important. On the other hand, many short-run investments, particularly in new stocks of inventories, depend very much on the current and expected rate of profit on sales. Moreover, one can argue about whether the profit rate should be investigated before taxes or after taxes. The profit rate before taxes reflects how capitalism actually behaves without government taxation. The profit rate after taxes reveals what business actually receives and has available for further investment. There is no right or wrong definition of the profit rate—before taxes or after taxes, as

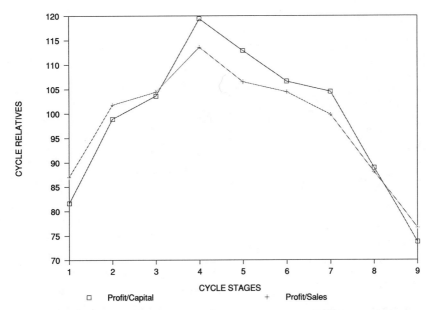

Fig. 12.8. Corporate Profit Rate before Taxes as Share of Capital and as Share of Sales: Amplitude by Stage Averaged across Three Cycles, 1970–1982 (from series A and B, Appendix E)

a ratio to sales or to capital. The most appropriate rate depends on the problem in which it is considered.

To allow the reader to judge the importance of these different definitions, in Figures 12.9, 12.10, 12.11, and 12.12, the four different definitions are all considered. What is perhaps most striking is how similar is the behavior of all four profit rates over the cycle. All of them move in the same direction in each segment (though there are slight deviations from that statement in individual cycles). All four profit rates rise in the first three segments of expansion, while all four profit rates fall in all segments of the contraction. With respect to the problem of the business cycle, it makes little difference which definition of the profit rate is used.

## COMPARISON WITH WEISSKOPF'S FINDINGS

For the 1950s and 1960s, it is correct to say that the rate of profit rises in the first half of expansion (the recovery phase), but then declines in the last half of expansion (the prosperity phase). In the contraction, there is also a profit rate lead before the trough, but not as marked. The leads of the profit rates tend to be less and less, however, in each successive cycle in this era.

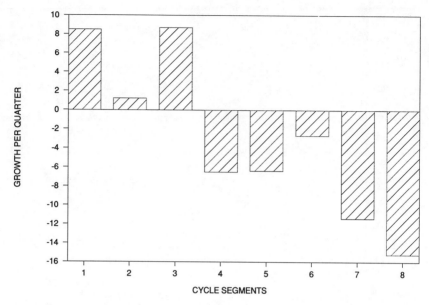

Fig. 12.9. Corporate Profit Rate as Share of Capital before Taxes: Growth by Segment Averaged across Three Cycles, 1970–1982 (from series A, Appendix H)

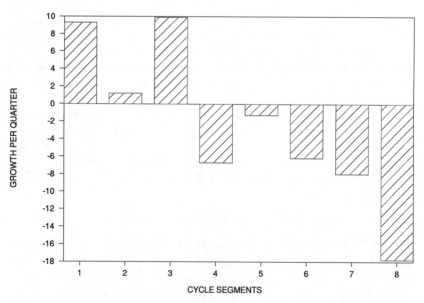

Fig. 12.10. Corporate Profit Rate as Share of Capital after Taxes: Growth by Segment Averaged across Three Cycles, 1970–1982 (from series B, Appendix H)

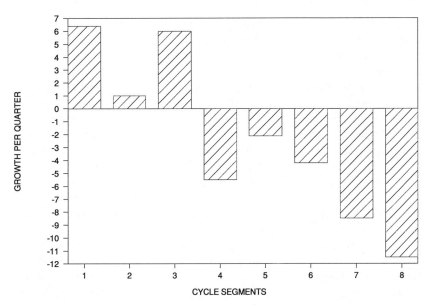

Fig. 12.11. Corporate Profit Rate as Share of Sales before Taxes: Growth by Segment Averaged across Three Cycles, 1970–1982 (from series C, Appendix H)

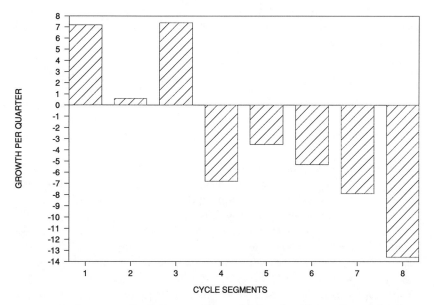

Fig. 12.12. Corporate Profit Rate as Share of Sales after Taxes: Growth by Segment Averaged across Three Cycles, 1970–1982 (from series D, Appendix H)

Weisskopf's finding that profit rates fall throughout the last half of expansion no longer holds in the 1970s and 1980s. In this era, the profit rate rises in most of the expansion and declines only slightly in the last segment of expansion.

Like all the other investigators, Weisskopf finds that the profit rate on capital moves similarly to the profit share of national income—though far from exactly the same because many other factors also affect the profit rate. The rising profit share in most of expansion supports the underconsumption theory—because a rising profit share causes a declining propensity to consume. Only after the profit rate starts to decline does the profit share start to decline, so it is only then that higher labor costs act as predicted by the reserve army theory. Since this is a very limited time period in the cycles of the 1970–1982 era, it is slim support for the reserve army theory in that era.

Weisskopf also finds that capacity utilization (reflecting demand) is the main factor causing the profit rate to rise in the first half of expansion. He also finds that it is the main factor lowering the profit rate in the first half of contraction. The findings in this chapter—and in Chapter 8, on the labor share—confirm Weisskopf's view of the importance of the capacity utilization ratio and its strongly procyclical behavior. The difference is that in the 1970–1982 era, this demand factor (as determined by Weisskopf's own method) was the dominant factor in most of the cycle because the time leads of profit rates before the cycle turning points were very short. The profit share rose until only shortly before the peak and fell until only shortly before the trough.

## DISAGREEMENT WITH WEISSKOPF'S THEORETICAL CONCLUSIONS

Weisskopf assumes that supply-side or demand-side factors (such as the labor share or capacity utilization) affect the profit rate with no time lag. At least, he looks only at simultaneous movements. While much of Weisskopf's work is extremely useful, this particular assumption is mistaken because most factors operate with a time lag in the business cycle.

If these factors do operate with a time lag, then analysis must be most concerned with what happened during the cycle phase before the downturn of profits, not after the downturn of profits. For example, in the expansion in both eras (1949–1970 and 1970–1982), the labor share declined in the phase before the profit rate began to decline. It follows that the declining labor share, with its negative effect on consumer demand, was an important factor influencing the decline of the profit rate. Thus Weisskopf's own data—as well as mine and Henley's—can be used in partial support of a demand-side theory point of view.

In addition, Weisskopf's elegant and innovative formula for the profit rate gave a boost to business cycle theory, but it is somewhat rigid and misleading, so its continued use may serve to restrict further cycle theory. As a result, this book has substituted, and focused on, a more general formula: Profit equals revenue minus cost. A full chapter was given to consumer spending as an element of revenue, while a separate chapter examined investment spending as an element of revenue (and later chapters will explore government spending, net exports, and credit stimulation with regard to revenue). Costs were examined in a full chapter devoted to labor costs as well as a chapter on costs of plant, equipment, and raw materials (with an analysis of interest costs still to come).

## Conclusion

The analysis in this chapter indicates that profits and profit rates are strongly procyclical. Their normal behavior includes a time lead at the cycle turning points. This behavior is governed by revenue and costs at all times, but revenue appears to be the more strongly moving factor in much of the cycle, though costs are important before the turning points. Briefly, in recovery, costs move sluggishly while revenue soars, so profit rates soar. In late prosperity, profits fall because revenue growth is very slow while costs are rising somewhat faster—and profit rates fall a little sooner and stronger because capital and sales are still slowly increasing. In the crisis, revenue falls rapidly, while costs are sluggish, so the profit rate falls rapidly. In late recovery, revenue bottoms out while costs are falling, so the profit rate begins to recover.

The next chapter presents a model that explains each of the main components of revenue and cost and then uses them to explain the rise and fall of profits and profit rates. It then uses that profit and profit rate behavior to explain the rise and fall of investment.

# CHAPTER 13

# Profit Squeeze
## (or Nutcracker) Theory of the Cycle:
## A Production-Realization Hypothesis

THE REVIEW of demand-side theories in Chapters 7 and 9, combined with the review of supply-side theories in Chapter 11, makes clear the opposing points of view. This chapter attempts a synthesis in which there is room for both the demand-side factors (which affect revenue) and the supply-side factors (which affect cost).

I call this theory the nutcracker theory because a downturn is caused by the closing of the jaws of the nutcracker on profits from the demand side as well as from the supply side. The hypothesis is that profits are limited both in the production of profits (through the purchase and use of inputs in the production process) and in the realization of profits (through the sale of the outputs).

A more precise and scholarly name for the theory might be a profit squeeze theory. The only problem with that name is that it has frequently been used in a careless way by advocates of various supply-side theories, especially the reserve army theory, who say that profit is squeezed by rising costs. But it is worth repeating that profit cannot be squeezed from one side only; it can only be squeezed from both sides. If, for example, costs rise 5 percent a year, that tells us nothing about the profit rate until we know whether revenue rose more or less than costs did. What if revenue rose 10 percent a year?

Elementary economics teaches that profits equal revenue minus costs. In an expanding economy, revenues are rising, so profits are squeezed only if costs rise faster than revenues. When supply-side theorists tell us nothing about demand or its effect on revenue, they cannot tell us a logically complete tale about the "squeeze" on profits. Similarly, if demand-side theorists tell us nothing about supply or its effect on costs, then they also cannot tell us a logically complete tale about the "squeeze" on profits. Thus, the term "profit squeeze" is used here to mean that profit is squeezed from both sides. To avoid misunderstanding, it should be noted that there can be several possible scenarios leading to a profit squeeze: (1) Revenue may be constant while costs rise; (2) revenue may rise but costs rise more; or (3) revenue may fall, but costs rise or remain constant or fall less than does revenue. The hypothesis here is that profit is squeezed in one of those three senses, usually the second sense, that costs rise faster than revenue in expansions.

## KARL MARX AND PROFIT SQUEEZE (OR NUTCRACKER) THEORY

Marx is explicit on the need to consider both costs and demand in a complete theory. He outlines three stages in the process of profit creation. First, the capitalist buys capital goods and labor power as cheaply as possible. Second, the capitalist uses these inputs in the production process, attempting to get labor to work as hard as possible, in order to produce surplus value (that is, all property income, or profit, rent, and interest). Third, the capitalist sells the product for as high a price as possible, in order to realize the surplus value (or profit) that is embodied in the product through production. Marx writes:

> The creation of . . . surplus value is the object of the direct process of production. . . . But . . . now comes the second act of the process. The entire mass of commodities . . . must be sold. If this is not done, or only partly accomplished . . . the laborer has been none the less exploited, but his exploitation does not realize as much for the capitalist.     (1909, vol. 3: 286)

If the profit rate declines, either because less profit is embodied in the product in the production process or because less profit is realized through sales, then there will be less new investment. Less new investment leads to a depression.

## JOHN MAYNARD KEYNES AND PROFIT SQUEEZE (OR NUTCRACKER) THEORY

According to Keynes, new investment is determined by the marginal efficiency of capital (MEC). The MEC is roughly the expected rate of profit on investment. Keynes conceptualizes the MEC as the difference between the expected flow of revenue and the expected flow of costs. Keynes emphasized the role of effective demand in determining revenue, but he also has an extensive discussion of the role of wage costs as well as the role of rising capital goods prices in the expansion (see Keynes 1936, 248).

Keynes asserts that the shape of the business cycle "is mainly due to the way in which the MEC fluctuates" (1936, 313). The downturn is due to pessimism over the future of the MEC: "The disillusion comes because doubts suddenly arise concerning the reliability of the prospective yield, perhaps because the current yield shows signs of falling off, as the stock of newly produced durable goods steadily increases. . . . Once doubt begins, it spreads rapidly" (Keynes 1936, 317). Keynes here stresses the objective behavior of current profits, though elsewhere he emphasizes subjective uncertainty that affects the animal spirits of capitalist investors. (An excellent analysis of Keynes on the business cycle, distinguishing objective and subjective influences on MEC, appears in Burkett and Wohar [1987].)

## WESLEY MITCHELL AND PROFIT SQUEEZE (OR NUTCRACKER) THEORY

Mitchell was influenced somewhat by Marx via Thorstein Veblen and he himself had some influence on Keynes, so it is not surprising that he also stressed the centrality of profits: "Since the quest for money profits by business enterprises is the controlling factor among the activities of men who live in a money economy, the whole discussion must center around the prospect for profits" (Mitchell 1941, xi). He visualizes profit as equal to price per unit times output, minus cost per unit times output. As discussed in Chapter 10, Mitchell painstakingly considers the course of each type of price and cost at each stage of the cycle in order to explain profit behavior. (Mitchell's work on cycles is discussed very favorably and in great detail by a number of writers in the collection by Burns [1952] and by Klein [1983].)

Mitchell calls the last half of expansion the "prosperity" phase, but it is a prosperity nurturing the seeds of its own downfall. He charts the rise of raw material prices, the rise of interest rates, the rise of wages, and the faltering of productivity growth. Prices do not rise as rapidly as costs, according to Mitchell, for several reasons: (1) public regulation of some prices; (2) long-run contracts for output; and (3) production of a vast new supply of goods, which may outrun consumer demand (though Mitchell says that he does not yet have sufficient evidence on this last point).

## KALECKI ON PROFIT SQUEEZE

Kalecki (1968) constructs an excellent endogenous, dynamic model of the business cycle, quite unlike the equilibrium-and-shock approach of the neoclassical economists. "The approach of Kalecki is generally concerned with the evolution of an economic system through time, without imposing any view that the system would reach some equilibrium position or that it would grow at some balanced equilibrium rate of growth" (Sawyer 1985b, 9).

At the heart of Kalecki's model is the influence of profits on investment; Kalecki's investment function includes the change in profits and the change in capital (which will affect the rate of profit). Unlike those who ignore one or the other, Kalecki always stressed the influence of both demand and supply on profits. He considered explicitly how the labor share influences consumer demand and how lack of consumer demand is one of the capitalist's problems. He also noted the importance of investment demand for profits. Yet he also emphasizes raw material prices and other costs.

Because he recognized both the demand and supply influences on profits, and because he recognized the interaction of profits and investment, Kalecki's model is far more sophisticated than many later ones. Although his theory was first stated in 1935, it remains one of the best places to begin to understand formal models of the business cycle. Kalecki's tradition has been carried on by many of the Post-Keynesians, such as Sawyer (1985b) and Eichner (1987).

## WEISSKOPF, BOWLES, AND GORDON ON PROFIT SQUEEZE

Weisskopf, Bowles, and Gordon (1985) contend that

> capitalist economic crisis may occur either because the capitalist class is "too strong" or because it is "too weak." When the capitalist class is too strong it shifts the income distribution in its favor, reducing the ratio of working-class consumption to national income and rendering the economy prone to crises of underconsumption or . . . a failure of aggregate demand. When the capitalist class is too weak, the working class . . . reduce the rate of exploitation, . . . reducing the level of investment. (p. 259)

They define the first type of crisis as a demand-type, or realization, crisis, while the second type is a production, or supply-type, crisis. They correctly observe that in "[b]oth types of crisis . . . the result . . . is ultimately the same—a decline in the rate of profit" (1985, 260). Thus, the term "profit squeeze" should be equally applicable or not applicable to either type of crisis. They argue that the Great Depression of the 1930s was a demand-type crisis, but that the recessions and depressions of the 1950s and 1960s were primarily due to supply-side problems. Note that the only type of supply side crisis they consider is a rise in wage costs.

In my opinion, this problem for capitalists—a rising wage share's reducing profits and causing decline—has been primary in a few extraordinary times, such as the railway booms of the nineteenth century. In the average expansion, capitalists are "too strong" because the labor share declines during most expansions till *after* the profit rate has begun to decline. Even in the 1950s and 1960s, when the labor share began to rise halfway through the expansion, the profit rate was already declining. Since the labor share usually declines until after the profit rate starts to decline, its rise should be viewed as an effect of declining profit rates, not a major cause. Moreover, from 1955 to 1982, the percentage of workers unionized was steadily dropping, so it seems more accurate to say that labor was steadily losing its economic and political strength relative to capital (except for cyclical changes).

Weisskopf, Bowles, and Gordon agree that either demand or supply problems may cause a crisis. (They further emphasize this point in Gordon, Weisskopf, and Bowles [1987].) This is a great advance over most writers, who concentrate on only one side of the problem and deny that the other side can ever cause a problem.

There remains a theoretical difference between their approach and the nutcracker, or profit squeeze, theory advocated in this chapter. Profit must be squeezed from both sides as a matter of logic, semantics, and economic analysis. It may be that in the 1930s the demand variables moved most, while the cost variables were less noticeable. But even in the 1930s, profit was still determined by the fact of the difference between revenue and cost. Assume that demand declined 10 percent in 1929 and cost did not change. One could talk about demand's being the more active side, but profit was still squeezed because demand fell while cost did not fall equally. Similarly, in the peak periods of the 1950s and 1960s, costs may have risen faster than did revenue, but the economist must explain why revenue did not rise further.

Unlike Weisskopf, Bowles, and Gordon, the theory in this chapter contends that one must always examine both sides of the forces squeezing profits. It is never correct—except in very loose popular talk—to speak as if one side or the other were the only problem.

More specifically, what is contended is that in most business cycle expansions, Wesley Mitchell was correct when he described wages and salaries as lagging behind selling prices (so that they are a source of profit)—while costs of capital goods, especially raw materials, rise faster than do the selling prices of finished goods (so that they hurt profits). The fact that selling prices and total sales do not increase faster is due to the limitations of demand. In most business cycle contractions, on the other hand, wages and salaries do not decline as much as does revenue, while costs of raw materials decline much faster than do finished goods' prices.

Even if economists are not persuaded by the empirical data supporting this hypothesis, it is hoped that at least economists will stop looking separately at demand or supply factors as the sole cause of a given cycle or of all cycles. It is hoped that it will be admitted—in theory—that one must trace and explain the path of both supply and demand factors before a profit decline in order to understand that decline. Let us now examine the nutcracker, or profit squeeze, theory in detail.

## Relationships of the Profit Squeeze (or Nutcracker) Theory

Henceforth, the term "profit squeeze" is used to define a theory that sees profit as determined by both revenue and cost. This theory may begin the usual way by stating that in equilibrium, output supplied (real national income) must equal output demanded by consumers and investors (leaving aside government and net exports):

$$Y_t = C_t + I_t. \tag{13.1}$$

It is worth emphasizing that any equilibrium is only momentary, at such times as supply catches up to demand. Moreover, the path traced by demand is neither constant nor steadily rising, but is cyclical. Even the notion that supply temporarily catches up to demand is unrealistic. In the expansion, supply is usually below demand because the money demand can rise rapidly, but physical production lags behind. In the contraction, money demand can fall rapidly, but physical production usually declines more slowly.

Of course, it is still the case that, by definition, national income ($Y$) equals labor income ($W$) plus property income ($R$).

### The Consumption Function

This model uses a consumption function that was developed in the underconsumptionist context. What is stressed is that consumption is not merely a function of national income, but is, in addition, influenced by the distribution of income, specifically, the share of labor in the national income. If the labor share rises, the average and the marginal propensity to consume will rise because labor's propensity to consume is higher than that of property owners. Conversely, a falling labor share will lead to a falling propensity to consume. Thus,

$$\text{Consumption } (C) = \text{function of National income } (Y)$$
$$+ \text{ function of Labor share } (W/Y). \tag{13.2}$$

Hence, consumer demand reacts positively to both higher national income and a higher share of labor in the national income. Chapter 5 presented evidence supporting this functional relationship.

### The Investment Function

This theory uses a broader investment function than that based on output demanded alone. In order to include not only demand but also the cost side of labor and capital goods, the theory assumes that new investment is a function of the change in the rate of profit:

$$\text{Investment } (I) = \text{function of change in Profit rate } (R/K). \tag{13.3}$$

Thus, investment demand is higher if the rate of profit is rising rapidly, but will fall when the rate of profit is stagnant or declining. Chapter 6 presented evidence supporting a positive relationship between investment and profits as well as profit rates. Investment is probably related both to the level of profit variables and to the growth or decline of these variables, though it is not easy to separate out the different influences.

## The Profit Function

It is crucial to this theory that the rate of profit be related both to demand and to supply variables. Thus, the profit rate is positively related to aggregate demand, reflected in capacity utilization (as the underconsumptionists would argue).

But the profit rate is also negatively related to the labor share and to the relative price of raw materials in comparison with finished output prices (as argued by the overinvestment theorists and the reserve army theorists). Thus, higher wages or a higher share of wages in the product will mean higher costs, while higher prices of raw materials relative to prices of finished goods will also mean a higher ratio of costs to revenue. Thus,

Profit rate $(R/K)$ = function of [Capacity utilization $(Y/Z)$,
Labor share $(W/Y)$,
Raw material prices/Finished
Goods prices $(M/P)$]. $\hspace{2cm}$ (13.4)

The fact that output demanded is a positive force on profits, while the labor share is negative from a cost viewpoint, helps to remind us of the dual nature of labor. If labor receives higher wages, this does mean higher costs, but it also means higher demand, according to equation 13.2. Demand increases revenue, but higher labor costs and higher materials costs will increase the cost of production.

It is clear that a change in wages has two separate and opposed effects on aggregate profits: the demand effect versus the cost effect. Which effect is greater? This cannot be determined by theory alone; theory can only show that both relationships exist. Which effect will be more powerful will be determined by (1) the actual values of the parameters in each relationship and (2) the time lags involved in each relationship. Testing the effects by simulation would require a model of considerable complexity and realism.

We can say, however, that in most of each expansion, real wages are rising, but profits rise even more—so perhaps the demand effect of high wages dominates over the cost effect. Similarly, in most of each contraction, real wages decline, but profits decline even more—so, again, the demand effect appears to dominate. These conclusions are compatible with the empirical findings of Weisskopf (1979). What happens around the turning points is more complex and is discussed below.

## The Distribution Function

The distribution of income in this model is represented by the labor share of national income. The labor share is assumed to be a negative function of capacity utilization, but also a negative function of unemployment. The fact that the labor share goes down when capacity utilization goes up reflects the underconsumptionist wage lag hypothesis that wages lag behind the property part of national income. But the labor share is also assumed to be a negative function of unemployment, in accordance with the reserve army theory. These assumptions are consistent with the evidence presented in Chapter 8.

Labor share $(W/Y)$ = a negative function of [Capacity
utilization $(Y/Z)$, Unemployment $(U)$].   (13.5)

Thus, the distribution function—like the profit function—combines those elements of both demand and supply theories found to be accurate.

## The Unemployment Function

Since the labor share is partly dependent on unemployment, we need to know how unemployment is determined. It was found in Chapter 8 that unemployment is a negative function of output demanded or national income:

Unemployment $(U)$ = negative function of National income $(Y)$.
(13.6)

As national income and output rise, unemployment declines. As national income and output decline, unemployment rises.

## The Capacity Utilization Function

Since the labor share is partly dependent on capacity utilization, we need to know how capacity utilization is determined. In Chapter 8 it was shown that capacity utilization is a positive function of output demanded or national income:

Capacity utilization $(Y/Z)$ = positive function
of national income $(Y)$          (13.7)

In expansion, rising national income leads to falling unemployment and rising capacity utilization, so there are two contradictory influences on the labor share. One influence is that lower unemployment raises the labor share, with a time lag. The dominant factor affecting the labor share, however, is the negative influence of rising capacity utilization, which moves in the same direction as does national income. Thus, there is no logical contradiction, merely a pull of two opposing forces. The labor share usually falls as national income rises because this reflects the greater strength of the demand or capacity utilization factors, as compared with the weaker and time-lagged influence of falling unemployment.

### The Capital Cost Function

For pre-World War II cycles, evidence was presented in Chapter 10 that the cost of capital goods (plant, equipment, and raw materials) rose faster than did the price of finished goods in expansions, while it fell faster than did the price of finished goods in contractions. In the period since World War II, there have been two changes: (1) The price of plant and equipment has moved roughly parallel to that of consumer goods, but raw material prices still move differently; and (2) there has been inflation even during recessions. What is still the case, however, in the cycles of the 1970s and 1980s is that the ratio of raw material prices to consumer prices has always risen in expansions and fallen in contractions. Thus, we may write:

$$\text{Cost of raw materials/Price of finished goods } (M/P)$$
$$= \text{positive function of National income } (Y). \qquad (13.8)$$

When this ratio of raw materials prices to consumer prices rises in expansions, it obviously has a negative effect on profit rates (as indicated in equation 13.4). This completes the relationships important for the profit squeeze theory; now we must examine how it actually operates to explain the cycle.

### OPERATION OF THE PROFIT SQUEEZE MODEL

To see how the model operates means to ask the usual questions as to why there is a cumulative expansion, why that expansion leads to a downturn, why there is a cumulative contraction, and why that contraction leads to a recovery.

### Why Does Recovery Lead to a Cumulative Expansion?

DEMAND

Real consumer demand rises most rapidly during recovery. This increase reflects the rise of national income, which also rises most rapidly in this phase. Real investment demand also rises more rapidly in recovery than at any other time. The reason is the rapid increase in expected profits, reflecting increases in present profits. New investment—via the multi-plier process of consumer respending—leads to even larger increases in national income. Increases in national income—via the accelerator—lead to higher levels of investment.

COST

Total real labor costs (wages, salaries, and so forth) rise more rapidly in recovery than at any other time. Real labor income, however, does not rise as rapidly as does property income, so its share declines. Positive influences on the labor share are the slow increase of wages per hour and the rapid increase in employment—though most of the increase in employment uses the unemployed, so there is little pressure on wages. But this is far outweighed by the large increase in productivity, which is more rapid in recovery than at any other time; the reasons for the increase in productivity were explored in great detail in Chapter 8. The increase in productivity goes automatically to increase capitalist profits; only with a time lag can workers struggle to renegotiate fixed wage and salary scales.

The rapid increase in production of finished goods means an even more rapid percentage increase in demand for raw materials. As the demand outstrips the supply, the price of raw materials begins to rise. Yet the price increase is held down somewhat at this period because there are reserves of raw materials and unused capacity from the depression phase.

PROFITS

In the recovery period, aggregate demand is increasing very rapidly. At the same time, the unit cost of supply is rising relatively slowly, partly because prices of inputs are rising only slowly, but especially because productivity is rising rapidly. As a result total profits, the profit share of income, the profit rate on sales, and the profit rate on capital are all rising rapidly. The effects of this rise in profitability are (1) rising availability of internal funds for investment and (2) rising profit expectations for the future. Therefore, investment also rises rapidly. Of course, new investment leads, via the multiplier, to more income and more consumption. The greater demand again raises profits, leading to more investment, more employment, more income, and so forth. Thus, there is a cumulative expansion and we move into the phase called prosperity.

## What Causes the Downturn or Crisis?

CONSUMER DEMAND

Real consumer demand rises more and more slowly in prosperity. National income growth also slows down, but not quite as much. Consequently, the average propensity to consume continues to decline. The continued decline of the average propensity to consume reflects mainly the continued decline of the labor share. Capitalists may also be saving a higher percentage of their increasing income. At any rate, the growth of consumer demand, the largest part of all demand, is very limited near the cycle peak.

Note that consumer demand will still be very limited in its growth near the peak even if the labor share flattens out or even grows slightly. One reason is that consumer demand reacts to changes in the labor share with a time lag—though not a long time lag. In fact, when the labor share begins to rise a little earlier in the expansion, as in the cycles of the 1950s and 1960s, then the average propensity to consume may also begin to rise slightly before the peak. This occurs, however, long after the profit rate has turned down in these cycles, so it is much too late to stop the downturn (the eventual rise in the labor share and the propensity to consume are effects of the downturn in profit rates, not causes of it).

COSTS

Real wages per hour are rising very slowly. Productivity is also rising very slowly, but still slightly faster than are hourly wages (as explained in Chapter 8). Consequently, the share of labor usually continues to decline, but very slowly (and is usually about constant before the peak). When the labor share stops declining, because of stagnant productivity, the average propensity to consume also stops declining (after a time lag). But profits and profit rates are already declining, so the process leading to contraction is already under way.

Why does productivity growth fall from its rapid pace in recovery to a much slower pace in prosperity? As Chapter 8 discussed in detail, overhead workers are now fully utilized, so no further easy gains are possible in this respect. Furthermore, as full capacity is approached, firms may reach or go beyond the optimum use of capacity (though most costs are constant in a wide range). Moreover, many small firms enter the market, some of which are quite inefficient.

Demand for raw materials continues to rise to the peak. But supply in many areas is limited to existing mines and farms (with particular amounts planted or born), so it takes much time to increase supply (often several years). Hence, the price of raw materials rises rapidly at this time.

PROFITS

Aggregate demand is rising more slowly in this phase. One important reason is that consumer demand is limited by a falling propensity to consume. The fall in the propensity to consume is caused mainly by a falling labor share, but with a time lag so that the propensity to consume continues to fall even after the labor share stops declining. Yet costs are rising rapidly because of the rising price of raw materials. Therefore, profits are squeezed more and more as the peak is approached. Geoffrey Moore (1983) writes: "Whereas at the beginning of an expansion, prices are typically rising faster than costs, at the end costs are typically rising faster than prices . . . putting a squeeze on profits" (p. 282).

It must be stressed once more that the reader should not confuse total profits with the profit share. The profit share always rises and falls exactly opposite to the movements of the labor share because they divide all income between them (leaving aside rent and interest for simplicity). Profits, however, are determined not only by labor costs (and the profit share of output), but also by other costs and by revenue, which is determined by demand.

This distinction is very important because, in the scenario related here, (1) profits determine investment, but (2) the profit share is only one of the factors determining profits (as shown clearly in Weisskopf). In the typical expansion, the labor share falls and the profit share rises for most of the expansion (since the effect of falling employment on wages is less important than demand factors and acts only with a long time lag). In this period, profits rise because demand rises faster than do costs.

Eventually, however, usually about a stage before the peak, costs (mainly raw material costs and interest costs) rise slightly faster than does demand (which is held down by a declining propensity to consume). At this point, therefore, real profit begins to decline slowly—and a recession becomes inevitable (for reasons discussed below).

Real wages may still inch up slowly (or be constant or even decline a little) so that the labor share stops declining and is about constant (or rises slightly or continues to fall slightly). The propensity to consume usually continues declining slowly to the peak because it is influenced by the labor share with a time lag. As a result, demand rises very slowly to the peak, while costs rise more rapidly. Thus, profits are declining, though the profit share may be about constant (or show a very slight rise or decline) to the peak.

Declining aggregate profits also mean a declining profit rate on capital. The reason is that the amount of capital (by the usual measurements, which are untrustworthy in theory and in calculation) moves extremely slowly relative to the rapid movements of profits. In all of the above discussion of profits, the term "profit rate" could be substituted for "profits" since they move almost identically over the cycle.

INVESTMENT

Why is a contraction inevitable once profits (and profit rates) begin to decline? The reason is that the decline in profits causes a delayed decline in investment. Actually, the profit decline first affects investment decisions (reflected in a reduction of new appropriations for plant and equipment), and then those decisions lead to a reduction of actual new investment. Thus, profits and profit rates turn down well before the peak, causing actual investment to turn down at the peak. The fall in investment sets off the contraction by causing a fall in employment and income.

### Why Does a Crisis Turn into a Cumulative Downturn?

DEMAND

Real consumer demand falls because real income is falling. But, the average propensity to consume begins to rise, so consumption falls less than income. The main reason that consumption falls less than income is that the labor share of income begins to rise. Real investment demand also falls rapidly in the crisis, reflecting the rapid decline of profit expectations and lack of available profits for reinvestment.

COST

Real aggregate wages decline in the crisis as a result of falling real wages per hour and rising unemployment (though unemployment usually lags behind output). Yet the labor share of income begins to rise. The labor share increases because although real hourly wages are falling, productivity is falling much faster. Productivity falls because employment does not decline as rapidly as does output. Although some unusually skilled workers may be retained, the main reason is that most overhead workers, such as bookkeepers or guards, cannot be fired when production fails.

Falling production lowers the demand for raw materials. The supply of raw materials, however, declines very slowly because its reduction involves closing mines and planting less crops for the following year. Therefore, prices of raw materials tend to decline in crises, often even when there is general inflation.

PROFITS

Aggregate demand is falling rapidly because of the decline in consumption demand and the very rapid fall in investment demand. Aggregate cost is falling more slowly because real wages and raw material prices decline very slowly at first. As a result aggregate profits and the rate of profit fall rapidly in the crisis. This decline in profits causes production and investment to fall even further (through the accelerator). The decline in production and investment lower employment, consumer demand, and income once again (through the multiplier process).

*What Causes the Upturn or Recovery?*

DEMAND

In the depression phase, real consumer demand continues to fall, but very slowly (and sometimes rises in mild cycles). The decline in consumption is very slow because income is declining slowly in this phase, but also because the average propensity to consume is rising. The propensity to consume rises mainly because the labor share is rising (though the labor share rises very slowly by the end of the depression because falling unemployment begins to affect it).

Real investment continues to decline in the depression so long as profits and profit rates decline—since this means lower profit expectations and less available internal funds. Toward the end of depression, profit expectations begin to rise, leading to a recovery in investment at the trough.

COST

In the depression, aggregate real wages, real hourly wages, and productivity are all falling, while unemployment rises. The share of labor, however, continues to rise slowly in the first part of depression. Near the trough, however, productivity may cease declining and begin to rise. The reason is that capitalist firms now fire every possible worker, even some very skilled and overhead workers. For this reason, the labor share stops rising and may be constant before the cycle trough.

In the depression, the price of raw materials continues to fall. Thus, by the end of the depression, total costs are falling rapidly.

PROFITS

Profits and profit rates continue falling in the early depression phase because demand falls faster than does the cost of supply. But, demand falls more and more slowly, while costs are still declining rapidly. Therefore, at some point—often before the trough, but not always—the profit rate and total profits will stop their decline, flatten out, and even rise a little. As soon as profit rates improve even slightly (or possibly if the rate of decline becomes very slight), profit expectations improve. The improved expectations lead to a rise in investment at the trough, marking the beginning of recovery.

EVALUATION OF THE PROFIT SQUEEZE (OR NUTCRACKER) THEORY

This model succeeds in its main purpose of combining the elements of revenue and cost in one simple model, but it has plenty of limitations and weaknesses.

The main problem with the theory stated in this chapter is that it still leaves out some very important variables. A complete model would need to incorporate the usual behavior of government, which is obviously vital to the U.S. economy. A complete model would have to incorporate an international sector, which becomes more important to the U.S. economy every day. A complete model would have to incorporate all of the financial factors in the economy, which alone can explain why expansions may become booms and why some recessions become deep depressions. Finally, a complete model would have to consider the impact of monopoly power on the economic behavior of the business cycle. With any of these factors left out, a model is extremely incomplete and is, at best, only a first approximation.

Another limitation of the model is its high level of aggregation; it does not consider different types of consumer demand (such as demand for goods versus demand for services), types of investment, degrees of competition in different sectors, and so forth; some of these issues are addressed in later chapters. The more formal limitations of the model are discussed in Appendix 13.1.

APPENDIX 13.1
A FORMAL MODEL OF THE PROFIT SQUEEZE (OR NUTCRACKER)
   THEORY

The simplest possible profit squeeze (or nutcracker) model begins with the statement that, in equilibrium, national product ($Y$) equals consumer demand ($C$) plus investment demand ($I$):

$$Y_t = C_t + I_t. \tag{13.1}$$

On the cost side, national product equals profit ($R$, all property income) plus wages ($W$, all labor cost) plus all material costs ($M$, analogous to Marx's constant capital):

$$Y_t = R_t + W_t + M_t. \tag{13.9}$$

Consumption is a function of property income and labor income:

$$C_t = a + bR_t + W_t. \tag{13.10}$$

All small letters are constants. The constant, $b$, is less than one. Investment is a positive function of the change in profits:

$$I_t = v(R_{t-1} - R_{t-2}). \tag{13.11}$$

Wage income, or all labor cost, is a positive function of output:

$$W_t = c + wY_t. \tag{13.12}$$

The constant, $w$, is less than one. Finally, material costs are a positive function of output:

$$M_t = g + mY_t. \tag{13.13}$$

The reduced form of this system of equations is:

$$Y_t = H + AY_{t-1} + BY_{t-2}. \tag{13.14}$$

In this equation, $H = a - bc - bg + c$, $A = w + (b + w)(1 - w - m)$, and $B = -v(1 - w - m)$. There are cycles where $A^2$ is less than $4B$.

### A More Realistic Profit Squeeze (Nutcracker) Model

If there is equilibrium (still ignoring government and net exports), then output, defined as national income $(Y)$, equals consumer spending $(C)$ plus investment spending $(I)$:

$$Y_t = C_t + I_t. \tag{13.1}$$

All variables are in constant dollars except prices.

Consumer spending is a function of output (or national income) plus the share of labor in national income $(W/Y)$ with a time lag:

$$C_t = a + bY_{t-1} + c(W/Y)_{t-1}. \tag{13.15}$$

This consumption function says that consumer demand will rise when workers get a higher proportion of national income.

Investment spending is a positive function of the change in the rate of profit $(R/K)$ with a time lag:

$$I_t = v(R/K_{t-1} - R/K_{t-2}). \tag{13.16}$$

A more realistic and complex investment function could also include total profits (as well as a separate credit variable), with each variable shown with distributed time lags.

The profit rate in this model reflects both revenue and cost elements. It is a positive function of the revenue elements and a negative function of the cost elements. Revenue may be conceptualized as consumer demand plus investment demand—represented by capacity utilization $(Y/Z)$. Cost in this model emphasizes the wage or labor share $(W/Y)$ plus the ratio of raw material prices $(M)$ to finished output prices $(P)$. Therefore,

$$R/K_t = p(Y/Z)_t - gW/Y_t - hM/P_t. \tag{13.17}$$

Although this profit function is still very oversimplified, it does teach us to remember both the demand and cost aspects of profitmaking.

The demand elements were explained above. Next, we explain the factors influencing costs. The share of labor, which influences both revenue and cost, is a negative function of both capacity utilization ($Y/Z$) and unemployment ($U$) with a time lag:

$$(W/Y)_t = w - z(Y/Z)_t - uU_t. \tag{13.18}$$

In order to keep the mathematics simple, time lags are ignored in this equation, but there is, in reality, a long time lag before unemployment affects the labor share.

We must now explain unemployment. Unemployment is a negative function of output:

$$U_t = j - kY_t. \tag{13.19}$$

There is probably some time lag involved in this function.

Capacity utilization is a positive function of output demanded ($Y$):

$$Y/Z_t = q + rY_t \tag{13.20}$$

Finally, the ratio of raw material prices ($M$) to finished goods prices ($P$) is a positive function of output, but rises and falls faster than does output:

$$M/P_t = m + nY_t. \tag{13.21}$$

By successive substitutions, we may arrive at one reduced-form equation, all in output:

$$Y_t = H + AY_{t-1} + BY_{t-2}, \tag{13.22}$$

where $H = a + c(w - zq - uj)$, $A = b + c(uk - zr) + v(pr + gzr - guk - hn)$, and $B = -v(pr + gzr - guk - hn)$. Although there are a large group of constants, this is still a second order difference equation to which the solution is known. There will be cycles if $A^2$ is less than $4B$. The cycles will be of constant amplitude if $B$ equals 1, explosive if $B$ is greater than 1, and damped if $B$ is less than 1.

### Some Limitations of the Model

First, the functions are stated as simply as possible in Appendix 13.1. A realistic model would allow for much more complex time lags, different for each variable, and distributed across several periods for some variables.

Second, the model in Appendix 13.1 uses only linear relationships. In reality, most relationships are not linear, but are nonlinear. A model with far more complex time lags and nonlinear relationships would be much more realistic, but much less easy to understand. Perhaps, what should be emphasized is that the reader may take the general relationships and functions seriously as a picture of the business cycle, but the precise forms of those relationships are not meant to be taken very seriously. A more general model in the next section clarifies this point.

Third, as noted in the chapter, this model leaves out government, international relations, financial factors, and monopoly power, all of which are discussed in the next part of this book.

Because of these limitations, this model—like the simpler models that came before it—is still not worth estimating in terms of its likely econometric values and predicted time path. It is still much too simple to be a useful tool for prediction. It is a model that helps to show why some policies (such as lowering wages to prevent a crisis) are erroneous, but more realism is needed before any strong policy statements can be made.

## A General Profit Squeeze Model

The functional relationships may be emphasized, along with more complex time lags, in a more general model, which does not attempt to specify the functional forms.

If there is equilibrium in this model (still ignoring government and trade), then output equals consumer demand plus investment:

$$Y_t = C_t + I_t. \tag{13.1}$$

Consumption is a function of both total income and the distribution of income, reflected by the labor share, with various time lags:

$$C_t = f^1(Y_{t-1} \ldots Y_{t-n}) + f^2(W/Y_{t-1} \ldots W/Y_{t-n}), \tag{13.23}$$

where $f^1$ and $f^2$ are positive functions.

Investment is a function of total profits and the profit rate, with various time lags:

$$I_t = f^3(R_{t-1} \ldots R_{t-n}) + f^4(R/K_{t-1} \ldots R/K_{t-n}), \tag{13.34}$$

where $f^3$ and $f^4$ are positive functions.

Profit is a function of revenue less cost. Revenue is consumption plus investment or total demand, reflected in capacity utilization. Cost in this model emphasizes the cost of labor, reflected in the labor share, and the cost of physical capital, reflected in part in the ratio of raw material prices to finished output prices:

$$R_t = f^5(Y/Z_t \ldots Y/Z_{t-n}) - f^6(W/Y_t \ldots W/Y_{t-n}) - f^7(M/P_t \ldots M/P_{t-n}), \tag{13.75}$$

where $f^5$ is positive, but $f^6$ and $f^7$ have a negative influence.

The behavior of the profit rate on capital is quite similar to that of total profits over the cycle because it is shaped by somewhat the same variables. In addition to their effect on profits, capacity utilization and raw material prices will affect the desirability of adding new capital. Thus, the profit rate may be assumed to be determined by the same three variables that determine profits, but with slightly different functions:

$$R/K_t = f^8(Y/Z_t \ldots Y/Z_{t-n}) - f^9(W/Y_t \ldots W/Y_{t-n})$$
$$- f^{10}(M/P_t \ldots M/P_{t-n}), \qquad (13.76)$$

where $f^8$ is a positive function, while $f^9$ and $f^{10}$ are negative.

What determines the labor share? It is assumed, as discussed in Chapter 8, that the labor share is a function of both the ratio of capacity utilization $(Y/Z)$ and the unemployment rate:

$$W/Y_t = -f^{11}(Y/Z_{t-1} \ldots Y/Z_{t-n}) - f^{12}(U_{t-1} \ldots U_{t-n}), \quad (13.27)$$

where $f^{11}$ and $f^{12}$ are both negative functions. Unemployment will influence the labor share with considerably longer time lags than those of capacity utilization.

The ratio $(M/P)$ of raw material prices to consumer goods prices, as noted in Chapter 10, rises and falls as the ratio of capacity utilization rises and falls:

$$M/P_t = f^{13}(Y/Z_{t-1} \ldots Y/Z_{t-n}), \qquad (13.28)$$

where $f^{13}$ is a positive function.

What determines capacity utilization? This ratio tends to rise and fall with the level of aggregate output:

$$Y/Z_t = f^{14}(Y_{t-1} \ldots Y_{t-n}), \qquad (13.29)$$

where $f^{14}$ is a positive function.

Finally, the unemployment rate usually moves in the opposite direction from that of aggregate output.

$$U_t = -f^{15}(Y_{t-1} \ldots Y_{t-n}), \qquad (13.30)$$

where $f^{15}$ is a negative function.

This general model does not have the mathematical limitations of the simple model stated earlier. To use this model for econometric testing would require some heroic (and unrealistic) simplifications. It may be useful, however, as a heuristic model to all economists who are trying to explain the endogenous business cycle. It contains as special cases the underconsumptionist, overinvestment, and reserve army models.

The model is still limited in that it does not explicitly consider finance and credit, international relations, government activity, or the impact of monopoly power. As each of these are considered in the next four chapters, it will be noted how the general model should be modified.

# PART THREE

# More Realistic Approximations

# CHAPTER 14

# Credit and Financial Crises

THIS CHAPTER EXPLORES the vital role of money, credit, and finance in the business cycle, including both its demand aspects and supply aspects. The main hypothesis of this chapter is that the downturn is initiated by the decline in profits, but the credit system plays a crucial role in determining whether a recession becomes a depression. As many other economists have argued, the economic system becomes more vulnerable and financially fragile in an expansion, so a small decline in profit expectations may set off a financial crisis, causing a depression. On the other hand, credit plays a positive role in recovery and early expansion. To evaluate this hypothesis, the chapter first examines its relationhship to existing theories, then turns to empirical data to test the theories.

## COMMON POINTS IN MARX, KEYNES, AND MITCHELL

This is an area of economics where Marx, Keynes, and Mitchell all agree on two basic points: (1) that the monetary and financial system is a precondition of the cycle; and (2) that the credit and financial system intensifies and exaggerates the cycle (on Keynes, see Tobin [1985]; on Marx and Keynes, see Crotty [1986, 1987] and Sardoni [1982]; on Mitchell, see Woodward [1987]). Marx, Keynes, and Mitchell all stress that capitalism requires the institutions of money and credit, with the use of money as a store of value, not just a medium of exchange. If Henry Ford produced a million autos, it would be absurd to think of his bartering each one for something else at an auction, as some theorists assume. On the contrary, Ford wants and needs money to act as capital in the next period. Therefore, money is used in this case to sell products, and then store away spending power until it is needed, so the logical basis of Say's law is destroyed. (Although Walrasian general equilibrium—the most sophisticated formulation of neoclassical economics—formally includes money, the role of money is indistinguishable from that of any other commodity. Thus, the system reduces to barter.)

Marx, Keynes, and Mitchell all emphasized that capitalism can be unstable because it is a monetary credit economy. Mitchell intended to make the monetary economy his main research project, of which the business cycle was only the first part. Mitchell took from Thorstein Veblen the distinction between industry (the useful making of things for people) and the pecuniary economy (the making of monetary profits). Veblen pointed out that in every contraction capitalists sabotage industry in the sense that they reduce production and employment. They make these reductions to protect their pecuniary profits. Mitchell stressed, time and again, that capitalists produce if, and only if, they can make a pecuniary profit.

This is one area where Keynes made an explicit and favorable reference to Marx (see Keynes 1979, 81). What Marx called a "barter" economy, Keynes sometimes called a "cooperative economy," which is assumed not to use money because people cooperate together without money (as in most primitive villages). What Marx called a "monetary" economy, Keynes sometimes called an "entrepreneur" economy to stress the monetary profit motive of the entrepreneur as the key to the economy.

Marx pointed out that when money ($M$) is first used in feudalism, it is merely the go-between to aid the exchange of one commodity ($C$) for another; thus the economic transaction is represented by $C$-$M$-$C$. But under capitalism, the capitalist starts with money ($M$), and then buys commodities ($C$) to produce more commodities ($C'$) in order to increase money ($M'$). It is now the commodity that plays the go-between; thus the economic transaction is represented by $M$-$C$-$M'$. Thus, Keynes (1979) writes:

> The distinction between a co-operative economy and an entrepreneur economy bears some relation to a pregnant observation made by Karl Marx. . . . He pointed out that the nature of production in the actual world is not, as economists often seem to suppose, a case of C-M-C, i.e., of exchanging commodity (or effort). That may be the standpoint of the private consumer. But it is not the attitude of business, which is the case of M-C-M', i.e., of parting with money for commodity (or effort) in order to obtain more money.     (p. 81)

This observation was at the heart of Keynes's attack on Say's law, in which he showed that it is sometimes rational not to use money immediately to buy more commodities.

## THE MARXIST APPROACH TO MONEY AND CRISIS

Marx had some more specific things to say about money and crisis (the fullest and clearest discussion of Marx on finance is Crotty [1987]). During a capitalist expansion period, credit is used to spend on investment beyond immediate income (going into debt) and beyond the objective prospects for profitmaking. Since it is beyond the objective conditions, this use of credit is called speculative by Marx; it postpones the decline, but produces a flood of goods that are beyond the objective limits of the market. Consumers also overestimate their prospects for future income, so they use credit to buy more than they can repay out of income. This increasing use of credit for consumption also postpones the decline, but increases vulnerability to personal bankruptcy.

When the contraction comes, consumers are unemployed or have lower real wages. Consumers are unable to buy and capitalists are unable to sell all the goods produced. The excessive debts of capitalist firms and of worker-consumers lead to corporate and personal bankruptcies in the contraction, so loans from banks cannot be repaid. In that case, banks cannot pay all their depositors, there are runs on banks, and they also go bankrupt. When the collapse comes, everyone wants money and no one wants goods.

What is interest, and how does it behave? According to Marx, interest is part of total profit (or total surplus value). The owner of industrial capital keeps a certain amount of profit in proportion to his or her equity. But profit also goes in the form of interest to the lenders of financial capital. Because interest is part of total profit, the interest rate is usually below the overall profit rate, except in a crisis.

The level of the interest rate reflects the struggle between the financial and industrial capitalists, under given customs, traditions, and laws, with given conditions of supply and demand. The relevant laws (such as usury laws, interest rate ceilings, and monetary policy) are also determined by that struggle. Marx emphasized the historical evolution of financial institutions. Before capitalism, loans were mostly made for luxuries, military expenditures, and other nonproductive items. Under capitalism, consumer credit remains important, but the key to investment, according to Marx, is credit lent by finance capitalists to industrial and merchant capitalists.

At the beginning of expansion, financial capitalists are in a weak bargaining position because there is an excess supply of money capital over the market demand for it. As the demand starts rising, because of better profit prospects and speculation, the interest rate rises. In the prosperity period, as investment fever takes over, there is much borrowing, accompanied by higher debts and higher interest rates (as credit demand passes supply).

After the downturn, demand for credit continues to rise for a while as people and firms need to borrow to pay old debts or routine expenses. Consequently, interest rates rise a little further. Thus, the interest rate tends to be a lagging cycle indicator. The high interest rate and credit rationing—due to the uncertain conditions—are seldom, if ever, the main cause of the downturn, but they often transform a mild recession into a severe depression.

In the depression, the decline in profit expectations leads to a rapid decline in business loans, hoarding and accumulation of money capital, and lower interest rates. Thus, when real profit expectations rise, the financial system is again ready to support a new recovery.

Marx was one of the first to recognize the usefulness of the truism reflected in the equation $MV = PT$, where $M$ is the quantity of money, $V$ is the velocity of money (the number of times money is respent in a period), $P$ is price, and $T$ is all transactions. Contrary to the classical quantity theory of money, which assumes that velocity is a constant changing ever so slowly in the long run, Marx expects velocity of money to fluctuate cyclically. When consumers and businesses are optimistic as a result of expansion, velocity of spending will climb. When consumers and businesses are pessimistic as a result of contraction, velocity will decline. Keynesians and institutionalists agree with many of Marx's points, but monetarists totally disagree. (It should be emphasized, however, that while Marx's comments on money and credit were extensive, they were mostly fragmentary, and did not constitute a systematic, well worked out theory. Marx's scattered views on money and credit are collected in De Brunhoff [1976].)

## Early Monetary and Monetary Overinvestment Theories

Theories making the existence of money the main cause of business cycles have been around a long time; Marx criticized such theories in the mid-nineteenth century. In the 1930s, R. G. Hawtrey argued the extreme view that changes in the flow of money are the sole cause of cyclical changes. (For a detailed discussion of Hawtrey and similar theorists, see Haberler [1960, ch. 3].) A rising flow of money (Money supply times Velocity of money) fuels the expansion. When banks make borrowing more difficult in late expansion, there is less money flow, causing less demand and leading to a downturn. A declining flow of money is reflected in recession or depression. When banks loosen up on credit in late depression, the flow of money increases, and a recovery ensues. There would be no problem if there were no limits to the quantity of money, but Hawtrey accuses the government of interference with the banking system in such ways as to limit money.

A related set of theories were the monetary overinvestment theories (see Haberler 1960, ch. 3). These theories held that during much of the expansion the market rate of interest is too low, that is, it is below an equilibrium rate that would make savings equal to investment. Consequently, entrepreneurs attempt to push investment beyond the available resources. Investment competes with consumption for resources; there is a "shortage of capital." This shortage of capital is reflected in lack of available funds to borrow and in higher interest rates. The shortage of capital leads to declining investment, which causes a recession or depression. Eventually, in the contraction, interest rates fall, the demand for new investment funds is less than the real resources available, there is an excess of capital, and a recovery begins.

## THE MONETARIST VIEW

The monetarists assume that competitive market capitalism automatically tends toward full employment, à la Say's law—or, in the modern version, toward the natural rate of unemployment. Beginning with Milton Friedman, there is a vast literature for and against monetarist views (Friedman and the rest of the monetarist literature are all cited in a promonetarist book on the business cycle by Courakis [1981]). For the monetarists, as for the classical economists, money is a medium of exchange between two commodities (goods or services), so demand equals supply, as in any barter economy. Since money is not hoarded, it does not cause an endogenous cycle problem. In fact, for the monetarists, the changes in money have no effect on the long-run values of real variables, such as real gross national product. Real GNP is determined solely by resources and technology.

The monetarists do believe that changes in the money supply determine nominal income and the price level. The money supply affects prices because (1) velocity does not change, except very slowly in the long run, and (2) real production is determined by resources and technology. In the short run, according to some monetarists, such as Milton Friedman, changes in the money supply and government spending may affect real GNP, but in the long run these must adjust to the levels given by real factors. On the other hand, rational expectations monetarists claim that even in the short run, if people have full information, they will adjust immediately. For example, people know that government spending leads to eventual inflation, so individuals immediately attempt to buy more goods before prices rise, thus causing immediate inflation. Thus, government spending results only in inflation, which soaks up all the spending, so there is no short-run effect on real GNP.

Since monetarists completely deny the role of a monetary credit entrepreneurial economy in causing business cycles, why are they called monetarists? Although they deny its role as an endogenous factor, monetarists do believe that changes in the money supply, determined exogenously by government policy, namely, Federal Reserve open market operations, do cause cycles. When government policy is mistaken, monetarists hold, too much money may cause inflation or too little money may lead to unemployment, inflicting these evils upon an economy that would otherwise be without them. Thus, while money and credit do not cause declines for internal or systemic reasons, exogenous changes in the money supply do cause temporary downturns and inflations, so money is the most vital policy factor.

## THE POST-KEYNESIAN VIEW

The Post-Keynesians oppose the monetarists and stress the following arguments by Keynes (for the best exposition, see Rousseas [1986]). Keynes stressed the uncertainty of the investment process. Even roulette, says Keynes, is based on probability, but economic outcomes cannot be assigned a probability, because the future cannot be predicted. For example, will there be a war or not? Will there be a new invention as important as the automobile? Technology and wars drastically affect the economy, but there is no calculable probability whatever to these and many other factors influencing the economy. "We simply do not know" (Keynes 1979, 213).

Whereas the neoclassical economists envision a barter economy with certainty (or certain probabilities), the Post-Keynesians see a monetary credit economy with uncertainty. Capitalists deal with uncertainty by (1) monopoly and collusion and (2) forward contracts, such as two- or three-year labor contracts. But these devices are insufficient to overcome the problems of an uncertain credit economy, so the economy is inherently unstable.

The fact of uncertainty makes people want to hold money rather than continuously circulate it. If not for uncertainty, why "should anyone outside of a lunatic asylum wish to use money as a store of wealth?" (Keynes 1979, 216). Rousseas says that money is "peculiar" as a commodity that may be stored without cost and used in the indefinite future (though we may be uncertain about repayment and about the value of the dollar). This peculiarity of money lets us postpone decisions in an uncertain world. The "peculiarity" of money and credit lets us borrow beyond our income. Thus, money can destabilize the economy.

### Post-Keynesian Theories of Endogenous Money Supply

According to Keynes, the demand for money is based on a preference for liquidity because of the need for money for current transactions, precautionary holding of reserves, and speculation over the uncertain future. On the other hand, Keynes assumed in the *General Theory* that the money supply is an exogenous factor, given by the government. Both monetarists and neoclassical-Keynesians agree that the government determines the money supply as a factor external to the economy.

The Post-Keynesians, however, view the money supply as determined by the economy (see Rousseas [1986] for an excellent discussion of this point). Thus, expansion of the business cycle increases output, which produces demand-side pressures for more credit in financial markets, which affect the amount of money and credit. These theorists posit that banks usually give credit as needed and only then worry about where to find enough reserves. But if that is the case, where does the banking system get more reserves when they are needed?

The Post-Keynesians have advanced two theories to answer this question. One theory says that the Federal Reserve (or central bank in another country) always accommodates to the banking system's needs because of the political pressure to do so (for a detailed and more realistic view of the politics of the Federal Reserve, see Greider [1987]). Remember one function of the Federal Reserve is to maintain "orderly" markets and to be a lender of last resort in emergencies, so it normally does all that it can do to prevent a large bank from failing, since it wishes to prevent a domino effect. In this view, the Federal Reserve controls the interest rate, but banks can get any amount they want at that rate.

The second theory says that whenever the Federal Reserve (or other central bank) cannot or does not accommodate business, then the private financial system finds a way to generate enough reserves through liability management and innovative new financial arrangements. It is generally believed, by the second group of theorists, that the Federal Reserve usually cannot fully accommodate business. The Federal Reserve has other pressures and constraints on it, such as the need to maintain currency stability. If the Federal Reserve were to just follow business desires, it might lead to inflation, which the Federal Reserve tries to prevent. Also, the Federal Reserve may make mistakes.

If the Federal Reserve is too restrictive, then the banks will find ways to move funds out of those liabilities that have high reserve requirements (such as demand deposits) to other types of liabilities with lower reserve requirements (such as Certificates of Deposit). Since banks use interest rates as a lure to push funds from one area to another, this practice tends to raise overall interest rates.

As reserve ratios tend to fall and their liabilities become more volatile and expensive, the banks become more vulnerable to economic downturns. Yet if the Federal Reserve fails to accommodate business, we get the monster called a credit crunch. It should also be noted that if innovative liability management does work, then the velocity of money has been increased (because there are more loans per deposit). Many Post-Keynesians believe that innovative liability management by the banks is a more important factor than Federal Reserve controls. Others stress that banks' ability to expand in innovative ways does have limits. If the profit rate declines and/or if the Federal Reserve limits liquidity, then banks may be unable to meet all credit needs, thereby helping to precipitate a downturn.

## Post-Keynesian Theories of Financial Fragility

Wolfson (1986, 188) argues that financial crises result from the convergence of two processes. On the one hand, there are business-cycle developments that are endogenous to the normal workings of any capitalist economy. On the other hand, there is the specific institutional structure of the financial system that has evolved historically. Once these two processes create the right conditions, any "surprise" shock may begin a financial crisis. The "surprise" events in the United States in the postwar period have been bank failures or government actions by the Federal Reserve, for example, the credit restrictions under President Carter in March 1980. These "surprise" events are also caused endogenously, but are unexpected by the financial system.

The long-run theory of financial fragility has been forcefully presented by Hyman Minsky (1986); also see Wojnilower (1988), but for a collection of divergent views, see Semmler (1989). Important contributions by Robert Pollin (1986, 1987) have analyzed fragility in terms of empirical trends in corporate and consumer credit. These writers have examined the long-run tendency toward increasing vulnerability of the financial system in recent decades, as discussed in the next section. In addition, the outstanding book by Wolfson (1986) and the excellent, comprehensive dissertation by Woodward (1987) have demonstrated how the financial system becomes more and more fragile in the expansion phase of each business cycle. Concretely, their work has shown that in each expansion, (1) the debt/equity ratio of corporations rises; (2) the periods allowed for debt repayment become shorter; and (3) there is less and less liquidity in corporate assets.

The implications of these facts may be noted briefly at this point. As was shown in detail in Chapter 12, toward the end of every capitalist expansion, real corporate profits decline for endogenous reasons. Since corporations have increased their debt burden, when their own profits start to decline, they have great difficulty paying back their debts. Money suddenly seems in short supply. The inability of corporations and consumers to pay back their debts leads to bank failures—caused initially by the fall in real profits. In the first part of the contraction, this "surprise" shock of bank failures may lead to a sudden financial crisis, which in turn may cause a deep depression. Although widespread bank failures may be traced to real factors, only a severe credit crunch or financial collapse can turn a recession (initiated by real factors) into a severe depression.

For confirmation or rejection of the various theories, let us now turn to the historical and empirical record.

## HISTORICAL CHANGES IN THE FINANCE SYSTEM

To understand the present situation, we must go back to the 1930s. The decline in profit rates, corporate failures, and consumers' lack of income beginning in 1929, plus a lack of financial regulation, led to the banking crisis of 1931–1933. The banking collapse made the depression much worse, in fact, made it the Great Depression. The Roosevelt administration felt it necessary to take action to prevent a recurrence. First, and perhaps most important, the Federal Deposit Insurance Corporation was created to guarantee bank accounts up to $2,500 (now $100,000), in order to prevent runs on banks. Second, many restrictions were put on the expansion of financial institutions, including stipulations that banks could not act like brokers, that brokers could not act like banks, that there could be no interstate banking, and that savings and loan institutions would mainly invest in home mortgages.

By the end of World War II, the United States had prosperity, high demand, high profits, and a low debt/equity ratio—debt had been liquidated in the depression, there were formal restrictions on expenditures during the war period, and there was nothing to buy or invest in during the war. The combination of the new regulations described above with these postwar conditions gave the United States a healthy financial system from 1945 to the mid-1960s. The relatively strong U.S. military and economic position after World War II, U.S. ability to impose the Bretton Woods system with the dollar as reserve currency, and the lack of economic destruction in the United States from the war all gave the United States international hegemony. This helped increase U.S. profits, which gave it an even more stable financial system.

By the mid-1960s, prosperity had led to less caution and more innovative ways around the restrictions. For example, funds were lured from regular deposits (with high reserve requirements) to certificates of deposit (with much lower reserve requirements). The larger certificates of deposit meant less protection by the FDIC because they were issued in amounts greater than the insurance limit. Also, there was more U.S. borrowing in the Eurodollar market.

Inflation in the late 1960s hurt the Savings and Loans because they had to borrow at high interest rates (due to deregulation of interest rate ceilings), but most of their funds were locked into long-run mortgage loans at low rates. Thus, some of the restrictions on permissible types of lending now became one cause of the disaster of the 1980s and 1990s.

The 1970s and 1980s witnessed increasing international competition, less U.S. productivity, and lower U.S. profit rates. There was increasing corporate debt, higher debt/equity ratios, and legislative attempts to remove restrictions. This resulted in increased vulnerability and an increasing number of bank failures. The Federal Reserve was used as a lender of last resort to prevent large failures and keep the system from collapsing in business contractions. One effect of this has been that debts were not wiped out in depressions, so they kept increasing in this period.

Total nonfinancial borrowing relative to GNP rose from the mid-1960s to the mid-1980s by 60 percent, including increases in household debt, corporate debt, and government debt. "What has occurred since the mid-1960s is that the proportion of the economy's total output (GNP) which is financed by borrowing has departed substantially from a long-term stable path, rising to an unprecedented level" (Pollin 1987, 146).

What has caused this large increase in corporate debt? First, one argument is that the rise in debt was due to inflation, which caused falling real interest rates. Second, some economists have argued that the boom psychology has led to corporate speculation. Third, it has been argued that limited profits in the 1970s and 1980s have driven corporations to borrow out of need to keep their growth up to the competition's. These three arguments refer to the demand for credit. A fourth argument says that innovative methods of financing, such as junk bonds for use in mergers, have been used to extend the supply of credit for all corporations (the best discussion of these alternative views is in Pollin [1986, 1987]).

The increase in corporate debt is an indicator of financial fragility. One result was a doubling in the rate of business failures from 1979 to 1985. Another result was that the number of banks listed as "problems" by the Federal Deposit Insurance Corporation (FDIC) has risen from 250 in 1983 to 1200 in 1986 (see Harrison and Bluestone 1988, 167). Finally, hundreds of savings and loans went bankrupt.

In addition to corporate debt, household debt has risen partly because the majority of households have needed credit merely to prevent their consumption from declining, while the rich have used credit to speculate. The result has been a massive increase in consumer debt (see Pollin 1987). Government has increased its debt through large deficits. Some of the deficits were caused by countercyclical activity in depressions, with much of this activity automatically required by law. Yet most of the deficits in the 1980s resulted from the Reagan administration's decisions to drastically lower taxes while greatly increasing military spending.

## FINANCIAL INTERNATIONAL TRENDS

International financial trends (including the trade deficit and the debt crisis) and their impact on cycles will be discussed in Chapter 16.

TRENDS IN THE INTEREST RATE

Some theories assume that all capital is borrowed and that the interest rate is the most important determinant of investment. In reality, not all capital is borrowed; industrial capitalists use large amounts of retained profits for reinvestment. Interest is paid on borrowed capital, but that is only one factor affecting costs.

Nominal interest rates were very low in the 1930s and grew very slowly until the 1960s, with very high rates only in the 1970s and 1980s. Thus, the average prime interest rate charged by banks grew in its average value for the whole cycle as follows in the seven business cycles since 1949: 2.7 percent in the 1949–1954 cycle; 3.6 percent in the 1954–1958 cycle; 4.4 percent in the 1958–1961 cycle; 5.6 percent in the 1961–1970 cycle; 7.5 percent in the 1970–1975 cycle; 9.4 percent in the 1975–1980 cycle; and 16.5 percent in the 1980–1982 cycle (see Bureau of Economic Analysis, U.S. Department of Commerce 1984, series 109). As might be expected, studies from the 1940s and 1950s found little or no empirical evidence of the impact of interest rates on investment (see Meyer and Kuh 1957, 181–89).

In the 1970s and 1980s, when nominal interest rates were very high, one might expect a significant negative effect on investment. In fact, price inflation was faster than the rise of the interest rate (and was a major cause of its rise), so real interest rates fell during most of this period. As noted earlier, some theorists have attributed much of the rise in borrowing for investment to the fact of a declining real interest rate. Yet the interest cost is only a small part of the profit picture on which investment borrowing is based, so it is only a small part of the explanation. One empirical study concludes that "the incentive for firms to borrow is bound up with their drive for profits and growth and their need to survive in a competitive environment. The cost of obtaining funds is surely a factor in this equation. But it is not the only factor or even the predominant one" (Pollin 1986, 228).

THE INCREASE IN CYCLICAL INSTABILITY

The mild cycles of the 1950s and 1960s were reflected in mild downturns in the financial variables. The more severe cycles of the 1970s and early 1980s were reflected in and exacerbated by more violent financial downturns. Table 14.1 reveals this change.

All of the financial variables listed in Table 14.1 declined more in the average contraction of the 1970–1982 period than in the 1949–1970 period. The following variables all declined in the earlier period, but declined more in the later period: the money supply (M1), the velocity of

TABLE 14.1
Increased Severity of Financial Downturns

|  | Contraction Amplitude Average of 4 Cycles, 1949–1970 | Contraction Amplitude Average of 3 Cycles, 1970–1982 |
|---|---|---|
| Money supply, M1, real (105) | −0.1 | −1.7 |
| Velocity, GNP/M1 (107) | −1.4 | −1.5 |
| Private credit, real (110) | −10.8 | −35.2 |
| Prime rate (109) | −15.5 | −37.7 |
| Short-run interest rate (67) | −15.2 | −34.3 |
| Corporate cash flow, real (35) | −6.4 | −13.6 |
| New orders for plant and equipment, real (20) | −13.2 | −22.1 |
| Money supply, M2, real (106) | 2.6 | −0.1 |
| Stock prices (19) | 3.5 | −0.7 |
| Composite financial index (917) | 0.5 | −3.1 |

Source: U.S. Department of Commerce, Bureau of Economic Analysis, *Handbook of Cyclical Indicators, A Supplement to the Business Conditions Digest* (Washington, D.C.: U.S. Government Printing Office, 1984).

Note: Numbers in parentheses indicate series numbers in source.

money, all private nonfinancial borrowing of credit, the prime interest rate charged by banks, the short-term interest rate charged by banks, the corporate cash flow, and new orders for plant and equipment. Three of the financial variables—the money supply (M2), the average price of 500 common stocks, and the composite index of money and financial flows—all actually rose a little in the average contraction of the earlier period, but fell a little in the average contraction of the later period. Thus, Table 14.1 provides quantitative measures of increased financial instability. This evidence of more severe cyclical behavior in financial variables suggests that credit crunches will be an increasingly important source of vulnerability for the advanced capitalist economy.

## CONTINUITY AND CHANGE IN FINANCIAL BEHAVIOR

The data presented in previous section show a change toward greater instability in the financial sector. But some things have remained relatively constant: The cyclical pattern and sequence of financial movements

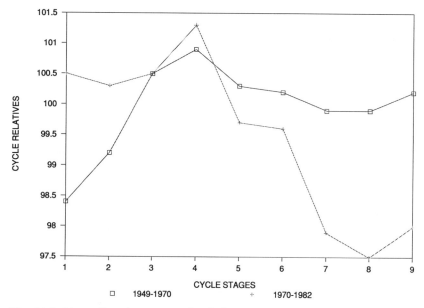

Fig. 14.1. Money Supply, M1: Amplitude by Stage Averaged across Four Cycles and Three Cycles, 1949–1970 and 1970–1982 (from series 105, Appendixes D and E)

have remained roughly the same in the two periods, even though the movements have become more violent. We now examine the cyclical pattern and sequence of turns in financial variables in three aspects: (1) money supply and velocity; (2) credit; and (3) interest rates. Each pattern is shown for both periods.

## MONEY SUPPLY AND VELOCITY

In the period since World War II, nominal money supply (M1, currency and demand deposits) as well as credit rose in both expansions and contractions, but rose far more rapidly in expansions (see B. Friedman 1986, 406). But real money supply and real credit supply actually fell in contractions. The velocity of money also rose and fell procyclically, according to B. Friedman (1986, 413).

The real money supply, both M1 and M2, is procyclical, rising in expansions and falling in contractions. The cyclical performance of M1 is pictured in Figure 14.1, while the data on M2 are presented in Appendixes A–H. The fact that its cyclical behavior conforms so well to the cycle is certainly compatible with the hypothesis that the money supply is an endogenous result of the cycle. For it to be both conforming to the

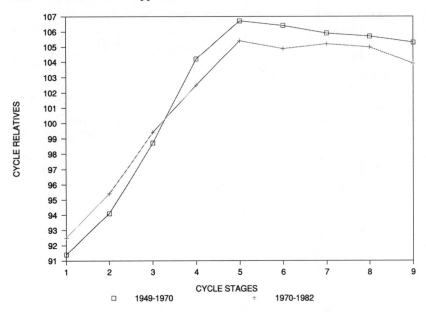

Fig. 14.2. Velocity of Money, M1: Amplitude by Stage Averaged across Four Cycles and Three Cycles, 1949–1970 and 1970–1982 (from series 107, Appendixes D and E)

cycle and still exogenous, one must believe that it is the totally dominant factor in the cycle, for which there is no good evidence. The monetarists do believe that the money supply is the dominant factor in the cycle, but the most comprehensive review of the empirical studies has found that the evidence is against them (see Woodward 1987).

The velocity of money, for both M1 and M2, is procyclical and is a coincident variable; it rises during the whole expansion, and it falls during the whole contraction. The cyclical behavior of the velocity of money for M1 is shown in Figure 14.2, while the data on the cyclical behavior of the velocity of money for M2 is presented in Appendixes A–H. The velocity of money rises in expansion because consumers are optimistic as to jobs and wages while capitalists are optimistic as to profit expectations. During the downturn, capitalists become pessimistic as to profit expectations, while consumers fear lower wages and loss of jobs, so the velocity of spending money declines. This result disproves the simple quantity theory of money as it applies to cycles, since that theory wrongly assumes a constant velocity. There is a more sophisticated version requiring only a slowly changing and predictable velocity, but that version of the quantity theory has also been criticized (see Woodward 1987).

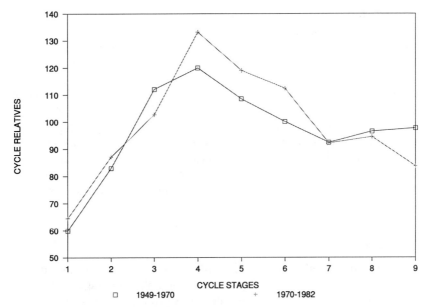

Fig. 14.3. Private Borrowing: Amplitude by Stage Averaged across Four Cycles and Three Cycles, 1949–1970 and 1970–1982 (from series 110, Appendixes D and E)

## TOTAL CREDIT

In the five business cycles from 1919 to 1938, the total loans of all banks under the Federal Reserve system rose 12.6 percent in the average expansion and fell by 14.2 percent in the average contraction (Mitchell 1951, 330). The cyclical performance of credit is depicted in Figure 14.3 for the post-World War II era.

Private borrowing, that is, the amount of funds raised by all private nonfinancial borrowers in credit markets, is procyclical. It rises in the expansion, but leads downward before the cycle peak. Thus, credit, like the money supply, rises and falls with the cycle, but with a small lead. It is worth noting that this measure of credit rises and falls far more rapidly than does the money supply. This can be seen by comparing Figures 14.1 and 14.3 or by looking at the data in Table 14.1. In the last three contractions, the real money supply declined 1.7 percent, but the real amount of all private borrowing declined by 35.2 percent. This is one reason to believe that the cyclical impact of credit is much greater than the impact of money.

Figure 14.3 also reveals that the total amount of private borrowing per quarter usually leads the cycle—that is, new borrowing decreases in amount, but it is still positive, so the total debt outstanding keeps rising until after the peak (the reasons for this decline in the rate of new borrowing are discussed below). The real amount of borrowing rises rapidly in stages 1 to 4, and then falls from stage 4 to 7, with only slight changes up or down after that.

The rapid increase of credit in the early and mid-expansion is a major engine of the growth of the economy. Much of this borrowing goes into business investment. Some of it is also borrowed by households to expand consumption. Thus, the growth of credit stimulates all sectors of the economy, allowing both consumers and investors to spend far beyond their present incomes. This stimulus is the direct cause of the economic boom—and it pushes the economy beyond the point it would have otherwise reached.

## BUSINESS CREDIT

While business credit acts as a great boon to economic expansion, it also eventually makes the economy more vulnerable and fragile. Wolfson (1986) has studied the cyclical aspect of this problem in great depth, examining a number of the most important financial ratios that indicate business health or weakness. He finds that the ratio of corporate debt to corporate equity (stockholders' ownership of capital) "has consistently increased as the cyclical peaks are approached" (1986, 135). The fact that debt is increasing faster than is capital means that the corporation is in a much weaker position if it must face a decline in its revenues. Paying back the debt becomes more difficult, interest takes a larger bite out of profits, and bankruptcy becomes that much more of a danger.

Wolfson also explores the cyclical behavior in other important ratios. First, the debt maturity ratio, which is the ratio of short-term loans to total credit of nonfinancial corporations, behaves procyclically. Its rise in expansion points to a greater need to refinance debt sooner than otherwise, and leaves the corporation vulnerable to higher interest rates when it must refinance (see Wolfson 1986, 135). Second, the liquidity rate, which is the ratio of liquid assets to short-term debt of nonfinancial corporations, behaves countercyclically. When it falls in an expansion, corporations have less liquid assets to pay back their due debts (1986, 136). Third, the interest coverage ratio, which is the ratio of (1) profits plus (2) depreciation plus (3) net interest receipts to the net interest paid by the corporation, behaves countercyclically. When it falls in expansions, it indicates that less interest can be "covered" by capital income (1986, 137).

All of these indicators show that corporations fall deeper into debt in the expansion relative to their assets and income. At the end of expansion, when revenues begin to decline, the corporation is far more vulnerable than it was at the beginning of expansion. Thus, a decline in profits and revenue has a greater chance of leading to bankruptcy than earlier in the cycle. If corporations cannot pay back all or even a portion of their debts to banks and other financial institutions, this fragile situation may lead to a bank and credit collapse, as it did in the Great Depression.

## CONSUMER CREDIT

The crucial ratio for consumers is the ratio of their debts to their income. Robert Pollin (1988a, 1988b) found that there has been a long-run trend upward in the ratio of household debt to household income. He found that this ratio rose rapidly from 1950 to 1965, flattened out from 1965 to 1975, and rose rapidly again from 1975 to 1985.

Pollin concluded that there were two major reasons for this trend. First, inflation has lowered real interest rates, making borrowing to buy assets, such as homes, somewhat more attractive as a speculative investment. Second, and most important, households have been forced by need to do more borrowing. He points out that from 1973 to 1985 real median household income fell by 4.9 percent, while the real median purchase price of individual family housing rose by 7.4 percent. Thus, some debt increase may have resulted from speculative actions by the rich, but most debt increase has been due to what Pollin calls "necessitous" borrowing by the poor (see also Wolfson 1986).

The ratio of consumer credit to personal income also fluctuates cyclically, though the trend in the 1950s and early 1960s overshadowed the cyclical movements. The average cyclical behavior of this ratio from 1970 through 1982 is portrayed in Figure 14.4. This figure shows that the ratio of consumer credit to income is procyclical, rising in expansions and falling in contractions. It lags behind the cycle by one stage, reaching its low point in stage 2 after the cycle trough, and reaching its high point in stage 6 after the cycle peak.

Why does consumer credit behave this way? In the expansion (from stage 2 to stage 5) more consumers have jobs and a steady income. Therefore, they become more optimistic than previously. Most consumers feel that they may use credit to buy necessities that they could otherwise not afford; they believe they will be able to pay the loans back when they are due. In this phase, therefore, the demand for consumer credit rises more rapidly than does consumers' personal income.

When the contraction begins, many consumers become unemployed or receive lower incomes. They cannot pay back their debts, so they rush to get new loans to pay back the old debts—and a few are still borrowing for current necessities, hoping the situation will still improve. Thus, be-

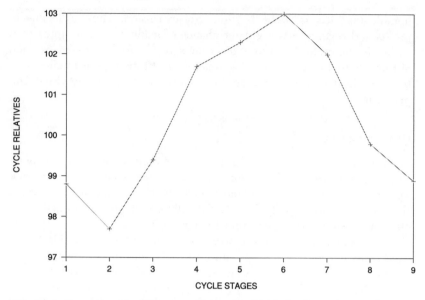

Fig. 14.4. Consumer Credit/Income Ratio: Amplitude by Stage Averaged across Three Cycles, 1970–1982 (from series 95, Appendix E)

cause of all this "necessitous" borrowing, the ratio of consumer debt to personal income rises still further in the first stage after the peak.

As the contraction deepens (stages 6 to 9), consumers are pessimistic about future income. They cut back on credit for that reason. Financial agencies may also be unwilling to lend to consumers with uncertain prospects (of course, some bad debts must be written off as households go bankrupt). For both supply and demand reasons, the ratio of outstanding consumer debt to personal income falls.

In the first stage of expansion, personal income grows rapidly. But consumers are still worried by the experience of the last recession or depression, so they do not contract new debts. Hence, the ratio of consumer debt to income continues to fall.

What impact does consumer credit have on the business cycle? In the expansion, optimistic consumers increase consumption faster than their current income increases. Consumer credit in this phase stimulates the economy. This positive stimulation continues—at a slower pace—even into the first stage of contraction, lessening the degree of deficient consumer demand.

In the rest of the contraction, however, the retrenchment of consumer credit pushes consumer demand and the economy downward even faster than current income decline would indicate. Consumers with high debt ratios at the peak are vulnerable to the recession, so they cannot pay back banks or loan companies. For individual consumers, this means loss of refrigerators, cars, and homes. These bad debts may also help lead to bankruptcy for some banks, moving them toward financial collapse. This negative effect continues even into the first phase of expansion, but it does little or no harm then because it is more than offset by the rapid rise of income.

## CYCLICAL BEHAVIOR OF INTEREST RATES

Wesley Mitchell (1951, 312–32) found that commercial paper rates in New York City in fourteen cycles (1858 to 1914) rose an average of 31.4 percent in expansions and fell by 33.9 percent in contractions. He also found that these commercial paper rates lag the cycle, not reaching a peak till stage 6, and not reaching a trough thereafter until stage 2 of the next cycle. Mitchell (1951, 312–32) also found that the weighted average of interest rates in eight northeastern U.S. cities in four cycles (from 1919 to 1933) rose by 5.0 percent in expansions and fell by 10.1 percent in contractions. He also found that these interest rates peaked in stage 6 and reached a trough in stage 2 of the next cycle, thus being a lagging indicator of cycles.

For the period from World War II to the present, the consensus of all studies is that short-run interest rates continue to be procyclical; they have a high conformity to the cycle, but tend to lag at peaks and troughs (see B. Friedman 1986, 408; Blanchard and Watson 1986, 123–82; and Zarnowitz and Moore 1986, 560–61). Long-run interest rates are also usually procyclical, but with much less amplitude and lower conformity. These views are confirmed by the data shown in Figures 14.5 and 14.6.

These figures show that both the prime interest rate for the most creditworthy borrowers and the bank rate on all short-term loans to business are procyclical, rising in the expansion and falling in the contraction. Why are interest rates procyclical? In expansion, there is (1) rising demand for business loans, consumer loans, and mortgage credit; (2) increasing expectation of inflation; and, consequently, (3) government attempts to restrict credit by higher interest rates (see Moore 1983, 140). In the contraction, there is decreasing demand for loans, there is less expectation of inflation, and the Federal Reserve may attempt to lower rates.

Most interest rates lag behind the cycle turns. Thus, in 1949–1970 the prime rate and the rate on short-term loans by banks to business do not peak till stage 6 (after the cycle peak). In the 1970–1982 period, both types of interest rate peak even later and do not reach a trough till early in the next expansion. The late turn for interest rates at the cycle peak

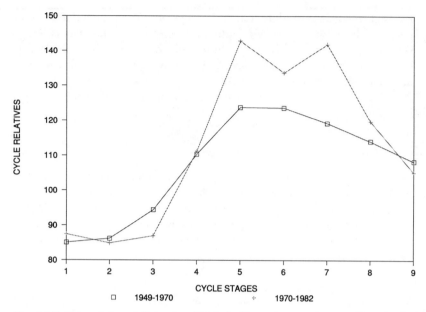

Fig. 14.5. Prime Interest Rate: Amplitude by Stage Averaged across Four Cycles and Three Cycles, 1949–1970 and 1970–1982 (from series 109, Appendixes D and E)

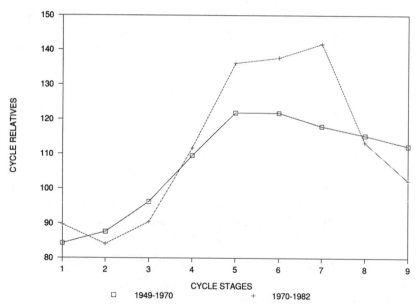

Fig. 14.6. Bank Rate on Business Loans: Amplitude by Stage Averaged across Four Cycles and Three Cycles, 1949–1970 and 1970–1982 (from series 87, Appendixes D and E)

occurs because firms and consumers desperately need credit at the beginning of the contraction, but credit is already severely restricted.

In early expansion, when jobs and profits are rising rapidly, the rate of interest is very low and rising slowly, or still declining, so its cost is easily borne and inconsequential. In the last half of expansion, limited profits and rising interest rates make the cost of interest a more significant negative factor, though far from the main cause of the profit squeeze. In the first half of contraction (the crisis phase), the still-rising interest rates are a heavy burden on firms with falling profits and on consumers with falling wages or unemployed. Thus, the cost of interest exacerbates the crisis. Finally, in the last half of the business cycle contraction (the depression phase), interest rates fall rapidly and are one of the factors preparing the conditions for recovery.

## The Timing of Real and Financial Factors

Each variable is subject to different leads and lags in different cycles, which are themselves of different length. Yet the sequence in which these variables follow one another remains about the same in all cycles. Table 14.2 presents the median number of months by which a variable leads (−) or lags (+) the cycle peak in the seven cycles of the period from 1949 to 1982.

Some variables almost always lead the cycle. The longest lead is in real corporate profits; profit rates have about the same lead. Part Two of this book discussed the factors leading to the decline of profits and profit rates. Once profit expectations grow dimmer, the next things to turn down are the financial variables: There is a decline in the real money supply, decline in the growth rate of consumer credit, and decline in the growth rate of business credit. The total new private borrowing declines, though it continues to be positive, so loans outstanding still grow. The falling profit expectations mean less desire for new business incorporations, which also decline. Finally, the lowered profit expectations, as well as the lower growth of credit and fewer new businesses, are reflected in reduced orders for plant and equipment.

The specific turning points in some variables are usually coincident with the reference cycle turning points. These variables include most indicators of output, including gross national product, sales of retail stores, the value of goods output, and nonresidential fixed investment, all in constant dollars. The coincident variables also include indicators of employment, including the number of employees on nonagricultural payrolls and the number of employee hours in nonagricultural businesses. One coincident financial indicator is the velocity of money, reflecting the fact that people and businesses are using more and more credit in expansions, but less and less credit in contractions.

TABLE 14.2

Timing of Real and Financial Variables, 1949–1982 (average, 7 cycles)

| Series | Median Number of Months of Lead ( − ) or Lag ( + ) |
|---|---|
| **Leading variables** | |
| 80. Real corporate profit after taxes | − 14 |
| 106. Real money supply, M1 | − 11 |
| 13. Number of new business incorporations | − 10 |
| 113. Net change in consumer credit | − 10 |
| 112. Net change in business loans | − 9 |
| 20. Orders for new plant and equipment | − 8 |
| **Coincident variables** | |
| 50. Real gross national product | 0 |
| 54. Real sales of retail stores | 0 |
| 49. Real value of goods output | 0 |
| 86. Real nonresidential fixed investment | 0 |
| 41. Employees on nonagricultural payrolls | 0 |
| 48. Employee hours in nonagricultural business | 0 |
| 107. Velocity of money, M1 | 0 |
| **Lagging variables** | |
| 109. Prime rate charged by banks | + 4 |
| 67. Bank rates on short-term loans | + 4 |
| 56. Real consumer credit | + 4 |
| 101. Real commercial and industrial loans | + 4 |
| 95. Ratio, consumer credit/personal income | + 4 |
| 70. Real manufacturing and trade inventories | + 6 |
| 77. Ratio, inventories/sales | + 8 |

Source: Same as Table 14.1, pp. 172–73.
Note: Series numbers refer to the source.

A number of the typically lagging variables are financial indicators. Interest rates lag by about one stage (or four months), including both the prime rate and the rates on all short-term bank loans to business. This lag occurs because there is an emergency need for loans in the crisis phase. Roughly the same time lag characterizes the quantity of credit variables, since these also reflect the urgent need for loans. Those credit variables peaking at the stage after the peak include business credit outstanding, consumer credit outstanding, and the ratio of consumer credit to personal income. Thus, credit props up the economy until one stage into the crisis (but at higher and higher interest rates); then credit declines rapidly, worsening the contraction.

Finally, there is a long lag before the peak in the real amount of manufacturing and trade inventories, which continue to pile up unplanned and unwanted well into the contraction. This reflection of the worsening situation is also shown in the even longer lag in the ratio of inventories to sales. While sales begin to decline at the cycle peak, inventories continue to rise (as an indicator of unsold goods). Only after a half a year into the contraction, on the average, do unwanted inventories start declining. Even then, unwanted inventories decline more slowly than do sales for a little while more. When the ratio of inventories to sales begins to decline at last, it sets the stage for recovery.

## CONCLUSION: THE CYCLICAL ROLE OF FINANCE

Before analyzing the role of finance in the business cycle, the reader may recall that Chapter 3 showed how the use of money is a precondition of the cycle. In looking at the specific causes of the business cycle, however, it was noted at the beginning of this chapter that credit (broadly defined) is a far larger amount than money (narrowly defined) and that credit fluctuates far more rapidly than does money in the cycle.

It is also worth remembering that the long-term trend was toward increased financial fragility from the 1949–1970 period to the 1970–1982 period. This trend may be one explanation of the deeper contractions of the latter period.

With this background we may ask a series of questions to focus on the controversial issues concerning finance and credit in the business cycle.

### 1. What Is the Role of Credit in the Cumulative Expansion?

With a brief time lag, credit responds to the rising profit expectations and rising personal income expectations. The enormous rise of credit in the expansion —both consumer credit and business credit—increases the growth of the economy at a far greater rate than the multiplier-accelerator mechanism would do if it were based on only real factors. In addition to the income derived from new investment (which is respent on consumption in the multiplier process), income is also increased by credit-financed spending since credit is multiplied far beyond current savings by the banking system. In addition to the investment that would be predicted by the accelerator based solely on the change in real income, the existence of credit easily available at relatively low interest rates increases investment beyond the amount of the prediction based on real factors alone.

## 2. What Is the Role of Credit in the Downturn?

Monetarist theories, stating that exogenous shocks causing a decline of money and credit are the main or even sole cause of downturns, are incorrect; Part Two of this book demonstrated in great detail that the real factors would lead to a downturn even if money and credit caused no problems. Moreover, credit is largely endogenously determined, and the amount of credit outstanding continues to expand, though more slowly, through late expansion and into the crisis period. Credit growth slows only *after* mostly real factors have caused a decline in profit expectations; credit declines drastically only one stage *after* a recession begins.

On the other hand, those theories that explain the beginning of the downturn solely by the action of real factors are also incorrect, or at least incomplete. The data presented in this chapter show that interest rates rise, with a time lag, throughout the expansion. Granted that interest rates rise because of demand for credit based on real factors (and false optimism spurred initially by real factors), it is still the case that rising interest rates do reduce the profit rate. Yet interest is only a small part of total cost to business, so it is only a small part of the negative factors leading to a downturn. The conclusion is that downturns would occur even if the cost and availability of credit were constant, but the reality is that the rising cost of credit does play a modest role (determined mostly endogenously) in causing the average downturn.

## 3. What Role Does Credit Play in the Cumulative Process of Contraction?

If real factors decline and profit expectations dim, a recession will result. But if there were no such thing as credit, it appears that all recessions would be mild. The financial system can turn potentially mild recessions into raging depressions. In the average contraction, after a brief time lag, the amount of consumer and business credit falls—while jobs and output are contracting. In this case, some consumers cannot repay loans to businesses or to banks, and some businesses also cannot repay banks—so some banks go bankrupt.

If the credit collapse is severe enough, it leads to a depression, since it greatly magnifies the decline caused by the multiplier-accelerator process. How bad the effect on the economy of the initial decline will be depends on the degree of financial fragility of economic units. This chapter described the endogenous process whereby financial fragility increases throughout the expansion. Businesses become more fragile as they are pressured to borrow more relative to capital, resort to shorter-term loans, use up their liquid assets, and pay higher interest rates. This means that when profits start declining the average business is up against the wall with very little in reserves — tending to cause more businesses to go bankrupt.

The rising ratio of consumer loans to personal income throughout the expansion means that consumer finances also become fragile. Consumers become more and more vulnerable to the loss of jobs or lower incomes, making it impossible to maintain loan payments.

Banks also tend to become more financially fragile throughout the expansion. To make optimal short-term profits, banks reflect their own optimistic expectations by higher and higher ratios of loans to reserves, and by making more loans to less creditworthy individuals or businesses. Thus, when consumers and businesses are unable to repay loans in a recession, banks are themselves more vulnerable to bankruptcy than in other cycle phases. In brief, the existence of increasing financial fragility in the expansion does not in itself cause a downturn, but it can decide the depth of the decline—and a high enough degree of financial fragility has the potential for another Great Depression.

### 4. What Is the Role of Credit in Causing an Upturn?

During a recession or depression interest rates fall (with a time lag). Declining interest rates reduce costs and are one small part of the factors helping profit rates to recover. Financial fragility also declines in the contraction—partly through bankruptcy of the weakest firms. As interest rates remain low in early recovery, they are a small part of the factors helping the recovery to gather steam.

### APPENDIX 14.1
### HOW DOES CREDIT MODIFY THE PROFIT SQUEEZE MODEL?

If one wished to formalize the profit squeeze (or nutcracker) model with the addition of financial variables, what modifications would be necessary?

The consumption function must include consumer credit as a positive influence on consumption. The changes in consumer credit may be explained by changes in consumer needs and expectations, as a function of employment and income.

The investment function must include not only the effect of internal funds, represented by profits, but also the effect of credit available to business. Both the demand and supply of credit to business are strongly influenced by the expected rate of profit, so all those factors influencing profit expectations may also be assumed to affect business credit in a different function.

Finally, the rate of profit—which influences investment—will be affected by interest costs, among other costs. Therefore, interest costs should be incorporated into the equation determining profit rates. Another equation would explain interest rates as a lagging function of output.

The overall effect of these financial additions and modifications would increase the amplitude of cycles. However, the basic shape and sequence of the endogenous cyclical movements would remain the same.

# CHAPTER 15

# Monopoly Power and Business Cycles

THE MAIN CONCERN of this chapter is the effect of monopoly power on the cyclical behavior of prices and profits. As a background, it begins by considering the long-run and cyclical behavior of average prices as well as the trends in monopoly power (the cyclical behavior of aggregate profits was considered in Chapter 12).

## PRICE BEHAVIOR

The Keynesian framework stresses that there may be price inflation if aggregate supply is less than aggregate demand (conceptualized as consumption, investment, government, and net exports). The monetary framework stresses that there will be inflation if aggregate supply (conceptualized as prices times output) is less than aggregate demand (conceptualized as the supply of money times the velocity of money). Although the two frameworks (both true by definition) emphasize different aspects of demand, both stress inflation as a demand-pull phenomenon, whereas some other theories stress inflation as a cost-push or profit-push phenomenon. We shall examine the facts in the light of these three types of theories.

## INFLATION IN WARTIME

The easiest type of inflation to explain is wartime inflation. The most spectacular inflations in U.S. history have occurred in wars. There was enormous inflation during the American Revolution, the War of 1812, the American Civil War, and World War I. During World War II, inflationary pressure was held back by strict price controls, but then inflation occurred when controls were lifted after the war. The Korean War and Vietnam War also resulted in inflation. Similarly, in other countries the most famous inflations have occurred during wars or their aftermaths, for example, in Germany after World War I, in Russia during and after the Revolution and civil war, and in China during its Revolution and civil war.

Prices rise in wartime because there is vast government spending, which competes for products and for workers with consumer spending and investment spending. Workers producing military supplies cannot eat bullets and tanks, so they spend their money for consumer goods, which are in short supply. The consumer goods are in short supply because labor has been taken to produce military goods. Private corporations producing nonmilitary supplies add to inflation by competing with military demand for the limited amounts of plant, equipment, and raw materials that are available. Yet governments cannot tax away enough of the military-generated wages and profits because they wish to maintain popular support and willingness to work.

## CYCLICAL INFLATION AND DEFLATION BEFORE WORLD WAR II

In most of U.S. history, prices tended to rise in every business cycle expansion and to fall in every business cycle contraction. The best index of U.S. wholesale prices reveals that prices moved in the same direction as did real production in twenty-three of the twenty-six cyclical expansions and contractions between 1890 and 1938 (see Mills 1946; for similar results, see Zarnowitz and Moore [1986, 526]). On the average for the eleven cycles between 1891 and 1914 and between 1921 and 1938, wholesale prices rose 8.7 percent in expansions and fell 8.9 percent in contractions (see Mitchell 1951, 312–21).

Why did prices usually rise in expansions and decline in contractions in this period? Most simply put, there was inflation in expansions because aggregate demand rose faster than did aggregate supply, while there was deflation in contractions because demand fell faster than did supply. In Keynesian terms, consumer demand and investor demand rose more rapidly than did output of those commodities in the expansion period and vice versa in contractions. In monetary terms, in expansions, the supply of money and the velocity of money rose (for endogenous reasons) faster than did the quantity of output, while the situation was the opposite in contractions.

## CYCLICAL PRICE BEHAVIOR SINCE WORLD WAR II

As in earlier expansions, the expansions since World War II have witnessed rising prices. Unlike previous cyclical contractions, however, the last seven contractions (1949 to 1982) all have shown increasing prices also. Although there have been years of no inflation, the inflationary tendency has persisted during the Korean War, the Vietnam War, and the period since then.

Table 15.1 illustrates several important facts. First, inflation in the 1950s and 1960s was generally very weak, but it was quite strong in the 1970s and 1980s. Second, as noted earlier, inflation continued even in contractions. The Keynesian and monetarist views both see inflation as

TABLE 15.1
Inflation in Expansion and Contraction
(Change in price per quarter as percentage of its cycle base)

| Cycle | Expansion | Contraction |
|-------|-----------|-------------|
| 1949–1954 | 0.4 | 0.3 |
| 1954–1958 | 0.8 | 0.6 |
| 1958–1961 | 0.5 | 0.1 |
| 1961–1970 | 0.8 | 1.5 |
| 1970–1975 | 1.5 | 2.7 |
| 1975–1980 | 1.9 | 2.7 |
| 1980–1982 | 2.2 | 1.2 |

Sources: Series #310, Implicit Price Deflator for GNP, from U.S. Department of Commerce, Bureau for Economic Analysis, *Handbook of Cyclical Indicators, A Supplement to the Business Conditions Digest* (Washington, D.C.: U.S. Government Printing Office, 1984).

the result of excess demand, so the phenomenon of rising prices in contractions seems to contradict their theory. They have pointed out, however, that although prices have risen, the rate of inflation has declined in contractions (for the United States, this is found by Moore [1983, 233]). Thus, they argue that as unemployment rises in contractions, the inflation rate declines, and vice versa.

Third, in four of the contractions (1954, 1958, 1961, and 1982) the inflation rate did decline, as predicted by orthodox demand-pull theory. Yet in three of the contractions (1970, 1975, and 1980) the inflation rate actually rose higher in the contraction than in the preceding expansion. In other words, in the 1950s and 1960s, unemployment and inflation mostly moved opposite to each other. In the 1970s, inflation perversely rose as unemployment rose and fell somewhat as unemployment fell. That inflation rose faster in a period of falling demand obviously contradicts any kind of demand-pull inflation theory. To explain this new phenomenon, other theories must be considered, such as the many types of cost-push and profit-push theories.

## DECLINING UNION STRENGTH

One popular cost-push explanation of inflation is that labor unions have too much power. But union strength has been declining. Total union membership included 36 percent of all nonagricultural workers in 1956, but dropped to only 18 percent in 1986 (see Freeman 1988, 64). In the private, nonagricultural sector, union membership dropped from 38 percent in 1956 to only 14 percent in 1986. Only in the public sector has union strength grown from 12 percent in 1956 to 40 percent in 1986. Obviously, the increase in unions in the public sector (which is much smaller than the private sector) has nowhere near offset the decrease in the private sector.

Explanations of the decline in union strength differ widely. Some of the favorites include divisions among unions, less aggressive union recruiting, more antilabor laws and antilabor intervention by government, and more aggressive antiunion drives by business. But these attitudinal changes must themselves be explained; one view is that the U.S. economy has tended toward a restructuring that is less favorable to unions. Another view is that the long, relatively smooth growth and prosperity from 1945 to the mid-1960s made unions "soft" and workers less receptive. (The best discussion of these arguments is by Robinson [1988], but also see Freeman [1988] and Reder [1988].)

Whatever the causes of the decline, the increasing weakness of labor unions has been a fact for the past three decades. Therefore, the explanation for increasing inflation (especially in recessions and depressions) cannot be labor union strength; it is no longer a persuasive theory. In fact, there is good evidence that wage shares in industries have declined when union strength has declined; Henley (1987a) finds a correlation of the wage share with union strength or weakness. Thus, declining union strength was more likely a factor in reducing inflation in this period. We must look elsewhere for the explanation of the inflation trends.

## THE INCREASE OF MONOPOLY POWER

As late as 1860, small farms and small businesses produced most of U.S. output. After the American Civil War had wiped out the slave owners, the capitalist class had no more rivals for power to rule. The northern industrialists ran the government through the Republican party and used government power to penetrate into the South and the West. For example, huge parcels of land—equal in total area to more than many European countries—were given to the railroads. At the same time, technological improvements made a much larger scale of production more profitable, so there was strong motivation to expand. Furthermore, improvements in transportation and communication made nationwide firms quite feasible.

In 1929, the 200 largest manufacturing corporations held 46 percent of all manufacturing assets. Except for a slight decline during World War II (when medium-sized corporations did very well), this index of overall concentration has been rising steadily. The share of the 200 largest manufacturing corporations rose from 47 percent in 1949 to 60 percent in 1973. By 1977 the 100 largest corporations produced 33 percent of all manufacturing net output by themselves (see Auerbach 1988, 150). *Fortune*'s 500 largest industrial corporations had 65 percent of sales, 70 percent of employment, and 84 percent of all assets in mining and manufacturing in 1984 (Munkirs and Knoedler 1987, 808).

Some of this increase in concentration was due to internal growth of the largest corporations, and some of it was due to mergers. Since 1950, one out of every five of the 1,000 largest manufacturing corporations has been swallowed by an even larger giant. The nature of these mergers has changed over time. In the 1890s and the 1900s, there was a wave of horizontal mergers, that is, mergers between competitors in the same industry. In the 1920s and the 1930s, there was a wave of vertical mergers, that is, mergers between a manufacturer and its suppliers or its retail dealers. There has been an enormous wave of conglomerate mergers in the late 1960s, 1970s, and 1980s, that is, mergers of unrelated firms. These conglomerate mergers have not been limited to manufacturing, but have occurred in every sector of the U.S. economy.

By 1963 (before most of the conglomerate mergers), in 40 percent of U.S. manufacturing industries, just four firms in each industry had over half the sales (see Blair 1972, 14). In another 32 percent of U.S. industries, just four firms in each industry had between 25 and 50 percent of all sales. Only 28 percent of the industries had less than 25 percent of the sales controlled by four firms. These data on concentration are very impressive, but they still greatly underestimate the concentration of economic power (the latest available data on conglomerates are analyzed in an excellent article by Dugger [1985]).

One problem is that the census industries are too broadly defined; that is, they include products that are not substitutes and do not compete. This reduces the reported degree of concentration. On the other hand, the reported concentration is increased by not including international competition. Adjusting for these two contrary biases (and some other less important biases), W. G. Shepherd found that in most industries concentration is higher than reported (1970, 274–80). A *concentration ratio* in this case may be defined as the percentage of total industry sales controlled by the four largest firms in the industry. In 1966 the official unadjusted concentration ratios were lower than Shepherd's adjusted ratios in all major industry groups except one. The changes were substantial; for example, the adjusted ratios rose from 16 to 46 for lumber, and from 32 to 64 for petroleum and coal products.

Second, each of the 100 largest conglomerates controls some of the biggest firms in several industries, so their power goes far beyond the

TABLE 15.2

Distribution of U.S. Corporate Assets, 1985

| Asset Size | Number of Corporations | Amount of Assets | Percent of Corporations | Percent of Assets |
|---|---|---|---|---|
| Less than $100,000 | 1,692 | $ 57 | 54.0% | 1.0% |
| $100,000–$1 million | 1,152 | 371 | 37.0 | 3.0 |
| $1 million–$25 million | 267 | 974 | 9.0 | 8.0 |
| $25 million–$250 million | 21 | 1,517 | 0.6 | 12.0 |
| $250 million or more | 4 | 9,852 | 0.1 | 77.0 |

Source: U.S. Internal Revenue Service, U.S. Statistics of Income: Corporation Tax Returns (Washington, D.C.: U.S. Government Printing Office, 1986).

Note: Table includes all U.S. corporations with at least $1 in assets. Amount of assets is given in billions of dollars. Number of corporations is given in thousands.

recorded concentration ratios. Using the census definition that best fits economic theory, there are 1,014 individual manufacturing industries. The concentration ratio was defined earlier as the percentage of sales controlled by the four largest firms in each of these industries. Yet in a majority of the manufacturing industries, at least one of the four largest firms in that industry is controlled by a large conglomerate (see Blair 1972, 53–54). By *large conglomerate* is meant one of the 100 largest firms in all of manufacturing.

Third, there are many interlocking directorates amongst the largest conglomerates, so that some of the same people sit on several boards to oversee their cooperation or collusion. In 1965, the 250 largest corporations had a total of 4,007 directorships, but these were held by just 3,165 directors (see Blair 1972, 76). Among the directors, 562 held two or more directorships, and five men held six each. There are also various groupings of corporations; for example, large blocks of stock in one group are held by the Rockefellers, whereas large blocks of stock in another are held by the Du Ponts.

Furthermore, banks are interlocked with many industrial corporations to form other important groups that work in a unified manner. Within the banking system itself, there is concentration of assets. In 1968, there were 13,775 commercial banks. Of these, a mere fourteen banks (not 14 percent, but just fourteen) held 25 percent of all deposits. The 100 largest banks held 46 percent of all deposits.

Finally, it is necessary to examine all U.S. corporations, including all sectors of business. Table 15.2 shows the statistics for 1985, the most recent available data. The table reveals that 1.7 million small corporations (54 percent of all corporations) have only $57 billion in assets (less than 1 percent of assets). The highest asset size level (over a quarter of a billion dollars) has just 4,000 corporations, but they have $9.9 *trillion* in assets (or 77 percent of all assets).

All of these data lead to two conclusions. Economic concentration among U.S. corporations is very high. Aggregate economic concentration among U.S. corporations, as defined by the percentage held by the 100 largest corporations, increased considerably in the 1970s and early 1980s. Industrial concentration, defined as the percentage of sales held by the top four in *each* industry, is much less clear in its trend, but did show a slight average increase in the last available data (though even this is controversial and depends on definitions). With these facts in mind, one can understand some of the evolution of price behavior of U.S. corporations.

## MONOPOLY POWER AND ADMINISTERED PRICES

Gardiner Means (1975) found what he called "administered" prices in the monopoly sector in the Great Depression of the 1930s and in the smaller depression of 1938. In the more concentrated industries, Means discovered, prices were not set in a competitive market, but were carefully administered or set in the best interests of the monopolies. He found that the competitive prices changed frequently, but that the administered or monopoly prices changed very seldom.

More specifically, prices in the competitive sector registered large declines in depressions, but administered prices in the monopoly sector declined very little. Leaving aside the middle 60 percent of industries, Means defines the competitive sector as the least concentrated 20 percent of industries and defines the monopoly sector as the most concentrated 20 percent. From 1929 to 1932, prices in the competitive sector fell 60 percent, but prices in the monopoly sector fell only 10 percent (Means 1975, 8–9). A few prices in the monopoly sector even rose a little in the face of the Great Depression.

In the expansion of 1933 to 1937, according to Means, competitive prices rose by 46 percent, whereas monopoly prices rose only 10 percent. In the depression of 1937 to 1938, competitive prices fell again by 27 percent, whereas monopoly prices fell only 3 percent. Monopoly prices are clearly more stable and are very resistant to the decline of demand during depressions. It will be shown that the stability (or increase) of monopoly prices is achieved at the expense of large price declines for small and competitive business, lower purchasing power for consumers, and high unemployment of workers.

Table 15.3 shows that even in the Great Depression the industries with great monopoly power lowered their prices very little. They kept prices

TABLE 15.3
Prices and Production in Depression, 1929–1932

| Industry | Decline in Prices | Decline in Production |
|---|---|---|
| Motor vehicles | 12% | 74% |
| Agricultural implements | 14 | 84 |
| Iron and steel | 16 | 76 |
| Cement | 16 | 55 |
| Automobile tires | 25 | 42 |
| Leather products | 33 | 18 |
| Petroleum products | 36 | 17 |
| Textile products | 39 | 28 |
| Final Food products | 39 | 10 |
| Agricultural products | 54 | 1 |

*Source*: National Resources Committee (under the direction of Gardiner Means), *The Structure of the American Economy* (Washington, D.C.: U.S. Government Printing Office, 1939), p. 386.

*Note*: Declines are given as a percentage of their 1929 base.

from dropping farther only by reducing their production by very large percentages. The more competitive industries had no choice but to let their prices be forced down by lack of demand. Production in the competitive sector declined less, because the lower prices brought greater demand. The monopoly sector thus held up its prices (and profit per unit) at the expense of great decreases in production and large-scale unemployment. The competitive sector lowered production less and fired fewer workers, but suffered much greater declines in prices and profits per unit. A highly monopolized economy is thus more apt to produce high rates of unemployment in every decline.

Data for more recent business cycles show similar patterns, taking inflation into account. The competitive sector is defined as all those industries in which concentration of sales by the top eight firms is under 50 percent. The monopoly sector is defined as all those industries in which concentration of sales by the top eight firms is over 50 percent. (This definition, like any definition with a particular dividing point, is purely arbitrary. A more accurate—but far more complex—analysis would look instead at the whole spectrum, from the least concentrated to the most concentrated for every statement about corporate performance.) The

TABLE 15.4

Expansion Amplitudes of Prices in Monopoly and Competitive Sectors

| Dates of Expansion | Prices in Monopoly Sector | Prices in Competitive Sector |
|---|---|---|
| October 1949–July 1953 | 13.6% | 11.1% |
| May 1954–August 1957 | 11.0 | 4.6 |
| April 1958–April 1960 | 2.1 | 3.0 |
| February 1961–December 1969 | 8.3 | 16.3 |
| November 1970–November 1973 | 10.2 | 23.4 |

Sources: Robert Lanzillotti, *Employment, Growth and Price Levels: Hearings before the Joint Economic Committee of the U.S. Congress* (Washington, D.C.: U.S. Government Printing Office, 1959), 2238; John Blair, "Market Power and Inflation," *Journal of Economic Issues* 8 (June 1974): 453–78; Kathleen Pulling, *Market Structure and the Cyclical Behavior of Prices and Profits, 1949 to 1975* (Ph.D. diss., University of California, Riverside, 1978).

Note: Expansion amplitude means rise from trough to peak as a percentage of cycle average.

hundreds of individual industries may be aggregated—by averaging all their concentration ratios, weighted by the value of shipments of each industry—into the two sectors.

The *expansion amplitude* of a price index is defined as its rise from initial trough to cycle peak, given as a percentage of its average level over the cycle. The average expansion amplitudes for all the prices in the monopoly sector and for all the prices in the competitive sector are given in Table 15.4 for the period 1949 through 1973. The results for the two cyclical expansions of 1949–1953 and 1954–1957 are unusual in that prices in the monopoly sector rose faster than did prices in the more competitive sector. In the three later expansions, 1958–1960, 1961–1969, and 1970–1973, the prices in the more competitive sector rose faster than did prices in the monopoly sector. This is the same pattern as in the expansion of 1933–1937. It will usually be the case that in expansions, prices in the more competitive sector rise somewhat faster than do prices in the monopoly sector. The theoretical reasons for this behavior are discussed in the next section.

Of most interest, however, are the relative price behaviors in contractions. Table 15.5 shows contraction amplitudes for the period 1948 through early 1975. As noted earlier, average prices for all sectors have behaved differently in recent contractions than in most previous recessions or depressions. They have risen instead of falling, so depression and unemployment no longer guarantee an end to inflation. For this reason,

TABLE 15.5

Contraction Amplitudes of Prices in Monopoly and Competitive Sectors

| Date of Contraction | Prices in Monopoly Sector | Prices in Competitive Sector |
|---|---|---|
| November 1948–October 1949 | −1.9% | −7.8% |
| July 1953–May 1954 | +1.9 | −1.5 |
| August 1957–April 1958 | +0.5 | −0.3 |
| April 1960–February 1961 | +0.9 | −1.2 |
| December 1969–November 1970 | +5.9 | −3.0 |
| November 1973–March 1975 | +32.8 | +11.7 |

Sources: Same as Table 15.4.

Note: Contraction amplitude means decline from peak to trough as a percentage of cycle average.

significant inflation has been continuous since 1967, though at different rates. The inflation began in the "normal" way with the spending during the Vietnam War, but its persistence through periods of falling demand indicates a new kind of animal. How much of this new phenomenon is associated with the competitive sector, and how much with the monopoly sector?

Various investigators have studied competitive and monopoly price behavior in the contractions since 1948. Their findings are summarized in Table 15.5. The *contraction amplitude* of a price index is defined as its change from the cycle peak to the cycle trough, given as a percentage of its average level over the whole business cycle. The table reveals that the pattern of the 1948 recession was the same as the pattern found by Gardiner Means (1975) for the 1929 and 1937 depressions. In all three cases, monopoly prices declined a little whereas competitive prices declined an enormous amount. In the 1954, 1958, and 1961 recessions we find the first indications of the new stagflation behavior (output stagnation plus price inflation). Competitive prices decline as usual, although by a small amount, but monopoly prices actually *rise* in the recessions, although again by a small amount. The new situation is very clear in the 1970 recession, in which competitive prices decline by a significant amount, whereas monopoly prices rise by a considerable amount. A finer division indicates even stronger price declines in the more competitive industries. Whereas prices in all industries under a 50 percent concentration ratio fell 3 percent, prices in industries under a 25 percent concentration ratio fell by 6.1 percent.

Price data on the 1973–1975 depression indicate that monopoly prices *rose* in the depression by an astounding percentage. This very large price increase throughout the now-dominant monopoly sector caused even competitive prices to show a small *rise* in the depression for the first time on record (because competitive firms have to buy some commodities from the monopoly sector). This undoubtedly caused great disruption in the competitive sector, decreased production, increased bankruptcies, and increased unemployment. Similar differences between competitive and monopoly price behavior have been found in Japan (see Kobayashi 1971).

## EXPLANATION OF PRICE BEHAVIOR

In almost all recessions before the 1950s, prices fell. That behavior was predictable and easily explained by traditional economic theory. Traditional microeconomic theory led us to expect that falling demand would cause *both* output and prices to decline. By a reduction of supply and also of prices in order to sell more of the supply, the amount of output supplied is brought back into equilibrium with the demand in each industry.

Similarly, in the aggregate, traditional macroeconomic theory in the 1950s predicted that an excess supply would lead to falling production, unemployment, and falling prices (or stable prices if there are "institutional rigidities" or monopoly power). On the other hand, traditional macroeconomic theory in the 1950s predicted price inflation only when there was an excess demand above the supply at full employment.

Traditional theory did not predict price inflation in the face of falling demand and unemployment, but this is what occurred in the monopoly sector in the recessions or depressions of 1954, 1958, 1961, 1970, 1975, 1980, and 1982. Of course, traditional theory would admit that firms with monopoly power could always set prices higher if they wished to restrict their supply enough to do so. But *why*, in the face of falling demand, should monopolies find it profitable to reduce their production so drastically as actually to increase prices?

Only a few economists—mostly in the Marxist, Post-Keynesian, and institutionalist traditions—have provided some answers to this question (see Kalecki 1968; Blair 1974; and Eichner 1973). In most of the monopoly sector, a single large firm in each industry sets prices; others simply follow this price leader. This "cost-plus" pricing by the large corporations has been confirmed by many empirical investigations (see Eichner 1973; Robinson 1979).

The giant corporations do *not* maximize their short-run profit by setting prices as high as possible at any given moment. Rather, they set prices with a profit margin that ensures their maximum long-run growth—and maximum long-run profits. This profit margin must, therefore, be enough to meet fully their expected needs for growth and expansion. Each corporation sets a *target* profit level, based on its previous record and the record of the leaders in its industry.

In a business expansion, to achieve their best long-run growth of profits, the giant corporations usually set their prices *below* what the market would pay in order (1) to discourage entry by rivals, (2) to gain acceptance of new products in a wider market, (3) to stop unions from claiming they have the ability to pay much higher wages, (4) to discourage government antitrust actions or attempts to put price controls on their products, and (5) to stabilize dividend payments (and stock prices) by preventing them from rising too high so that they won't fall as much in the next recession. This holding down of prices thus gives the monopoly or oligopoly firms more power to maintain or even raise prices in the following contraction—because the giant firm has acquired a larger market, fewer rivals, less government control, and so forth.

What happens if a giant corporation finds its sales revenue falling in a recession or depression? The firm will try to obtain enough revenue to reach its target profit by means of a higher price markup on the remaining sales. This process has been ably illustrated in an arithmetic example in an excellent article by Wachtel and Adelsheim (1976):

> For example, say a firm operating in a concentrated industry has direct costs (raw material and labor) of $200 per unit of output and sets its profit markup above direct costs at 20 percent, therefore selling the product for $240 per unit and making a profit of $40 per unit. Let us say the firm has a target level of profits of $40,000; to realize this profit level it will have to sell 1,000 units at $240 per unit. Now we have unemployment and a recession which causes the volume of sales to fall, say, to 960 units. But if the firm still has a target profit level of $40,000, which it wants to attain, it will have to raise its prices to slightly over $242 per unit from the previous level of $240 per unit. It does this by raising its percentage markup over costs to 21 percent compared to the previous 20 percent. Having increased their profit per unit, the firm now achieves its target profit level, but the resultant manifestation in the economy is the simultaneous occurrence of inflation and unemployment. (p. 15)

This illustration assumes little or no further decrease in demand when the price is marked up. But Wachtel and Adelsheim point out that their conclusion, that monopolies with these policies will raise prices in a recession, holds true even if the price increases cause some further decline in demand. Of course, even the tightest monopoly in reality will lose a few customers from any price rise, but most of them have a strong enough market control—and a strong enough image from advertising—

to ensure that they will not lose many customers. Just how high a price they can set is a function of their degree of monopoly.

More specifically, their degree of monopoly power over price has three main constraints. First, if the industry raises its prices (led by the price leader), how many customers are willing or able to switch to a substitute product? Second, if the price and profit margins are raised, how many new firms will be able to enter the industry, or how high are the barriers to such new entrants? Third, what is the realistic likelihood of any government intervention if the price gouging becomes too obvious to be overlooked?

It follows from this "cost-plus" behavior that such oligopoly firms do not change their prices as frequently as do competitive firms. Even if there is rapid inflation of prices and costs, these firms usually keep one price for quite a while, and then raise it to the new level dictated by their usual profit margin above costs. Thus, there is considerable evidence that in periods of business expansion and rapid inflation, it is the prices of the more competitive firms that rise more rapidly and change from day to day.

In a recession, however, the small, competitive firms are forced to drop their prices rapidly as demand falls (because none of them can restrict the industry supply) *regardless* of the effect on their profit rates. This is not true of the large, oligopoly firms. In the recession, if costs per unit of oligopoly firms remain the same (as they do in physical terms over a wide range of output), then the oligopolies may keep their prices the same to maintain a profit rate as near constant as possible. Of course, that entails extra reduction of production and the unemployment of many more workers than in a similar competitive industry, but that is not their worry.

Indeed, in recent recessions or depressions, when total sales were declining, the firms with monopoly power actually raised prices as far as they believed was necessary to maintain their profit margins and total profit. In order to make these price increases in the face of declining demand, they very drastically reduced their production, thereby worsening unemployment.

## MONOPOLY AND PROFIT RATES

If our economy operated under pure and perfect competition, then capital would flow immediately from areas of low profit rates to areas of high profit rates. It follows that the rate of profit would be equal in all industries. The rate of profit, however, is not equal in all industries. It is consistently higher in industries with greater monopoly power.

In this case, define a *concentration ratio* as the percentage of industry sales controlled by the eight largest firms. The ratio for each industry group is a weighted average of the ratios in each of its component industries. The *monopoly sector* is defined as all those industry groups with over 50 percent concentration in all the census years from 1949 to 1973 whereas the *more competitive sector* is all those groups with under 50 percent concentration in all the census years from 1949 to 1973. The *rate of profit* used here is the percentage of profit to sales in each industry group (other studies have found the exact same results when the rate of profit is defined as the percentage of profits to capital [see Sherman 1968, ch. 3]). The average rate of profit on sales for the monopoly sector (over 50 percent concentration) was 11.2 percent for the average of the years from 1949 to 1973. The average rate of profit on sales for the more competitive sector (under 50 percent concentration) was only 6.2 percent for the average of the years from 1949 to 1973; the difference between the two sectors was statistically significant (see Pulling 1978).

Why does the monopoly sector have higher profit rates than those of the competitive sector? In the first place, monopoly power means the ability to restrict supply and keep prices higher than in the competitive sector (within the three constraints discussed in the preceding section). The higher prices mean lower real wages for all worker-consumers. The profits of small, competitive businesses and farmers are also hurt by monopoly prices to the extent that they must purchase producer goods from the monopoly sector. Some large firms in the monopoly sector also have extra market power as large buyers of commodities from small competitive businesses, forcing down the prices charged by these small suppliers.

Large firms in the monopoly sector may also have extra power in the labor market, so they may add to profits by buying labor at a rate lower than the average wage. This factor may, of course, be somewhat offset by trade union action. In U.S. manufacturing, the wage share is lower in industries with high concentration, but is higher in industries with high unionization (see Henley, 1987a); where both factors operate, they partially offset each other. In the modern world, wages are not automatically determined by supply and demand in the market. They are determined by the bargaining strength of capital and labor (under given conditions of supply and demand), with monopoly capital usually in the stronger position. Workers are thus squeezed from both sides by monopoly. On the one hand, monopolies can charge workers higher prices as consumers; on the other hand, the monopolies can pay lower money wages by exerting their power in the labor market. (In reality, however, wage rates are usually higher in more concentrated industries because it is easier for unions to organize larger units and because monopolies usually find it easier to hand on higher wages to consumers as higher prices than to fight with unions.)

TABLE 15.6
Long-Run Profit Rate on Investment for All U.S. Manufacturing
Corporations, 1956–1975

| Size (by Assets) | Profit Rate (Profit before Taxes Divided by Stockholders' Capital) |
| --- | --- |
| $0–$1 million | 3.7% |
| $1 million–$5 million | 5.3 |
| $5 million–$10 million | 6.7 |
| $10 million–$50 million | 7.4 |
| $50 million–$100 million | 8.1 |
| $100 million–$250 million | 8.5 |
| $250 million–$1 billion | 8.8 |
| $1 billion and over | 11.7 |

Source: U.S. Federal Trade Commission, Quarterly Report of U.S. Manufacturing Corporations (Washington, D.C.: U.S. Government Printing Office, 1956–1975).

Additional monopoly profits come from lucrative government military contracts, which are financed from the workers' tax money, thus again increasing total profits. Extra-high returns from foreign investments abroad also add to monopoly profits; that is, profits are extracted from workers in foreign countries. In summary, monopolies or oligopolies make profit far above the average rate in several ways: (1) selling at higher prices to consumers, thereby lowering the real wage; (2) selling at higher prices to small businesses and farmers; (3) buying at lower prices from small businesses and farmers; (4) buying labor at lower wages from workers (but this is often offset by union organization, as noted above); (5) selling to the government at higher prices; and (6) buying labor power and materials at lower prices in foreign countries. Through these relatively high prices and low costs (always relative to a competitive firm in the same situation), the monopoly or oligopoly firms extract more profits from the worker-consumer-taxpayer here and abroad; they also transfer some profits from small businesses and farmers to themselves.

Table 15.6 shows the long-run profit rate on the capital investment of all stockholders averaged for the years 1956 through 1975. Each group of corporations is shown by the size of total assets, from the smallest (below a million) to the largest (over a billion). The relationship in Table 15.6 is very clear. The profit rate on investment rises monotonically as the size of the corporation increases.

The higher profit rate with size is explained by all the reasons given earlier for the higher profit rate resulting from monopoly power. To a large extent, large size means monopoly power, though there are industries where there are so many giant firms that the concentration ratio by four or eight appears low, and there are industries small enough for a medium-sized firm to have monopoly power. Moreover, when we examine behavior by size alone, this eliminates some of the distortion of the concentration ratios caused by one conglomerate's controlling subsidiaries in a number of different industries. The large size also directly affects profitability through economies of scale in production, in distribution, and in nationwide advertising. The large manufacturing corporation may also own its own natural resources. Moreover, the large corporation may have much cheaper access to finance either because of its credit rating or through a direct tie-in with a financial institution.

MONOPOLY PROFIT RATES OVER THE CYCLE

We have seen that the large monopoly corporations have higher profit rates in the long run than do small competitive firms. We have also seen that in expansions, the large monopoly firms raise their prices more slowly in order to increase their share of the market. In contractions, the large monopoly firms keep their prices from falling or actually raise them, whereas competitive firms have to reduce prices or raise them much less than do the monopolies. Given this difference in price conduct, what is the difference in performance of profit rates in the two sectors over the cycle? Table 15.7 shows the cyclical amplitudes of the monopoly and competitive profit rates.

In Table 15.7 the monopoly sector includes all major industry groups with concentration ratios greater than 50 percent in all of the Census of Manufactures years: 1954, 1958, 1967, and 1972. The competitive sector includes those groups with concentration ratios of less than 50 percent in all the same years. An expansion amplitude measures the peak value minus the initial trough value as a percentage of the cycle average. The contraction amplitude is the final trough minus the peak as a percentage. The profit rate is the total profit divided by sales (but very similar results have been found using the profit rate on capital [see Sherman 1968, ch. 6]).

Table 15.7 shows quite clearly that profit rates in the more competitive sector normally rise and fall more violently than do profit rates in the monopoly sector—which is the same pattern as that of price behavior. Profit rates in the more competitive sector of manufacturing rose faster than in the monopoly sector in four out of four expansions from 1949 to

TABLE 15.7
Amplitudes of Monopoly and Competitive Profit Rates

| Cycle | Monopoly Sector | | Competitive Sector | |
|---|---|---|---|---|
| | Expansion Amplitude | Contraction Amplitude | Expansion Amplitude | Contraction Amplitude |
| 1949–1954 | 32.1 | − 30.8 | 45.8 | − 56.9 |
| 1954–1958 | 21.6 | − 41.3 | 32.1 | − 47.8 |
| 1958–1961 | 33.5 | − 28.6 | 36.6 | − 47.1 |
| 1961–1970 | 25.0 | − 35.1 | 49.0 | − 32.3 |
| Average | 28.0 | − 34.0 | 40.9 | − 46.0 |

Source: Federal Trade Commission data compiled by Kathleen Pulling, *Market Structure and Cyclical Behavior of Prices and Profits, 1949–1975* (Ph.D. diss., University of California, Riverside, 1977).

1970. And profit rates in the more competitive sector fell further in three out of four contractions.

If we examine the cyclical amplitude of profit rates by size of corporation, the pattern is very similar. Table 15.8 shows the profit rate on sales by size of assets of corporations for the four cycles of 1949 to 1970 and the profit rate on capital by size of corporate assets for the three cycles of 1970 to 1982. The two different definitions of the profit rate are used to show that the change in definition does not change the results.

Table 15.8 reveals that the profit rates of the larger corporations rise less in expansions and fall less in contractions than do the profit rates of the smaller corporations. When we combine these findings with the similar findings on monopoly and competitive sectors shown in Table 15.7, the conclusion is that the profit rates of large monopoly corporations are far more stable than those of small competitive corporations.

Why do the large monopoly corporations have more stable profit rates in both boom and bust? First, they attempt to set their prices so as to maintain a stable profit rate. Second, their monopoly power allows them to set their prices at those levels. They maintain those prices in contractions by restricting their production (and employment). In expansion, they raise prices only slowly while rapidly increasing their production (and employment) to obtain or keep a high share of the expanding market. Third, the costs per unit of the largest corporations remain fairly constant over a wide range of output below full capacity. The unit costs of small corporations rise rapidly when they drop below optimum capacity. Fourth, the interest burden of small corporations, as compared to large corporations, is greater both because they pay higher interest rates and because they borrow a higher percentage of their capital. Fifth, and

TABLE 15.8
Amplitude of Profit Rates by Size

| Asset Size | Expansion Amplitude | Contraction Amplitude |
|---|---|---|
| PART A. Average of Four Cycles, 1949–1970 | | |
| Less than $250,000 | +83% | −83% |
| $250,000–$1 million | +39 | −55 |
| $1 million–$5 million | +37 | −52 |
| $5 million–$100 million | +28 | −27 |
| $100 million and over | +22 | −27 |
| PART B. Average of Three Cycles, 1970–1982 | | |
| Less than $5 million | +49 | −58 |
| $5–$25 million | +38 | −39 |
| $25–$100 million | +34 | −41 |
| $100–$1 billion | +25 | −37 |
| $1 billion and over | +24 | −33 |

Source: U.S. Census Bureau, Quarterly Financial Reports of Manufacturing Corporations (Washington, D.C.: U.S. Government Printing Office, 1949–1988).

Note: Profit rate for 1949–1970 is percentage of profit (before taxes) to sales for all U.S. manufacturing corporations. Profit rate for 1970–1982 is percentage of profit (before taxes) to stockholders' equity for all U.S. manufacturing corporations. All amplitudes are for specific cycles.

very important, the small corporations have all their eggs in one basket (with no reserves) whereas the large conglomerates are very diversified, with some investments in industries that may happen to grow despite a contraction (and an ability to shift reserve capital from one area to another).

There is also some evidence that crises hit the small competitive firms long before they hit the large monopoly firms. In the business expansions in the period 1949–1961, the profit margins of the monopoly industries (defined as those with over 50 percent concentration of sales by eight firms) did not feel the squeeze for 4 months beyond the average, turning down only 2.2 months before the expansion peak.

In summary, it appears that the increased monopolization of the economy increases the stability of prices and profits in the sector of high monopoly power, but reduces the stability of output and employment in that sector. Also, the stability of monopoly prices further destabilizes prices in the competitive sector. The instability of the competitive sector is the prime factor setting off each new crisis of overproduction and contraction. But the drastic decline of output and employment in the monopoly sector (used to keep prices high) greatly deepens the crisis.

## CONCENTRATION BY MULTINATIONAL (OR GLOBAL) FIRMS

The present high degree of economic concentration of assets in the whole capitalist world by a few enormous multinational, or global, corporations constitutes a new structural stage of international capitalism. The term "multinational" suggests management from many countries, whereas the truth is that each firm is governed mostly by the nationals of one developed capitalist country. The term "global corporation" may be less misleading; also, some economists are now using the more precise term "transnational corporations." The one viewpoint uniting all these corporations is the notion that the whole globe is their oyster, that vast profits may be made by control of markets in several countries.

In pursuit of profit, U.S.-based global corporations have been rapidly expanding abroad. In 1957, investment in plant and equipment by U.S. firms abroad was already 9 percent of total U.S. domestic investment in plant and equipment; but by 1970 that investment abroad rose to 25 percent of domestic investment. In terms of total assets of U.S. industries, by 1974 about 40 percent of all consumer goods industries, about 75 percent of the electrical industry, about 33 percent of the chemical industry, about 33 percent of the pharmaceutical industry, and over half of the $100 billion petroleum industry were located outside the United States (Barnet and Muller 1974, 17).

It is worth stressing, however, that the United States' former dominance of the global corporations has ended, and its share has dramatically declined. Whereas U.S.-based firms held two-thirds of all direct foreign investment in 1961–1970, the share of U.S.-based firms fell to less than half in 1976–1980 (Auerbach 1988, 243). At the same time, the share of West German- and Japanese-based firms rose dramatically. Thus one of the most important international facts today is the competition faced by U.S. firms.

It is also important to note that many transactions within and between capitalist countries are conducted solely between subsidiaries of the same parent corporation. A large-scale sample found that over 50 percent of total foreign trade transactions in the capitalist world are of this nonmarket intracorporate variety between subsidiaries of the same company (Muller 1975, 194). This means that taxes can be shifted to those countries where the rates are lowest. It also means that taxation policies may not operate—or may operate mainly to the benefit of the global giants.

Several studies show that the global corporations based in the United States absorb a disproportionate part of all U.S. government spending and tax reductions designed to stimulate the economy (Muller 1975, 188).

The global manufacturing corporations are served by global banks with tentacles almost everywhere (Auerbach 1988, 195–201). At their urging, additional credit has been created as a new currency, the huge pool of Eurodollars (and the special drawing rights, which also act as currency). Since there are no reserve deposit requirements on the Eurodollars, they are particularly unstable and contribute a strong impetus to inflationary pressures by further credit creation. This international credit expansion plus rapid monetary flows between corporate subsidiaries across borders make it less possible than ever for any capitalist nation to control its money supply by any conceivable monetary policies.

It should also be noted that union bargaining power has been further weakened by the power of the global corporations to shift production rapidly from areas of high wages to low-wage areas. For example, if the United States has high wages, they shift to Mexico, and if even Mexican wages are considered too high, they shift to Hong Kong.

The multinational or global firms are the present instrument whereby enormous profits are extracted from the neocolonial countries and sent back to the imperialist countries. For example, U.S. firms' profits from abroad were only 7 percent of total U.S. corporate profits in 1960, but had risen to 30 percent by 1974 (Muller 1975, 183). The top 298 U.S.-based global corporations earn 40 percent of their entire net profit overseas, and their rate of profit from abroad is much higher than their domestic profit rate. Moreover, (1) the rate of profit in U.S. investments abroad is several times higher in the less developed than in the advanced capitalist countries; and (2) the less developed neocolonial countries generously make a good-sized contribution to U.S. capital accumulation (the same facts could be shown for European and Japanese investments in the Third World).

Finally, the international concentration of investment decisionmaking in a relatively small number of corporations plus the very intimate ties of international trade and investment among all the capitalist countries bind these economies closely together. Therefore, as will be explained in detail in Chapter 16, a contraction begun in one country or in just a few global corporations spreads at lightning speed to the others.

## Conclusion

The phenomenon of inflation appears in recessions now because of the vast increase in concentrated monopoly power (both in the U.S. economy and worldwide). In several recessions of the 1950s and 1960s, though competitive prices dropped in each contraction, monopoly prices rose. In the depressions of 1975 and 1980, general inflation increased competitive prices a little, whereas monopoly prices soared. As a result of the monopolists' control over prices—as well as some other factors associated with absolute size—the monopoly profit rates are relatively stable, declining relatively little in recession or depression. The small competitive firms, however, bear the full burden of the profit decline in depression (although workers shoulder an even larger burden through reduced real wages). Hence, increasing monopoly has caused greater declines of production and unemployment, while raising prices through that very restriction of supply.

The existence of monopoly, therefore, increases cyclical unemployment to a higher level than it would be if there were no monopoly. Unlike the neoclassical view, however, the rest of this book has shown that there would continue to be cyclical unemployment even if there were competitive capitalism (with no rigidities or monopoly power).

## Appendix 15.1
### A Profit Squeeze (Nutcracker) Model with Monopoly Power

How should the profit squeeze (or nutcracker) model of Chapter 13 be modified to reflect the reality of monopoly power? Monopoly power affects price behavior. Monopoly power affects profit behavior, wage behavior, and investment behavior—each of which is different in large corporations in concentrated industries than in small firms in more competitive industries. Moreover, by affecting income distribution (as shown by Kalecki [1968, ch. 1]), monopoly power affects consumption, and thereby changes the value of the multiplier. By affecting investment behavior, monopoly power changes the value of the accelerator.

In brief, the behavioral functions of every variable are different in the monopoly sector (meaning more concentrated industries) than in the competitive sector (meaning more competitive industries). Therefore, the simplest modification is to disaggregate the model into two sectors, each having all the behavioral functions, but also showing how the two sectors will affect each other and will aggregate together in the whole economy. The monopoly sector may be defined as all industries above a certain concentration ratio, while the competitive sector may be defined as all industries below a certain concentration ratio.

As complex as such a model would be it may be criticized for simplicity. First, concentration ratios are not a very good indicator and certainly not the only indicator of monopoly power. Other indicators, such as barriers to entry, would be needed to create an index of monopoly power for each industry. Second, there are not two clearly distinct sectors, but a range from the largest firms in the most concentrated industries to the smallest firms in the most competitive industries. Instead of a two-sector model, an $n$-sector model would be needed to show the full spectrum of behavior from competitive to monopoly behavior. Such a model would illustrate the important differential behavior of industries according to monopoly power over the business cycle, but it would not change the overall behavior of the endogenous business cycle model.

### Bibliographic Essay on Monopoly Power

The best single study of monopoly power, prices, and profits is by Joseph Bowring (1986). An important, pioneering Marxist study of monopoly power is by Baran and Sweezy (1966). A thorough follow-up on the pros and cons of the Baran and Sweezy thesis is by John Foster (1986). For a Marxist view of monopoly power completely opposed to Baran and Sweezy's views—and opposed to the views of this author—see Willi Semmler (1982). A beautifully and clearly written popular book by a left-wing liberal on monopoly and inflation is by John Case (1981). There is a comprehensive and incisive presentation of the Post-Keynesian view in Alfred Eichner (1976). A very interesting and useful discussion of monopoly and inflation is by Malcolm Sawyer (1982). There is an excellent survey of theories of monopoly capitalism by Malcolm Sawyer (1988). A brilliant book on the evolution of monopoly power in the United States is by John Munkirs (1985). A powerful collection of institutionalist articles on monopoly power is in Wallace Peterson (1988b). The merger movement is analyzed clearly in Du Boff and Herman (1989). A very useful survey and contribution to the Marxist debate on monopoly power is in Amitava Dutt (1987). The best discussion of conglomerates is in William Dugger (1985). For neoclassical views of mergers and antitrust policy, see Steven Salop (1987); Laurence White (1987); and Richard Schmalensee (1987). For neoclassical views of takeovers, see Hal Varian (1988); Shleifer and Vishay (1988); Michael Jensen (1988); Jarrell, Brickley, and Netter (1988); and F. M. Scherer (1988).

# CHAPTER 16

# The International Economy and Business Cycles

THIS CHAPTER REMOVES the unreal assumption that the U.S. economy is isolated and self-sufficient. The closed economy assumption was useful till now to clarify the domestic aspects of the business cycle; but its unreal nature is emphasized by Dernberg (1989), who says: "Since there is no such thing as a closed economy . . . it follows that much of macroeconomics [using that assumption] is not only incomplete, but it is also incorrect" (p. 1). This chapter examines how the U.S. business cycle behaves in the real world of international trade, investment and finance (an outstanding collection of articles on these issues is MacEwan and Tabb [1989]). The chapter begins with the dramatic history of the rise and fall of U.S. economic power. In that historical context, the chapter turns to theories of international transmission of cycles, followed by empirical analysis of what actually happens. The hypothesis of this chapter is that the close international integration of the capitalist economies has increased instability.

## RISE OF THE U.S. EMPIRE

Until the Civil War, U.S. capitalism was far behind European capitalism. It had the advantage, however, of having no feudal or semifeudal encumbrances. After the Civil War, it also abolished slavery and opened the whole country to capitalism. Moreover, the U.S. economy was relatively short of labor, so it was forced to use the most advanced technology. As a result, U.S. industrialization proceeded very rapidly after 1870, and it eventually overtook and passed British and other European industry. Finally, the two world wars devastated much of Europe, but stimulated the U.S. economy. By 1945 the United States had emerged completely dominant in the capitalist world, though this situation lasted only a brief time in a historical perspective. From 1945 till the mid-1960s, the U.S. economy was far more powerful than Europe's or Japan's, while U.S. military power played policeman trying to maintain imperialist control of the Third World (for an insightful discussion of theories of imperialism, see Griffin and Gurley [1985]).

Between 1945 and 1950, the U.S. gross domestic product (GDP) was equal to that of the whole rest of the world combined. Thus, in 1950 the French GDP was only 10 percent of the U.S. GDP; West Germany's, only 8 percent; Italy's, only 5 percent; Japan's, only 4 percent; the United Kingdom's, only 13 percent—and all five, only 39 percent of the U.S. GDP. In 1950, the United States produced 82 percent of all the world's passenger vehicles, produced 55 percent of the world's steel, and consumed 50 percent of the world's energy (see Syzmanski 1975, 65–70).

In the 1950s and early 1960s, U.S. firms also extended their control over much of European industry. By 1965, U.S. firms or their subsidiaries owned 80 percent of computer production, 24 percent of the motor industry, 15 percent of the synthetic rubber industry, and 10 percent of the production of petrochemicals within the entire European Common Market. Furthermore, it is well to remember how concentrated this ownership was. About 40 percent of all U.S. direct investment in Britain, France, and West Germany was owned by Ford, General Motors, and Standard Oil of New Jersey. (For most of the data in this section, see Mandel [1970].)

From World War II to the early 1960s, U.S. firms maintained a relative superiority over Western European firms because of (1) greater size of capital assets, (2) greater total U.S. savings, and (3) greater technological advances. The size advantage of U.S. corporations was indicated by the fact that of the hundred largest global corporations, sixty-five were based in the United States, eleven in the United Kingdom, eighteen in other Common Market nations, and five in Japan. Because they had greater size and financial power, U.S. firms were able to do more technological research in this period. Furthermore, the continued enormous U.S. military spending subsidized much technological research for U.S. firms. U.S spending on research per capita was three to four times European research spending. Finally, the United States drained away many of the best brains in Europe (after they were trained in Europe). Between 1949 and 1967, about 100,000 of the best doctors, scientists and technicians left Western Europe for the United States.

DECLINE OF THE U.S. EMPIRE, MID-1960s TO THE PRESENT

In spite of all these initial advantages, the superiority of the U.S. economy in world production faded away and has now been replaced by competition by European and Japanese firms, frequently superior in size, research, and industrial innovation. The capitalist economies of Japan and Western Europe began in 1945 with a skilled labor force but devastated factories. As their industry was rebuilt from scratch, they used the latest technology and began the long march to catch up with the U.S. economy. Whereas the data show that the United States ruled supreme in the early 1950s, it was being challenged by the growing power and competition of Japan and Western Europe in every market by the early

1970s—and they have surpassed the U.S. economy in many areas in the 1980s.

By the 1970s, the United States was still the largest economy, but it no longer was far larger than the combination of all the rest. Thus, by 1972 the French gross domestic product (GDP) had risen to 17 percent of U.S. GDP, West Germany's had risen to 22 percent, Italy's, to 10 percent, Japan's, incredibly, to 24 percent, and the United Kingdom's, to 14 percent—all five of these together now had a GDP equal to 86 percent of U.S. GDP. In specific areas of basic production, the U.S. share of the world total fell between 1950 and 1972 from 82 percent to 29 percent of passenger vehicles, from 55 percent to 20 percent of steel production, and from 50 percent to 33 percent of world energy production.

In the 1970s and 1980s, the competitive position of Japan and Western Europe was further strengthened by the fact that their productivity per labor hour rose much faster than did U.S. productivity. On the other hand, Japanese and West European wage levels also rose faster than did U.S. wage levels, which hurt their competitive position.

The decline of the U.S. empire had several obvious results. First, U.S. corporations can no longer easily sell excess production abroad, so it is no longer possible to increase exports to avoid recession. Second, U.S. corporations have lost some degree of control in some of the Third World, so prices of some raw materials—mainly oil—greatly increased in the 1970s (though oil prices have now declined). A third result of relative U.S. decline is that foreigners have now vastly increased their investments in the U.S. economy. Foreign investments had risen to $481 billion, or almost half a trillion dollars, by 1980 (data from U.S. Department of Commerce, discussed in Tamalty 1981, 1). Of these investments, 50 percent were held by West Europeans, 7 percent by Canadians, 7 percent by Japanese, and 21 percent by others, including Middle Easterners. Since profits from these investments fluctuate with the U.S. economy, they also help transmit U.S. depressions abroad.

Of course, U.S. investments abroad are still vast (but foreign investment in the U.S. economy grew faster in the last ten years). U.S. private investment abroad was $12 billion assets abroad in 1950, but had risen to $214 billion assets abroad by 1980. In 1950, U.S. firms repatriated $1.5 billion in profits to the United States, but this had risen to $43 billion in profits by 1980 (see Harrison and Bluestone 1988, 27). Thus, if the rest of the world suffers recession, less profits flow back to the United States. Since these profits are now relatively very important to the U.S. economy, recession abroad may cause a major depressing effect on the U.S. economy.

Fourth, in the 1950s and 1960s, the United States was the largest net creditor and supplier of capital to the rest of the world. Now, the United States is the largest net debtor in the world. In 1981 the net U.S. international investment was $141 billion, but by 1987 it was minus $403 billion (see MacEwan 1989, 17). This is a momentous transformation.

Fifth, when the United States was the dominant economic power in the 1950s and 1960s, it was able to maintain a fixed exchange ratio of its currency to gold. Other currencies kept their reserves in dollars and used the dollar as their base. When the U.S. economy relatively weakened in the 1970s, it was forced to go to a flexible exchange ratio. Since the value of the U.S. dollar could then change rapidly, this action greatly increased international financial instability.

Sixth, another reflection of reduced U.S. economic strength versus West European and Japanese competitors is the deficit in the U.S. trade balance. In the 1950s and 1960s the United States exported vastly more than it imported, so all other countries complained of a "shortage of dollars," while the United States had a flow of dollars into it. The surplus of dollars from exports was used up by (1) huge U.S. investments abroad plus (2) enormous U.S. military spending and military aid abroad.

The competition of Europe and Japan then reduced the share of the U.S. economy in world exports. The U.S. share of world exports fell from 21 percent in 1957 to 14 percent in 1983 (see Harrison and Bluestone 1988, 27). In the same period, U.S. imports of oil and other products rose in value. Therefore, a trade deficit developed, which has persisted and grown. This deficit rose from $25 billion in 1980 to $160 billion in 1987 (for an insightful analysis, see MacEwan [1989]). The effect of this deficit is that instead of demand flowing into the United States to pay for net exports, there is actually demand flowing out of the United States to pay for net imports.

It is worth tracing this change in export and import patterns in some detail, as background for the cyclical analysis to follow. According to the official data (Council of Economic Advisers 1988), from 1960 through 1969, U.S. imports averaged 3.1 percent of GNP, while exports were 3.7 percent of GNP, so the United States had a comfortable trade surplus; that is, net exports were 0.6 percent of GNP (having been 0.7 percent in the 1950s). There was a drastic change in the 1970s. From 1970 through 1979, imports rose to 5.9 percent of GNP, while exports rose only to 5.4 percent, so there was a trade deficit; that is, net exports averaged −0.5 percent of GNP. The situation worsened in the 1980s. From 1980 through 1987, U.S. imports grew to an average 8.5 percent of GNP, while exports rose to only 6.3 percent of GNP, so net exports reflected a large deficit, at −2.2 percent of GNP. Thus, trade became much more important, while the balance of trade changed from a surplus to a large deficit.

## Theory of Business Cycle Spread

The channels for international transmission of business cycles are (1) international trade, (2) international investment, and (3) the international financial system.

The channel of transmission of cycles through international trade works like this. Suppose there is a growth in U.S. exports so that exports become greater than imports (a *favorable* balance of trade). This means a net increase in demand for U.S. products; it will raise income and output if the economy has been below full employment. Of course, if there already was full employment, the increased demand could lead only to higher prices. Alternatively, suppose the United States increases its imports till it has fewer exports than imports (an unfavorable balance of trade). In this case, the U.S. loses buying power to foreign countries, causing less demand and more unemployment.

Suppose the U.S. economy is in a depression and the rest of the world is not. Then since U.S. citizens have less income, the United States will import less from other countries. In that case, the other countries will have a decrease in the demand for their commodities, causing depressive effects on their industries. Since the rest of the world then will have less income, part of its adjustment will be made by getting fewer imports from the United States. Thus, the process is cumulative.

Just the opposite cumulative process occurs if one country begins to recover from a depression. If U.S. income begins to rise, U.S. citizens have more money to spend, and foreign goods look more attractive. Therefore, the United States imports more of both consumer and investment goods, leading finally to increased income and increased imports in other countries. Of course, in either expansion or depression, we should keep in mind that the cumulative process, whereby changes in imports and exports have a multiple effect as they pass from country to country, requires a finite amount of time for each new round of trading. Moreover, not all the increased income that a country gets from increased exports will be respent for imports; some of it will leak into internal spending and will not rebound to increase the exports of another country.

If a government imposes trade barriers that lessen trade between countries (in order to protect its own industry in a contraction), such trade barriers may intensify an international contraction. The most famous U.S. action was the very high Smoot-Hawley tariff, which further reduced international trade in the Great Depression. Of course, other countries may retaliate by raising their tariffs against U.S. goods. If the retaliation is of the same magnitude, then the U.S. tariffs will reduce U.S. imports, but foreign tariffs will equally reduce U.S. exports. The result will be lower world trade, world output, and world employment, but no change in the U.S. balance of trade.

## INVESTMENT AND SPREAD OF CYCLES

The second major means of transmitting the business cycle is via international investment. If Japan loans or invests in the United States, then usually part of the money is spent in Japan on equipment and part is spent in the United States on installation and operation of equipment, as well as wages of labor. This transaction will have several effects. It will immediately result in some increase in demand in Japan and some in the United States. To the extent that the money is respent, there will again result cumulative and multiple effects, which may increase a boom or aid a revival from depression. We may note that there will be secondary effects not only on imports and exports of goods and capital, but also to some extent on internal consumption and investment.

Some observers have stressed that investment abroad means less excess of savings at home; thus, "the stability of capital-exporting countries with high rates of saving has . . . been dependent on the recurrent appearance of new opportunities for investment abroad" (League of Nations 1945, 3; also see Severn 1974; Miller and Whitman 1973). But this very important source of investment opportunities is also very fluctuating and cyclical in nature. The fact that it has even greater fluctuations than those of domestic investment is due to the greater sensitivity of investment abroad to changes in the business outlook in other countries. The greater sensitivity is due, in turn, to the greater uncertainty because of distances, different laws, customs, and political trends. Among the most often mentioned problems of international investment are (1) difficulties of management owing to long lines of communication and transportation, (2) inadequate legal protection, (3) ignorance of language and customs, and (4) risk of transfer restrictions on profits or outright confiscation. These factors account for the uncertainty and sensitivity that lead to wide cyclical fluctuation of foreign investments.

The approach of classical economics stressed the ability of foreign investments to raise the average rate of profit of the home country. J. S. Mill mentions investment abroad as

> the last of the counter-forces which check the downward tendency of profits. . . . This is, the perpetual overflow of capital into colonies or foreign countries, to seek higher profits than can be obtained at home. . . . In the first place, it carries off a part of the increase of capital from which the reduction of profit proceeds. Secondly, the capital so carried off is not lost, but is chiefly employed . . . in founding colonies which become large exporters of cheap agricultural produce. (Mill [1848] 1920, Book 4, ch. 4: 736)

In his view, the rate of profit of the capital-exporting country would be raised by having less competition at home, higher profits from abroad, and a supply of cheap raw materials for its industries. In this context it is possible, if a depression started in a capital-importing country, that the lesser returns on investment would have depressing effects abroad.

The income from investments abroad also has an effect on demand because it is equivalent to an invisible export. The receiver of investment income receives money or credit from the debtor. If that money or credit is immediately reinvested in the debtor country, then the effect will be expansionary (though most profits are usually repatriated to the home country). In a depression period, creditors are more likely than ever to withdraw those funds from the debtor country back to their own country.

Every investment must eventually produce a supply of goods on the market. Thus, though the original effect of an international investment will be to increase demand for the factors of production, it is often claimed that its later effect will be to compete with the industry of the home country. This depends on the type of goods produced and where they are marketed. If the goods are of the same type as already produced by either the capital exporter or importer and are sold in the market of the previously established industries, then, of course, the effect may very well be depressing at a future time. On the other hand, if the goods are raw materials needed by the capital exporter, then their production and sale may even cause the rate of profit in the capital exporter country to rise.

There does seem to be a considerable degree of agreement on the main points of the trade and investment transmission mechanisms, which might be summed up as follows: If a depression begins in a country that imports a large amount of goods relative to world supply, then the rest of the world feels a sudden decline in the demand for many kinds of goods. This seems initially to be the main instrument of spreading the depression. Subsequently, however, in the exporting countries the lower demand for their goods lowers their income, their consumption, and the investment opportunities in their countries. When the effects reach back to the initiating countries, not only may there be some drop in demand for their finished goods exports, but usually the demand for their capital export drastically declines in view of the drying up of investment opportunities abroad.

## BEHAVIOR OF INVESTMENT AND TRADE IN THE GREAT DEPRESSION

In the Great Depression, the flow of U.S. investment abroad declined from over $1.3 *billion* in 1929 to $1.6 *million* in 1932 (League of Nations 1934, 220–30). During a depression, countries may still desire most intensively to find or conquer new markets for goods and capital export, as Britain did in the nineteenth century, but this easy road to recovery has seldom been open in the twentieth century. (As one exception, it is possible that massive U.S. aid to Europe during the Marshall Plan period moderated early postwar U.S. recessions.) In fact, markets have narrowed with the increase of government ownership in large areas of the world, for example, after the Soviet revolution of 1917. Usually, the world must await the expansion of income and increase of imports in the industrially advanced capitalist countries before recovery can spread around the world.

As might be expected, the U.S. depression of the thirties had the worst effect on (1) those in debt to the United States, who had been paying back principal, interest, and dividends by exports to the United States; (2) exporters of producers' goods (especially raw materials) because these had constituted 85 percent of U.S. imports in the previous period; and (3) those who exported consumer goods to the United States (mostly food), which constituted the other 15 percent of U.S. imports. For this reason, Argentina and Australia, large exporters of raw materials, were immediately among the hardest hit and were the first to go off the gold standard. On the other hand, the immediate detrimental effects of the Great Depression did force a positive long-run adjustment in some countries. For example, several Latin American countries, such as Brazil, (1) defaulted on their debts, and (2) shifted to import-substituting industrialization, which led to a growth spurt in the postwar period. The growth in Latin America eventually led to more U.S. exports to that area.

When there is a period of expansion in the United States, some of the increased income also appears to be used for increases both in the import of finished products for consumption, which are mostly luxuries, and in the import of producers' goods for new investment, most of which are raw materials. Though U.S. imports were a small portion of U.S. income in 1929, a decrease of U.S. income meant a larger than proportional decrease of imports. This was because a larger than proportional part of the increase in income was devoted to investment in raw materials (because of the acceleration principle) and to consumption of luxuries (because demand for these items reacts most strongly to changes in income). Therefore, in the boom of the twenties, imports increased faster than did national income; while in the depression of the thirties, imports decreased even faster than did the rapidly falling national income.

In the sixteen business cycles from 1867 to 1938 (excluding the war-dominated period from 1914 to 1920), imports rose by 26 percent in the average expansion and fell by 19 percent in the average contraction (see Mitchell 1951, 312–32). By contrast, there was much less cyclical movement in U.S. exports because these were related to the cyclical movements of national income in other countries, which were only partly synchronized with U.S. national income. Thus, in the same sixteen business cycles, U.S. exports rose 15 percent in the average expansion and fell only 1 percent in the average contraction.

Since imports rose more than did exports in expansions, it followed (by definition) that net exports fell in expansions. Since imports fell more than did exports in contractions, net exports tended to rise in contractions. Thus, net exports were countercyclical. Since net exports were falling long before the peak, they exacerbated the downturn in profits by a reduction in demand. On the other hand, the usual rise in net exports in the depression helped set the stage for recovery.

It is the underdeveloped countries that are hardest hit by these wide fluctuations in trade. International investment and international trade in primary products—that is, in raw materials, both agricultural and mineral—show the greatest fluctuations. Therefore, it was observed of the Great Depression "that any country whose economy is intimately dependent on foreign investment or whose trade is greatly dependent on primary commodities will be seriously affected by swings of business arising outside its own borders" (League of Nations 1945, 92). Of course, this is still true.

The physical output of agriculture was stable or showing a slow rise during the entire 1920s and the 1930s. Manufactured products, on the other hand, rose up to 1929, and then dropped off rapidly. In 1933 world manufacturing output was only about 40 percent of that of 1929; it then rose slowly until manufacturing reached the 1929 level in 1938, only to fall off again. Mining activity and the output of minerals in world statistics show even greater fluctuation. In the period from 1918 to 1939, mineral production rose about as fast as did manufacturing in expansions, but minerals fell faster than did manufacturing in depressions (League of Nations 1945, 80). In price terms also, the fluctuations of raw materials are much greater than those of finished products. During the expansion of the twenties, raw material prices rose faster than did finished goods prices, then dropped much faster to the depression trough of 1933, and then rose more slowly till 1938; in the 1938 recession, raw material prices again dropped faster. In the world market, the *prices* of iron and steel had quite small fluctuations in this period, but the *prices* of both nonferrous metals and farm products had very large cyclical variations. Since raw materials are relatively expensive in the boom, the Third World raw materials producing countries tend to have a favorable balance of trade and good terms of trade in expansions. In the Great Depression, however, the Third World countries suffered both an unfavorable balance of trade and poor terms of trade. Moreover, although their exports were cut back in the depression, most of their imports were necessities, which could not be cut back so easily.

The drop in demand for commodities exported can have two effects, either lowering the price or lowering the amount, or both. The physical output and amount taken of most agricultural products for consumers are relatively stable because on the demand side they are necessities of life and on the supply side they are largely governed by nature and produced under extremely competitive conditions. Therefore, almost the total drop in food products, such as crops and livestock, is a drop in prices. Consequently, there is a proportionate drop in the people's income in these countries even though they still do the same amount of production.

The situation with minerals and industrial crops, which are used as raw materials for which the demand fluctuates very greatly, is quite different. In the case of raw materials—minerals most obviously—there is a great drop in output and employment as well as in price and income. In the brief recession of 1937 to 1938, for example, not only did the amount of tin exported from Bolivia (its main export) drop precipitously, but the price of tin fell by 45 percent.

## CYCLICAL PATTERN OF IMPORTS AND EXPORTS SINCE WORLD WAR II

When the demand of other countries for imports rises, then the United States can export more. Thus, one quantitative study in the 1950s concluded: "During expansions in world imports, U.S. export quantities, prices, and values rose; during contractions in world imports, they fell (or rose at a slower rate)" (Mintz 1959, 305). It is still true today that a rise in world income results in more imports from the United States.

Thus, U.S. exports rise in the expansion phase of other countries. "U.S. exports to Canada, the United Kingdom, West Germany, and Japan, for example, grew six times as fast when those countries were in an expansion phase of their growth cycle than when they were in a contraction phase" (Klein and Moore 1985, 306; also see Klein 1976). In a later section, however, it will be shown that the cycles of the leading capitalist countries tend to move together. Therefore, U.S. exports tend to expand in U.S. expansions because these foreign economies are expanding. U.S. exports tend to fall in U.S. contractions because these foreign economies are contracting. Thus, Dornbusch and Fischer (1986, 462) find that U.S. exports are roughly procyclical from 1950 to 1980.

What about U.S. imports? When U.S. income is expanding in a cyclical expansion, our imports rise because we demand more of foreign goods. Thus, for Canada, the United Kingdom, West Germany, and Japan, "exports out of those countries to the United States (our imports from them) grew more than three times as fast as during upswings in the

TABLE 16.1
U.S. Exports and Imports

| Variable | Expansion Amplitude | Contraction Amplitude |
|---|---|---|
| PART A. Average, 7 Cycles, 1949–1982 | | |
| Imports (257) | 28.4 | −4.8 |
| Exports (256) | 23.5 | −2.6 |
| Net exports (256–257) | −5.1 | −2.2 |
| PART B. Average, 4 Cycles, 1949–1970 | | |
| Imports (257) | 31.1 | 0.6 |
| Exports (256) | 20.8 | −0.4 |
| Net exports (256–257) | −10.3 | −1.0 |
| PART C. Average, 3 Cycles, 1970–1982 | | |
| Imports (257) | 27.1 | −11.9 |
| Exports (256) | 24.8 | −5.6 |
| Net exports (256–257) | −2.3 | 6.3 |

Source: U.S. Department of Commerce, Bureau of Economic Analysis, *Handbook of Cyclical Indicators, A Supplement to the Business Conditions Digest* (Washington, D.C.: U.S. Government Printing Office, 1984).

Note: The numbers in parentheses are the series numbers in the source.

U.S. growth cycle as during its downswings" (Klein and Moore 1985, 306). Thus, U.S. imports tend to be procyclical because they are a function of U.S. income; Dornbusch and Fischer find that imports conform to the cycle better than exports (1986, 462).

Table 16.1, Part A, reveals that in the seven cycles in the period from 1949 to 1982, U.S. imports and exports were both procyclical. Imports rose more rapidly in expansions and fell more rapidly in contractions. Net exports are equal to exports minus imports, so they measure the net flow of demand into the United States. Since imports rose and fell faster than exports, net exports were countercyclical, falling in expansions and rising in contractions.

Why do imports tend to rise more rapidly than exports do and also fall more rapidly than exports do? The reason is that U.S. imports are closely tied to the U.S. cycle because they are a function of U.S. income. U.S. exports, however, are only indirectly related to the U.S. cycle. U.S. exports fluctuate procyclically only to the degree that other countries' cycles are synchronous with the U.S. cycle in timing and in amplitude. Foreign cycles are not in perfect timing synchronization with U.S. cycles. Moreover, the United States—which is the largest and most advanced capitalist economy—is subject to greater economic instability, reflected in higher cyclical amplitudes in production and income than those of other capitalist countries (described below). Since the rest of the world is not perfectly synchronous with the U.S. economy and since the U.S. economy has greater fluctuations, it follows that U.S. exports have a smaller cyclical amplitude than that of U.S. imports.

Thus, net exports tend to be countercyclical (this analysis is also supported by Dornbusch and Fischer [1986, 462]). This means that the flow of money demand out of the U.S. economy rises faster than does the flow of money demand into the U.S. economy in the average expansion. Net export demand, as a result, declines in the expansion and appears to be a depressing factor on the whole. On the other hand, net exports tend to rise in the contraction, so they appear to be a stimulating factor at that time.

Parts B and C of Table 16.1 also show some differences between the 1949–1970 period and the 1970–1982 period. In both periods, in the average expansion, imports rose faster than did exports, so net exports declined. In the mild cycles of the 1950s and 1960s, however, U.S. personal disposable income and consumption continued to rise slowly in contraction—so U.S. imports also rose slowly in contractions in that period. Since imports rose and exports fell, net exports continued to fall in contractions, being a mildly depressing factor.

The 1970–1982 period reverted to the usual cyclical pattern, with both imports and exports falling in contractions. Imports fell twice as fast as exports did, so net exports rose in contractions. This behavior is shown in more detail in Figure 16.1 and Figure 16.2. These figures bear out the picture already discussed, adding one new fact. In this particular period, in the last segment of expansion, exports rose faster than did imports, so net exports were a leading indicator, turning upward before the peak.

It would appear in the 1970s and early 1980s, net exports were a depressing factor in the first three quarters of expansion, and then added to demand just before the peak and during the contraction. This appearance, however, is misleading. Throughout this period, the United States suffered a trade deficit, or negative net exports. Therefore, the proper conclusion is that the large trade deficit was a strongly negative factor, meaning a net reduction of U.S. domestic demand, in all phases of the cycle. It was just a little less negative at the end of expansion and in the contraction.

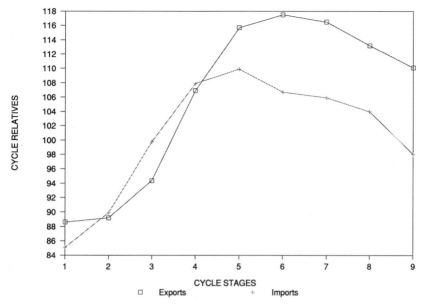

Fig. 16.1. Imports and Exports: Amplitude by Stage Averaged across Three Cycles, 1970–1982 (from series 257 and 258, Appendix E)

## INTERNATIONAL FINANCE AND TRANSMISSION OF CYCLES

The third major transmission belt for international instability and cycles is the financial system (see the classic study by Morgenstern [1959]).

After World War II, the U.S. dominance in production and trade carried over into financial dominance (see the excellent studies by Magdoff [1969, 1979]). One reflection of this dominance was the negotiation of the Bretton Woods agreement in the way desired by the United States, making the U.S. dollar the international currency. U.S. banks also spread their branches and influence around the world. In the 1970s and 1980s, however, since the decline of U.S. production and trade relative to other countries, the U.S. has also lost some of its financial dominance. This loss of dominance is reflected in many ways, including stiff competition in finance from banks of other countries.

The evidence on the present high degree of international integration of finance is clear but there is a considerable controversy as to its effects. One major characteristic of financial integration is mobility of capital across international frontiers. Most economists in this area have argued that international capital mobility has increased (see the excellent article by Epstein and Gintis [1988], but see the qualifications by Zevin [1988]). There has also been a large body of literature arguing that explanations

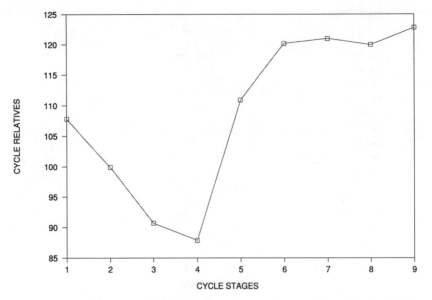

Fig. 16.2. Net Exports: Amplitude by Stage Averaged across Three Cycles, 1970–1982 (from series 258 − 257, Appendix E)

of saving and investment that assume a closed economy are obsolete. Rather, it is argued, all macroeconomics must be considered anew in an international model (see, for example, Dornbusch 1980; also see Dernberg 1989). In practical terms, the globalization of finance means an increase in the power of business to shift to other countries, as well as a decrease in the power of governments to control their own economies. As one example, the early Mitterand government attempted to expand the French economy by increasing buying power, but most of the added spending went into imports, not domestic sales.

Increases in financial integration are also reflected in the growth of the market in Eurodollars, greater use of computer-facilitated information flow, opening up of stock markets to foreign nationals, the increase in international banking cited above, and various reductions in government controls on capital flows. It is certainly true that the age of electronic miracles has made information flow around the world almost instantaneous. But this has not resulted in a new international equilibrium mechanism wherein all capitalist firms and countries adjust smoothly and flexibly to all changes in a financially integrated world. On the contrary, careful studies by MacEwan (1986) and by Gordon (1988) find a world in which the world financial system is highly integrated, but integration exacerbates economic problems because the instability of one country is rapidly transmitted to all other countries. For example, in the stock market collapse of October 1987, the news traveled immediately; as a result, U.S., Japanese, and European markets all fell in unison (though at very different rates). In this example, close financial integration did not result in equilibrium, but in the spread of instability. As Dernberg (1989) states: "[T]he combination of flexible exchange rates and a high degree of international capital mobility have created a climate in which macroeconomic shock transmission from one country to another is enormous" (p. 7).

The tendency toward spreading instability has been very clear since the old U.S.-dominated financial order disappeared in the mid- to late 1960s, to be replaced by anxious competition and considerable chaos. Gordon (1988) points out: "Because of movement toward flexible exchange rates after the collapse of the Bretton Woods system in 1971, there was an increasing synchronization of business cycles among the advanced countries after 1971, leading to increasingly volatile fluctuations of economic activity. When one economy sneezed, others echoed" (p. 11).

In addition to stock market shocks and violent exchange rate fluctuations, another mechanism for spread of business cycle instability is through the banking system. MacEwan (1986) comments:

> There is substantial disagreement over the causes of the Great Depression of the 1930s, but there is little dispute over the fact that the failure of the capitalist world's financial system made a major contribution to the depth and duration of the economic crisis. When Austria's Kreditanstalt failed in 1931, international financial markets spread the impact through a run on German banks, a depreciation of sterling, extensive liquidation of dollars for gold, and eventually the widespread bank closings in the U.S. (p. 178)

The phenomenon of bank failures leading to other bank failures is not new, but the spread of bank branches all over the world and the almost instantaneous flow of information may make the international repercussions even greater today than previously.

One other mechanism of transmission of instability is especially important at the present time: the enormous mound of debt in the Third World owed to U.S. and European banks. The crisis in the Third World debt, and its effects, is analyzed in detail by MacEwan (1986); George (1988); and Pollin (1989). Repayment of these debts is improbable because they are so large relative to export earnings—especially in Brazil, Mexico, and Argentina, where in 1984 the ratios of debt to merchandise exports were, respectively, 45 percent, 69 percent, and 141 percent (MacEwan 1986, 180). If these debts are not repaid, they must be written off as bad debts by the banks, which makes the banks' own position visibly weaker. An excellent book on these issues, with policy suggestions, is Pool and Stamos (1989).

## Previous Empirical Studies of Synchronization of Business Cycles

So far, this chapter has found increased integration of trade, investment, and finance in the capitalist world. These increasingly integrated economies transmit instability very quickly from one to another. As a result, we would expect increased synchronization of production cycles. Moreover, if the production cycle in the leading capitalist countries is closely synchronized, the transmission mechanisms described above may have more violent effects as results of instability reverberate from one country to another. To what degree has increased synchronization occurred?

There have been several excellent studies of the degree of synchronization of the business cycle in various capitalist countries (see Morgenstern 1959; Mintz 1959, 1967; Hickman and Schleicher 1978; MacEwan 1984; and Klein and Moore 1985). Klein and Moore comment that "to varying degrees these researchers discovered evidence of synchronized economic movements among developed countries" (1985, 286). It is worth noting that in the nineteenth century, (1) as countries became industrialized they joined the international business cycle, and (2) countries that became colonies of the industrialized countries also became part of the international business cycle. Chapter 3 of this book discussed in detail Wesley Mitchell's extensive studies of how synchronization of cycles increased among countries as capitalism spread, with almost worldwide synchronization in the Great Depression of 1929.

Klein and Moore (1985) constructed an international composite coincident index, composed of the coincident indexes for seven countries (the United States, Canada, the United Kingdom, West Germany, France, Italy, and Japan). They found that much the same indicators (both coincident and leading) were consistent in performance in the seven countries. They found that their index showed clear business cycles, with troughs in 1958, 1961, 1963, 1967, 1971, and 1975, though some of these, such as 1963 and 1967, were only declines in the rate of growth and not absolute declines.

Klein and Moore found very little deviation from the international dates by the individual countries. In fact, they checked to see how many months each of ten capitalist countries was in phase with the international cycle. They found that Japan was in phase 86 percent of the time; Canada, 88 percent; France, 83 percent; the United Kingdom, 78 percent; the United States, 77 percent; the Netherlands, 77 percent; Belgium, 68 percent; Italy, 66 percent; and Sweden, 48 percent; with an average of 75 percent.

By far the best study of how much the synchronization of the cycle has increased in the 1970s and 1980s over that in the 1950s and 1960s is by Arthur MacEwan (1984). He examines monthly data, using three-month moving averages, for the United States, Japan, West Germany, France, Italy, the United Kingdom, and Canada, based on both the index of industrial production and the coincident composite index for each country. He begins by examining the simple question of how often various pairs of countries' composite indexes move in the same direction. For the 1950s and 1960s, he finds *no* statistically significant synchronization of cycles between the U.S. economy and any of the others, except for Canada, which does usually fluctuate with the U.S. economy. For 1970 through June 1981, however, he finds statistically significant synchronization of U.S. downturns with every country except Italy (MacEwan 1984, 67). This is an impressive confirmation of the hypothesis that synchronization has increased in this period. Also for the 1970s and early 1980s, he finds a statistically significant synchronization of U.S. upturns with Japan, West Germany, and Canada and some nonsignificant synchronization with France and the United Kingdom, but again little synchronization with Italy.

MacEwan also finds increased synchronization among the United States, Japan, and Europe when he uses upturns and downturns of indexes of industrial production, regression analysis based on composite indexes, and regression analysis based on indexes of industrial production. Within Europe, however, synchronization was high in the 1950s and 1960s, but did not increase in the 1970s. His findings indicate that increasing synchronization and rising economic integration are related: "The high degree of integration within Europe was associated with a relatively high degree of synchronization early on, and the growing synchronization of the United States and Japan within the group more recently has been associated with their growing integration into the world economy" (MacEwan 1984, 75). He cautions that trade integration is a large part of the story, but is not the only important aspect of integration. He puts a heavy emphasis on expansion of international credit and movements of liquid financial capital, as well as growing financial integration.

## DATA ON SYNCHRONIZATION OF BUSINESS CYCLES

The simplest way to compare the degree of synchronization among the advanced capitalist countries is to examine their cyclical amplitudes and cyclical patterns over the reference cycle dates for U.S. business cycles.

TABLE 16.2
Amplitudes of Industrial Production by Country
(in percentages of cycle base)

| Country | Average, 4 Cycles, 1949–1970 | | Average, 3 Cycles, 1970–1982 | |
|---|---|---|---|---|
| | Expansion | Contraction | Expansion | Contraction |
| United States (47) | 24.5 | −8.5 | 18.9 | −11.2 |
| Canada (723) | 28.4 | −0.9 | 15.4 | −8.7 |
| Japan (728) | 63.5 | 8.0 | 20.3 | −7.7 |
| OECD[a] (721) | 31.6 | 2.0 | 10.4 | −4.5 |
| West Germany (725) | 30.1 | 5.2 | 9.5 | −6.3 |
| United Kingdom (722) | 15.3 | 0.1 | 6.4 | −3.8 |
| Italy (727) | 33.5 | 5.8 | 15.1 | −6.6 |
| France (726) | 25.7 | 6.4 | 10.9 | −3.6 |

*Source*: Same as Table 16.1.

*Note*: The numbers in parentheses are the series numbers in the source.

[a] OECD is the Organization for Economic Development and Cooperation, which is the economic organization of the Western European countries.

Table 16.2 examines the cyclical amplitudes of industrial production in the leading capitalist countries.

Table 16.2 reveals striking differences between the mild cycles of the 1950s and 1960s and the more severe cycles of the 1970s and 1980s. In both periods, U.S. production rises and falls procyclically, though the average expansion is less and the average decline is greater in the latter period (1970–1982). In the case of Canada, in the 1970–1982 period, the expansion is almost half as much as in the earlier period, while the contraction is more than nine times as much as in the earlier period. In all the other countries (in Japan and Western Europe), the difference between the two periods is even clearer. In every case, the later expansions are much less than the earlier ones. In every case, there is a continued rise (though at a slower rate) in the contractions of the 1949–1970 period. But in every case, there are actual declines in the contractions of the 1970–1982 period.

The causes of this behavior are not mysterious. After World War II, Japan and Western Europe had very little production capacity and needed everything. Therefore, to the extent that financing was available (and much came from the United States), production grew rapidly in the 1950s and 1960s. Thus, even during U.S. recessions, when their exports to the United States declined, these countries continued to grow, though at a slower pace.

In the later period, the 1970s and 1980s, demand no longer grew so rapidly, so they were more vulnerable to economic recessions spreading from the United States. Furthermore, ties to the U.S. economy continued to grow stronger, both in trade and in reciprocal investment.

Figures 16.3, 16.4, and 16.5 compare the average cyclical behavior or industrial production in the United States, Japan, and the OECD countries of Western Europe in the 1970–1982 period. The similarity of behavior is striking. All three averages rise during U.S. reference cycle expansions, while all three decline during the last three-quarters of U.S. reference cycle contractions. The only difference is that Japanese and OECD industrial production indexes turn down one stage (about one quarter) later than the U.S. index does—possibly because they are pushed into recessions by the U.S. recession, with a time lag. At any rate, they are closely synchronized. It is worth repeating that MacEwan (1984) found the same result in econometric tests.

CONCLUSION

This chapter noted the decline and fall of U.S. domination over the world. Relevant international trends in the later period include (1) foreign competitors with higher sales and productivity growth than those of the U.S. economy; (2) the change to flexible exchange rates; (3) the change of the U.S. economy from net creditor to net debtor; (4) an enormous rise in the U.S. trade deficit; and (5) a huge Third World debt to U.S. banks, with many defaults occurring or expected. These long-run international trends have increased the vulnerability of the U.S. economy (for further discussion, see MacEwan [1990]).

This chapter analyzed and described empirically three major channels of transmission of instability and cycles. First, the simplest mechanism is the fluctuations of imports and exports; a relative decline in other countries' imports (because their income is contracting) results in less demand for U.S. exports. Second, foreigners may increase or decrease their direct investment in the United States, depending on their own investment resources or needs—while U.S. firms may make more or less profits abroad and may invest more or less abroad. Third, there are several mechanisms for transmission of instability in the financial sector—(i) one stock market collapse may lead to another; (ii) one bank failure may lead to another; (iii) violent exchange rate fluctuations may adversely affect trade; and/or (iv) bad debts of some countries may lead to bank failures in another country. It is important to remember that these mechanisms do not operate only between independent firms in different countries, but also

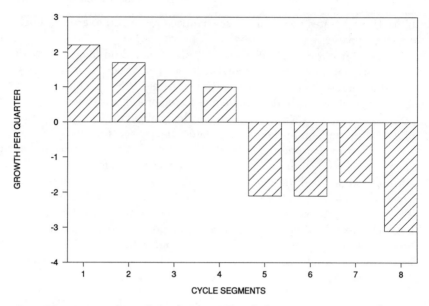

Fig. 16.3. U.S. Industrial Production: Growth by Segment Averaged across Three Cycles, 1970–1982 (from series 47, Appendix H)

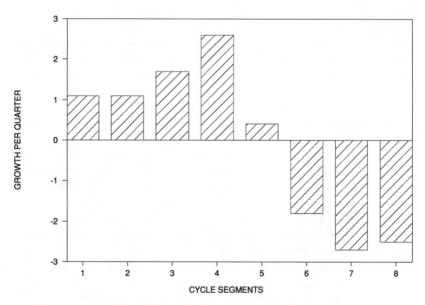

Fig. 16.4. Japanese Industrial Production: Growth by Segment Averaged across Three Cycles, 1970–1982 (from series 728, Appendix H)

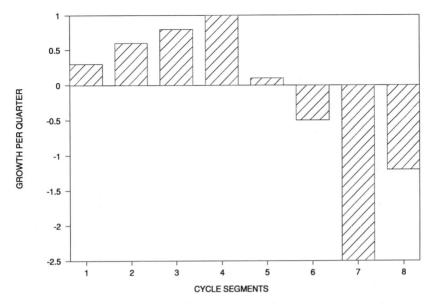

Fig. 16.5. OECD Industrial Production: Growth by Segment Averaged across Three Cycles, 1970–1982 (from series 721, Appendix H)

within and through the large conglomerate global firms that now dominate the global economy (as detailed in Chapter 15).

Capitalist economies are more highly integrated than in previous periods, so these transmission mechanisms operate rapidly to spread instability. As a result, boom and bust periods of the capitalist countries are more closely tied together than ever before. In the 1950s and 1960s, the U.S. economy was subjected to only minor cycles (while it was the dominant economic power). Almost all other capitalist economies showed continued growth with no absolute declines, but with lower growth rates in U.S. recessions. In the 1970s and early 1980s, however, the U.S. economy suffered severe downturns. These U.S. downturns were echoed by synchronized declines in the West European and Japanese economies (as well as in most Third World economies)—and these downturns worsened the U.S. contractions. Thus, all of the transmission mechanisms for international instability cited above were working furiously with dramatic effect in the latter period.

When all of these economies decline together, the negative effects reverberate and cause cumulative international decline—but they also tend to recover together in a cumulative international expansion. As shown in the survey of long-run trends and in the section on financial transmission mechanisms, there is both more financial fragility and quicker transmission in this period, so downturns may be more severe and recoveries more difficult. At any rate, the close international economic relationships are a factor for increased instability at this time.

International trends and the synchronized instability make effective capitalist government responses by any single government very difficult (as will be discussed in Chapter 17).

APPENDIX 16.1
FORMAL MODEL OF INTERNATIONAL CYCLES

There have been many models of two-country interactions, with income and price elasticity effects, which may be tied to multiplier-accelerator models. One way to model the approach used here would be to set up the United States as one economy with the rest of the advanced capitalist world as a second economy. Each would have the complete profit squeeze (or nutcracker) set of equations as in Appendix 13.1, modified by the financial system as in Appendix 14.1, and by monopoly power as in Appendix 15.1. We could then observe how the two react to each other through the international trade, investment, and finance variables. Each could be the catalyst for a downturn or recovery in the other. Each would add to the cumulative expansion process but also to the cumulative contraction process in the other.

To complete the model would require separate sectors for the underdeveloped Third World economies and for the socialist countries, each with quite different laws of movement not discussed in this book.

# CHAPTER 17

# Government Fiscal Behavior and the Business Cycle

THE MAIN HYPOTHESES of this chapter are that government fiscal behavior is an endogenous part of the business cycle, and that it has a significant impact on the business cycle, but that it is far from the most important factor in peacetime cycles.

## THE ENDOGENEITY OF GOVERNMENT BEHAVIOR

The endogeneity of government monetary behavior was discussed in Chapter 14; this chapter focuses exclusively on the question of the endogeneity of fiscal behavior (that is, government spending and taxation). There are two aspects to this question. The political aspect raises the question of what determines government behavior; the economic question is whether there is a roughly constant pattern of behavior over every cycle.

Most neoclassical economists have no theory of government behavior (other than the rational choice of individual voters), leaving that issue to political scientists. The dominant theory in political science for a long time (still popular in most textbooks) was the pluralist theory. The pluralists assert that the U.S. government is not dominated by an economic class, but is a democracy reflecting many different interest groups, and that power is not held by one group, but is held plurally by many groups. They assert that the "power structure of the United States is highly complex and diversified (rather than unitary and monolithic), that the political system is more or less democratic . . . that in political processes the political elite is ascendant over and not subordinate to the economic elite" (Rose 1967, 492). Notice that in arguing for the proposition that the United States is democratic in nature, the pluralists find it necessary to emphasize that political power is, to a large degree, independent of and superior to economic power. The reason for this insistence is that economic power is so extremely unequally distributed. If political power exactly followed economic power, the degree of inequality would leave little to be called democracy.

Pluralists consider a long list of interest groups, including not only rich and poor, debtors and creditors, unions and big business, but also advocates of gun control and the National Rifle Association, women's rights groups and antifeminist groups, Protestants, Jews, Catholics, and so forth. The pluralist view is that all of these compete in the political arena. The democratic process chooses representatives from among them all according to their success with the voters. The resulting government compromises and reconciles all the competing interests. For a powerful critique of pluralism by a former pluralist, see Lindblom (1977); for an excellent Marxist critique, see Miliband (1969); for a critique of pluralism by this author, see Sherman (1987).

Whereas neoclassical economists and political pluralists view government economic behavior as external to the economic system, Marxists view it as an endogenously determined part of a unitary political-economic system. For a comprehensive discussion of Marx's complex view of the relations between politics and economics, see Avineri (1968) and Draper (1977). Marxists have emphasized two ways in which class economic interests determine government fiscal behavior. First, economic power translates into political power through ability to give money to candidates, ownership and control (through advertising) of the media by the wealthy, lobbying by business interests, more political participation and voting by the wealthy, and lack of participation and voting by most of the lower-income workers and unemployed—in fact, half of Americans don't vote. Some excellent empirical discussions of the impact of class economic power on politics are in Piven and Cloward (1988); Burnham (1982); Green (1972); and Stern (1988).

Second, even if candidates opposed to the power of the capitalist class are elected, the structure of the capitalist economy forces most representatives to support capitalist interests—witness the giveaway in 1989 of $66 billion to bail out the savings and loan institutions. The extensive contemporary Marxist debate on the process and degree of endogenous control of government behavior is discussed thoroughly in Szymanski (1978) and Carnoy (1984); also see Sherman (1987); Marxists' views on fiscal policy are surveyed clearly in Miller (1986).

The endogenous interaction of political and economic power has also been analyzed by many radical institutionalists, beginning with Thorstein Veblen. For example, when the underconsumptionist John Hobson suggested raising the income of the working class to increase consumer demand, Veblen commented: "the contemplated move was manifestly chimerical in any community, such as the modern industrial communities, where public policy is with growing singleness of purpose guided by business interests with a naive view to an increase of profits" (Veblen [1904] 1975, 13). Many institutionalists, such as John Kenneth Galbraith, have analyzed in detail the symbiosis between big business and government (see the comprehensive exposition of radical institutionalism in

Dugger [1989]). There is also a large Post-Keynesian literature—some of it based on the pioneering work of Michal Kalecki—on the endogeneity of fiscal and monetary policy (see Rousseas 1986; see also various issues of the *Journal of Post Keynesian Economics* during the last decade).

This book is not the place to explore the determinants of government behavior in detail, but a working assumption will be that it is endogenously determined. Government fiscal behavior reflects the interest of the capitalist class—influenced more or less by conflict with working-class interests—reacting to a given phase of the business cycle. What will be explored in detail in this chapter is the fairly regular pattern of government fiscal activity over the business cycle, reflecting these class interests.

## THE LIMITED IMPACT OF FISCAL BEHAVIOR

Few, if any, economists until the 1930s blamed the peacetime business cycle on government fiscal policy. In fact, it was impossible for fiscal policy to cause the business cycle, at least until the 1930s, for two reasons. First, total government spending was a tiny proportion of GNP. Second, most of it was state and local spending, which was controlled by forty-eight different governments, and which was usually balanced even in the 1930s (these issues are discussed very thoroughly in Miller [1982, 1986]). In 1929, on the eve of the Great Depression, federal spending was only 1 percent of GNP. Federal spending rose a little in the 1930s, then grew enormously during World War II, and has remained very significant ever since, as discussed below.

So-called automatic fiscal policy was largely enacted in the 1930s. Instituted, or greatly increased, were unemployment compensation, farm and business subsidies, and various welfare spending, all of which automatically increase in contractions and automatically decrease in expansions. On the other side, corporate and personal income taxes became important, and these automatically increase as a percentage of GNP in expansions and automatically decrease as a percentage of GNP in contractions. As a result, the government deficit (spending minus taxes) tends to increase in contractions, but decrease in expansion, as discussed in detail below. Discretionary fiscal policy since the 1930s has tended to reinforce this pattern.

It is the hypothesis of this chapter that there would be a business cycle in capitalism even with no government fiscal activity—as shown by the fact that the cycle did exist before the 1930s though government fiscal activity was negligible. Since World War II, fiscal activity was stimulative in every peacetime contraction; whereas in expansions it was either depressing or less and less stimulative—but the hypothesis is that it was not the determining factor in cycle turns.

A completely different hypothesis is the political business cycle theory. This theory argues that politicians manipulate fiscal policy before elections to stimulate the economy and please voters, and then depress the economy after the election to reduce inflation. Although there are a few obvious examples of such attempts, the evidence in this chapter will indicate that the business cycle and the fiscal reaction to it remain mostly determined by the whole capitalist system.

The hypothesis of this chapter is also quite contrary to the monetarist view that the cycle is primarily due to exogenous fiscal-monetary shocks. The hypothesis is also opposed, however, to the notion that the government can eliminate the business cycle by disinterested fine-tuning of the economy through fiscal (and monetary) policies. These and other policy views are discussed in detail in Chapter 18.

### LONG-RUN TRENDS IN FISCAL BEHAVIOR

How does the government actually act? Aside from the jumps in spending during the two world wars, total government spending (federal, state, and local) has risen fairly continuously in the twentieth century. Total government spending was 7.7 percent of GNP in 1902, rising to 8.1 percent in 1913 on the eve of World War I. It continued to rise, reaching 21 percent of GNP in 1940 (see Ransom 1980, 2). After World War II, total government spending rose from 26 percent of GNP in the 1949–1954 cycle to 37 percent in the 1980–1982 cycle. It generally rose through conservative as well as liberal administrations. Ironically, the biggest jump in federal spending as a percentage of GNP came during the conservative Reagan administration. Although government spending was only a small influence in 1902, by 1982, at 37 percent of GNP, it implied a whole new stage of capitalism in symbiosis with government. Fiscal policy can and does change the distribution of income, the allocation of resources, the inflation rate, and the course of the business cycle. When most people think of the growth of government spending, they think of federal spending. In wartime that is correct, but otherwise it is much less true. Federal spending was only 1 percent of GNP in 1929 before the Great Depression. During World War II, government spending (almost all military) rose to the incredible height of 42 percent of GNP in 1944, thereby producing full employment. Trends since then are shown in Table 17.1.

Total government spending rose enormously in the 1949 to 1982 period (from 26 percent to 37 percent of GNP), but not much of that rise was due to the federal government. Most of the increased spending was

TABLE 17.1
Government Spending (as percentage of GNP)

| Cycle | Federal Purchases of Goods and Services | Federal Spending | State and Local Spending | Total Spending |
|---|---|---|---|---|
| 1949–1954 | 12.1 | 18.0 | 7.5 | 25.5 |
| 1954–1958 | 11.4 | 18.0 | 8.6 | 26.6 |
| 1958–1961 | 11.1 | 19.1 | 9.8 | 28.9 |
| 1961–1970 | 10.6 | 19.4 | 11.4 | 30.8 |
| 1970–1975 | 8.4 | 20.5 | 13.7 | 34.2 |
| 1975–1980 | 7.5 | 21.8 | 13.7 | 35.5 |
| 1980–1982 | 8.2 | 23.8 | 13.1 | 36.9 |

Source: All series from U.S. Department of Commerce, Bureau of Economic Analysis, *Handbook of Cyclical Indicators: A Supplement to the Business Conditions Digest* (Washington, D.C.: U.S. Government Printing Office, 1984).

Note: Definitions and series numbers: Federal purchases of goods and services as percentage of GNP is series #265. All federal spending (including purchases and transfers) is #502. State and local spending is #512. Total government spending is #502 plus #512. GNP is #50. All are in constant dollars.

by state and local governments, whose spending almost doubled in this period as a percentage of GNP. In this period, federal government purchases of goods and services actually *declined*, from 12.1 percent to 8.2 percent of GNP. Total federal spending did rise, but not because of more purchases of goods and services. Federal expenditures have grown because of the growth of transfer payments, especially social security and interest payments. Transfer payments simply transfer income from those being taxed to the recipients of government payments. Most federal interest payments arise from debt due to military spending, and are paid to the wealthy. Federal interest payments equaled 20 percent of the personal income tax in 1980, but had risen to 38 percent in 1986 (Harrison and Bluestone 1988, 152), a major redistribution of income from taxpayers to wealthy bondholders.

## Taxation

The personal income tax is called progressive because it charges higher rates in higher income brackets. The corporate income tax is also somewhat progressive (assuming that the corporation pays it, rather than passing it along to the consumer). By the end of World War II official tax rates on the wealthiest taxpayers rose to 90 percent, but effective rates were always much lower because of legal loopholes. The social security payroll tax is regressive because those in lower income brackets pay a higher percentage of their income. State and local sales taxes are also regressive (see Pechman 1985, 6–7).

Reformers in U.S. history have always talked about the tax system's redistributing income to reduce the extreme inequality. But, as of 1985, if one adds up all the effects of progressive and regressive taxes, "it is clear that the tax system has very little effect on the distribution of income" (Pechman 1985, 5). Pechman's study is careful and detailed, and reaches roughly the same conclusion on alternative assumptions about tax incidence.

For the period of his study—between 1966 and 1985—Pechman finds a decline in the importance and/or progressivity of corporate taxes and personal income taxes (both progressive taxes). At the same time, the regressive payroll tax became more important. As a result, "the effect of these changes was to reduce the progessivity of the tax system" (Pechman 1985, 8). What is even more interesting, in light of the important effect of class income on consumption, is the fact that in 1966 the taxes paid by capital were higher than those paid by labor. But by 1985 the tax burden on labor was substantially higher than on capital (Pechman 1985, 9).

### Growth of the Deficit

The increase in interest payments in the 1980s was partly due to higher interest rates, but also partly due to the increase in the national debt. A deficit measures an increase in the debt in one year, while a surplus measures the decrease of the debt in a year. In the 1950s and 1960s, there were five years with surpluses; but in the 1970s and 1980s, there was a deficit every year. The average deficit grew relative to GNP: The deficit was 0.4 percent of GNP in the 1950s (in seven deficit years); the deficit was 0.8 percent of GNP in the 1960s (in eight deficit years); the deficit averaged 2 percent of GNP in all of the 1970s; but the deficit averaged 4 percent of GNP from 1980 through 1987 (Council of Economic Advisers 1988).

### Military Spending

Much of the deficit was due to the increase in military spending. Total military spending was well over a trillion dollars during the Reagan administration. The U.S. Department of Defense is the largest planned economy in the world except for the USSR—and it spends more than the net income of all U.S. corporations. But military spending goes far beyond Department of Defense spending. A careful study of military spending by Cypher (1972) defined military spending to include half of all "international affairs" spending, veterans' benefits, atomic energy and space appropriations (mostly military-related), and 75 percent of the interest on the public debt (since at least 75 percent of the debt was used to pay for wars). Other military costs on which it is impossible to get exact data are major parts of the budget for research and development, the CIA and other intelligence agencies—and, of course, the deaths, wounds, and alienation of young Americans.

The most important measure of military spending is as a percentage of gross national product (GNP). From 1947 to 1971 it ranged, in Cypher's estimates, from a low of 10.1 percent of GNP in 1948 to a high of 21.9 percent in the Korean War year of 1952. For the whole 1947 to 1971 period, direct military spending averaged 13.2 percent of GNP according to this estimate. Yet this amount of direct military spending still underestimates the impact of military industries. Economists measure the secondary effects of military spending by the *government multiplier*, which measures the ratio of the total increase in all spending to every dollar of increase in government spending. Estimates of the multiplier from military spending range from about $1.85 to $3.50 of total spending for every dollar of military spending (see Cypher 1974; also see Griffin, Wallace, and Devine 1982). If we take a conservative estimate that the indirect effects equal the direct effects, then direct military spending of 13.2 percent of GNP might generate 26.4 percent of GNP.

Big business benefits strongly from the high level of military spending, a fact that affects fiscal policy. This incentive is based on the fact that the rate of profit is very high in military production and that most of these profits go to a few very large firms. Almost all military contracts go to some 205 of the top 500 corporations, and just 100 of them get 85 percent of all military contracts.

Military profits are mostly understated because, in reporting to the government, the military firms overstate their costs. Because they do not operate under competition but in a close relationship with the Pentagon, they probably overstate costs more than do most firms. Still, a study by the General Accounting Office (GAO) of the U.S. government definitely spelled out their high profit rates (see Cypher 1972, ch. 5). First, the GAO asked eighty-one large military contractors by questionnaire what their profit rates were for 1966 through 1969. The replies, which were limited by self-interest, still admitted an average profit rate of 24.8 percent—much higher than nonmilitary profits in the same industries. But spot checks by the GAO showed that these profit rates were still very much underreported, so the GAO did its own audit of the books of 146 main military contractors. The study found that the profit rate of these contractors was a fantastic 56.1 percent rate of return on invested capital.

There is a controversy over the cyclical impact of military spending. Tom Riddell (1988) argues that military spending is used to boost profit rates whenever they decline, while others emphasize that military spending is pushed by the military-industrial complex at all times (see Melman 1988). These issues can be clarified by looking at the actual pattern of government spending.

## CYCLICAL SPENDING PATTERNS IN WAR AND PEACE

There is a vast difference in the pattern of federal government spending during war-dominated cycles and peacetime cycles. The Korean War dominated the 1949–1954 cycle, while the Vietnam War dominated the cycle of 1961–1970. In the average of these two war-dominated cycles, the index of military equipment production rose 1.1 percent per quarter in expansions, but fell 5.8 percent per quarter in contractions (U.S. Department of Commerce, Bureau of Economic Analysis 1984, series #557). Since military spending is the largest part of federal purchases of goods and services, the huge rise and decline in military production caused a similar rise and fall in federal purchases. Thus, in the average of the two war-dominated cycles, real federal purchases of goods and services rose 3.1 percent per quarter in expansions and fell by 5.0 percent per quarter in contractions (U.S. Department of Commerce, Bureau of Economic Analysis 1984, series #253). It appears, therefore, that in these two cycles, the rise of military spending was the major cause of the expansion, while the postwar decline of military spending was a major cause of the contraction.

When we move from the two war cycles to the five peacetime cycles (1954–1958, 1958–1961, 1970–1975, 1975–1980, and 1980–1982), the role of military spending is less important. Moreover, military spending changes from procyclical to countercyclical: In the average peacetime expansion, military production rose only 0.3 percent per quarter, while government purchases of all goods and services rose only 0.1 percent per quarter. During the average peacetime business contraction, military production rose to 0.5 percent per quarter, while all federal purchases of goods and services rose to 0.7 percent per quarter. It thus appears that military spending and other federal purchases during peacetime were used to bolster the economy during recessions, but were cut back in expansions. Military spending, however, puts billions of dollars into bombs, poison gas, and other weapons of mass destruction. The question, therefore, is whether it is ethical, or even economically rational, to use wasteful military spending to prop up the economy in recessions.

## TOTAL FEDERAL EXPENDITURES

Goods and services are only part of federal spending. Let us now turn to total federal expenditures, which include goods and services, but also include all kinds of transfer payments. We shall examine data for each of

TABLE 17.2
Federal Government Expenditure (rate of growth per quarter, constant dollars)

| Cycle | Expansion | | Contraction | |
|---|---|---|---|---|
| | Rate | Politics | Rate | Politics |
| | PART A. Two War Cycles | | | |
| 1949–1954 | 4.0 | Truman, Korea | −4.1 | Eisenhower |
| 1961–1970 | 1.1 | Johnson, Vietnam | 0.9 | Nixon |
| Average | 2.6 | | −1.6 | |
| | PART B. Five Peacetime Cycles | | | |
| 1954–1958 | 0.3 | Eisenhower | 3.2 | Eisenhower |
| 1958–1961 | 0.1 | Eisenhower | 1.9 | Kennedy |
| 1970–1975 | 0.4 | Nixon | 2.9 | Ford |
| 1975–1980 | 0.9 | Carter | 3.0 | Carter |
| 1980–1982 | 0.8 | Reagan | 2.1 | Reagan |
| Average | 0.5 | | 2.6 | |

Source: Series #502, from same source as Table 17.1.

the war cycles and each of the peacetime cycles. Table 17.2 shows spending rates of growth in expansion and contraction for each cycle.

Not surprisingly, given the enormous increase in military spending, federal government expenditures rose at 2.6 percent per quarter in the average wartime expansion but only at 0.5 per quarter in the average peacetime expansion. In the two contractions following wars, expenditures *fell* by an average 1.6 percent per quarter. By contrast, in the five peacetime contractions, government expenditures *rose* by an average 2.6 percent per quarter. The impact in contractions, therefore, was procyclical in the average war cycle, but countercyclical in the average peacetime cycle.

What is fascinating is that there is no evidence that it matters which party, Republicans or Democrats, is in power. There is no evidence whatsoever that Republicans spend less than Democrats do in business contractions. In every one of the five peacetime cycles, regardless of who was in power, the pattern is the same: a slow rise of federal government spending in expansions, followed by a rapid rise in federal spending in contractions. This pattern is shown graphically for the last three cycles, 1970 to 1982, in Figure 17.1.

Why does federal spending rise slowly in expansions, and then rapidly

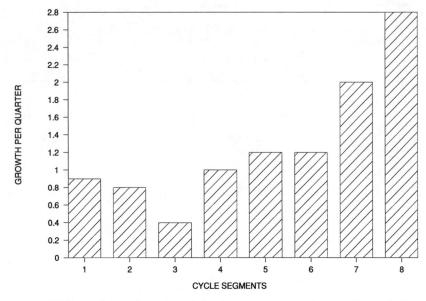

Fig. 17.1. Federal Spending: Growth by Segment Averaged across Three Cycles 1970–1982 (from series 502, Appendix H)

in contractions? The slow rise in expansions reflects the long-run increases in military spending and in constructive spending on goods, services, business subsidies, welfare, and interest on the debt. The far more rapid rise of spending in contractions is mostly not discretionary policy, but is automatic under present laws. Some of the expenditures that automatically increase in every recession or depression are farm subsidies, unemployment compensation, and business subsidies. One result is that personal income falls more slowly than does GNP, thus supporting more consumer spending.

## FEDERAL RECEIPTS AND DEFICITS

In addition to spending, government fiscal impact is determined by receipts (mostly taxes). Table 17.3 presents federal receipts, as well as resulting deficits, in terms of their cyclical amplitude as a rate of growth per quarter for each cycle.

Receipts behave about the same in wartime and peacetime. They rise in every expansion and decline in every contraction, mainly reflecting the rise and fall of corporate and individual income. This functional relation is strong enough to outweigh most discretionary policy changes due to war and peace or changes in political administration. Figure 17.2 reveals

TABLE 17.3
Federal Receipts and Deficits (rate of growth per quarter, constant dollars)

| Cycle | Expansion | | | Contraction | | |
|---|---|---|---|---|---|---|
| | Receipts | Deficit | Politics | Receipts | Deficit | Politics |
| | PART A. | Two War Cycles | | | | |
| 1949–1954 | 0.6 | 3.4 | Truman, Korea | −4.2 | 0.0 | Eisenhower |
| 1961–1970 | 1.3 | −0.2 | Johnson, Vietnam | −2.5 | 3.7 | Nixon |
| Average | 1.0 | 1.6 | | −3.4 | 1.9 | |
| | PART B. | Five Peacetime Cycles | | | | |
| 1954–1958 | 1.3 | −1.0 | Eisenhower | −3.2 | 6.3 | Eisenhower |
| 1958–1961 | 2.4 | −2.3 | Eisenhower | −0.8 | 2.7 | Kennedy |
| 1970–1975 | 1.4 | −1.0 | Nixon | −1.0 | 3.9 | Ford |
| 1975–1980 | 1.2 | −0.3 | Carter | −0.9 | 4.2 | Carter |
| 1980–1982 | 1.7 | −0.9 | Reagan | −2.0 | 4.0 | Reagan |
| Average | 1.6 | −1.1 | | −1.6 | 4.2 | |

Source: Same as Table 17.1.
Note: Definitions: Receipts are series #501. Deficit is expenditures (#502) minus receipts (#501).

for the last three cycles the dramatic procyclical behavior of federal revenues.

Contrary to popular opinion, the federal deficit also behaves somewhat the same in all peacetime cycles, regardless of which party is in power. Thus, the deficit rose (or the surplus declined) in every contraction of peacetime—under Eisenhower, Kennedy, Ford, Carter, and Reagan. The deficit fell (or the surplus rose) in every expansion of peacetime—under Eisenhower, Nixon, Carter, and Reagan. In spite of the Vietnam War, the same cyclical pattern held for the deficit in the 1961–1970 cycle (under Johnson and Nixon). Only the very rapid rise and fall of military spending in the Korean War cycle, 1949–1954, under Truman and Eisenhower, reversed the normal pattern. Figure 17.3, showing the federal deficit during the last three cycles, reveals the clearly countercyclical pattern of the deficit in peacetime. Therefore, we may assume as a stylized fact of the cycle that the federal deficit is countercyclical, that is, that it falls in expansion and rises in contraction. The implications of this important fact are discussed in a later section after we have examined state and local fiscal behavior and total government fiscal behavior.

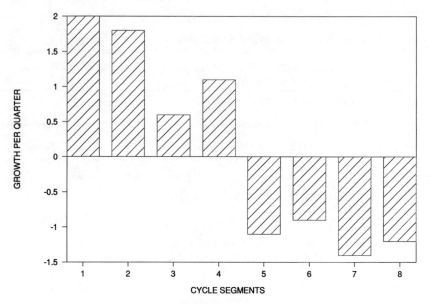

Fig. 17.2. Federal Receipts: Growth by Segment Averaged across Three Cycles, 1970–1982 (from series 501, Appendix H)

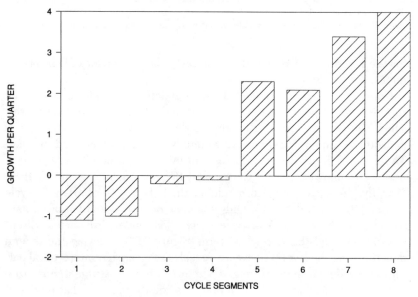

Fig. 17.3. Federal Deficit: Growth by Segment Averaged across Three Cycles, 1970–1982 (from series 502 − 501, Appendix H)

TABLE 17.4
State and Local Spending, Receipts, and Deficits
(rate of growth per quarter, constant dollars)

| Cycle | Expenditures | Revenues | Deficits |
|-------|-------------|----------|----------|
| PART A. Expansions | | | |
| 1949–1954 | 1.2 | 1.1 | 0.1 |
| 1954–1958 | 1.5 | 1.5 | 0.0 |
| 1958–1961 | 1.0 | 1.7 | −0.7 |
| 1961–1970 | 1.6 | 1.7 | −0.1 |
| 1970–1975 | 1.0 | 1.4 | −0.4 |
| 1975–1980 | 0.4 | 0.8 | 0.4 |
| 1980–1982 | −0.7 | −0.2 | −0.5 |
| Average | 0.9 | 1.1 | −0.3 |
| PART B. Contractions | | | |
| 1949–1954 | 2.4 | 0.9 | 1.5 |
| 1954–1958 | 2.7 | 1.9 | 0.6 |
| 1958–1961 | 2.4 | 1.9 | 0.5 |
| 1961–1970 | 2.8 | 1.8 | 1.0 |
| 1970–1975 | 1.0 | −0.1 | 1.4 |
| 1975–1980 | −0.2 | −0.1 | −0.1 |
| 1980–1982 | 0.2 | 0.0 | 0.2 |
| Average | 1.6 | 0.9 | 0.7 |

Source: Same as Table 17.1.
Note: Definitions: Receipts are series #511, expenditures are series #512, and deficits are expenditures minus receipts.

## STATE AND LOCAL FISCAL BEHAVIOR OVER THE CYCLE

Table 17.4 shows the behavior of state and local expenditures, receipts, and deficits, cycle by cycle. The table is not split into war and peacetime cycles because there is no noticeable change in cyclical behavior between those two categories.

State and local revenues (mostly sales and property taxes) grew rapidly in both expansions and contractions in the 1950s and 1960s. Revenues grew far more slowly in the 1970s and 1980s as the economy expanded more slowly. Spending grew at about the same rate as did taxes in the first two cycles in the expansions, so budgets were balanced. After that spending grew less than did taxes in expansions (or declined more in the 1980–1981 weak expansion), so deficits declined in expansions. In every contraction (except one) spending rose more rapidly than did revenues because of the need to help those hurt by the contractions. Hence, in every contraction (except one) the deficit rose and was countercyclical in effect. The only exception was the crisis situation in the 1980 contraction, when revenue fell, forcing state and local governments to lower spending even more, which worsened the decline of income.

When behavior is averaged over the last three cycles, as shown in Figures 17.4, 17.5, and 17.6, it can be seen that the average state and local fiscal behavior in the 1970–1982 period was basically countercyclical—a pattern similar to that of federal activity. Spending rose somewhat more rapidly in contractions than in expansions. Revenues rose rapidly in expansions, declined in crisis phases, and rose a tiny bit in depressions. The result, spotlighted in Figure 17.6, was that the state and local deficit fell throughout the average expansion and rose throughout the average contraction of this period. Thus it did contribute to the countercyclical effect of the federal government.

## CYCLICAL BEHAVIOR OF TOTAL GOVERNMENT FISCAL ACTIVITY

Total government activity includes federal, state, and local activity. For the three business cycles from 1970 through 1982, Table 17.5 and Figures 17.4, 17.5, and 17.6 reveal the cyclical behavior of total government spending, receipts, and deficits (all in constant dollars, as in the last two sections). Table 17.5 also shows the breakdown of federal, state, and local activity.

In the average for the 1970–1982 period, Figure 17.7 shows that total real government expenditures rise moderately in recovery, then rise more slowly in prosperity, pick up speed again in the crisis, and rise most rapidly in the depression phase. Thus, they rise faster in contractions than in expansions.

By contrast, Figure 17.8 depicts the fact that total real government receipts rise most rapidly in recovery, and then less rapidly in prosperity. The receipts actually decline in crisis and depression, so they are very procyclical. Receipts follow the pattern of real national income, but rise and fall somewhat faster, mostly because income taxes are a higher percentage in higher income brackets.

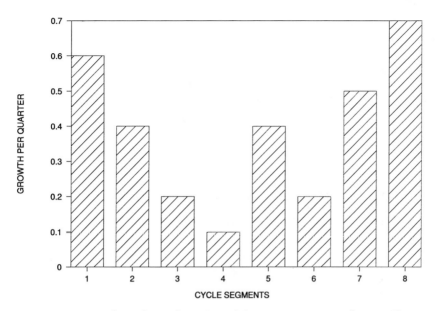

Fig. 17.4. State and Local Spending: Growth by Segment Averaged across Three Cycles, 1970–1982 (from series 512, Appendix H)

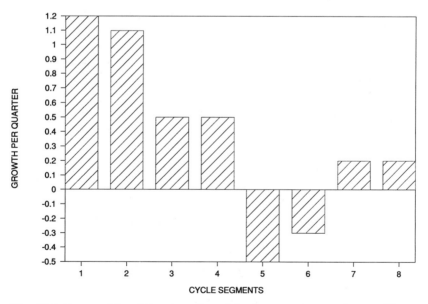

Fig. 17.5. State and Local Receipts: Growth by Segment Averaged across Three Cycles, 1970–1982 (from series 511, Appendix H)

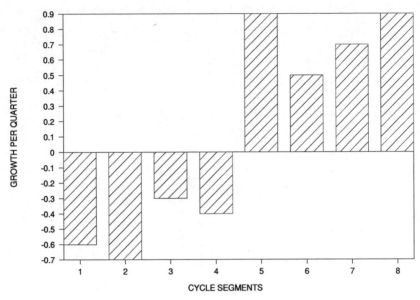

Fig. 17.6. State and Local Deficit: Growth by Segment Averaged across Three Cycles, 1970–1982 (from series 512 – 511, Appendix H)

As a result of the spending and taxing pattern, total real government deficits fall at a considerable pace in recovery (when receipts rise much faster than does spending), as shown in Figure 17.9. In prosperity, when receipts rise only a little faster than does spending, total government deficits fall only very slightly. In the crisis, total government deficits rise rapidly (because spending is rising while taxes are falling in real terms). In the depression phase, total government deficits rise most rapidly (because spending rises rapidly, while receipts are still falling). Thus, total government deficits fall in expansions and rise in contractions, being a significant countercyclical factor. As noted earlier, this pattern is changed very little (if at all) by the declared fiscal ideology of the party in power.

CONFLICTING INTERPRETATIONS OF THE FISCAL DATA

In the peacetime cycles, total government deficits—the aggregate result of federal, state, and local fiscal decisions—fall in business expansions and rise in business contractions. Since a high deficit stimulates the economy (if Keynes is correct), this means that government tends to stimulate the economy in contractions, but tends to reduce stimulation in expansions.

Liberal Keynesians will applaud this countercyclical behavior of the deficit. In the Keynesian view, a rising deficit in contractions will tend, all other things being equal, to decrease unemployment and encourage

TABLE 17.5
Cyclical Pattern of Fiscal Activity
(average, 3 cycles, 1970–1982, rate of growth per quarter, constant dollars)

|  | Expansion | Contraction |
|---|---|---|
| Expenditures |  |  |
| Federal (502) | 0.8 | 1.8 |
| State and local (512) | 0.3 | 0.5 |
| Total government (502 + 512) | 0.6 | 1.1 |
| Receipts |  |  |
| Federal (501) | 1.4 | −1.2 |
| State and local (511) | 0.6 | −0.1 |
| Total government (501 + 511) | 1.2 | −0.7 |
| Deficits[a] |  |  |
| Federal | −0.6 | 3.0 |
| State and local | −0.4 | 0.5 |
| Total government | −0.5 | 1.8 |

Source: Same as Table 17.1.
[a] Expenditures minus receipts.

recovery. The falling deficit in expansions will tend to prevent overheating and inflation.

On the other hand, monetarists will point out that the rising deficit in contractions may lead to higher interest rates. This view is the monetarist "overcrowding" argument, which says that government demand for loans drives up interest rates for all borrowers (this argument is evaluated in Chapter 18). Monetarists have also decried the fact that deficit spending has continued in recent cycles during expansions (though at a declining rate of growth). The existence of deficit spending over the whole cycle means to monetarists that the government is continually pumping money into the economy. In their view, this action may be the major cause of the long-run inflationary trend in the economy (this argument is also evaluated in Chapter 18).

Those with a strong underconsumptionist perspective should praise the government for its continued deficit spending since 1970, since this deficit helps bolster inadequate demand. Underconsumptionists should also approve of the fact that the deficit did increase in all contractions, presumably aiding recovery. Underconsumptionists, however, could ar-

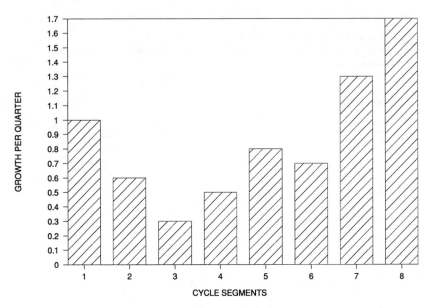

Fig. 17.7. Total Government Spending: Growth by Segment Averaged across Three Cycles, 1970–1982 (from series 512 + 502, Appendix H)

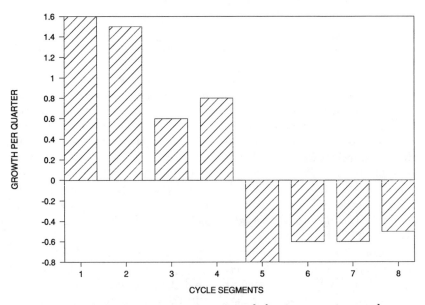

Fig. 17.8. Total Government Receipts: Growth by Segment Averaged across Three Cycles, 1970–1982 (from series 511 + 501, Appendix H)

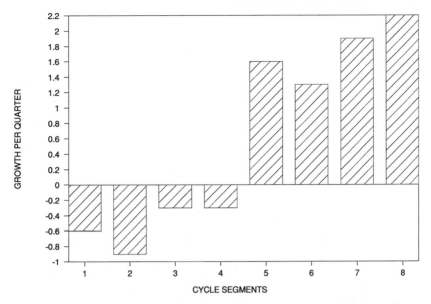

Fig. 17.9. Total Government Deficit: Growth by Segment Averaged across Three Cycles, 1970–1982 (from series [512 + 502] − [511 + 501], Appendix H)

gue that the deficits should have been much greater because the U.S. economy has been far below full employment during this period. In support of the underconsumptionist theory, it may be noted that the Reagan administration ran record deficits since 1982 and that the expansion, beginning in 1983, was unusually long.

Some neoclassical economists believe that by not reducing the deficit to zero in every expansion, the government causes the business cycle downturn. They argue that a continuing deficit leads to inflation, that inflation causes wages to rise faster than do profits, and that this leads to reduction of output and downturn. Some Marxists agree that higher wages cause a problem for business, but believe that government tries to help business to prevent full employment by depressive fiscal measures before the peak, which help cause a downturn. They point to the fact that most downturns are preceded by rising government surpluses or, at least, falling government deficits.

CONCLUSIONS

To clarify some of these issues, let us go back to the most clearly established facts. In the war-dominated cycles, it is obvious that government has a massive impact. In the expansions during World War II, the Korean War, and the Vietnam War, government military spending was the single largest and most rapidly rising factor. After each war, there was a recession caused in part by the decline of military spending.

In the average peacetime cycle, however, the government role is quite different. In the recovery phase, while the private economy is booming (with rapidly rising output and profits), the government deficit declines rapidly. This action (mostly automatic under present law) removes an unnecessary source of expansion and may reduce inflationary pressures.

In the prosperity period, however, when the private economy is slowing its rate of growth, the further decline of deficit spending removes more support for expansion, so it helps set the stage for a business contraction. Since there is some deficit spending continuing, one cannot say that government fiscal actions cause the downturn, but the slight decline in the deficit does further reduce the rate of growth of demand. The deficit decline in prosperity is inherent in the present fiscal structure, and that structure is designed to represent business interests (by not pushing the economy all the way to full employment, which would raise wages too far, in the business view). Therefore, government fiscal policy does play an endogenous role—and its reduction of stimulation is a factor in the events leading to the downturn. Yet the downturn is caused by the private economy because the private sector declines even though the government is still stimulative, albeit with a weaker and weaker force.

In the whole contraction—including both the crisis and depression phases—the government deficit increases relatively rapidly. Thus, the present fiscal structure is countercyclical in the contraction and operates as one endogenous cause of the recovery. It provides a major support to the cyclical tendency of the private economy to recover at that point (again, obviously moving in the direction encouraged by and favorable to business interests). Thus, the two main hypotheses of this chapter—the endogeneity of fiscal activity and its limited but significant impact in peacetime cycles—are confirmed by the evidence of the present historical period.

It is also worth emphasizing that, earlier in U.S. history, the private economy both rose in expansions and declined in contractions long before fiscal policy was quantitatively significant enough to affect the economy with enough impact to cause upturns or downturns. Government spending and taxation in peacetime was not that significant until the 1930s—and there were many business cycles before then.

APPENDIX 17.1
GOVERNMENT IN A FORMAL CYCLE MODEL

In a business cycle model, government spending is an element of demand, which increases profits by allowing their realization through sales.

Government taxes reduce demand, which reduces profits. Government fiscal policy will affect the consumption function as well as the investment function, with the relative impact depending on the type of spending and the type of taxes.

In light of its fairly regular cyclical behavior, the easiest way to depict government fiscal activity is as a function of unemployment. The deficit is a positive function of unemployment; it rises as unemployment rises, but declines as unemployment falls. If the two factors in the deficit are separated, then two functions are needed. One could say that government revenue is a negative function of unemployment, rising as unemployment falls, and vice versa. Government spending may be seen as a positive function of unemployment; its growth rate rises as unemployment rises, but its growth rate declines as unemployment falls. These functions would reflect the endogenous role of government fiscal behavior in the business cycle. The addition of these equations to the nutcracker model would modify it, but would not change the basic hypothesis that cycles are endogenous.

# PART FOUR

# Policy

# CHAPTER 18

# Can Reform Policies Lessen
# the Business Cycle under Capitalism?

## Fiscal, Monetary, and Income Policies

THE ANALYSIS in the earlier parts of this book produced certain conclusions important for policy:

1. Say's law is incorrect.
2. The business cycle is primarily endogenous.
3. Effective demand is a very important determinant of the cycle.
4. Income distribution is an important determinant of consumer demand.
5. But the cost of supply is also important to the determination of profits.

### SOME IMPLICATIONS OF THE ANALYTIC CONCLUSIONS

Given these findings, there are some policy views that must be rejected. First, there is the supply-side notion that taxes on wealthy capitalists should be reduced to increase investment. This is incorrect because the fact of more saving does not necessarily mean more investment (as Keynes demonstrated). Second, there is the argument that unemployment could be cured by reducing wages because lower wages will encourage investment. This is incorrect because (1) consumer demand is an important determinant of investment and (2) lower wages mean less consumer demand. Third, there is the argument that higher wages would reduce unemployment by raising consumer demand. This is incorrect because (1) costs are an important determinant of investment (via profits) and (2) wages are the largest component of costs.

In the light of the analytic conclusions, the rest of this chapter examines the rest of the proposals usually made for fiscal, monetary, and income policies.

### NEOCLASSICAL-KEYNESIAN FISCAL POLICY

In the 1950s and 1960s, there was an overwhelming consensus among most U.S. economists and most U.S. politicians on a demand-oriented fiscal policy, usually considered to be "liberal" and "Keynesian." In its textbook description, it relied on two simple government policies to fine-tune the economy, prevent inflation, and prevent cyclical contractions. In the first case, if there is unemployment (and no inflation), increase government spending, reduce government taxes, and allow the resulting deficit spending to stimulate demand. In the second case, if there is inflation (and no unemployment), reduce government spending, increase taxes, and let the resulting surplus soak up excess demand.

In the modern U.S. context, these policies are said to be liberal because they would increase government activity in order to prevent the evils of unemployment and inflation. Policies are called conservative in the modern U.S. context if they would reduce government anticyclical activity, relying on the private capitalist system to automatically correct any problems.

These policies were often called Keynesian, but Paul Samuelson renamed them the policies of the neoclassical-Keynesian synthesis because (1) they are Keynesian in the sense of requiring government activity to prevent unemployment and inflation, but (2) they are neoclassical in the sense that once full employment is restored, it is assumed that the private enterprise economy performs in an optimal way. The analysis was also neoclassical in the sense of positing that adjustment to full employment was prevented only by wage-price rigidities or imperfections in the competitive process. Since these analyses and policies were far from what she considered to be Keynes's own view, Robinson (1979) called them "bastard Keynesian" analyses and policies.

Whether or not this view was called a neoclassical-Keynesianism, it held strongly that fiscal policy could fine-tune the economy to eliminate the business cycle. There were many statements by noted economists in the 1960s that the business cycle had disappeared. Modigliani (1977) stated that the dominant view was that "a private enterprise economy using an intangible money *needs* to be stabilized, *can* be stabilized, and *should* be stabilized by appropriate monetary and fiscal policy" (p. 27). Paul Samuelson said that in "the writings of Solow, Tobin, and myself, attention was focused on a managed economy which through skillful use of fiscal and monetary policy channeled the Keynesian forces of effective demand into behaving like a neoclassical model" (quoted in Lekachman 1960, 30).

There are three kinds of limitations on this liberal, neoclassical-Keynesian synthesis of fiscal policy: (1) administrative inadequacies; (2) political constraints based on class interests; and (3) inherently conflicting economic goals.

## ADMINISTRATIVE CONSTRAINTS UPON FISCAL POLICY

In reality, administration of these liberal policies is difficult (as conservatives frequently note) because it requires precise and prompt government planning within a chaotic and unplanned capitalist economy. First, there is the information-gathering problem. There is always delay before available data can reveal changes in unemployment and inflation. Second, there is a much longer delay for interpretation of the data. Some government economists must determine that rising unemployment or inflation or both exist before something can be done about it. Third, there is a further delay in order to decide what to do about it. Economists must estimate how much of an increase or cut in spending or an increase or cut in taxes, or both, is required to meet the goals. This is not only time-consuming, but extremely difficult. No two economists agree on the amounts, and government estimates are always totally inaccurate (a conclusion for which past evidence is overwhelming). If there is to be spending for the purchase of equipment or construction, engineers must also make plans.

A fourth administrative delay must occur while Congress goes through the lengthy process of deliberation (that is, class conflict in more or less polite debates) and legislation. A fifth administrative delay must occur before the plans can be put into effect. A plan to build a new battleship does not put money into circulation immediately, but slowly over many years. An "immediate" tax cut still requires time for the estimated amount to be spent by consumers or investors.

As a result of these five delays (information gathering, interpretation, planning, legislation, and execution), as well as the gross mistakes in planning, the results seldom have any resemblance to the plans. In fact, it has frequently happened that new spending, designed to end a recession, actually helps overstimulate an expansion. Similarly, tax cuts to stimulate the economy may occur in time to increase inflation.

## POLITICAL CONSTRAINTS UPON FISCAL POLICY

The political constraints on fiscal policy are much worse problems for the process than the administrative constraints. As shown in Chapter 17, capitalist class interests are dominant in the budget process. These interests frequently conflict with the pleasant goals assumed by liberal economists. For example, full employment—defined as a situation with no one unemployed—would provide labor with a much greater power to raise wages, so it is never an actual goal of U.S. fiscal policy (though liberals have gotten Congress to adopt some pious statements, with no enforcement procedure). In practice, the U.S. government has usually adopted the conservative view that some unemployment is "natural," such as 6 or 7 percent (of course, if unemployment is "natural," it is good).

Increases or decreases in government spending hurt some groups and help others. Increases or decreases in taxes hurt some groups and help others. There is no class-neutral fiscal policy—just as there is no button marked "government waste" to push for painless cuts. The question is always this: spending or cuts for whom? The ability to ignore this issue is the greatest weakness of liberal fiscal policy.

Not only is the distribution of income directly affected; so also is the allocation of resources. Fiscal policies determine the use of private resources (such as Cadillacs) versus public resources (mass transit). They determine spending for hospitals or schools versus bombs or battleships. Again, none of this is class neutral, but strongly affects distribution of income.

Suppose that by some miracle a large majority agrees on a certain amount of government spending to combat unemployment. The prime political question, however, is spending on what, for it is here that vested interests come into play. For example, even small vital expenditures on free medical care have sometimes been defeated by the American Medical Association. Powerful vested interests oppose almost every item in the civilian budget as soon as economic expansion proceeds beyond the necessary minimum. What kinds of interests must be defeated to have the necessary spending to fill the enormous deficiency in demand in an economic contraction? Constructive projects, such as the Tennessee Valley Authority, could develop dams, irrigation, and cheap power, but these have been fought tooth and nail by the private power interests because they might lower profit rates. There could be large-scale public housing, but private contractors have long kept such programs to a minimum.

There might be other constructive spending—for example, on hospitals and schools. The rich, however, see these as subsidies to the poor for things that the rich can buy for themselves out of their own pockets. Proposals to increase unemployment compensation or lower taxes paid by the poor encounter even greater resistance because they would transfer income from the rich to the poor. Likewise, billions could usefully be spent in aid and loans to the less developed world, where poverty and human suffering are so widespread. That, however could be passed on a massive scale only over the bodies of hundreds of members of Congress, who well represent the wishes of their self-interested constituents and have no concept of the long-run gain to world trade and world peace. If any of these measures is allowed to some extent, it is only after a long political fight and certainly not promptly enough to head off a developing depression.

The dominant capitalist interests will not tolerate government competition with private enterprise, measures that undermine the privileges of the wealthy, or policies that significantly alter the relative distribution of income. They therefore tend to oppose all government nonmilitary spending—except business subsidies. The only major exception to this generalization is government spending on highways, which is actively promoted by the largest lobbying effort of any single industry after defense: the automobile producers.

From all of the facts just given, it must be concluded that peaceful constructive spending on a large enough scale for full employment is opposed by too many special interests to be politically feasible. On the other hand, military spending does not violate any vested interests. Military spending is considered an ideal antidepression policy by big business for three reasons. First, such expenditures have the same short-run effect on employment and profits as would expenditures on more socially useful projects. Second, military spending means big and stable profits for big business, whereas welfare spending may shift income from rich taxpayers to poor recipients. Third, the long-run effect of military spending is even more favorable because no new productive equipment is created to compete with existing facilities. (On the other hand, most studies conclude that military spending provides fewer jobs per dollar than nonmilitary spending.)

It is an historical fact that only the military spending of World War II brought the United States out of the Great Depression. It is a historical fact that the strong expansions and mild contractions of the 1950s and the 1960s were strongly supported by the high level of cold war spending in the Korean War and in the Vietnam War. Yet, writing just after the Vietnam War, the liberal Paul Samuelson (1973) claimed that it would be easy to replace military spending by nonmilitary spending:

> However true it might have been in the turn-of-the-century era of Lenin . . . it is definitely no longer the case in the age of Keynes that prosperity of a mixed economy (i.e., capitalism plus government) depends on cold-war expenditures and imperialistic ventures. . . . Does building missiles and warheads create jobs? . . . Then so too will building new factories, better roads and schools, cleaning up our rivers, and providing minimum income-supplements for our aged and handicapped. (pp. 823–24)

Certainly it is true that jobs could be created in all these constructive ways rather than the destructive ways of warfare.

But it is naive to ignore the fact that vested interests can and will obstruct government programs that might harm them. For the government to build new factories means direct competition with private industry. Free public education means use of money for the education of poorer citizens. Cleaning up the rivers means forcing private industry to spend money on purifying its wastes. Giving to the aged and handicapped means shifting income to the poor. The political reality is that vested interests oppose each of these programs with violent rhetoric and successful political pressure.

Paul Samuelson says that Marxists have asked: "Politically, will there be as much urgency to spend what is needed for useful, peacetime full-employment programs as there is urgency and willingness to spend for hot- and cold-war purposes?" And he answers: "It was proper to ask this question back in the 1950s. But . . . experience since then has shown that modern electorates have become very sensitive to levels of unemployment that would have been considered moderate back in the good old days. And they do put effective pressure at the polls on their government" (Samuelson 1973, 824–25). But in the first place, the pressure is only to get jobs—not necessarily to get constructive rather than warfare jobs. Hence, both Republican and Democratic administrations continue military spending to avoid unemployment—and do not do large amounts of constructive spending.

In the second place, Samuelson just assumes that "the people" or "the electorate" successfully put on pressure for their needs and interests. In Chapter 17 it was shown that this has not been true, that the U.S. government has been dominated by capitalist interests opposed to the interests of the majority. Since Samuelson wrote, the Nixon, Ford, Carter, and Reagan administrations have not shown any anticapitalist tendencies. The U.S. government did not replace Vietnam War expenditures with a new flood of income supplements to the aged and handicapped, government-built factories, roads and schools, or huge expenditures to clean up our rivers. The historical record shows, contrary to Samuelson's expectations, that there was high unemployment in most of the 1970s and early 1980s and that the U.S. government did not eliminate it by vast increases in peaceful government spending. On the contrary, the Nixon, Ford, Carter, and Reagan administrations all talked about the need for fiscal conservatism, and—in the midst of high unemployment—cut various social programs.

The Reagan administration merely followed the same policies as the Carter administration in a more drastic manner. The 1981 Reagan budget is a classic example of class interests at work. It made huge increases in military spending. At the same time (with continued high unemployment), the largest cuts in spending were in public service job programs, while the job-producing Young Adult Conservation Corps was eliminated. Other spending cuts tending to reduce employment were in the following: education programs, aid to disadvantaged children, specific health programs, Medicaid payments to states, Medicare for the elderly, public housing (with increases in rents), food stamps, mothers' and infants' nutrition, school lunches, day care, Aid to Families with Dependent Children, the Economic Development Administration, the Appalachian Regional Administration, urban development action grants, the Consumer Product Safety Commission, mass transit aid, funds for water cleanup projects, funds for more parks, funds for arts and humanities, funds for legal services for the poor, funds for the postal service, funds for public broadcasting, and funds for community action programs. There were no cuts in subsidies to big business (a point mentioned to a reporter by David Stockman [1985], head of the Office of Management and Budget).

On the tax side, there was an equal percentage cut in all personal income taxes, which means that the rich got much larger cuts than did the poor, in addition to which the maximum rate was reduced from 70 percent to 33 percent. The personal income tax system had more loopholes and was less progressive than before. Representative Robert Michel, Republican leader in the House, while on national television just before the tax cuts were voted, told a conference of House Republican members to be sure to remind their wealthy constituents that the new tax law would be less progressive than the old. At the same time, many kinds of business taxes were reduced an enormous extent. The acceleration of depreciation schedules tremendously reduced the taxation of corporate profits. An immense extra tax cut was given to the oil companies. Finally, to help the "truly needy" wealthy (though Reagan talked about helping the truly needy poor), all gift and inheritance taxes suffered huge cuts.

Some lessons are clear. Instead of increases for the constructive spending items that Samuelson thought would be easy to increase, these types of spending were cut. The cuts in spending fell most heavily on the poor and the working class, and some spending cuts hurt the middle class. Most of the tax cuts, as well as the increase in military spending, increased the aftertax profits of the whole capitalist class. A cautious summary of the tax bill said: "Although the bill contains massive tax cuts for business and a host of tax breaks for special interests, there are only a handful of changes to help the average worker" (United Press International 1981, 1).

It is important to remember that this anti–working class, procapitalist budget was written by the conservative Republican party. Yet it is also important to remember that (1) it passed only because many Democrats supported it, and (2) the budget proposal of the liberal Democrats also made enormous cuts in all nonmilitary pro–working class programs, even though these cuts were less than the Republican ones.

## ECONOMIC CONSTRAINTS UPON FISCAL POLICY

To understand why both U.S. liberals and U.S. conservatives end up with remarkably similar fiscal policies (and to understand why these policies have not been very effective), one must understand the economic constraints set on policy by the structure of capitalism. The four major constraints within the system are as follows: (1) Redistribution to the poor may reduce capitalist incentives to invest; (2) government competition may reduce investment in private enterprise; (3) conflict may occur between policies to reduce the internal deficit and policies to reduce the trade deficit; and (4) there may be conflict between antiunemployment and antiinflation policies. In addition, there is the alleged conflict between government borrowing and private investment borrowing. All of these problems are seen as barriers to any government activism by conservative economists. To the extent that these barriers are real—and not just rhetoric to stop social action—they point to conflicts within the system and the need to change the system (but that is left to the next chapter).

## Crowding Out?

The liberal Keynesian policy leads to deficit spending in depressions; indeed, this is an automatic, built-in effect under present laws. Conservatives argue that government borrowing raises interest rates, thereby reducing or crowding out private borrowing for investment. Thus, they argue, government spending reduces private spending by an equal amount and has no other effect. It appears reasonable to argue that government borrowing may raise interest rates. But how much? Is the increase significant? Is it far overshadowed by other effects?

Chapter 14 also referred to the fact that most empirical studies have found no statistically significant negative effect of interest rates on investment. The historical record of the business cycle (see particularly Chapters 14 and 17) shows why one would not expect to find good evidence that deficit spending raises interest rates or that higher interest rates lower investment. In the average expansion, the government deficit declines (mainly because of rising revenues), yet interest rates rise (mainly because of rising private demand), while private investment rises (mainly because of improved profit expectations). On the other hand, in the average contraction the government deficit rises, yet interest rates fall, while private investment also falls.

Thus, the evidence that government spending crowds out private spending is not convincing. It does seem clear that deficit spending has a net stimulative effect because the demand effect (through the multiplier) is far greater than the effect of higher interest costs.

Although deficit spending has stimulated the economy in every war period, it has had its most dramatic effects in two periods. First, during World War II, under President Roosevelt, the government bought 40 percent of GNP. Given that enormous new demand for goods and services, the vast unemployment of the Great Depression disappeared. By

1943, the official unemployment rate had fallen to 1 percent. The expansion lasted till the end of the war.

Second, in the years from 1980 to 1988, under President Reagan, military spending was vastly increased, while taxes were considerably reduced. The result was a historically unprecedented deficit. This deficit helped the recovery from depression and continued to feed an unusually long expansion. Thus, President Reagan provided the best evidence available in support of Keynes's theories for a peacetime period (with a military buildup).

### Redistribution of Income

Keynes said that capitalism is at fault because of (1) "failure to provide for full employment" and (2) "its arbitrary and inequitable distribution of wealth and income" (Keynes 1986, ch. 24, quoted in Rousseas 1986, 372). Keynes argued that fiscal policy should redistribute income to the poor (see Hotson 1976, 13–14) and that this would help alleviate the lack of effective demand. If, however, a drastic reduction of income inequality by fiscal means were to be legislated by a liberal or mildly radical government, then capitalists might refuse to invest. This sabotage of the U.S. economy—"sabotage" was how Thorstein Veblen referred to capitalist decisions not to invest—has generally not resulted from minor reforms increasing taxes or welfare spending. But a really drastic redistribution policy might lower "business confidence" and make capitalists hoard or flee the country with their capital. Such flight did occur in Chile under the socialist government of Salvadore Allende and also in the first year of the socialist government of François Mitterand in France.

Another more immediate problem of redistribution is the fact that the enormous national debt of the United States means enormous interest payments from the average taxpayer to the rich holders of Treasury bonds. The huge deficits of the Reagan administration, at high interest rates, thus greatly increased the inequality of income.

### Competition with Private Enterprise

If the U.S. government sponsored a successful energy corporation, the lower prices would compete with present private energy corporations. These private energy corporations might then go on strike by not investing or by fleeing overseas. As conservatives frequently and correctly point out, *any* peaceful constructive direct investment by government does compete with private capital. Therefore, enough government investment might cause an investment strike or capital flight. Of course, one remedy would be still more government investment, but that would lead to socialism, would it not?

The same constraint may apply to competition with elite professionals. If free national health care were instituted, doctors might get reasonable payments instead of outrageous monopoly revenues. Doctors might also flee, but where would they go? Every other industrialized country (except South Africa) already has free national health care.

### Government Deficit versus Trade Deficit

When the U.S. economy is stimulated, income grows. Higher incomes lead to an increase in imports. If exports do not change (and that does not depend on the U.S. economy), then this causes net exports to decline—which causes the trade deficit to increase. Thus, if the economy improves, so that the government deficit declines, the trade deficit may increase. Yet a higher trade deficit means lower demand for U.S. products.

A related problem is the fact that a stronger U.S. economy leads to a higher exchange rate for the U.S. dollar. But a higher exchange rate reduces U.S. exports. Again, internal policy may conflict with trade policy.

### Inflation and Unemployment

Perhaps the most difficult problem for U.S. fiscal policy is that policies to reduce unemployment tend to increase inflation. But in the 1970s and early 1980s, the U.S. economy was faced with both unemployment and inflation. In the early 1970s, Paul Samuelson said that economists knew how to prevent either unemployment or inflation, but he sadly admitted that there was no liberal policy to solve both: "Experts do not yet know . . . an income policy that will permit us to have simultaneously . . . full employment and price stability" (Samuelson 1973, 823). Typical liberal Keynesian policies for full employment stimulate the economy with a high level of demand, but the usual Keynesian policy to reduce inflation is to reduce demand. It is impossible to do both at once.

It is true that unemployment and inflation sometimes moved together in the 1970s. Closer examination, however, reveals that they sometimes increased together, but almost never decreased together, so they cannot be cured with the same policy. A drastic enough rise in demand to cause full employment would also probably lead to more inflation. A drastic enough fall in demand to cause zero inflation or stable prices would also cause much more unemployment.

MONETARY POLICY

Monetary policy can affect demand by increasing or decreasing the available credit. The Federal Reserve system uses three major tools: (1) reserve requirement changes; (2) controlling the discount rate; and (3) open market operations. Before considering policy alternatives, let us review the use of these well-known tools.

Bank reserves must be held against all liabilities of banks, with the legal minimum set by the *reserve requirement*, which is expressed as a certain percentage of each type of liability. Raising or lowering this reserve requirement will substantially affect the amount of new bank lending and money/credit creation that results from new reserves being provided to the banking system. For example, when the reserve requirement on demand deposit liabilities is raised, this reduces the amount of new bank loans. Thus raising the reserve requirement reduces credit; lowering the reserve requirement increases credit.

Banks are also allowed to borrow reserves from the Federal Reserve System through the discount window. The interest rate charged on such loans by banks is called the discount rate. By raising or lowering the discount rate, the Federal Reserve can discourage or encourage the borrowing of bank reserves.

Neither of these two policy options has been used much by the Federal Reserve in the past, except in extreme circumstances. Reserve requirement changes are thought to be too drastic and have seldom been used for policy reasons. Reserve requirements have gradually been lowered over the years, partly in response to pressure applied by commercial banks. The Federal Reserve does change the discount rate periodically, but this usually merely reflects changes in market interest rates. Often the discount rate is below competing market rates because, ideally, banks are supposed to borrow only emergency loans from the discount window, and it is felt that this rate should not be a penalty rate. The discount rate has been used aggressively as a macropolicy instrument only on a few occasions.

Open market operations are the true vehicle for implementing monetary policy. These operations are used daily by the Federal Reserve system with the explicit intent of accomplishing policy objectives. Open market operations are overseen by the Federal Reserve Bank of New York. It is here that traders buy and sell U.S. Treasury securities. When the Federal Reserve buys U.S. bonds from banks in return for money, bank reserves are increased. But when the Federal Reserve sells bonds to banks, money reserves are decreased. An increase in bank reserves allows more bank loans to be made. This means that bank liabilities, including demand deposits, a component of the money supply, grow.

These operations, therefore, influence levels of credit, money, and interest rates in the economy. The primary tool of implementing Federal Reserve policy is open market operations. This tool has been used almost exclusively in the past and probably will continue to be the dominant tool in the future.

### Strict Monetarism

Strict monetarism advocates the adoption of a monetary "rule" (see Friedman 1968). The rule means that the money supply should be forced to grow at some designated rate, say 4 percent to 5 percent, regardless of economic circumstance. A monetary expansion should not be used to counteract a recession, so the Federal Reserve should do no countercyclical activity. Interest rates should be determined entirely by the market, so the Federal Reserve should not try to influence interest rates.

The money supply, according to this school of thought, will be controlled by carefully controlling either the level of bank reserves or the monetary base (bank reserves plus currency in the hands of the nonbank public) through open market operations. Through empirical research, the *money multiplier*, which establishes the connection between bank reserves and the money supply, will be determined. Once this multiplier is determined, open market operations will be conducted at a pace sufficient to allow reserves to grow at the rate sufficient to produce exactly the desired growth in the money supply.

For example, the Federal Reserve might decide to control total bank reserves in its open market operations. Staff economists might conclude, from their research, that if reserves were to grow at a 3.5 percent annual rate, then the M1 money supply would grow at 4 percent. Presumably, the trading desk at the Federal Reserve Bank of New York would be instructed to purchase Treasury securities gradually at a rate that would allow bank reserves to expand 3.5 percent annually. This they would do faithfully and passively, regardless of market conditions.

If, after a period of time, they discovered that they had guessed incorrectly about the multiplier, so that the money supply growth rate was too fast or too slow, they would presumably adjust the reserve growth rate to compensate. For example, if the Federal Reserve was controlling reserves and the growth rate of reserves was 3.5 percent, but the money supply was growing at 5 percent instead of the desired 4 percent, then the allowed growth rate of reserves might be dropped down a bit until the money supply target was approximately reached.

Regardless of the practical operating plans of strict monetarism, the policy has one fundamental feature that distinguishes it from any discretionary monetarism: In the conduct of open market operations, there is to be no response whatsoever to prevailing economic conditions. It is *not* the job of the Federal Reserve (or any other central bank) to pursue stabilization or countercyclical policies. This is the purest form of a laissez-faire policy. The free market economy is to work without intervention.

Strict monetarists justify their policy as the most *workable* monetary policy. In their opinion, the Federal Reserve system can't hope to control interest rates and the two or three measures of monetary aggregates simultaneously. Furthermore, monetarists argue, variations in the money supply growth rate will undoubtedly produce variations in the level of spending, but the lags and amplitudes between money and spending are quite variable, so an expansionary discretionary monetary stimulus might overstimulate or understimulate, producing more confusion and harm than assistance. It is far simpler to have one easy target and use one simple procedure in pursuit of a very elementary objective—to make it easy for the private sector of the economy to solve its own problems. It is assumed that Say's law operates, so that the private economy automatically reaches full employment. Moreover, strict monetarists contend that discretionary policy unavoidably ends up being inflationary policy. Inflation, monetarists insist, would absolutely be a thing of the past in the presence of a monetary rule.

### Discretionary Monetarism

Advocates of a discretionary monetary policy (such as Paul Volcker, when he headed the Federal Reserve) also identify money as the most important financial variable influencing the level of nominal spending in the economy; it is the primary, if not the exclusive, variable that the Federal Reserve system should attempt to control. These monetary theorists also have considerable faith in the free enterprise system, but they regard it as less stable than do their pure monetarist colleagues, so they hold that it is occasionally in need of a countercyclical stabilization policy.

The Volcker policy was certainly a type of discretionary monetarism. Volcker's policy gave primary emphasis to the control of monetary aggregates, with most attention given to M1. Secondary attention, however, was given to the behavior of interest rates. Strict monetarists would not allow this. An ideal discretionary monetarist policy would always state its objective in meeting monetary targets. The monetary targets, however, rather than being held constant, would be raised and lowered as economic conditions dictated.

The more Keynesian-oriented critics of monetarism have a number of complaints against both forms of monetarism and especially the monetarist "rule." Generally, the rule is regarded as too inflexible. The traditional Keynesian position is that one of the many roles of the government is to implement countercyclical stabilization policies and that the government can do this successfully if appropriate policies are implemented. Rather than regarding the economy as a smoothly running machine needing an occasional few drops of monetary oil, they see the private sector as prone to all sorts of disturbances, calamities, and economic mishaps. The monetary rule simply ties the hands of one of the most potentially potent public agencies, rendering it ineffective during times of economic crises. If the finance markets are inherently unstable, with volatile demands for credit, episodic bursts of harmful speculation, and lapses in rational decisionmaking, then monetarist policies are ill advised. The closer the Federal Reserve moves toward emphasis on narrow monetary growth rate targets, the greater the interest rate volatility is going to be. Without the intervention of the Federal Reserve, any sudden jump in credit demand is likely to drive interest rates up.

Economists who have been influenced by the argument that the money stock is endogenous, such as the Post-Keynesians (discussed in Chapter 14), are also highly critical of monetarism. In the long run, monetarist policies will simply be ineffective, they argue. If a monetary rule is adopted, for example, and either private or government credit demand continues to grow, the resulting high interest rates will introduce a fertile environment for the development of new financial instruments. These new instruments initially are money substitutes and eventually begin to serve money functions, at least at some levels of commerce. With such a development, the instruments that the Federal Reserve actually controls (such as M1) become increasingly irrelevant to the level of spending. This phenomenon might appear as a rise in velocity—that is, the ratio of spending to the officially defined money supply will shoot up. Velocity increases because the money supply, which the Federal Reserve is controlling with its rule, becomes less important to the level of spending in the economy (while credit becomes more important).

### Controlling Wide Aggregates and Credit

Some Keynesian-oriented monetary economists, who are critical of monetarism's focus on narrow monetary aggregates, advise the monitoring and targeting of much wider liquidity aggregates, such as some measure of credit. It is felt by these theorists that these inclusive aggregates of credit are much more closely correlated to levels of spending than money (see, for example, Earley, Parsons, and Thompson 1976).

Such ideas are certainly consistent with the endogenous money stock argument. If near-money substitutes that begin to function as money are developed, wider financial aggregates are more likely to include those instruments (such as money market funds) that begin to serve as money.

Hence, an aggregate credit policy is less likely to be "surprised" by inflation if the endogenous money stock argument is correct. Advocates of these policies point out that the velocities of wide credit aggregates have tended to be nearly constant for two decades, whereas the velocity of money has fluctuated sharply. This provides strong evidence, in their opinion, that the long-run relationship between wide credit aggregates and spending is far more exact.

Creditists, as they might be called, stress that both the level of spending and the extension of new credit are both *flows* (whereas the monetary aggregates are stocks). Any variation in credit flows will *directly* cause a variation in spending, whereas expenditures can grow without changes in the money stock. Moreover, changes in the money stock need not necessarily lead to changes in spending. A rise or fall in the demand for money as a financial asset can disturb the connection between money and spending, but a rise in the amount of credit extended will almost certainly generate new spending. When inflation is a problem, the creditists believe that controls over credit are more likely to succeed than a reduction in the rate of growth of the money supply.

## IMPACT OF MONETARY POLICY

The monetarists view government fiscal and monetary shocks to the economy as the main destabilizing factors in the U.S. political-economic system. On the contrary, Part Two of this book shows how the private capitalist economy endogenously generates the business cycle. Of course, the same evidence of a continuing endogenous business cycle—with severe contractions in 1975 and 1982—also disproves the hypothesis that the government is able to stabilize the economy by fine-tuning it with fiscal and monetary policy.

The evidence presented in Chapters 14 and 17 indicates that fiscal behavior and monetary (or credit) behavior are endogenous to the economic system (in the sense of being determined by the conjuncture of the business cycle phase and long-term capitalist interests). This behavior also has a significant, but usually limited impact (except in war-driven cycles and a few exceptional instances). In peacetime contractions, the government usually stimulates the economy (1) by running a deficit, and (2) by loosening up on credit to encourage borrowing. Thus, government behavior is one of the factors helping the private economy to recover. In peacetime expansions, the declared foe is usually inflation, so fiscal policy is less and less stimulating as the expansion progresses. In the usual expansion, monetary policy is at first accommodating to business, but usually becomes more restrictive towards the peak. The monetary restrictions are usually effected after the rate of profit has begun to decline, so the private economy is merely pushed along the path it has already taken. Thus, the government usually allows a downturn, but then encourages the recovery. It is an actor, but not the prime actor—and its acts are mostly predictable.

## LIMITATIONS OF MONETARY POLICY

Many liberals believe that monetary policy could be effective under the right policies. Even Hyman Minsky, who emphasizes the vulnerability of the capitalist economy and the incorrect policies of the Federal Reserve, says: "Once endogenous economic processes take the economy to the brink of crisis, Federal Reserve intervention can abort the development of a full-fledged crisis and debt deflation" (quoted in Rousseas 1986, 114). But there are many reasons to be skeptical about the efficacy of any monetary policy.

Suppose that there is a liberal U.S. administration and a liberal Keynesian head of the Federal Reserve committed to full employment as well as stable prices. Suppose that there is careful coordination of monetary and fiscal policy. Suppose that there are no practical problems interfering with the Federal Reserve's ability to control monetary and credit aggregates (though this is probably contrary to the theory and reality of an endogenous money and credit supply). Nevertheless, there are clear limitations to monetary policy (some of the political and practical issues are detailed in Epstein [1981]).

First, take the case of inflation. It is true that sufficiently strong measures will cure inflation. For example, in the winter of 1980, both the Carter administration and the Federal Reserve agreed to strong measures to reduce credit. These measures succeeded in reducing inflation from about 18 percent to 8 percent in a few months. The trouble is that such measures must be so harsh in order to have any effect on inflation that they depress the economy. In 1980 the result was a recession and a very considerable rise in unemployment. (The same policies appear to have increased unemployment in England under the Thatcher administration and in the United States under the Reagan administration.)

Second, take the case of severe unemployment. Many neoclassical-Keynesians would support low interest rates and easy credit. Yet Post-Keynesians emphasize that the interest rate required for a full employment equilibrium may be so low as to be unattainable. That interest rate might be below the minimum level for speculation, in which case speculative investors would hold back because they would expect it to return to a higher level. The equilibrium (full employment) interest rate might even be negative if profit expectations were negative—that is, if losses were expected, a business would borrow only if a bank paid it to borrow.

For these reasons, the Post-Keynesians see monetary policy as at best an adjunct to (or co-partner with) fiscal policy in a deep depression. Low interest rates cannot alleviate unemployment at all if expected profit rates are below zero.

Finally, the realistic situation in the 1990s is the existence of *both* inflation and unemployment in U.S. capitalism. In this case, what should a liberal neoclassical-Keynesian monetary policy be? Should it ease credit and lower interest rates sufficiently to stimulate the economy and reduce involuntary unemployment to zero? If it works (which is questionable), this will cause inflation. Should it reduce credit and raise interest rates in order to reduce inflation to zero? If it is drastic enough to be effective, it will cause severe unemployment.

## MONETARY POLICY, WAGES, AND INFLATION

In every expansion phase, as soon as real wages start to rise, many neoclassical economists begin to worry that higher wages will cause inflation and will weaken the U.S. competitive position so as to worsen the trade deficit. For example, Laurence Summers (Professor of Economics at Harvard) worries: "Workers who accepted real wage reductions in 17 of the last 20 quarters will start demanding and receiving wage increases in excess of past price increases, setting off a wage-price spiral" (1988, 1). Summers pays no attention to the evidence that the power of unions steadily declined in this period. He also pays no attention to the whole analysis of effective demand by Keynes and returns to the pre-Keynesian position that favors lowering wages, "reducing consumption and increasing national saving" to cure all evils. He gives it a modern twist by arguing that "reduced consumption can make room for increased demand for American products, which will come as the trade deficit declines" (1986, 1). In other words, if only workers are wise enough to accept even lower wages (after wages fell in seventeen of the last twenty quarters), there will be economic growth, no trade deficit, and no federal deficit, and the Federal Reserve will not have to slow down the economy.

Similarly, in a synthesis of opinions of many neoclassical economists, John Berry (1988) concludes: "The compensation of American workers . . . is increasing at the fastest pace in three years, raising concerns of an acceleration in inflation in coming months" (p. 1). Notice that economists do not seem concerned with wage cuts, only with wage increases. Berry (1988) reports that economists are also concerned over falling unemployment because this allows wage increases (which represent "about two-thirds of all business costs"). In this context, Berry notes that "Federal Reserve Chairman Alan Greenspan warned Congress . . . that if an expected slowdown in the economy does not occur, . . . the Fed will be forced to continue to increase interest rates in order to prevent a new surge in inflation" (p. 11).

Thus, whenever endogenous forces expand the economy and increase employment and wages, the desire of capitalists to hold down wages is reflected in tighter Federal Reserve policies. But these policies help cause a crisis of realization and a recession or depression, so they must be considered a failure as an anti–business cycle policy. We turn now to the more obvious attempt to hold down inflation by reducing real wages through direct controls, a policy last used by the Nixon administration.

## INCOME POLICY: DIRECT CONTROLS ON WAGES AND PRICES

This chapter has demonstrated that neither fiscal policy nor monetary policy (nor their combination) can end a situation of unemployment plus inflation. Therefore, when the combination of unemployment and inflation became an obvious evil in the early 1970s, even the conservative Nixon administration decided to try the drastic solution of military spending plus an income policy, that is, direct wage and price controls. Because direct controls are a possible addition to monetary and fiscal policy, it is very instructive to examine this episode as a case study (relying on the excellent study by Harris [1978]).

On August 15, 1971, President Nixon announced a new economic policy designed to save America and increase corporate profits. Phase 1 ran for ninety days, from August to November 1971. All wages, prices, and rents were frozen. Profits were not frozen. In actuality, all wage increases were prevented, but some prices continued to creep upward.

Phase 2 lasted from November 1971 until January 1973. The freeze was ended, but there were mandatory controls of wages, prices, and rents, though not of profits. Under this system, inflation continued, though at a reduced rate of "only" about 4 percent per year. Unemployment, according to the official definition, fell from its highest level of about 6 percent in the 1970 recession down to about 5 percent.

Phase 3 was supposed to "phase out the economic stabilization program and move back to the free market, since the price target was being achieved," according to administration spokespersons. It removed all controls over prices in all industries except food, health, and construction and substituted voluntary controls. The voluntary controls were no controls at all because they had no enforcement procedure. Therefore, business paid no attention to them, so prices skyrocketed, rising at about 8 percent a year. The first part of phase 3 lasted only from January to June 1973. A striking feature of it was the pressure kept on the unions to abide by voluntary controls and the extent to which the unions did restrain workers from asking for wage raises. As a result, there was a very slight rise in money wages, and the real earning power of workers declined. Again there were no controls on profits, which continued to soar.

Near the end of phase 3, the swift rise in prices led to a new freeze. The second part of phase 3 was a second freeze, from June to August 1973. All prices were frozen, but there were no controls on unprocessed food or on rents. Neither wages nor profits were frozen, but wages remained under phase 3 voluntary controls.

Phase 4 began in August 1973 and ended in April 1974. It was again a mandatory system of controls over prices, wages, and rents, but not over profits. It was very effective in holding down wages, but prices continued to rise at about 10 percent per year.

In all of 1973, the actual buying power of workers declined by 4 percent, whereas profits rose rapidly. In the first half of 1974, unemployment rose to 6 percent, real gross national product declined, and the rate of inflation rose to 12 percent. According to the usual definitions, the U.S. economy was in a recession in the midst of an inflation. President Nixon, however, denied that it was a recession, preferring to call it a slight readjustment. Much later, President Ford finally admitted it was a recession, but not a depression, even though unemployment was over 9 percent. President Ford still resisted any attempts to cure unemployment until late 1974; even in October 1974, he was still talking about *raising* taxes.

The year 1975 was a year of recession, high unemployment, and declining real wages owing to inflation. Because of the wage-price controls and the continuing inflation and unemployment, the actual buying power of workers reached a peak in 1972 and declined during the next four years. Thus, the real weekly wages of an urban worker with three dependents declined from $96.64 in 1972 to $90.53 in 1975 (in constant 1967 dollars).

## Controls Cause Inefficiency and Corruption

Economists of most ideological views criticized the controls, but for different reasons. The neoclassical economists, such as Milton Friedman, were horrified at the violation of the First Commandment of laissez-faire economics: Thou shalt not interfere with the market process of setting wages and prices (1971, 45). They have always argued that resources, including capital and labor, cannot be efficiently allocated if prices are not set by competition in the market. If the government arbitrarily sets prices, how can a businessperson calculate most efficiently what to produce or what technology to use? If a businessperson does follow the arbitrary prices set by the government, then he or she will not produce what consumers desire and will not produce it in the cheapest possible way. It will not be produced as cheaply as possibly because those prices do not correctly reflect the true scarcities of resources. Moreover, it will not be the combination of goods that consumers desire because those prices do not correctly reflect true consumer preferences. Thus, wage-price controls doom a capitalist economy to inefficiency.

It is probably true that direct controls do not mix well with capitalism since they would mean a combination of bureaucratic planning with private greed in a market economy. The controls might improve the situation over a pure market economy at times (such as rapid inflation), but this is not a stable combination, as shown below.

### Controls Increase Inequality

One reason that the combination is unstable is that it means political control of relative incomes. Given the strength of the capitalist class, political determination of relative incomes will always tend to increase the inequality of income. It was demonstrated above that during the Nixon administration's controls, wages were restricted while profits soared. This should not have surprised anyone because, in his speech announcing the wage-price controls, President Nixon stated: "All Americans will benefit from more profits. Profits fuel the expansion . . . mean more investment . . . and . . . mean . . . more tax revenues. That's why higher profits in the American economy would be good for every person in America" (Nixon 1971). Vice-President Agnew argued the same theory in favor of the controls, saying: "Rising corporate profits are needed more than ever by the poor" (Agnew 1971). The Nixon administration was successful in limiting wages and raising profits.

The mechanism for setting wages was a Pay Board, to which Nixon appointed an equal number of business representatives, "public" representatives, and union representatives. Eventually, the union representatives from the AFL-CIO resigned. They pointed out that the so-called "public" representatives appointed by Nixon were always more aggressively opposed to wage increases than the business representatives, so labor lost every vote by a 2 to 1 margin. This specific result reflected the particular administration in power, but the general tendency would be the same in any capitalist country—though a very strong labor movement with a socialist party, as in Sweden, could certainly lead to a more progressive result.

### A COHERENT LIBERAL MACRO POLICY

Many liberal economists have advocated an integrated use of fiscal policy, monetary policy, and income policy, where "income policy" means direct wage-price controls (see for example, Tobin 1985, 16). John Kenneth Galbraith has consistently advocated controls, and the AFL-CIO has advocated controls at various times. It was a liberal Democratic Congress that gave the control powers to President Nixon, though it did so only because it did not expect him to exercise the powers. The conservative Nixon had always opposed controls, but saw them as necessary for his short-term goals. Nixon not only used direct controls to hold down inflation (and distribute income to capitalists), but also increased military spending to hold down unemployment. During the 1980 primary elections, Senator Edward Kennedy advocated the same basic stabilization policies, with different distribution and allocation policies.

A coherent liberal statement of this policy might be as follows:

1. In order to achieve full employment, use higher government spending on peaceful, constructive programs.
2. In order to achieve full employment, reduce taxes of the poor, the workers, and the middle class to stimulate consumer demand.
3. In order to achieve full employment, use monetary policy to lower interest rates.
4. In order to eliminate inflation, put direct controls on the prices of all monopoly corporations, with stiff enforcement penalties.

No controls are needed for small business prices, which will follow monopoly prices. No controls are needed for wages, which only try to catch up to prices. Controls only on the prices of the top thousand corporations could be efficiently administered and involve less bureaucracy—while the lack of controls on wages would make it difficult to have anti-working class distribution effects.

The most liberal form of public spending would be a very strong full employment act (to replace the act sponsored by Senator Humphrey and Representative Hawkins, which was weakened till in its final form it had no effect). A real full employment act would provide that any unemployed person could get work with the government (local, state, or federal) as the employer of last resort. The wage would automatically be set equal to the wage for comparable work in the private sector.

This liberal reform can be argued on the basis that if, and only if, private enterprise failed to provide jobs, then the government would be forced to provide jobs. It should appeal, however, to some conservatives in that (1) unemployment compensation could be ended forever (so people would no longer be paid not to work), and (2) all welfare payments to people who are able to work could be ended forever. (Of course, child care payments would be needed for working women with children, and the ill or disabled need care.)

The work done need *not* be wasteful work. The United States badly needs to replace old bridges, replace old roads, replace and expand mass transit, replace old sewer systems, clean up rivers and lakes, build new hospitals and provide more health care personnel, expand and better maintain national parks, provide more educational personnel, and so forth. There are plenty of jobs to be done; it is just that these are not areas for big private profits.

## PROBLEMS WITH THE LIBERAL PROGRAM

Such a program could be relatively successful for some length of time. In the first place, however, if there are to be any controls, political reality will result in wage-price controls, not only on all prices but also on all wages. Even Senator Kennedy and the AFL-CIO favored this compromise, provided, of course, that there would be strong promises that the controls would not be used to distribute income in an anti–working class manner. This is probably the best possible liberal program that could be enacted.

For how long could such a program successfully move toward full employment, stable prices, class-neutral income distribution, and a reasonably efficient economy? Suppose that a liberal administration enacted such a program. All of our experience with controls—in World War II, the Korean War, and the Nixon administration—and all economic theory indicate that it could succeed to some degree for six months to a year. Then it would reach a crossroad.

First, the conservative issue of efficiency would become more and more difficult. Prices could be almost frozen for six months to a year, but by then domestic supply and demand conditions, technology, and foreign conditions would have changed considerably, so big readjustments would become more and more necessary. One choice would be to dismantle controls slowly, as the Nixon administration did. The other choice would be to move toward some form of planning.

Second, since the economy would have been stimulated to full employment, with much higher government spending and much higher resulting consumer demand, the inflationary pressures would be enormous. Again, one answer would be to (1) end price controls and (2) end guaranteed full employment. This would mean going back to the same old business cycle, in which inflation is eventually "cured" by depression and large-scale unemployment. The other alternative would be some form of planning.

A third problem would be the battle over income distribution. Imagine an economy at full employment, but where wages and profits are determined by government boards. Labor and capital would have to fight in the political arena to control these boards. If capitalist political power proved stronger than that of the labor movement, wages would be frozen while prices rose. The economic results would lead to conflict, possibly followed by repression.

If, on the other hand, labor developed enough political power to get strong price controls, but continuous wage increases, this would mean reducing the rate of profit. Falling rates of profit would make capitalists react by reducing their investments. This would further lower employment in the private sector. The loss of business "confidence" and collapse of the private sector would again lead to enormous pressure to dismantle the controls. The alternative would be more public saving, public employment, and some form of national economic planning. Thus, the liberal program could ameliorate the business contraction for a short while—in the long-run, however, the realistic alternatives are return to market capitalism (in which there will always be cyclical contractions) or progress to democratic planning (as discussed in the next chapter).

## SUGGESTED READINGS

There is a vast body of literature on policy from various points of view. For the most reactionary, see George Gilder (1981). The supply-side view is given by Arthur Laffer (1982). For the monetarist view, see Milton Friedman (1968); but also see Franco Modigliani (1977). Middle of the road views are expressed by Charles Kindleberger (1978) and by James Tobin (1981). A Post-Keynesian view of government policy is given by John Hotson (1976) and by Hyman Minsky (1986). An institutionalist view is stated by Wallace Peterson (1987); and Marxist views of fiscal policy are given by David Gold (1977) and by John Miller (1986). Some coherent left policy programs are presented in Bowles, Gordon, and Weisskopf (1983); Ferleger and Mandle (1987); and Dugger (1989). A variety of views on Keynes and policy are stated in a collection by Harold Wattel (1985).

# CHAPTER 19

# Can the Business Cycle Be Eliminated?

## Economic Democracy and Democratic Planning

FROM THE EVIDENCE in this book, it appears that the business cycle is caused by the capitalist system. To eliminate the business cycle, it follows that it is necessary to change to an alternative economic system. This chapter proposes a system based on economic democracy and democratic planning, as defined below. This chapter contains only a brief sketch of such a system; full discussion of all of the problems would require a long book. The issues raised by this solution are discussed in detail in Sherman (1987) and the problems of alternative economic systems are compared in Zimbalist, Sherman, and Brown (1989).

### ECONOMIC DEMOCRACY

There are three problems related to the structure of industry that are relevant to the problem of the business cycle. First, as explained in Chapter 15, monopoly power tends to make unemployment worse and also tends to worsen inflation. Second, as shown in Chapter 8, equality of income distribution is important in determining effective demand, but the concentration of ownership and concentration of corporate assets makes the distribution of income more unequal. Third, the institution of democratic planning must be built on the basis of a democratic structure. In other words, a democratic process of planning cannot be coupled with undemocratic capitalist control and ownership by a tiny elite through a relatively small number of giant corporations. The two are incompatible because (1) the goal of democratic planning is the maximum benefit for the country, but the goal of private enterprise is maximum private profit; and (2) the corporations would control the planning process through economic power.

To overcome these three problems, it is proposed that the thousand largest U.S. corporations—all having monopoly power—be publicly owned and be run as cooperatives by the workers in them. Each worker's having one vote in the direction of the corporation is, by definition, a democratic procedure for running the giants of U.S. industry. This would automatically end the most extreme concentration of ownership and greatly reduce the inequality of income distribution.

Each cooperative would have a board of directors elected by the workers. There should be one government representative on the board of directors for (1) direct access to information, (2) influence for enforcement of safety laws, and (3) influence for enforcement of environmental laws. Thus, the general public interest would constrain the local interest to some extent. Otherwise, however, the cooperatives would operate to maximize their profits by selling their products through the market mechanism. The board of directors would appoint a manager, who would be in charge of output, technology, prices, and so forth. As always, the manager's own wage would depend largely on the profit to the cooperative. The manager and board could expand the cooperative's capital by reinvestment of profits.

Some of the largest corporations are presently several times larger than necessary for optimal efficiency. Therefore, such firms could and should be broken into smaller pieces of optimum size before being remade into cooperatives. On the other hand, a few firms may be too small. For example, since all U.S. airlines and airports are closely linked in the national network by controllers, there should probably be only one enterprise in the U.S. airline industry to ensure safety as well as efficiency. That firm would be run as a cooperative by the airline employees, but with close federal supervision on safety matters—as well as price regulation if it is a monopoly.

If society is to control the economy democratically, then it must control the financial system. The Federal Reserve should be democratized by ending its semiindependent status and making it a normal government agency under Congress and the President. The banking system is the one industry that should be publicly owned so that credit can be controlled directly by the Federal Reserve, which would run the banking industry.

Economic democracy means the extension of democratic control to the economy. If the financial system were owned and controlled by the public through the government, and if all of the large corporations were controlled by workers' cooperatives, then most of the economy would be under economic democracy. Since capitalists would have lost ownership and control of most of the economy, it would no longer be capitalism; it could be called economic democracy—or democratic socialism if that name is preferred (but "socialism" is a pejorative term in the United States).

## DEMOCRATIC PLANNING

Democratic planning means that the people of the United States, through their duly elected government, would plan the overall macroeconomic direction of the economy. Before explaining the concept in detail, it is worth noting what other economists have said about the idea. All neoclassical economists reject the need for public planning because they argue that the private economy automatically adjusts to an optimum path—but this view is refuted by the facts of recessions, depressions, and cyclical unemployment. It is not credible to say that a system with millions of people unemployed is optimal for human beings.

Of course, Karl Marx and most Marxist economists have advocated a degree of planning. It is less well known that Thorstein Veblen and many of his institutionalist followers have advocated democratic planning in the United States (see Dugger 1988). It is even less well known that John Maynard Keynes did not merely advocate fiscal and monetary policy to combat unemployment and inflation, but also emphasized the need for direct planning of investment.

## Keynes's Socialization of Investment

Keynes (1936) prescribed "a somewhat comprehensive socialization of investment" (ch. 24, discussed in Hotson 1976, 13–14). Since the rapid rise and fall of investment is the key to the business cycle, it is no surprise that Keynes believed that the government must have ultimate control over investment if it is to combat the business cycle. But what exactly did Keynes mean by the socialization of investment?

In a fascinating article, Robert Lekachman (1985) brings out the details of this radical side of Keynes, showing a considerable commitment to planning. In 1939, Keynes wrote: "In contemporary conditions we need, if we are to enjoy prosperity and profits . . . much more central planning than we have at present. . . . The intensification of the trade cycle and the increasingly chronic character of unemployment have shown that private capitalism was already in its decline as a means of solving the economic problem" (quoted in Lekachman 1985, 32). Keynes's statement of 1943 makes the point clearer: "If two-thirds or three-quarters of total investment is carried out or can be influenced by public or semi-public bodies, a long-term programme of a stable character should be capable of reducing the potential range of fluctuation to much narrower limits than formerly" (quoted in Lekachman 1985, 33).

Keynes certainly endorsed some type of investment planning, but he does not clarify how much is to be "carried out" directly by public bodies and how much is to be "influenced" by the public and carried out by private enterprise. Regardless of what Keynes meant to say, this chapter advocates (1) influencing investment in the large cooperatively owned enterprises (and the small remaining private enterprises) by fiscal policy and monetary policy, as well as (2) doing all necessary remaining investment to bring the economy to full employment through public agencies.

## *The Investment Process*

In the economy envisioned here, all of the largest firms would be cooperatives and the rest would still be private enterprises. Obviously, each of these firms would continue to have the right to invest, but control could be exercised in various ways and in various degrees. The U.S. government (through the Council of Economic Advisors) would propose plans for investment to the U.S. Congress Joint Economic Committee. This plan would then be implemented in part through the present mechanisms: (1) the fiscal process of government spending and taxation, and (2) the monetary policies of the government. Moreover, the Federal Reserve would be ordered by Congress to implement monetary policies, not only through its usual tools, but mainly by direct control of credit through its ownership of the banking system. The government (through the Federal Reserve) would offer credit at low rates directly to the largest cooperatives for expansion in their own areas. This would be similar to the way that the Japanese government gets the banks to offer credit to industry in specific areas—except that in Japan the loans are made to big business and here it would be to workers' cooperatives. New workers' cooperatives would also receive credit in order to encourage the growth of this democratic economic form.

In addition, however, the U.S. government would add its own investments—on the basis of its open and democratic planning process—when it was necessary to stimulate the economy. The government could also decrease its investments when necessary to reduce the speed of growth. In some cases, these investments could go to existing enterprises, but they could also form entirely new enterprises, especially in areas requiring new research and development or new innovations. These new firms would immediately be turned over to the workers in them to be run as cooperatives, so the government would *not* get into the business of microeconomic planning of existing enterprises—what the government would plan would be the volume of investment, not its nature, except when starting new enterprises.

### INTERNATIONAL IMPLICATIONS

It would be best if international economic planning were done by the United Nations, but that is probably a utopian dream at present. The U.S. planning mechanism, suggested above, would be helpful, however, in curing the U.S. trade deficit. It could help the U.S. economy compete better internationally in several ways. First, our present monopolies clearly feel no competitive pressure to innovate until they are suddenly passed by foreign competitors. The large cooperative enterprises would be in close contact with those government agencies concerned with technical progress and trade, so they could be more easily pressured in the direction of innovation (and they would have a government representative on their governing boards).

Second, the existing cooperatives could be given credits specifically for innovation, while new cooperatives could be set up with the specific purpose of technological innovation in mind. The main reason for the U.S. trade deficit has been U.S. lack of technological programs vis-à-vis other countries. If that lack is cured, so too will the trade deficit be cured.

## DEMOCRATIC PLANNING VERSUS SOVIET PLANNING

The type of planning described above would be strikingly different from previous Soviet planning. First, Soviet planning, until recently, was undemocratic. The basic directions of Soviet planning were decided by a few leaders at the top, and these leaders were self-appointed by a small group. Because it was undemocratic, Soviet planning did not follow the wishes of the population as to the allocation of resources. Moreover, since citizens could not criticize the top leaders, their enormous mistakes went by without comment until a new leader took over many years later, so we may assume there was much waste of resources. Of course, Gorbachev is trying to change this feature by his policies of openness, or *glasnost*, and decentralized reconstruction, or *perestroika* (see Gorbachev 1987).

Any U.S. planning would be directed by our elected leaders and completely open to storms of criticism. Thus, the basic outlines of plans would have to follow the desires of the majority of the population—or else the leaders would be unemployed as a result of the democratic process. Mistakes would be instantly discussed by everyone, especially the opposition party. Presumably, macroeconomic plans would be formulated by the Council of Economic Advisors and presented to the Joint Economic Committee of Congress for consultation and to begin any necessary legislative procedures.

A second feature of Soviet planning is its extreme centralization. Gorbachev (1987) has discussed this feature extensively and has documented its very high level of inefficiency. The present Soviet system is inevitably inefficient because it tries to plan on a microeconomic level. It is as if a planner in Moscow could know every nail, every nut and bolt, in every enterprise in the whole Soviet Union. Even with the most advanced computers imaginable, such a thing is impossible and unnecessary.

In contrast, the U.S. system of planning proposed here would make no microeconomic decisions; those decisions would be left up to the individual firms in the marketplace, whether government run, cooperative, or private. The planning would be for macroeconomic balanced growth. As noted, it would use fiscal policy, monetary policy, standby price controls, direct credit to enterprises, or, as required, direct new investments. The government investments would add to old cooperatives or set up new cooperatives, but would not set up government-run enterprises, except in unusual circumstances. Thus, the firms would continue to make all microeconomic decisions, but within a planned macroeconomic environment (and, of course, in the context of safety and environmental regulations).

## FULL EMPLOYMENT: INSTITUTIONS, LAWS, AND PERFORMANCE

In the previous chapter, it was noted how fiscal and monetary policy may be used to a limited extent under monopoly capitalism to attempt to produce full employment and price stability. But it was also shown that such policies face constraints, limits, and inherent contradictions in the present institutional system.

Only basic changes in institutions can make democratic, macroeconomic planning a feasible possibility. First, monopoly power and income distribution should be totally changed by transforming the largest corporations into publicly owned, cooperatively run enterprises. Second, the government should undertake investment planning.

This new institutional structure should have as its goal full employment and stable prices as a normal result of good planning, not of extraordinary measures. For example, under a system of market capitalism, price controls would be difficult to legislate against private interests, would be very difficult to enforce, and would eventually be in conflict with the underlying system of private decisionmaking. In a democratic (or socialist) economic system with institutionalized macroeconomic planning, it would be reasonable to maintain the power of standby price controls.

If macroeconomic planning were perfect, the price controls would not be needed. Emergency situations might arise, however, from time to time, as a result of mistakes or unexpected events, where price controls might be needed to prevent inflation in a limited sector for a relatively brief time—so that power should always be available.

Another suggested reform under market capitalism is a constitutional right of every adult person to full employment, with the government as the employer of last resort. Under present institutions, such a reform has proven impossible to legislate. Even if it were put into the Constitution, it would be in basic conflict with private enterprise because it would change the fundamental rules of the capitalist labor market—wherein firms must always have more power than workers. Moreover, in each depression, government would be competing with private enterprise and slowly replacing it.

Under the proposed institutions, there would be no reason for opposition to a constitutional right to full employment as a standby power for help to individuals. If planning worked correctly, however, there would be little or no occasion for individuals to exercise that right. Planned full employment as a normal condition under given institutions is obviously better than emergency correction. At any rate, the combination of planning and the right to a job should make photos of unemployed workers an exhibit only for museums and unemployment compensation an exotic subject for historians. This is *not* a prediction of utopia because many other problems will persist, but the pathological condition known as unemployment can and should be eradicated.

# Definitions of Variables

ALL DEFINITIONS, unless specified otherwise, are based on U.S. Department of Commerce, Bureau of Economic Analysis, *Handbook of Cyclical Indicators, A Supplement of the Business Conditions Digest* (Washington, D.C.: U.S. Government Printing Office, 1984). The definitions are given briefly here, but are further elaborated in the source. The number before each definition refers to the series number (#) in the source.

20. *New Orders for Plant Equipment.* Contracts and orders for plant and equipment in 1972 dollars.

30. *Inventory Investment.* Change in business inventories in 1972 dollars.

43. *Unemployment Rate.* The ratio of the number of persons unemployed to the civilian labor force, expressed as a percent.

47. *Index of Industrial Production.* The index, based on 1967 = 100, covers manufacturing, mining, gas, and electric utilities.

50. *Gross National Product.* The market value, in 1972 dollars, of goods and services from labor and property supplied by labor and property.

64. *Labor Share.* Compensation of employees as a percentage of national income, that is #280/#220.

77. *Ratio, Inventory to Sales.* The ratio of inventories in manufacturing and trade to sales in manufacturing and trade in 1972 dollars.

82. *Capacity Utilization.* The ratio of output, calculated by the Federal Reserve Board, to total capacity, estimated by FRB surveys.

86. *Gross Nonresidential Investment.* Gross private nonresidential fixed investment (structures plus producers' durable equipment) in 1972 dollars.

105. *Money Supply, M1.* Consists of currency, travelers' checks, demand deposits, and interest-earning checkable deposits in 1972 dollars.

109. *Prime Interest Rate.* The interest rate that banks charge their most creditworthy business customers for short-term loans.

110. *Private Nonfinancial Borrowing.* All funds raised (net of repayment) by private nonfinancial borrowers in credit markets, adjusted for inflation by author.

220. *National Income.* Incomes of all U.S. residents in production of goods and services received for labor or for property, adjusted for inflation by author.

231. *Total Consumption.* Personal consumption expenditures in 1972 dollars, that is, all goods and services purchased (or received in kind) by individuals.

233. *Consumer Durables*. Personal consumption expenditures for durable goods in 1972 dollars.

238. *Consumer Nondurables*. Personal consumption expenditures for nondurable goods in 1972 dollars.

239. *Consumer Services*. Personal consumption expenditures for services in 1972 dollars.

280. *Labor Income*. All compensation to employees, including wages, salaries, bonuses, tips and all supplementary benefits.

286. *Corporate Profits before Taxes*. Corporate profits before taxes with inventory valuation and capital consumption allowances, adjusted for inflation by author.

320. *Consumer Price Index*. Measures the average cost (1967 = 100) of a fixed market basket of goods and services purchases by all urban consumers.

331. *Price of Crude Materials*. This is the producer price index (1967 = 100) for all crude materials, including imports, used for further processing.

346. *Hourly Wages*. Index of average hourly compensation for all employees in the nonfarm business sector in 1972 dollars.

358. *Product per Hour*. Index of output divided by hours for all persons in the nonfarm business sector in 1972 dollars.

501. *Federal Government Receipts*. Includes all taxes, fees, and contributions to social insurance.

502. *Federal Government Expenditures*. Includes purchases of goods and services, transfer payments, net interest paid, and subsidies, less profits of government enterprises.

910. *Index of Leading Indicators*. An average of twelve series that usually lead the cycle (series 1, 5, 8, 12, 19, 20, 29, 32, 36, 99, 106, and 111).

920. *Index of Coincident Indicators*. An average of four series that usually turn roughly at cycle turns (series 41, 47, 51, and 57).

930. *Index of Lagging Indicators*. An average of six series that usually lag the cycle (series 62, 77, 91, 95, 101, and 109).

Series from Bureau of Census, *Quarterly Financial Report on Manufacturing, Mining, and Trade Corporations* (Washington, D.C.: U.S. Government Printing Office, 1970–1983):

A. *Profit Rates (before Tax) on Capital*. Ratio of profit before tax to stockholders' equity.

B. *Profit Rate (after Tax) on Capital*. Ratio of profit after tax to stockholders' equity.

C. *Profit Rate (before Tax) to Sales*. Ratio of profit before tax to sales in the same sector.

D. *Profit Rate (after Tax) to Sales*. Ratio of profit after tax to sales in the same sector.

# APPENDIX B: Cycle Bases in Seven Cycles

A CYCLE BASE is defined by Mitchell as the average of a variable over the whole cycle. It is an absolute level of activity, around which we measure relative cyclical movements. Thus, (1) it provides the reader with a base or context for examining the cyclical movements; and (2) if we are given the cyclical bases for several cycles in a row, they provide a trend line from which all cyclical activity has been removed. This appendix presents the cycle bases for many variables for the seven cycles from 1949 to 1982 (using all quarterly data and quarterly cycle dates).

| SERIES | | CYCLE | | | | | | |
|---|---|---|---|---|---|---|---|---|
| | | 1<br>1949–1954 | 2<br>1954–1958 | 3<br>1958–1961 | 4<br>1961–1970 | 5<br>1970–1975 | 6<br>1975–1980 | 7<br>1980–1982 |
| 19. | Index of 500 Common Stock Prices | 26 | 45 | 60 | 89 | 106 | 108 | 136 |
| 43. | Unemployment Rate (percentage) | 3.6 | 4.8 | 6.0 | 4.7 | 5.7 | 7.0 | 8.4 |
| 44. | Unemployment Rate, Persons Unemployed 15 Weeks and Over (percentage) | 0.7 | 1.1 | 1.7 | 1.1 | 1.2 | 1.9 | 2.5 |
| 47. | Index of U.S. Industrial Production (1967 = 100) | 36 | 43 | 47 | 67 | 88 | 100 | 107 |
| 50. | Gross National Product, Real ($ trillions) | 1.4 | 1.5 | 1.6 | 2.1 | 2.6 | 3.0 | 3.3 |
| 64. | Compensation of Employees/ National Income (percent) | 67 | 68 | 69 | 70 | 73 | 73 | 75 |

(Continued on following page)

APPENDIX B: Cycle Bases in Seven Cycles (*Continued*)

| | | | | CYCLE | | | |
|---|---|---|---|---|---|---|---|
| SERIES | 1<br>1949–1954 | 2<br>1954–1958 | 3<br>1958–1961 | 4<br>1961–1970 | 5<br>1970–1975 | 6<br>1975–1980 | 7<br>1980–1982 |
| 67. Rates on Short-Term Business Loans (percentage) | 3.3 | 4.1 | 4.9 | 6.0 | 8.1 | 10.1 | 16.4 |
| 77. Manufacturing & Trade Inventories to Sales (Ratio) | 1.54 | 1.51 | 1.52 | 1.50 | 1.56 | 1.60 | 1.66 |
| 82. Capacity Utilization Rate, Manufacturing FRB (percentage) | 85 | 84 | 79 | 85 | 82 | 80 | 75 |
| 86. Gross Private Nonresidential Investment, Real ($ billions) | 131 | 153 | 153 | 221 | 290 | 336 | 379 |
| 95. Consumer Installment Credit/ Personal Income (percentage) | 6.7 | 9.1 | 9.9 | 11.9 | 12.8 | 13.0 | 12.2 |
| 109. Prime Interest Rate Charged by Banks (percentage) | 3.0 | 3.6 | 4.4 | 5.6 | 7.5 | 9.5 | 16.3 |
| 110. Private Nonfinancial Borrowing, Real ($ billions) | 17.7 | 27.6 | 32.9 | 58.1 | 134.5 | 232.0 | 251.4 |
| 114. Treasury Bonds, Short-Term Yield (percentage) | 1.6 | 2.1 | 2.8 | 4.4 | 5.8 | 7.2 | 12.2 |

APPENDIX B:  Cycle Bases in Seven Cycles (*Continued*)

| SERIES | | 1 1949–1954 | 2 1954–1958 | 3 1958–1961 | 4 1961–1970 | CYCLE 5 1970–1975 | 6 1975–1980 | 7 1980–1982 |
|---|---|---|---|---|---|---|---|---|
| 117. | Municipal Bond Yield (percentage) | 2.2 | 2.8 | 3.4 | 4.1 | 5.6 | 6.6 | 11.0 |
| 230/220 | Consumption/National income (percentage) | 77 | 77 | 78 | 76 | 76 | 78 | 80 |
| 231. | Total Consumption, Real ($ trillions) | 0.8 | 0.9 | 1.0 | 1.3 | 1.6 | 1.9 | 2.1 |
| 233. | Consumption, Durables, Real ($ billions) | 75 | 91 | 94 | 135 | 198 | 245 | 250 |
| 238. | Consumption, Nondurables, Real ($ billions) | 372 | 421 | 456 | 551 | 662 | 732 | 766 |
| 239. | Consumption, Services, Real ($ billions) | 320 | 376 | 430 | 574 | 766 | 912 | 1030 |
| 241. | Gross Private Domestic Investment, Real ($ billions) | 219 | 242 | 253 | 350 | 461 | 503 | 495 |
| 310. | GNP Price Deflator Index | 25 | 28 | 30 | 35 | 49 | 70 | 95 |
| 320. | Consumer Price Index | 79 | 82 | 88 | 99 | 132 | 193 | 275 |

(Continued on following page)

APPENDIX B: Cycle Bases in Seven Cycles (*Continued*)

| SERIES | | CYCLE | | | | | | |
|---|---|---|---|---|---|---|---|---|
| | | 1<br>1949–1954 | 2<br>1954–1958 | 3<br>1958–1961 | 4<br>1961–1970 | 5<br>1970–1975 | 6<br>1975–1980 | 7<br>1980–1982 |
| 331. | Crude Materials, Producer Price Index | 109 | 99 | 100 | 101 | 153 | 233 | 323 |
| 346. | Index of Real Wages per Hour (1977 = 100) | 56 | 65 | 71 | 83 | 95 | 99 | 96 |
| 358. | Index of Real Output per Hour (1977 = 100) | 60 | 65 | 70 | 83 | 94 | 99 | 99 |
| 502. | Federal Government Spending, Real ($ billions) | 266 | 266 | 305 | 410 | 539 | 648 | 758 |
| 721. | Index of Industrial Production, OECD (1975 = 100) | 26 | 39 | 48 | 66 | 92 | 101 | 105 |
| 728. | Index of Industrial Production, Japan (1975 = 100) | 7 | 13 | 19 | 47 | 91 | 103 | 120 |
| 910. | Index of Leading Indicators (1967 = 100) | 56 | 64 | 71 | 95 | 121 | 136 | 139 |
| 920. | Index of Coincident Indicators (1967 = 100) | 58 | 66 | 68 | 91 | 120 | 136 | 142 |
| 930. | Index of Lagging Indicators (1967 = 100) | 49 | 62 | 71 | 92 | 111 | 113 | 122 |

*Source:* U.S. Department of Commerce, Bureau of Economic Analysis, *Handbook of Cyclical Indicators, A Supplement to the Business Conditions Digest* (Washington, D.C.: U.S. Government Printing Office, 1984).

APPENDIX C: Cycle Relatives, Average, Seven Cycles, 1949–1982

| SERIES | | 1 | 2 | 3 | 4 | 5 | 6 | 7 | 8 | 9 |
|---|---|---|---|---|---|---|---|---|---|---|
| | | | | | | STAGES | | | | |
| 20. | New Orders for Plant and Equipment, Real | 82.5 | 89.2 | 102.6 | 112.9 | 112.1 | 109.3 | 102.4 | 97.7 | 95.1 |
| 30. | Inventory Investment, Real | 67.5 | 97.6 | 118.9 | 113.7 | 112.7 | 97.1 | 84.1 | 80.7 | 55.6 |
| 43. | Unemployment Rate | 115.7 | 108.4 | 93.1 | 84.3 | 83.9 | 91.4 | 106.9 | 122.5 | 133.1 |
| 50. | Gross National Product, Real | 89.6 | 93.9 | 100.1 | 104.7 | 106.4 | 105.8 | 104.7 | 104.3 | 104 |
| 77. | Ratio, Inventory to Sales | 104.4 | 99.2 | 97.8 | 99.1 | 100.3 | 101.8 | 103.9 | 105.7 | 106.1 |
| 82. | Capacity Utilization, Manufacturing, FRB | 91.7 | 97 | 103.3 | 104.1 | 104.1 | 101.3 | 97.4 | 92.9 | 90.8 |
| 105. | Money Supply, M1 | 99.3 | 99.7 | 100.5 | 101.1 | 100 | 99.9 | 99 | 98.9 | 99.2 |
| 109. | Prime Interest Rate Charged by Banks | 86.1 | 85.6 | 91.2 | 110.8 | 132 | 127.9 | 129 | 116.5 | 107 |
| 110. | Private Nonfinancial Borrowing, Real | 61.9 | 84.8 | 108.1 | 125.7 | 113 | 105.4 | 92.3 | 95.7 | 91.7 |
| 233. | Consumer Durables, Real | 84.7 | 92.4 | 101.4 | 106 | 107.3 | 105.9 | 104.4 | 102.6 | 101.8 |

(Continued on following page)

APPENDIX C: Cycle Relatives, Average, Seven Cycles, 1949–1982 (*Continued*)

| SERIES | | 1 | 2 | 3 | 4 | STAGES 5 | 6 | 7 | 8 | 9 |
|---|---|---|---|---|---|---|---|---|---|---|
| 238. | Consumer Nondurables, Real | 93.3 | 95.5 | 99.5 | 103.1 | 104.4 | 104.2 | 104.1 | 104.3 | 104.6 |
| 239. | Consumer Services, Real | 91.3 | 93.8 | 98.3 | 103.6 | 106.2 | 106.4 | 106.9 | 108.1 | 108.9 |
| 910. | Index of Leading Indicators | 86.6 | 94.6 | 101.8 | 105.5 | 104.4 | 102.6 | 100.3 | 98.7 | 100 |
| 920. | Index of Coincident Indicators | 86.6 | 91.4 | 100.4 | 107.1 | 109.4 | 108.1 | 105.5 | 102.1 | 100.4 |
| 930. | Index of Lagging Indicators | 93.2 | 89.8 | 96.3 | 105.5 | 111 | 112.8 | 113.3 | 111.3 | 108.8 |

*Source*: U.S. Department of Commerce, Bureau of Economic Analysis, *Handbook of Cyclical Indicators, A Supplement to the Business Conditions Digest* (Washington, D.C.: U.S. Government Printing Office, 1984).

APPENDIX D:  Cycle Relatives, Average, Four Cycles, 1949–1970

| SERIES | | 1 | 2 | 3 | 4 | 5 | 6 | 7 | 8 | 9 |
|---|---|---|---|---|---|---|---|---|---|---|
| | | | | | | STAGES | | | | |
| 20. | New Orders for Plant and Equipment, Real | 78.3 | 87 | 104.9 | 112.6 | 110 | 107.9 | 100.6 | 97.5 | 96.8 |
| 64. | Employee Compensation/National Income | 100.1 | 98.4 | 98.7 | 100.8 | 102.3 | 102.9 | 103.1 | 102.9 | 102.9 |
| 67. | Bank Rates on Short Term Business Loans | 84.3 | 87.6 | 96.2 | 109.5 | 121.9 | 121.8 | 118 | 115.3 | 112.3 |
| 86. | Gross Private Nonresidential Investment, Real | 84.3 | 89 | 101.8 | 106.5 | 111.2 | 109.5 | 107.6 | 106.1 | 104.3 |
| 95. | Consumer Installment Credit to Personal Income | 90.6 | 90.4 | 100.4 | 103.2 | 107.1 | 107.9 | 108.4 | 108.6 | 108.3 |
| 105. | Money Supply, M1 | 98.4 | 99.2 | 100.5 | 100.9 | 100.3 | 100.2 | 99.9 | 99.9 | 100.2 |
| 107. | Velocity of Money, GNP to M1 | 91.4 | 94.1 | 98.7 | 104.2 | 106.7 | 106.4 | 105.9 | 105.7 | 105.3 |
| 109. | Prime Interest Rate Charged by Banks | 85.1 | 86.2 | 94.4 | 110.4 | 123.8 | 123.7 | 119.3 | 114.1 | 108.3 |
| 110. | Private Nonfinancial Borrowing, Real | 59.9 | 83 | 112.1 | 120 | 108.5 | 100.1 | 92.4 | 96.5 | 97.7 |
| 220–280. | Property Income | 90 | 96.4 | 103.3 | 103.4 | 101.5 | 99.1 | 97.8 | 96.5 | 97.3 |
| 231/220 | Consumption/National Income | 103.2 | 101.2 | 98.5 | 98.6 | 99.4 | 100.2 | 101.2 | 102 | 102.4 |

(Continued on following page)

APPENDIX D:  Cycle Relatives, Average, Four Cycles, 1949–1970 (*Continued*)

| SERIES | | STAGES | | | | | | | | |
| --- | --- | --- | --- | --- | --- | --- | --- | --- | --- | --- |
| | | 1 | 2 | 3 | 4 | 5 | 6 | 7 | 8 | 9 |
| 231. | Total Consumption, Real | 90.5 | 93.4 | 98.8 | 104.2 | 107 | 107.2 | 107.3 | 107.8 | 108 |
| 280. | Employee Compensation | 87 | 90.8 | 99.3 | 106.2 | 109.7 | 109.6 | 108.7 | 108.2 | 107.8 |
| 286. | Corporate Profit, before Tax | 82.3 | 98.7 | 107.9 | 105.3 | 101.1 | 94.2 | 87.5 | 86.2 | 84.9 |
| 346. | Hourly Wages, Real | 92.4 | 94.7 | 99 | 103.1 | 105.2 | 105.4 | 105.7 | 106.2 | 106.3 |
| 358. | Product per Hour, Real | 93.4 | 96.1 | 99.9 | 102.3 | 103.3 | 103.1 | 103.5 | 104.3 | 104.5 |

*Source*: U.S. Department of Commerce, Bureau of Economic Analysis, *Handbook of Cyclical Indicators, A Supplement to the Business Conditions Digest* (Washington, D.C.: U.S. Government Printing Office, 1984).

| SERIES | | STAGES | | | | | | | | |
| --- | --- | --- | --- | --- | --- | --- | --- | --- | --- | --- |
| | | 1 | 2 | 3 | 4 | 5 | 6 | 7 | 8 | 9 |
| A. | Profit before Taxes on Capital | 79.6 | 103.7 | 113.2 | 102.5 | 99.0 | 87.5 | 81.4 | 76.0 | 73.9 |
| B. | Profit before Taxes on Sales | 91.7 | 105.0 | 106.6 | 99.8 | 94.1 | 89.5 | 85.8 | 83.3 | 82.1 |

*Source*: Bureau of Census, U.S. Department of Commerce, *Quarterly Financial Report on Manufacturing, Mining, and Trade Corporations* (Washington, D.C.: U.S. Government Printing Office, 1949–1983).

APPENDIX E: Cycle Relatives, Average, Three Cycles, 1970–1982

| SERIES | | STAGES | | | | | | | | |
|---|---|---|---|---|---|---|---|---|---|---|
| | | 1 | 2 | 3 | 4 | 5 | 6 | 7 | 8 | 9 |
| 20. | New Orders for Plant and Equipment, Real | 88.1 | 92.2 | 99.5 | 113.3 | 114.9 | 111.1 | 104.8 | 98 | 92.8 |
| 43. | Unemployment Rate | 103.7 | 102.6 | 95.4 | 86.5 | 86.3 | 92.5 | 102.6 | 114.1 | 127 |
| 47. | U.S. Industrial Production | 90.1 | 94 | 100.8 | 106.7 | 108.5 | 106.4 | 103.9 | 101.5 | 98.3 |
| 64. | Employee Compensation/National Income | 101.1 | 99.8 | 99.3 | 99 | 98.9 | 100 | 101.6 | 101.8 | 101.9 |
| 67. | Bank Rates on Short Term Business Loans | 89.6 | 84.1 | 90.4 | 111.7 | 136.1 | 137.7 | 141.7 | 113.3 | 102.3 |
| 82. | Capacity Utilization, FRB | 95.2 | 98.1 | 102.8 | 106.1 | 105.1 | 102.3 | 98.6 | 95.6 | 91.8 |
| 86. | Real Gross Private Nonresidential Investment | 90.6 | 90.9 | 97.7 | 108.3 | 112.2 | 111.6 | 107 | 103.4 | 100.5 |
| 95. | Consumer Installment Credit to Personal Income | 98.8 | 97.7 | 99.4 | 101.7 | 102.3 | 103 | 102 | 99.8 | 98.9 |
| 105. | Money Supply, M1 | 100.5 | 100.3 | 100.5 | 101.3 | 99.7 | 99.6 | 97.9 | 97.5 | 98 |
| 107. | Velocity of Money, GNP to M1 | 92.5 | 95.4 | 99.4 | 102.5 | 105.4 | 104.9 | 105.2 | 105 | 103.9 |

(Continued on following page)

APPENDIX E:  Cycle Relatives, Average, Three Cycles, 1970–1982 (Continued)

| SERIES | | STAGES | | | | | | | | |
| --- | --- | --- | --- | --- | --- | --- | --- | --- | --- | --- |
| | | 1 | 2 | 3 | 4 | 5 | 6 | 7 | 8 | 9 |
| 109. | Prime Interest Rate Charged by Banks | 87.5 | 84.9 | 87 | 111.3 | 142.9 | 133.7 | 141.9 | 119.8 | 105.2 |
| 110. | Private Nonfinancial Borrowing, Real | 64.5 | 87.2 | 102.8 | 133.2 | 119 | 112.4 | 92.2 | 94.5 | 83.7 |
| 220. | National Income | 92.9 | 95.7 | 100.1 | 104.4 | 105.4 | 104.6 | 102.5 | 101.4 | 100.6 |
| 220–280. | Property Income | 90.1 | 96.3 | 102 | 107.3 | 108 | 104.7 | 97.9 | 96.4 | 95.5 |
| 231. | Total Consumption, Real | 93.1 | 95.6 | 100 | 103 | 103.5 | 102.9 | 102.7 | 103 | 103.7 |
| 231/220 | Consumption/ National Income | 101 | 100.2 | 99.4 | 98.4 | 98.3 | 99 | 100.8 | 101.9 | 103.3 |
| 241. | Real Gross Private Domestic Investment | 83.5 | 92.7 | 105.2 | 112.3 | 113.3 | 108 | 99.2 | 94.6 | 85.3 |
| 256. | Exports, Real | 88.6 | 89.2 | 94.4 | 106.9 | 115.7 | 117.5 | 116.5 | 113.2 | 110.1 |
| 256–257. | Net Exports | 107.8 | 99.9 | 90.7 | 87.9 | 110.9 | 120.2 | 121 | 120 | 122.8 |
| 257. | Imports, Real | 85.1 | 89.9 | 99.8 | 107.9 | 109.9 | 106.7 | 105.9 | 104 | 98 |
| 280. | Employee Compensation, Real | 93.9 | 95.5 | 99.4 | 103.4 | 104.5 | 104.6 | 104.1 | 103.3 | 102.4 |
| 286. | Corporate Profit, before Taxes | 88.6 | 99.3 | 106.4 | 111.7 | 111.7 | 109.1 | 95.4 | 91.2 | 84.2 |

| SERIES | | 1 | 2 | 3 | 4 | STAGES 5 | 6 | 7 | 8 | 9 |
|---|---|---|---|---|---|---|---|---|---|---|
| 320. | Consumer Price Index | 87.2 | 90.2 | 94.9 | 102 | 109 | 110.5 | 114 | 117.4 | 118.2 |
| 331. | Crude Materials, Producer Price Index | 83.3 | 87.8 | 92 | 107.1 | 117 | 118.8 | 115.4 | 121.6 | 118 |
| 331/320 | Ratio, Price of Crude Materials/ Consumer Price Index | 95.7 | 97.5 | 97.1 | 105.3 | 108 | 108.1 | 101.7 | 103.6 | 99.7 |
| 346. | Hourly Wages, Real | 97.8 | 98.7 | 100.5 | 100.9 | 99.4 | 99.1 | 99.6 | 99.6 | 100.1 |
| 358. | Product per Labor Hour | 96.6 | 98.8 | 100.7 | 101.4 | 100.9 | 100.3 | 99.6 | 99.7 | 100 |
| 501. | Federal Government Receipts | 91.7 | 93.1 | 100.6 | 106 | 107.6 | 106.8 | 105.6 | 103.7 | 102 |
| 501–502. | Federal Government Deficits | 117 | 127.6 | 81.5 | 52.2 | 48 | 63.9 | 92.1 | 136.5 | 190 |
| 502. | Federal Government Expenditures | 93.5 | 95.6 | 98.2 | 100.4 | 102.3 | 103.5 | 105 | 107.4 | 110.2 |

*(Continued on following page)*

APPENDIX E: Cycle Relatives, Average, Three Cycles, 1970–1982 (*Continued*)

| SERIES | | | | | STAGES | | | | |
|---|---|---|---|---|---|---|---|---|---|
| | | 1 | 2 | 3 | 4 | 5 | 6 | 7 | 8 | 9 |
| 721. | OECD, Industrial Production | 94.8 | 95.6 | 98.9 | 103.2 | 105.6 | 105.7 | 105.3 | 101.9 | 100.7 |
| 728. | Japan, Industrial Production | 89.7 | 92.3 | 97.3 | 105.2 | 110.6 | 111 | 108.3 | 104.8 | 102.3 |

*Source:* U.S. Department of Commerce, Bureau of Economic Analysis, *Handbook of Cyclical Indicators, A Supplement to the Business Conditions Digest* (Washington, D.C.: U.S. Government Printing Office, 1984).

| SERIES | | | | | STAGES | | | | |
|---|---|---|---|---|---|---|---|---|---|
| | | 1 | 2 | 3 | 4 | 5 | 6 | 7 | 8 | 9 |
| A. | Profit/Capital, before Tax | 81.6 | 98.9 | 103.6 | 119.4 | 112.9 | 106.6 | 104.5 | 88.9 | 73.7 |
| B. | Profit/Sales, before Tax | 87 | 101.8 | 104.4 | 113.6 | 106.5 | 104.4 | 99.8 | 88.1 | 76.6 |

*Source:* Bureau of Census, U.S. Department of Commerce, *Quarterly Financial Report on Manufacturing, Mining, and Trade Corporations* (Washington, D.C.: U.S. Government Printing Office, 1970–1983).

APPENDIX F: Growth per Quarter, Average, Seven Cycles, 1949–1982

| SERIES | | SEGMENTS | | | | | | | |
|---|---|---|---|---|---|---|---|---|---|
| | | 1-2 | 2-3 | 3-4 | 4-5 | 5-6 | 6-7 | 7-8 | 8-9 |
| 13. | Number of New Incorporations | 2.3 | 2.4 | 1.3 | 0.2 | -1.1 | -2.3 | -0.7 | 3.8 |
| 19. | Index of 500 Common Stock Prices | 5.1 | 2.3 | 0.8 | -1.5 | -3.2 | -4.1 | 3.3 | 7.3 |
| 20. | Contracts and Orders for Plant and Equipment, Real | 2.8 | 2.6 | 1.8 | -0.7 | -2.8 | -6.6 | -3.5 | -2.6 |
| 30. | Inventory Investment, Real | 10.1 | 4.2 | -1 | -0.3 | -15.6 | -13 | -3.4 | -25.1 |
| 35. | Corporate Net Cash Flow, Real | 5.9 | 1.9 | -0.1 | 0 | -2.1 | -4.2 | -0.1 | 1.7 |
| 43. | Unemployment Rate | -2.9 | -3.3 | -1.5 | -0.3 | 7.5 | 14.8 | 14.1 | 10.6 |
| 50. | Gross National Product, Real | 1.4 | 1.2 | 0.9 | 0.6 | -0.6 | -1.1 | -0.3 | -0.3 |
| 50/106 | Velocity of Money, GNP/M2 | 0.4 | 0.6 | 0.2 | 0.6 | -0.7 | -0.9 | -0.9 | -1 |
| 67. | Bank Rates on Short-Term Business Loans | -0.8 | 5 | 3.4 | 4 | 4.1 | -4.7 | -11.3 | -6.2 |
| 77. | Inventory/Sales | -1.7 | -1.3 | -0.3 | 0.4 | 1.5 | 2 | 1.9 | 0.4 |
| 82. | Capacity Utilization Index | 2.2 | 1.5 | 0.2 | 0 | -3.2 | -3.9 | -4.2 | -2.6 |
| 86. | Nonresidential Investment, Real | 1 | 2 | 1.5 | 1.3 | -1 | -3.1 | -2.5 | -2.2 |
| 105. | Money Supply, M1, Real | 0.2 | -0.1 | 0.1 | -0.6 | -0.1 | -0.9 | -0.1 | 0.4 |
| 106. | Money Supply, M2, Real | 0.9 | 0.5 | 0.5 | -0.1 | 0.2 | -0.1 | 0.6 | 0.7 |
| 107. | Velocity of Money, GNP/M1 | 1.1 | 1.2 | 0.8 | 1.2 | -0.4 | -0.1 | -0.3 | -0.7 |

(Continued on following page)

|  | | | | | | SEGMENTS | | | |
| --- | --- | --- | --- | --- | --- | --- | --- | --- | --- |
| SERIES | 1–2 | 2–3 | 3–4 | 4–5 | 5–6 | 6–7 | 7–8 | 8–9 |
| 109. Prime Interest Rates Charged by Banks | 2.6 | 3.1 | 3.7 | 8 | −4 | −0.2 | −11.7 | −9.6 |
| 110. Private Borrowing by Nonfinancial Borrowers | 11.4 | 2.6 | 6.3 | −8.2 | −7.6 | −13.8 | 5.3 | −4 |
| 114. Yield on Short-Term Treasury Bonds | 9.1 | 4.5 | 7.6 | 3.3 | −7.8 | −18.1 | −17.5 | −12.9 |
| 115. Yield on Long-Term Treasury Bonds | 2.6 | 1.5 | 2.4 | 4.4 | −0.8 | −2.8 | −2.6 | −4.6 |
| 116. Yield on High-Grade Corporate Bonds | 2.5 | 1.1 | 3.2 | 4.5 | −1.2 | −2.2 | −4.1 | −4.7 |
| 117. Yield on 20 Municipal Bonds | 1.8 | 0.6 | 2.7 | 6.1 | −1 | −0.1 | −2.3 | −3.7 |
| 220. National Income, Real | 1.4 | 1.3 | 0.9 | 0.5 | −0.8 | −1.5 | −0.6 | −0.6 |
| 231. Total Consumption | 0.9 | 1 | 0.9 | 0.6 | −0.2 | −0.1 | 0.3 | 0.4 |
| 233. Consumer Durables | 2.6 | 1.8 | 0.9 | 0.5 | −1.5 | −1.5 | −1.8 | −0.7 |
| 238. Consumer Nondurables | 0.7 | 0.8 | 0.7 | 0.4 | −0.2 | −0.1 | 0.2 | 0.3 |
| 239. Consumer Services | 0.8 | 0.9 | 1.1 | 0.9 | 0.2 | 0.5 | 1.2 | 0.7 |
| 286. Corporate Profit before Taxes | 4.7 | 1.7 | 0.2 | −0.8 | −5.1 | −9.7 | −2.5 | −3.7 |

Growth per Quarter, Average, Seven Cycles, 1949–1982 (*Continued*)

| SERIES | | SEGMENTS | | | | | | | |
|---|---|---|---|---|---|---|---|---|---|
| | | 1–2 | 2–3 | 3–4 | 4–5 | 5–6 | 6–7 | 7–8 | 8–9 |
| 910. | Index of Leading Indicators | 2.6 | 1.5 | 0.7 | −0.4 | −1.8 | −2.3 | −1.5 | 1.2 |
| 917 | Composite Index of Money and Financial Flows | 1 | 0.8 | 0.3 | −0.5 | −0.7 | −0.8 | 0 | 1.1 |
| 920. | Index of Coincident Indicators | 1.6 | 1.8 | 1.3 | 0.8 | −1.3 | −2.6 | −3.4 | −1.7 |
| 930. | Index of Lagging Indicators | −1.1 | 1.3 | 1.8 | 1.9 | 1.8 | 0.5 | −2 | −2.5 |

*Source*: U.S. Department of Commerce, Bureau of Economic Analysis, *Handbook of Cyclical Indicators, A Supplement to the Business Conditions Digest* (Washington, D.C.: U.S. Government Printing Office, 1984).

| SERIES | SEGMENTS | | | | | | | |
|---|---|---|---|---|---|---|---|---|
| | 1–2 | 2–3 | 3–4 | 4–5 | 5–6 | 6–7 | 7–8 | 8–9 |
| Profit Rate before Taxes on Capital | 8.9 | 1.7 | 2.2 | −3.4 | −9.3 | −4.7 | −8 | −7.7 |

*Source*: Bureau of Census, U.S. Department of Commerce, *Quarterly Financial Report on Manufacturing, Mining, and Trade Corporations* (Washington, D.C.: U.S. Government Printing Office, 1949–1983).

APPENDIX G:  Growth per Quarter, Average, Four Cycles, 1949–1970

|  |  | SEGMENTS | | | | | | | |
| SERIES | | 1–2 | 2–3 | 3–4 | 4–5 | 5–6 | 6–7 | 7–8 | 8–9 |
|---|---|---|---|---|---|---|---|---|---|
| 30. | Inventory Investment, Real | 15.9 | 13.7 | 2 | 5.9 | −16.6 | −7 | −6.3 | −3.3 |
| 47. | United States, Index of Industrial Production | 2.3 | 1.9 | 1.1 | 1.0 | −2.2 | −3.0 | −2.0 | −1.1 |
| 48. | Hours Worked | 0.9 | 1 | 0.6 | 0.5 | −0.5 | −1 | −1.6 | −0.3 |
| 64. | Labor Share, that is, Labor Income/National Income | −0.6 | 0 | 0.4 | 0.5 | 0.7 | 0.2 | −0.1 | 0 |
| 77. | Inventory/Sales | −2.4 | −0.4 | −0.1 | 0.2 | 1.6 | 2.5 | 2.0 | 1.0 |
| 86. | Nonresidential Investment, Real | 1.7 | 2.1 | 0.8 | 1.4 | −1.3 | −2 | −1.7 | −1.8 |
| 220. | National Income | 1.5 | 1.3 | 0.8 | 0.6 | −0.8 | −1 | −0.4 | −0.4 |
| 220–280 | Total Property Income | 2.1 | 1.3 | 0.1 | −0.6 | −2.4 | −1.3 | −0.1 | −0.4 |
| 220–280/220 | Property Share | 0.6 | 0 | −0.7 | −1.2 | −1.6 | −0.3 | 0.3 | 0 |
| 231. | Total Consumption | 1 | 0.9 | 0.9 | 0.8 | 0.2 | 0.1 | 0.5 | 0.2 |
| 231/220 | Average Propensity to Consume, that is, Consumption/National Income | −0.7 | −0.5 | 0 | 0.3 | 0.8 | 1 | 0.8 | 0.5 |
| 241. | Real Gross Private Domestic Investment | 4.3 | 1.9 | 0.1 | −0.4 | −3.5 | −4.4 | −0.9 | −0.6 |

APPENDIX G: Growth per Quarter, Average, Four Cycles, 1949–1970 (*Continued*)

| SERIES | | 1–2 | 2–3 | 3–4 | 4–5 | 5–6 | 6–7 | 7–8 | 8–9 |
|---|---|---|---|---|---|---|---|---|---|
| | | | | | SEGMENTS | | | | |
| 256. | Exports | 0.4 | 1 | 1.4 | 2.1 | −0.4 | −1.1 | −0.2 | −1.4 |
| 256–257. | Net Exports | −0.2 | −0.9 | −0.2 | −0.3 | 0.3 | 0.1 | −0.3 | −0.9 |
| 257. | Imports | 0.6 | 1.9 | 1.6 | 1.9 | −0.7 | −1.2 | 0.1 | 2.3 |
| 280. | Total Labor Income, Real | 1.2 | 1.3 | 1.2 | 1.1 | −0.1 | −0.9 | −0.5 | −0.4 |
| 282. | Proprietors' Income, Real | 1 | 0 | 0 | 0 | −0.6 | −0.2 | −0.6 | −0.4 |
| 284. | Rental Income, Real | 0.1 | −2.4 | −7.6 | 0 | −0.4 | 0.3 | −0.1 | 0.9 |
| 286. | Corporate Profit before Tax | 5.4 | 1.6 | −0.4 | −1.4 | −6.5 | −6.7 | −1.3 | −1.2 |
| 288. | Interest Income, Net, Real | 1.9 | 0.9 | −7.6 | 2.2 | 1.5 | 3.9 | 4.1 | 1.7 |
| 346. | Real Hourly Wages | 0.8 | 0.7 | 0.7 | 0.7 | 0.2 | 0.3 | 0.5 | 0.1 |
| 358. | Productivity, that is, Real Output per Hour | 0.9 | 0.6 | 0.4 | 0.3 | −0.2 | −0.3 | 0.8 | −0.2 |
| 721. | OECD, Industrial Production | 1.4 | 1.8 | 1.9 | 2 | 1.4 | 1.2 | 0.7 | 0.4 |
| 722. | United Kingdom, Index of Industrial Production | 1.0 | 0.8 | 0.7 | 1.0 | 0.4 | 1.2 | 0.3 | 0.1 |
| 723. | Canada, Index of Industrial Production | 1.2 | 2.0 | 1.7 | 0.4 | −0.2 | −0.9 | 0.4 | 0.3 |
| 725. | West Germany, Index of Industrial Production | 1.4 | 1.7 | 1.8 | 2.6 | 1.1 | 2.3 | 1.8 | 0.8 |

(Continued on following page)

APPENDIX G: Growth per Quarter, Average, Four Cycles, 1949–1970 (*Continued*)

| SERIES | | 1–2 | 2–3 | 3–4 | 4–5 | 5–6 | 6–7 | 7–8 | 8–9 |
|---|---|---|---|---|---|---|---|---|---|
| | | | | | **SEGMENTS** | | | | |
| 726. | France, Index of Industrial Production | 0.4 | 1.1 | 1.2 | 1.5 | 2.4 | 2.6 | 1.5 | 1.1 |
| 727. | Italy, Index of Industrial Production | 1.8 | 1.5 | 2.6 | 2.0 | 5.1 | 0.5 | 1.3 | 0.4 |
| 728. | Japan, Index of Industrial Production | 1.6 | 2.9 | 4.3 | 5.1 | 2.3 | 3 | 1.6 | 0.4 |

*Source:* U.S. Department of Commerce, Bureau of Economic Analysis, *Handbook of Cyclical Indicators, A Supplement to the Business Conditions Digest* (Washington, D.C.: U.S. Government Printing Office, 1984).

| SERIES | 1–2 | 2–3 | 3–4 | 4–5 | 5–6 | 6–7 | 7–8 | 8–9 |
|---|---|---|---|---|---|---|---|---|
| | | | | **SEGMENTS** | | | | |
| A. Profit Rate before Taxes on Capital | 9.1 | 2.2 | −2.7 | −1.1 | −11.5 | −6.1 | −5.4 | −2 |
| B. Profit before Tax/Sales | 7.1 | 0.4 | −1-5 | −1.5 | −6.4 | −2.4 | −1.7 | −1.7 |

*Source:* Bureau of Census, U.S. Department of Commerce, *Quarterly Financial Report on Manufacturing, Mining, and Trade Corporations* (Washington, D.C.: U.S. Government Printing Office, 1970–1983).

APPENDIX H: Growth per Quarter, Average, Three Cycles, 1970–1982

| SERIES | | | | SEGMENTS | | | | |
|---|---|---|---|---|---|---|---|---|
| | 1–2 | 2–3 | 3–4 | 4–5 | 5–6 | 6–7 | 7–8 | 8–9 |
| 47. United States, Index of Industrial Production | 2.2 | 1.7 | 1.2 | 1.0 | −2.1 | −2.1 | −1.7 | −3.1 |
| 48. Hours Worked | 0.6 | 0.8 | 0.9 | 0.7 | −0.4 | −0.6 | −1.3 | −1 |
| 64. Labor Share, that is, Labor Income/National Income | −0.8 | −0.2 | −0.1 | −0.1 | 0.8 | 1.2 | 0.2 | 0.1 |
| 86. Nonresidential Investment | 0.1 | 1.3 | 2.7 | 2 | −0.6 | −3.5 | −2.8 | −2.9 |
| 220. National Income | 1.6 | 1.1 | 1.1 | 0.5 | −0.8 | −2.1 | −1 | −0.9 |
| 220–280. Total Property Income | 3.1 | 1.4 | 1.3 | 0.6 | −3.3 | −6.8 | −1.5 | −1 |
| (220–280)/220 Property Share | 1.5 | 0.3 | 0.2 | 0.1 | −2.5 | −4.7 | −0.5 | −0.1 |
| 231. Total Consumption | 1.4 | 1 | 0.9 | 0.3 | −0.6 | −0.2 | 0.3 | 0.7 |
| 231/220 Average Propensity to Consume, that is, Consumption/National Income | −0.5 | −0.2 | −0.2 | −0.1 | 0.7 | 1.4 | 0.8 | 1.4 |
| 241. Real Gross Private Domestic Investment | 5.1 | 3.1 | 1.8 | 0.5 | −5.3 | −6.8 | −3.5 | −9.3 |
| 256. Exports | 0.1 | 2 | 2.5 | 3.3 | 1.8 | −0.9 | −2.5 | −3.1 |
| 256–257. Net Exports | −2.9 | −0.4 | −0.1 | 2.2 | 5 | 0.4 | −0.3 | 2.9 |
| 257. Imports | 3 | 2.4 | 2.6 | 1.1 | −3.2 | −1.3 | −2.2 | −6 |

(Continued on following page)

| SERIES | | 1–2 | 2–3 | 3–4 | 4–5 | 5–6 | 6–7 | 7–8 | 8–9 |
|---|---|---|---|---|---|---|---|---|---|
| | | | | | | SEGMENTS | | | |
| 280. | Total Labor Income | 0.8 | 0.9 | 1 | 0.4 | 0.1 | 0.4 | -0.7 | -0.8 |
| 282. | Proprietors' Income, Real | 2.1 | 0.3 | -0.4 | -0.7 | -5.8 | -6.1 | 2 | -0.3 |
| 284. | Rental Income, Real | 3.2 | -1.7 | 2.9 | 2.6 | 3.6 | -15.3 | -1 | 8.1 |
| 286. | Corporate Profit before Taxes | 6.2 | 1.8 | 1.3 | -0.1 | -2.6 | -10.5 | -3.2 | -7 |
| 288. | Interest Income, Real | 1.5 | 2 | 2.9 | 5.5 | 2.1 | 2.5 | -1.1 | -1 |
| 320. | Consumer Price Index | 1.7 | 1.5 | 1.9 | 3.3 | 1.5 | 2.9 | 2.5 | 0.8 |
| 331. | Index, Price Crude Materials | 2.7 | 1.2 | 3.3 | 4.2 | 1.8 | -2.5 | 5.4 | -3.7 |
| 331/320 | Ratio, Price of Crude/CPI | 1.2 | 0.4 | 1.4 | 0.8 | 0.1 | -4.9 | 2.1 | -3.9 |
| 346. | Real Hourly Wages | 0.5 | 0.4 | 0.1 | -0.7 | -0.3 | 0.4 | 0 | 0.5 |
| 358. | Productivity, that is, Real Output per Hour | 1.1 | 0.5 | 0.2 | -0.3 | -0.5 | -0.7 | 0.1 | 0.3 |
| 501. | Federal Government Receipts, Real | 2 | 1.8 | 0.6 | 1.1 | -1.1 | -0.9 | -1.4 | -1.2 |
| 501 + 511. | Total Government Receipts, Real | 1.6 | 1.5 | 0.6 | 0.8 | -0.8 | -0.6 | -0.6 | -0.5 |
| 502. | Federal Government Spending, Real | 0.9 | 0.8 | 0.4 | 1 | 1.2 | 1.2 | 2 | 2.8 |

APPENDIX H: Growth per Quarter, Average, Three Cycles, 1970–1982 (*Continued*)

| SERIES | | SEGMENTS | | | | | | | |
|---|---|---|---|---|---|---|---|---|---|
| | | 1–2 | 2–3 | 3–4 | 4–5 | 5–6 | 6–7 | 7–8 | 8–9 |
| 502–501 | Federal Government Deficit, Real | −1.1 | −1 | −0.2 | −0.1 | 2.3 | 2.1 | 3.4 | 4 |
| 502 + 512. | Total Government Spending, Real | 1 | 0.6 | 0.3 | 0.5 | 0.8 | 0.7 | 1.3 | 1.7 |
| (502 + 512) − (501 + 511) | Total Government Deficit | −0.6 | −0.9 | −0.3 | −0.3 | 1.6 | 1.3 | 1.9 | 2.2 |
| 511. | State and Local Receipts, Real | 1.2 | 1.1 | 0.5 | 0.5 | −0.5 | −0.3 | 0.2 | 0.2 |
| 512. | State and Local Spending, Real | 0.6 | 0.4 | 0.2 | 0.1 | 0.4 | 0.2 | 0.5 | 0.7 |
| 512–511. | State and Local Deficit, Real | −0.6 | −0.7 | −0.3 | −0.4 | 0.9 | 0.5 | 0.7 | 0.9 |
| 721. | OEDC, Industrial Production | 0.3 | 0.6 | 0.8 | 1 | 0.1 | −0.5 | −2.5 | −1.2 |
| 722. | United Kingdom, Index of Industrial Production | −1.3 | 0.2 | 1.2 | 0.7 | −2.4 | 0.6 | −1.8 | −0.6 |
| 723. | Canada, Index of Industrial Production | 1.8 | 0.9 | 1.9 | 0.0 | −0.3 | −2.7 | −1.1 | −2.5 |
| 725. | West Germany, Index of Industrial Production | 0.4 | 0.5 | 0.5 | 1.0 | −0.4 | −1.1 | −2.0 | −2.0 |

(*Continued on following page*)

APPENDIX H: Growth per Quarter, Average, Three Cycles, 1970–1982 (Continued)

| SERIES | | SEGMENTS | | | | | | | |
| --- | --- | --- | --- | --- | --- | --- | --- | --- | --- |
| | | 1–2 | 2–3 | 3–4 | 4–5 | 5–6 | 6–7 | 7–8 | 8–9 |
| 726. | France, Index of Industrial Production | 0.3 | 0.4 | 0.9 | 0.7 | 1.0 | −1.0 | −1.8 | −1.1 |
| 727. | Italy, Index of Industrial Production | 1.0 | 1.0 | 0.6 | 2.0 | 0.9 | −0.2 | −5.7 | −1.2 |
| 728. | Japan, Index of Industrial Production | 1.1 | 1.1 | 1.7 | 2.6 | 0.4 | −1.8 | −2.7 | −2.5 |

*Source:* U.S. Department of Commerce, Bureau of Economic Analysis, *Handbook of Cyclical Indicators, A Supplement to the Business Conditions Digest* (Washington, D.C.: U.S. Government Printing Office, 1984).

| SERIES | | SEGMENTS | | | | | | | |
| --- | --- | --- | --- | --- | --- | --- | --- | --- | --- |
| | | 1–2 | 2–3 | 3–4 | 4–5 | 5–6 | 6–7 | 7–8 | 8–9 |
| A. | Profit Rate before Taxes on Capital | 8.5 | 1.2 | 8.7 | −6.5 | −6.4 | −2.7 | −11.4 | −15.2 |
| B. | Profit Rate after Taxes on Capital | 9.3 | 1.2 | 9.9 | −6.7 | −1.3 | −6.2 | −8 | −17.8 |
| C. | Profit Rate before Taxes on Sales | 6.4 | 1 | 6 | −5.5 | −2.1 | −4.2 | −8.5 | −11.5 |
| D. | Profit Rate after Taxes on Sales | 7.2 | 0.6 | 7.4 | −6.8 | −3.5 | −5.3 | −7.9 | −13.6 |

*Source:* Bureau of Census, U.S. Department of Commerce, *Quarterly Financial Report on Manufacturing, Mining, and Trade Corporations* (Washington, D.C.: U.S. Government Printing Office, 1970–1983).

# References

Abromowitz, Moses. 1950. *Inventories and Business Cycles*. New York: National Bureau of Economic Research.

AFL-CIO Executive Committee. 1973. *The National Economy*. Washington, D.C.: AFL-CIO.

Agnew, Vice-President Spiro. 1971. Speech at National Governors' Conference, September 4.

Alchian, Armen. 1969. "Information Costs, Pricing, and Resource Unemployment." *Western Economic Journal* 7 (June): 107–29.

Amott, Teresa. 1989. "Re-slicing the Pie." *Dollars and Sense*, No. 146 (May): 10–11.

Ando, A., and Franco Modigliani. 1963. "The Life Cycle Hypothesis of Saving." *American Economic Review* 53 (March): 55–84.

Arcela, Francisco, and Allan Metzler. 1973. "The Markets for Housing and Housing Services." *The Journal of Money, Credit, and Banking* 5 (February): 78–99.

Arestis, P., and C. Driver. 1980. "Consumption out of Different Types of Income in the U.K." *Bulletin of Economic Research* 32: 23–36.

Auerbach, Paul. 1988. *Competition, The Economics of Industrial Change*. New York: Basil Blackwell.

Avineri, Shlomo. 1968. *The Social and Political Thought of Karl Marx*. Cambridge: Cambridge University Press.

Bain, Joe S. 1939. "The Relation of the Economic Life of Equipment to Reinvestment Cycles." *Review of Economics and Statistics* 21 (May): 79–88.

Baran, Paul. 1957. *The Political Economy of Growth*. New York: Monthly Review Press.

Baran, Paul, and Paul Sweezy. 1966. *Monopoly Capital*. New York: Monthly Review Press.

Barnet, Richard, and Ronald Muller. 1974. *Global Reach*. New York: Simon and Schuster.

Barro, Robert J., ed. 1989. *Modern Business Cycle Theory*. Cambridge, Mass. Harvard University Press.

———. 1980. "The Equilibrium Approach to Business Cycles." In Robert J. Barro, ed., *Money, Expectations, and Business Cycles*, 41–78. New York: Academic Press.

Bell, Peter. 1977. "Marxist Theory, Class Struggle, and the Crisis of Capitalism." In Jesse Schwartz, ed., *The Subtle Anatomy of Capitalism*, 170–94. Santa Monica, Cal.: Goodyear Publishers.

Bernanke, Ben, and James Powell. 1986. "The Cyclical Behavior of Industrial Labor Markets." In Robert Gordon, ed., *The American Business Cycle*, 583–638. Chicago: University of Chicago Press.

Bernstein, Michael A. 1987. *The Great Depression.* New York: Cambridge University Press.

Berry, John. 1988. "Labor Costs Raise Fears of Inflation." *Washington Post*, July 27, 1, 11.

Bils, Mark. 1987. "The Cyclical Behavior of Marginal Cost and Price." *American Economic Review* 77 (December): 838–55.

Black, Fischer. 1987. *Business Cycles and Equilibrium.* Hagerstown, Md.: Basil Blackwell.

Blair, John. 1974. "Market Power and Inflation." *Journal of Economic Issues* 8 (June): 453–78.

———. 1972. *Economic Concentration.* New York: Harcourt, Brace, Jovanovich.

Blanchard, Oliver, and Mark Watson. 1986. "Are Business Cycles All Alike?" In Robert Gordon, ed., *The American Business Cycle*, 123–82. Chicago: University of Chicago Press.

Bleany, Michael. 1976. *Underconsumption Theories.* New York: International Publishers.

Blinder, Alan S. 1988. "The Challenge of High Unemployment." *American Economic Review* 78 (May): 1–15.

———. 1976. "Intergenerational Transfers and Life-Cycle Consumption." *American Economic Review* 66 (May): 87–93.

———. 1975. "Distribution Effects of the Aggregate Consumption Function." *Journal of Political Economy* 83: 446–61.

Blinder, Alan, and Douglas Holtz-Eakin. 1986. "Inventory Fluctuations in the United States Since 1929." In Robert Gordon, ed., *The American Business Cycle*, 183–236. Chicago: University of Chicago Press.

Boddy, Raford, and James Crotty. 1975. "Class Conflict and Macro-Policy." *Review of Radical Political Economics* 7 (Spring): 1–17.

Boskin, Michael. 1978. "Taxation, Saving, and the Rate of Interest." *Journal of Political Economy* 86 (April): 503–27.

Bowles, Samuel, and Herbert Gintis. 1982. "The Crisis of Liberal Democratic Capitalism." *Politics and Society* 11: 69–79.

———. 1981. "Structure and Practice in the Labor Theory of Value." *Review of Radical Political Economics* 12 (Winter): 1–27.

Bowles, Samuel, David Gordon, and Thomas Weisskopf. 1983. *Beyond the Wasteland.* New York: Doubleday.

Bowring, Joseph. 1986. *Competition in A Dual Economy.* Princeton, N.J.: Princeton University Press.

Brenner, Harvey. 1976. *Estimating the Social Costs of National Economic Policy: Implications for Mental Health and Criminal Aggression.* Prepared for the Joint Economic Committee, U.S. Congress, Washington, D.C.: U.S. Government Printing Office.

Bureau of Economic Analysis, U.S. Department of Commerce. 1984. *Handbook of Cyclical Indicators, A Supplement to the Business Conditions Digest.* Washington, D.C.: U.S. Government Printing Office.

Burkett, Paul, and Mark Wohar. 1987. "Keynes on Investment and the Business Cycle." *Review of Radical Political Economics* 19 (Winter): 39–54.

Burmeister, E., and P. Taubman. 1969. "Labor and Non-Labor Income Saving Propensities." *Canadian Journal of Economics* 2: 1–15.

Burnham, Walter Dean. 1982. *The Current Crisis in American Politics*. New York: Oxford University Press.

Burns, Arthur, ed. 1952. *Wesley Clair Mitchell: The Economic Scientist*. New York: National Bureau of Economic Research.

Burns, Arthur, and Wesley Mitchell. 1946. *Measuring Business Cycles*. New York: National Bureau of Economic Research.

Buttrell-White, Betsy. 1978. "Empirical Tests of the Life Cycle Hypothesis." *American Economic Review* 68 (September): 547–60.

Carnoy, Martin. 1984. *The State and Political Theory*. Princeton, N.J.: Princeton University Press.

Case, John. 1981. *Understanding Inflation*. New York: Penguin Books.

Chandler, Lester. 1970. *America's Greatest Depression, 1929–1941*. New York: Harper and Row.

Cherry, Robert. 1981. "What Is So Natural about the Natural Rate of Unemployment?" *Journal of Economic Issues* 15 (September): 729–44.

———. 1980. *Macroeconomics*. Reading, Mass.: Addison-Wesley.

Cherry, Robert, et al., eds. 1987. *The Imperiled Economy*, Book 1. New York: Union for Radical Political Economics.

Cochrane, D., and G. H. Orcutt. 1949. "Application of Leasat Squares Regression to Relationships Containing Autocorrelated Error Terms." *Journal of the American Statistical Association* 44 (May): 32–61.

Costrell, Robert M. 1981–1982. "Overhead Labor and the Cyclical Behavior of Productivity and Real Wages." *Journal of Post Keynesian Economics* 4 (Winter): 277–90.

Council of Economic Advisers. 1988. *Economic Report of the President, 1988*. Washington, D.C.: U.S. Government Printing Office.

Courakis, Anthony, ed. 1981. *Inflation, Depression, and Economic Policy in the West*. Totowa, N.J.: Barnes and Noble.

Crotty, James. 1987. "The Role of Money and Finance in Marx's Crisis Theory." In Robert Cherry et al., eds., *The Imperiled Economy*, Book 1, 71–82. New York: Union for Radical Political Economics.

———. 1986. "Marx, Keynes, and Minsky on the Instability of the Capitalist Growth Process." In Suzanne Heldurn and Daird Bramhall, eds., *Marx, Schumpeter, and Keynes*, 297–327. Armonk, N.Y.: M. E. Sharpe.

Crotty, James R., and Jonathan P. Goldstein. 1988. "A Marxian-Keynesian Theory of Investment Demand: Empirical Evidence." Paper presented at Conference on International Perspectives on Accumulation and Profitability, at New York University, New York, September 1988.

Crow, John A. 1948. *The Epic of Latin America*. Garden City, N.Y.: Doubleday.

Cypher, James. 1974. "Capitalist Planning and Military Expenditures." *Review of Radical Political Economics* 6 (Fall): 1–19.

———. 1972. "Military Expenditures and the Performance of the Post-War Economy, 1947–1971." Ph.D. diss., University of California, Riverside, Cal.

Darity, William, and Wanda Marrero. 1981. "Distribution, Effective Demand, and the Orthodox Macromodel." *Journal of Macroeconomics* 3 (Fall): 455–87.

Davidson, Paul. 1978. *Money and the Real World.* New York: Wiley.

De Brunhoff, Suzanne. 1976. *Marx on Money.* New York: Urizen Books.

De Leeuw, F. 1962. "The Demand for Capital Goods by Manufacturers: A Study of Quarterly Time Series." *Econometrica* 30, No. 3 (July): 407–23.

Dernberg, Thomas. 1989. *Global Macroeconomics.* New York: Harper and Row.

Devine, James. 1987. "Cyclical Over-Investment and Crisis in a Labor-Scarce Economy." *Eastern Economic Journal* 13 (July-Sept.): 271–80.

———. 1983. "Underconsumption, Over-Investment, and the Origins of the Great Depression." *Review of Radical Political Economics* 15 (2): 1–27.

Dornbusch, Rudiger. 1980. *Open Economy Macroeconomies.* New York: Basic Books.

Dornbusch, Rudiger, and Stanley Fischer. 1986. "The Open Economy." In Robert J. Gordon, ed., *The American Business Cycle.* Chicago: University of Chicago Press.

Draper, Hal. 1977. *Karl Marx's Theory of Revolution.* New York: Monthly Review Press.

Du Boff, Richard, and Edward Herman. 1989. "The Promotional-Financial Dynamic of Merger Movements." *Journal of Economic Issues* 23 (March): 107–34.

Duesenberry, J. 1949. *Income, Saving, and the Theory of Consumer Behavior.* Cambridge, Mass.: Harvard University Press.

Dugger, William, ed. 1989. *Radical Institutionalism.* New York: Greenwood Press.

———. 1985. "Centralization, Diversification, and Administrative Burden in U.S. Enterprises." *Journal of Economic Issues* 19 (September): 687–701.

Dutt, Amitava Krishna. 1987. "Competition, Monopoly Power, and the Uniform Rate of Profit." *Review of Radical Political Economics* 19 (Winter): 55–72.

Earley, James, Robert Parsons, and Fred Thompson. 1976. "Money, Credit, and Expenditures." *The Bulletin* 3. New York: NYU Graduate School of Business: 2–38.

Edsall, Thomas. 1986. "More than Ever, the Electorate Is Polarized on Economic Lines." *Washington Post National Weekly Edition,* January 6.

Eichner, Alfred. 1987. *Macrodynamics of Advanced Market Economies.* Armonk, N.Y.: M. E. Sharpe.

———. 1976. *The Megacorp and Oligopoly.* Armonk, N.Y.: M. E. Sharpe.

———. 1973. "A Theory of the Determination of the Mark-up Under Oligopoly." *Economic Journal* 83 (December): 1184–99.

Eichner, Alfred, and J. A. Kregal. 1975. "An Essay on Post-Keynesian Theory: A New Paradigm in Economics." *Journal of Economic Literature* 13 (December): 1293–1314.

Einarsen, Johan. 1938. *Reinvestment Cycles.* Oslo: J. Chr. Gundersens Boktrykkeri.

Eisner, Robert. 1978. *Factors in Business Investment.* Cambridge, Mass.: Ballinger.

Epstein, Gerald. 1981. "Domestic Inflation and Monetary Policy." In Tom Ferguson and Joel Rogers, eds., *The Hidden Election*, 141–95. New York: Pantheon.

Epstein, Gerald, and Herbert Gintis. 1988. "An Asset Balance Model of International Capital Market Equilibrium." Paper presented at Conference on Financial Openness (WIDER), Helsinki, July 1988. Revised paper presented at Conference on International Perspectives on Profitability and Accumulation, at C. V. Starr Center for Applied Economics and New York University, New York, September 1988.

Evans, Michael K. 1969. *Macroeconomic Activity*. New York: Harper and Row.

Evans, Paul. 1987. Book review of *How Real Is the Federal Deficit?*, by Robert Eisner. *Journal of Economic Literature* 25 (September): 1345–46.

Ferleger, Lou, and Jay Mandle. 1987. "Democracy and Productivity in the Future American Economy." *Review of Radical Political Economy* 19 (Winter): 1–15.

Fichtenbaum, Rudy. 1985. "Consumption and the Distribution of Income." *Review of Social Economy* (October): 234–44.

Fine, Ben, and Lawrence Harris. 1976. "Controversial Issues in Marxist Economic Theory." In R. Miliband and J. Seville, eds., *The Socialist Register*, 141–178. New York: Monthly Review Press.

Fisher, Franklin. 1987. "Horizontal Mergers." *Journal of Economic Perspectives* 1 (Fall): 23–40.

Foley, Duncan. 1983. "Say's Law in Marx and Keynes." Paper presented at Conference on Heterodoxy in Economic Thought: Marx, Keynes, and Schumpeter, at University of Paris X-Nanterre, Paris, June 3–5, 1983.

Foster, John B. 1987. "What Is Stagnation?" In Robert Cherry et al., eds., *The Imperiled Economy*, Book 1. New York: Union for Radical Political Economics.

———. 1986. *The Theory of Monopoly Capital*. New York: Monthly Review Press.

———. 1985. "Sources of Instability in the U.S. Political Economy and Empire." *Science and Society* 49 (Summer): 167–93.

Freeman, Richard B. 1988. "Contraction and Expansion: The Divergence of Private Sector and Public Sector Unionism in the United States." *Journal of Economic Perspectives* 2, No. 2 (Spring): 63–88.

Friedman, Benjamin. 1986. "Money, Credit, and Interest Rates in the Business Cycle." In Robert Gordon, ed., *The American Business Cycle*, 395–458. Chicago: University of Chicago.

Friedman, Milton. 1982. *Capitalism and Freedom*. Chicago: University of Chicago Press.

———. 1971. "Price Controls." *Newsweek*, August 30, 81.

———. 1968. "The Role of Monetary Policy." *American Economic Review* 72 (January): 1–24.

———. 1957. *A Theory of the Consumption Function*. Princeton, N.J.: Princeton University Press.

Frumkin, Norman. 1987. *Tracking America's Economy*. Armonk, N.Y.: M. E. Sharpe.

Galbraith, John Kenneth. 1989. "A Look Back." *Journal of Economic Issues* 23 (June): 413–16.

―――. 1972. *The Great Crash*. Boston: Houghton-Mifflin.

―――. 1967. *The New Industrial State*. Boston: Houghton-Mifflin.

Gans, Herbert. 1988. "Is Voting Just for Upscale People?" *Washington Post*, July 8, 1.

Gapinski, James. 1982. *Macroeconomic Theory*. New York: McGraw-Hill.

Geary, P. T., and J. Kennan. 1982. "The Employment-Real Wage Relationship." *Journal of Political Economy* 90 (August): 854–71.

George, Susan. 1988. *A Fate Worse than Debt: The World Financial Crisis and the Poor*. New York: Grove Press.

Gilder, George. 1981. *Wealth and Poverty*. New York: Basic Books.

Glyn, Andrew, and Bob Sutcliffe. 1972. *British Capitalism, Workers, and the Profit Squeeze*. London: Penguin.

Gold, David. 1977. "The Rise and Decline of the Keynesian Coalition." *Kapitalstate* 6 (Fall): 1–18.

Gorbachev, Mikhail. 1987. *Perestroika*. New York: Harper and Row.

Gordon, David M. 1988. "The Global Economy: New Edifice or Crumbling Foundations?" *New Left Review* 168 (March/April): 24–65.

Gordon, David, Thomas Weisskopf, and Samuel Bowles. 1987. "Power, Accumulation and Crisis." In Robert Cherry et al., eds., *The Imperiled Economy*, Book 1, 43–58. New York: Union for Radical Political Economics.

―――. 1983. "Long Swing and the Nonproductive Cycle." *American Economic Review* 73 (May): 152–57.

Gordon, R. A. 1961. *Business Fluctuations*. 3d ed. New York: Harper and Row.

―――. 1952. "Investment Opportunities in the United States." In R. A. Gordon, ed., *Business Cycles in the Post-War World*. New York: Oxford University Press.

Gordon, Robert J., ed. 1986. *The American Business Cycle*. Chicago: University of Chicago Press.

Gordon, Robert J., and John Veitch. 1986. "Fixed Investment in the American Business Cycle, 1919–1983." In Robert J. Gordon, ed., *The American Business Cycle*. Chicago: University of Chicago Press.

Gottlieb, Manuel. 1963. "Long Swings in Urban Building Activity." In *43rd Annual Report of the NBER*. New York: NBER.

Green, Francis. 1984. "A Critique of the Neo-Fisherian Consumption Function." *Review of Radical Political Economics* 16, Nos. 2 and 3: 95–114.

―――. 1980. "A Note on the Overestimated Importance of the Constant U.S. Savings Ratio." *Southern Economic Journal* 47, No. 2: 510–16.

Green, Mark. 1972. *Who Runs Congress?* New York: Bantam.

Greider, William. 1987. *Secrets of the Temple: How the Federal Reserve Runs the Country*. New York: Simon and Schuster.

Griffin, Keith, and John Gurley. 1985. "Radical Analyses of Imperialism, the

Third World, and the Transition to Socialism." *Journal of Economic Literature* 23 (September): 1089–1143.

Griffin, L. J., M. Wallace, and J. Devine. 1982. "The Political Economy of Military Spending." *Cambridge Journal of Economics* 6 (March): 1–14.

Grilliches, Z., and N. Wallace. 1965. "The Determinants of Investment Revisited." *International Economic Review* 6, No. 3 (September): 311–29.

Guttentag, J. M. 1961. "The Short Cycle in Residential Construction." *American Economic Review* 51 (June): 292–308.

Haberler, Gottfried. 1960. *Prosperity and Depression*. 4th ed. Cambridge, Mass.: Harvard University Press.

Hahn, Frank. 1983. *Money and Inflation*. Cambridge, Mass.: MIT Press.

Hahnel, Robin, and Howard Sherman. 1982a. "Income Distribution and the Business Cycle." *Journal of Economic Issues* 16 (March): 49–73.

——. 1982b. "The Profit Rate over the Business Cycle." *Cambridge Journal of Economics* 6 (June): 185–94.

Hansen, Alvin. 1964. *Business Cycles and National Income*. New York: Norton.

Harris, Joe. 1978. "The Impact of the 1971–1974 Wage and Price Controls on Profit Levels and Distribution of Income." Ph.D. diss., University of California, Riverside, Riverside, Cal.

Harrison, Bennett, and Barry Bluestone. 1988. *The Great U-Turn: Corporate Restructuring and the Polarizing of America*. New York: Basic Books.

Hayek, Frederick. 1939. *Profits, Interest, and Investment*. London: Routledge.

Heilbroner, Robert. 1989. "Rereading 'The Affluent Society.' " *Journal of Economic Issues* 23 (June): 367–78.

Henley, Andrew. 1987a. "Trade Unions, Market Concentration and Income Distribution in United States Manufacturing Industry." *International Journal of Industrial Organization* 5: 193–210.

——. 1987b. "Labour's Shares and Profitability Crisis in the United States." *Cambridge Journal of Economics* 11 (December): 315–30.

Heskel, Mitchell, Robert Pinkham, and Doris Robinson. 1982. "The Empirical Consumption-Wage Bill Ratio." *Journal of Post-Keynesian Economics* 5 (Fall): 66–77.

Hickman, Bert. 1959. "Diffusion, Acceleration, and Business Cycles." *American Economic Review* 49 (September): 535–65.

Hickman, Bert, and Stefan Schleicher. 1978. "The Interdependence of National Economies." *Weltwirtschaftsliches Archiv* 114: 642–708.

Hicks, John R. 1950. *A Contribution to the Theory of the Trade Cycle*. Oxford: Oxford University Press.

Hobson, John A. 1922. *The Economics of Unemployment*. London: George Allen and Unwin.

Holbrook, Robert, and Frank Stafford. 1971. "The Propensity to Consume Separate Types of Income: A Generalized Permanent Income Hypothesis." *Econometrica* 39 (January): 1–21.

Hotson, John. 1976. *Stagflation and the Bastard Keynesians*. Waterloo, Canada: University of Waterloo Press.

Hultgren, Thor. 1965. *Costs, Prices, and Profits: Their Cyclical Relations*. New York: National Bureau of Economic Research.

Jarrell, Gregg, James Brickley, and Jeffry Netter. 1988. "The Market for Corporate Control." *Journal of Economic Perspectives* 2 (Winter): 49–68.

Jensen, Michael. 1988. "Takeovers." *Journal of Economic Perspectives* 2 (Winter): 21–48.

Joint Economic Committee of the U.S. Congress. 1986. *The Concentration of Wealth in the United States*. Washington, D.C.: U.S. Government Printing Office (July).

Jorgenson, Dale. 1971. "Econometric Studies of Investment Behavior: A Survey." *Journal of Economic Literature* 9: 1111–47.

Jorgenson, Dale, and M. Hall. 1963. "Capital Theory and Investment Behavior." *American Economic Review* 53, No. 2 (May): 247–59.

Kahn, R. F. 1931. "The Relation of Home Investment to Unemployment." *Economic Journal* (June): 25–44.

Kalecki, Michal. [1935] 1968. *Theory of Economic Dynamics*. New York: Monthly Review Press.

Keynes, John M. 1979. *Collected Writings*, 29. London: Macmillan.

———. 1939. "Mr. Keynes on the Distribution of Incomes and 'Propensity to Consume': A Reply." *Review of Economics and Statistics* 27 (August): 128–30.

———. 1936. *The General Theory of Employment, Interest and Money*. New York: Harcourt Brace Jovanovich.

Kindleberger, Charles. 1978. *Manias, Panics and Crashes: A History of Financial Crisis*. New York: Basic Books.

King, M. A. 1975. "The United Kingdom Profits Crisis: Myth or Reality?" *The Economic Journal* 85 (March): 33–54.

Klein, Lawrence. 1962. *An Introduction to Econometrics*. Englewood Cliffs, N.J.: Prentice-Hall.

Klein, Lawrence, and A. S. Goldberger. 1955. *An Econometric Model of the United States, 1929–1952*. Amsterdam: North Holland Publishers.

Klein, Philip. 1989a. "Institutionalism Confronts the 1990s." *Journal of Economic Issues* 23 (June): 545–54.

———. ed. 1989b. *Analyzing Modern Business Cycles*. Armonk, N.Y.: M. E. Sharpe.

———. 1983. "The Neglected Institutionalism of Wesley Clair Mitchell." *Journal of Economic Issues* 17 (December): 867–99.

———. 1976. *Business Cycles in the Postwar World*. Boston: University Press of America.

Klein, Philip, and Geoffrey Moore. 1985. *Monitoring Growth Cycles in Market-Oriented Countries*. Cambridge, Mass.: Ballinger.

Kloby, Jerry. 1987. "The Growing Divide." *Monthly Review* 39 (September): 1–9.

Kobayashi, Yoshihiro. 1971. "Movements of Price and Profits in the Periods of Rapid Growth in the Japanese Economy." *Economic Studies Quarterly* 6 (August): 14–36. In Japanese.

Kotz, David. 1987. "Long Waves and Social Structures of Accumulation." *Review of Radical Political Economics* 19 (Winter): 16–38.

Kuznets, Simon. [1932] 1967. *Secular Movements in Production and Prices*. New York: A. M. Kelley.

Laffer, Arthur. 1982. *Supply-Side Economics*. Pacific Palisades, Cal.: Goodyear.

League of Nations. 1945. *Economic Stability in the Post-War World*. Geneva: League of Nations.

———. 1934. *Statistical Yearbook, 1932–1934*. Geneva: League of Nations.

Lee, Maurice W. 1955. *Economic Fluctuations*. Homewood, Ill.: Irwin.

Lekachman, Robert. 1985. "The Radical Keynes." In Harold Wattel, ed., *Policy Consequences of John Maynard Keynes*, 30–38. Armonk, N.Y.: M. E. Sharpe.

———. 1960. *Keynes' General Theory*. London: Macmillan.

Leontief, Wassily. 1985. "Theoretical Assumptions and Unobserved Facts." In W. Leontief, ed., *Essays In Economics*, 272–82. New Brunswick, N.J.: Transaction Books.

Lindblom, Charles. 1977. *Politics and Markets*. New York: Basic Books.

Long, C. D. 1939. "Long Cycles in the Building Industry." *Quarterly Journal of Economics* 51 (May): 371–403.

Long, John, and Charles Plosser. 1983. "Real Business Cycles." *Journal of Political Economy* 91 (February): 39–69.

Lucas, Robert. 1986. "Models of Business Cycles." Paper prepared in mimeo for the Yrjo Jansson Lectures. Helsinki, Finland (March).

———. 1981. *Studies in Business Cycle Theory*. Oxford: Basil Blackwell.

———. 1977. "Understanding Business Cycles." In Karl Brunner and Alan Metzler, eds., *Stabilization of the Domestic and International Economy*. Amsterdam: North Holland Publishers.

———. 1975. "An Equilibrium Model of the Business Cycle." *Journal of Political Economy* 83 (December): 1113–44.

Maccini, Louis, and Robert Rossana. 1981. "Investment in Finished Goods Inventories." *American Economic Review* 71 (May): 392–401.

MacEwan, Arthur. 1990. *Debt and Disorder*. New York: Monthly Review Press.

———. 1989. "International Trade and Economic Instability." *Monthly Review* 40 (February): 10–21.

———. 1986. "International Debt and Banking: Rising Instability within the General Crisis." *Science and Society* 50 (Summer): 177–209.

———. 1984. "Interdependence and Instability: Do the Levels of Output in the Advanced Capitalist Countries Increasingly Move Up and Down Together?" *Review of Radical Political Economics* 16: 57–79.

MacEwan, Arthur, and William Tabb, eds. 1989. *Instability and Change in the World Economy*. New York: Monthly Review Press.

Mack, Ruth. 1956. *Consumption and Business Fluctuations: A Case Study of the Shoe, Leather, Hide Sequence*. New York: National Bureau of Economic Research.

Magdoff, Harry. 1979. *Imperialism: From the Colonial Age to the Present*. New York: Monthly Review Press.

———. 1969. *Age of Imperialism*. New York: Monthly Review Press.

Magdoff, Harry, and Paul Sweezy. 1987. *Stagnation and the Financial Explosion.* New York: Monthly Review Press.

Mandel, Ernest. 1970. *Europe vs. America: Contradictions of Imperialism.* New York: Monthly Review Press.

Mankiw, N. Gregory. 1989. "Real Business Cycles: A New Keynesian Perspective." *Journal of Economic Perspectives* 3 (Summer): 79–90.

Marglin, Stephen. 1984. *Growth, Distribution, and Prices.* Cambridge, Mass.: Harvard University Press.

Marglin, Stephen, and Amit Bhaduri. 1990. "Profit Squeeze and Keynesian Theory." In Stephen Marglin, ed., *The Golden Age of Capitalism: Lessons for the 1990s.* London: Oxford University Press.

Martin, Henry. 1987. "Financial Instability in the U.S. Economy." In Robert Cherry et al., eds., *The Imperiled Economy,* Book 1, 139–44. New York: Union for Radical Political Economics.

Marx, Karl. [1905] 1952. *Theories of Surplus Value.* New York: International Publishers.

———. 1909. *Capital,* vol. 3. Chicago: Charles Kerr.

———. 1907. *Capital,* vol. 2. Chicago: Charles Kerr.

———. [1867] 1903. *Capital,* vol. 1. Chicago: Charles Kerr.

Mayer, Thomas. 1972. *Permanent Income, Wealth, and Consumption: A Critique of the Permanent Income Theory, The Life-Cycle Hypothesis, and Related Theories.* Berkeley: University of California Press.

Means, Gardiner. 1975. "Inflation and Unemployment." In John Blair, ed., *The Roots of Inflation.* New York: Burt Franklin.

Melman, Seymour. 1988. "Economic Consequences of the Arms Race: The Second-Rate Economy." *American Economic Review* 78 (May): 55–59.

———. 1970. *Pentagon Capitalism.* New York: McGraw-Hill.

Metzler, Lloyd. 1947. "Factors Governing the Length of Inventory Cycles." *Review of Economics and Statistics* 29 (February): 1–15.

———. 1941. "Nature and Stability of Inventory Cycles." *Review of Economics and Statistics* 23 (August): 113–29.

Meyer, John, and Edwin Kuh. 1957. *The Investment Decision.* Cambridge, Mass.: Harvard University Press.

Miliband, Ralph. 1969. *The State in Capitalist Society.* New York: Basic Books.

Mill, John Stuart. [1848] 1920. *Principles of Political Economy.* Edited by W. L. Ashley. London: Longmans, Green.

Miller, John. 1986. "The Fiscal Crisis of the State Reconsidered: Two Views of the State and the Accumulation of Capital in the Postwar Economy." *Review of Radical Political Economics* 18, Nos. 1 and 2 (Spring and Summer): 236–60.

———. 1982. "The State, Cycles, and Crises: A Critical Examination of the Fiscal Revolution in the United States." Ph.D. diss., University of Pittsburgh, Pa.

Miller, Norman, and Marina Whitman. 1973. "Alternative Theories and Tests of U.S. Foreign Investment." *Journal of Finance* 28 (December): 1131–50.

Mills, Frederick. 1946. *Price-Quantity Interactions In Business Cycles.* New York: National Bureau of Economic Research.

Minsky, Hyman. 1986. *Stabilizing an Unstable Economy*. New Haven: Yale University Press.

Mintz, Ilse. 1967. *Cyclical Fluctuations in the Exports of the United States since 1879*. New York: National Bureau of Economic Research.

———. 1959. *Trade Balance During Business Cycles*. New York: National Bureau of Economic Research.

Mirowski, Philip. 1986. "Mathematical Formalism and Economic Explanation." In Philip Mirowski, ed., *The Reconstruction of Economic Theory*, 179–240. Boston: Kluwer-Nijhoff.

———. 1985. *The Birth of the Business Cycle*. New York: Garland Publishing Co.

Mitchell, Wesley C. 1951. *What Happens during Business Cycles*. New York: National Bureau of Economic Research.

———. 1913. *Business Cycles*. Berkeley: University of California Press.

Mitchell, Wesley C., and W. L. Thorp. 1926. *Business Annals*. New York: National Bureau of Economic Research.

Modigliani, Franco. 1977. "The Monetarist Controversy Or, Should We Forsake Stabilization Policies?" *Economic Review*, 21–35. San Francisco: Federal Reserve Bank of San Francisco.

———. 1975a. "The Consumption Function in a Developing Economy and the Italian Experience." *American Economic Review* 65 (December): 825–42.

———. 1975b. "The Life-Cycle Hypothesis of Saving Twenty Years Later." In Michael Parkin and A. R. Nobay, eds., *Contemporary Issues in Economics*. Proceedings of the Conference of University Teachers of Economics. Manchester, N.H.: Manchester University Press.

Modigliani, Franco, and Charles Steindel. 1977. "Is a Tax Rebate an Effective Tool for Stabilization Policy?" *Brookings Papers on Economic Activity* 1: 175–209.

Moore, Geoffrey. 1983. *Business Cycles, Inflation, and Forecasting*. 2d ed. Cambridge, Mass.: Ballinger.

———. 1962. "Tested Knowledge of Business Cycles." In *42nd Annual Report of the National Bureau of Economic Research*. New York: National Bureau of Economic Research.

Morgenstern, Oskar. 1959. *International Financial Transactions and Business Cycles*. New York: National Bureau of Economic Research.

Moseley, Fred. 1985. "The Rate of Surplus Value in the Post-war U.S. Economy: A Critique of Weisskopf's Estimates." *Cambridge Journal of Economics* 9 (January): 43–51.

Muller, Ronald. 1975. "Global Corporations and National Stabilization Policy." *Journal of Economic Issues* 9 (June): 183–84.

Mullineux, A. W. 1984. *The Business Cycle after Keynes*. Totowa, N.J.: Barnes and Noble.

Munkirs, John. 1985. *The Transformation of American Capitalism*. Armonk, N.Y.: M. E. Sharpe.

Munkirs, John, and Janet Knoedler. 1987. "The Dual Economy: An Empirical Analysis." *Journal of Economic Issues* 21 (June): 803–11.

Munley, Frank. 1981. "Wages, Salaries, and the Profit Share." *Cambridge Journal of Economics* 5 (April): 235–42.

Murfin, A. J. 1980. "Saving Propensities from Wage and Non-Wage Income." *Warwick Economic Research Papers*, no. 174: 1–19.

Musgrove, Philip. 1980. "Income Distribution and the Aggregate Consumption Function." *Journal of Political Economy* 88 (June): 504–25.

Nixon, President Richard. 1971. Speech on television, August 15.

Oi, Walter. 1962. "Labor as a Quasifixed Factor." *Journal of Political Economy* 70 (December): 538–55.

Orsberg, Lars. 1988. "The 'Disappearance' of Involuntary Unemployment." *Journal of Economic Issues* 22 (September): 707–28.

Pechman, Joseph. 1985. *Who Paid the Taxes, 1966–1985*. Washington, D.C.: The Brookings Institution.

Perlo, Victor. 1976. "The New Propaganda of Declining Profit Shares and Inadequate Investment." *Review of Radical Political Economics* 8 (Fall): 53–64.

Perry, Charles. 1970. "Changing Labor Markets and Inflation." *Brookings Papers on Economic Activity* 3: 411–41.

Peterson, Wallace. 1988a. *Income, Employment, and Economic Growth*. 6th ed. New York: W. W. Norton.

———, ed. 1988b. *Market Power and the Economy*. Norwell, Mass.: Kluwer Academic Publishers.

———. 1987. "Macroeconomics: Where Are We?" *Review of Social Economy* 45 (April): 64–76.

Piven, Frances Fox, and Richard Cloward. 1988. *Why Americans Don't Vote*. New York: Pantheon Books.

Plosser, Charles. 1989. "Understanding Real Business Cycles." *Journal of Economic Perspectives* 3 (Summer): 51–78.

Pollin, Robert. 1989. "Abyss of Third World Debt." *Monthly Review* 40 (June): 54–58.

———. 1988a. "The Growth of U.S. Household Debt: Demand-side Influences." *Journal of Macroeconomics* 10 (Spring): 231–48.

———. 1988b. *Deeper in Debt: The Changing Financial Conditions of U.S. Households*. Report prepared for Joint Economic Committee, U.S. Congress, Washington, D.C.: U.S. Government Printing Office.

———. 1987. "Structural Change and Increasing Fragility in the U.S. Financial System." In Robert Cherry et al., eds., *The Imperiled Economy*, Book 1, 145–58. New York: Union for Radical Political Economics.

———. 1986. "Alternative Perspectives on the Rise of Corporate Debt Dependency." *Review of Radical Political Economics* 18 (Spring and Summer): 205–35.

Pool, John Charles, and Stephen Stamos. 1989. *International Economic Policy: Beyond the Trade and Debt Crisis*. Lexington, Mass.: Lexington Books.

Pulling, Kathleen. 1978. "Cyclical Behavior of Profit Margins." *Journal of Economic Issues* 12 (June): 1–24.

Ransom, Roger. 1980. "In Search of Security: The Growth of Government in the

United States, 1902–1970." *University of California, Riverside Working Papers*, no. 40 (January).

Rebitzer, James. 1987. "Unemployment, Long-term Employment Relations, and Productivity Growth." *Review of Economics and Statistics* 69 (November): 627–35.

Reder, Melvin W. 1988. "The Rise and Fall of Unions." *Journal of Economic Perspectives* 3, No. 2 (Spring): 89–110.

Ricardo, David. [1817] 1891. *The Principles of Political Economy and Taxation*. London: Gonner, Bell, and Sons.

Riddell, Tom. 1988. "U.S. Military Power, the Terms of Trade, and the Profit Rate." *American Economic Review* 78 (May): 60–65.

Robinson, J. Gregg. 1988. "American Unions in Decline: Problems and Prospects." *Critical Sociology* 15, No. 1 (Spring): 33–56.

Robinson, Joan. 1979. "Solving the Stagflation Puzzle." *Challenge* (November-December): 40–46.

Rodbertus, Karl. 1898. *Overproduction and Crisis*. New York: Scribner's.

Rose, Arnold. 1967. *The Power Structure*. New York: Oxford University Press.

Rosen, Lewis. 1973. "Stock Market Capital Gains and Consumption Expenditures." *Journal of Finance* 28 (December): 1376–89.

Rousseas, Stephen. 1986. *Post Keynesian Monetary Economics*. New York: M. E. Sharpe.

Ruccio, David. 1988. "The Merchant of Venice or Marxism in the Mathematical Mode." *Rethinking Marxism* 1 (Winter): 36–68.

Russakoff, Dale, and Cindy Skrzycki. 1988. "Growing Pains in the 'Contingent Work Force.' " *Washington Post*, February 11, 1, 18.

Salop, Steven. 1987. "Symposium on Mergers and Antitrust." *Journal of Economic Perspectives* 1 (Fall): 3–12.

Samuelson, Paul. 1973. *Economics*. 9th ed. New York: McGraw-Hill.

———. 1971. "Price Controls." *Newsweek*, August 30, 82.

———. 1939. "Interaction between the Multiplier Analysis and the Principle of Acceleration." *Review of Economic Statistics* 21 (May): 75–78.

Sardoni, Claudio. 1982. *Marx and Keynes on Economic Recession*. New York: New York University Press.

Sawyer, Malcolm. 1988. "Theories of Monopoly Capitalism." *Journal of Economic Surveys* 2, No. 1: 47–76.

———. 1985a. "Toward a Post-Kaleckian Macroeconomics." In Philip Arestis and Thanos Skouras, eds., *Post Keynesian Economic Theory*. Armonk, N.Y.: M. E. Sharpe.

———. 1985b. *The Economics of Michal Kalecki*. Armonk: N.Y.: M. E. Sharpe.

———. 1982. *Macroeconomics in Question: The Keynesian-Monetarist Orthodoxy and the Kaleckian Alternative*. Armonk, N.Y.: M. E. Sharpe.

Scherer, F. M. 1988. "Corporate Takeovers." *Journal of Economic Perspectives* 2 (Winter): 69–82.

Schmalensee, Richard. 1987. "Horizontal Merger Policy." *Journal of Economic Perspectives* 1 (Fall): 41–54.

Schor, Juliet, and Samuel Bowles. 1987. "Employment Rates and the Incidence of Strikes." *Review of Economics and Statistics* 45 (November): 580–96.

Schultze, Charles. 1964. "Short-Run Movements and Income Shares." In National Bureau of Economic Research, *The Behavior of Income Shares*. Princeton, N.J.: Princeton University Press.

Schumpeter, Joseph A. 1939. *Business Cycles: A Theoretical, Historical, and Statistical Analysis of the Capitalist Process*. New York: McGraw-Hill.

Semmler, Willi, ed. 1989. *Financial Dynamics and Business Cycles*. Armonk, N.Y.: M. E. Sharpe

———. 1982. "Competition, Monopoly, and Differential Profit Rates." *Review of Radical Political Economics* 13 (Winter): 39–52.

Severn, Alan. 1974. "Investor Evaluation of Foreign and Domestic Risk." *Journal of Finance* 29 (March): 545–50.

Shaikh, Anwar. 1978. "An Introduction to the History of Crisis Theories." In Union for Radical Political Economy, ed., *U.S. Capitalism in Crisis*, 219–48. New York: Monthly Review Press.

Shepherd, William. 1970. *Market Power and Economic Welfare*. New York: Random House.

Sherman, Howard. 1987. *Foundations of Radical Political Economy*. Armonk, N.Y.: M. E. Sharpe.

———. 1986. "Changes in the Character of the U.S. Business Cycle." *Review of Radical Political Economics* 18, Nos. 1 and 2: 190–204.

———. 1971. "Marxist Models of Cyclical Growth." *History of Political Economy* 3 (Spring): 28–55.

———. 1968. *Profits in the United States*. Ithaca, N.Y.: Cornell University Press.

Sherman, Howard, and Gary Evans. 1984. *Macroeconomics: Keynesian, Monetarist, and Marxist Views*. New York: Harper and Row.

Sherman, Howard, and Thomas Stanback. 1962. "Cyclical Behavior of Profits, Appropriations, and Expenditures." *Proceedings of the American Statistical Association* 59 (September): 274–86.

Shleifer, Andrei, and Robert Vishay. 1988. "Value Maximization and the Acquisition Process." *Journal of Economic Perspectives* 2 (Winter): 7–20.

Sismondi, J.C.L. Simonde de. [1815] 1946. "Industrial Crisis: The Result of Laissez-Faire." In Donald D. Wagner, ed., *Social Reformers*, 151–53. New York: Macmillan.

Solow, Robert M. 1960. "On a Family of Lag Distributions." *Econometrica* 28, No. 2 (April): 393–406.

Stanback, Thomas. 1963. *Post-war Cycles in Manufacturers' Inventories*. New York: National Bureau of Economic Research.

Steindel, Charles. 1977. "Personal Consumption, Property Income, and Corporate Saving." Ph.D. diss., MIT.

Steindl, Joseph. 1952. *Maturity and Stagnation in American Capitalism*. New York: Monthly Review Press.

Stern, Philip M. 1988. *The Best Congress Money Can Buy*. New York: Pantheon.

Stockman, David. 1986. *The Triumph of Politics*. New York: Harper and Row.

Summers, Laurence. 1988. "Good News on the Trade Deficit, But . . ." *New York Times*, May 20, 1.

Sweezy, Paul. 1942. *Theory of Capitalist Development*. New York: Monthly Review Press. Reprinted 1970.

Szymanski, Albert. 1978. *The Capitalist State and the Politics of Class*. Cambridge, Mass.: Winthrop.

———. 1975. "The Decline and Fall of the U.S. Eagle." In David Mermelstein, *The Economic Crisis Reader*. New York: Random House.

———. 1974. "Productivity, Growth, and Capitalist Stagnation." *Science and Society* 48 (Fall): 295–322.

Tamalty, Karen. 1981. "Foreigners' Investments in U.S. Rise." *Los Angeles Times*, November 15, 1.

Taylor, Lester. 1971. "Saving Out of Different Types of Income." *Brookings Papers on Economic Activity* 2: 383–416.

Tobin, James. 1985. "Keynes Policies in Theory and Practice." In Harold Wattel, ed., *The Policy Consequences of John Maynard Keynes*. Armonk, N.Y.: M. E. Sharpe.

———. 1981. "The Monetarist Counter-Revolution Today—An Appraisal." *Economic Journal* 71 (March): 321–37.

Turner, Marjorie. 1989. *Joan Robinson and the Americans*. Armonk, N.Y.: M. E. Sharpe.

United Press International. 1981. "Tax Cut Seen Having Small Initial Impact." *Honolulu Advertiser*, August 5, 1.

United States Bureau of the Census. 1986. *Money, Income, and Poverty Status of Families and Persons in the United States*. Washington, D.C.: U.S. Government Printing Office (August).

United States Department of Commerce. Bureau of Economic Analysis. 1984. *Handbook of Cyclical Indicators*. Washington, D.C.: U.S. Government Printing Office.

United States Internal Revenue Service. 1935–1955. *Statistics of Income, Corporate Income Tax Returns*. Washington, D.C.: U.S. Government Printing Office.

Valentine, Lloyd M. 1987. *Business Cycles and Forecasting*. 7th ed. Cincinnati, Ohio: Southwest Publishing Co.

Varian, Hal. 1988. "Symposium on Takeovers." *Journal of Economic Perspectives* 2 (Winter): 3–5.

Veblen, Thorstein. [1904] 1975. *The Theory of Business Enterprise*. New York: Augustus Kelly.

Wachtel, Howard, and Peter Adelsheim. 1976. *The Inflationary Impact of Unemployment: Price Markups during Postwar Recessions, 1947–1970*. Report prepared for U.S. Congress, Joint Economic Committee. Washington, D.C.: U.S. Government Printing Office.

Walbank, F. W. 1956. *The Decline of the Roman Empire in the West*. London: Cobbett Press.

Wattel, Harold, ed. 1985. *Policy Consequences of John Maynard Keynes*. Armonk, N.Y.: M. E. Sharpe.

Weeks, John. 1989. *A Critique of Neoclassical Macroeconomics*. New York: St. Martin's Press.

Weintraub, Sidney. 1978. *Keynes, Keynesians, and Monetarists*. Philadelphia: University of Pennsylvania Press.

———. 1958. *An Approach to the Theory of Income Distribution*. Philadelphia: Chilton.

Weisskopf, Thomas. 1979. "Marxian Crisis Theory and the Rate of Profit in the Postwar U.S. Economy." *Cambridge Journal of Economics* 3 (December): 341–78.

———. 1978. "Marxist Perspectives on Cyclical Crisis." In Union for Radical Political Economics, ed., *U.S. Capitalism in Crisis*, 241–260. New York: Monthly Review Press.

Weisskopf, Thomas, Samuel Bowles, and David Gordon. 1985. "Two Views of Capitalist Stagnation." *Science and Society* 49 (Fall): 259–86.

———. 1983. "Hearts and Minds: A Social Model of U.S. Productivity Growth." *Brookings Papers on Economic Activity* 2: 381–441.

White, Laurence. 1987. "Anti-trust and Merger Policy." *Journal of Economic Perspectives* 1 (Fall): 13–22.

Winnick, Andrew. 1989. *Toward Two Societies: The Changing Distribution of Income and Wealth in the U.S. since 1960*. New York: Praeger.

Wojnilower, Albert. 1988. "The Central Role of Credit Crunches in Recent Financial History." *Brookings Papers on Economic Activity* 2: 277–326.

Wolfson, Martin. 1986. *Financial Crises*. Armonk, N.Y.: M. E. Sharpe.

Wonnacott, Paul. 1974. *Macroeconomics*. Chicago: Irwin.

Wood, Adrian. 1975. *A Theory of Profits*. Cambridge: Cambridge University Press.

Woodward, Kenneth. 1987. "Money, Profits, Credit, and Business Cycles." Ph.D. diss., University of California, Riverside, Riverside, Cal.

Yaffe, David. 1973. "The Crisis of Profitability." *New Left Review* 80 (July/August): 1–21.

Zarnowitz, Victor. 1985. "Recent Work on Business Cycles in Historical Perspective." *Journal of Economic Literature* 23 (June): 523–80.

Zarnowitz, Victor, and Geoffrey Moore. 1986. "Major Changes in Cyclical Behavior." In Robert J. Gordon, ed., *The American Business Cycle*, 519–82. Chicago: University of Chicago Press.

Zevin, Robert. 1988. "Are World Financial Markets More Open?" Paper presented at Conference on Financial Openness (WIDER), Helsinki, July 1988.

Zimbalist, Andrew, Howard Sherman, and Stuart Brown. 1989. *Comparing Economic Systems*. San Diego: Harcourt Brace Jovanovich.

# Index

434 · Index